# INTERNATIONAL ACTION AGAINST
## RACIAL DISCRIMINATION

# International Action Against Racial Discrimination

MICHAEL BANTON

CLARENDON PRESS · OXFORD

1996

Oxford University Press, Walton Street, Oxford OX2 6DP

Oxford New York

Athens Auckland Bangkok Bombay
Calcutta Cape Town Dar es Salaam Delhi
Florence Hong Kong Istanbul Karachi
Kuala Lumpur Madras Madrid Melbourne
Mexico City Nairobi Paris Singapore
Taipei Tokyo Toronto
and associated companies in
Berlin Ibadan

Oxford is a trade mark of Oxford University Press

Published in the United States
by Oxford University Press Inc., New York

British Library Cataloguing in Publication Data
Data Available

Library of Congress Cataloging in Publication Data
Banton, Michael P.
International action against racial discrimination / Michael Banton.
Includes bibliographical references.
1. United Nations. General Assembly. Committee on the
Elimination of Racial Discrimination. 2. Race discrimination.
3. Race discrimination—Law and legislation. 4. Human rights.
I. Title
HT1521.B335 1996 305.8—dc20 95–47057

ISBN 0–19–828061–0

1 3 5 7 9 10 8 6 4 2

Typeset by BookMan Services, Oxford
Printed in Great Britain
on acid-free paper by
Biddles Ltd, Guildford and King's Lynn

Dedicated
to my colleagues on the Committee for the Elimination
of Racial Discrimination, from whom I have learnt so much
and with whom I have been engaged in the exploration
and implementation of a historic innovation in
international affairs.

# PREFACE

REPRESENTATIVES of the world's many nations assemble under United Nations auspices in New York and Geneva. They are more accustomed to disagreeing than to agreeing with one another. So it was remarkable that in 1965 they should have decided unanimously to adopt the International Convention on the Elimination of All Forms of Racial Discrimination (ICERD) and that within twenty-five years three-quarters of the world's states should have declared themselves willing to be bound by it.

The Convention takes the form of a treaty between states. On accession, a state assumes a variety of obligations, one of which is to report every two years on what it has been doing to implement the Convention's provisions. State reports are laid before a committee of eighteen individuals whom the states themselves elect. This is the Committee on the Elimination of Racial Discrimination, often referred to as CERD (in distinction from ICERD). States which are parties to the Convention should know whether other states are keeping to their side of the contract, so CERD can be seen as the agent of the body of states parties in monitoring implementation by individual states. Those who drafted the Convention decided that CERD should report on its examination of state reports to the General Assembly rather than to the states parties. They saw the Convention as an expression of the UN's desire to increase respect for human rights. Nevertheless, the states parties have responsibilities distinct from those of the General Assembly.

Studying in retrospect how the Convention attracted so much support, it becomes apparent that certain of the assumptions about the nature and causes of racial discrimination current in the UN in the early 1960s were influenced by the political circumstances of the period. Most of the state representatives thought that racial discrimination was characteristic of states other than their own. Governments acceded to the Convention for reasons of foreign, not domestic, policy; many nominated diplomats, as their specialists in foreign affairs, for election to CERD. Most of those elected were inclined to construe the Committee's mandate very strictly, which was beneficial in the 1970s because at that time CERD was pioneering an advance into virgin territory and its activities were regarded with suspicion by states jealous of their sovereignty. In the early 1960s UN resolutions could refer, as does the Convention itself, to 'the necessity of speedily eliminating racial discrimination throughout the world'. Thirty years later any observer could see that racial and ethnic tensions within states were more frequently the causes of armed conflict than such tensions between states. Nor did such an observer need to be a lawyer to see that racial discrimination as defined in ICERD article 1.1 was not something that could be speedily eliminated, or that the Convention's provisions reached deep into the domestic policies of any state party. (Its text is reproduced as Appendix I.) Had the scope of the Convention been apparent to them at the outset, maybe fewer states would have acceded to it.

CERD has now been joined by five other committees monitoring implementation of UN human-rights treaties, so that comparisons can be drawn between the approaches of these different treaty bodies. CERD's approach is still influenced by ideas about the Convention formed in an earlier period; they have delayed the development of its jurisprudence, though in some other respects the Committee has been innovative. Freed from the constraints of the Cold War, it has responded to new challenges by taking steps that would have been inconceivable before 1990.

To give the reader an understanding of CERD's contribution, this book has first to sketch the place of action against racial discrimination within the broader movement for the protection of human rights. It has to describe the relation of CERD to other UN bodies with similar responsibilities. A narrative of the Committee's activities has therefore to take account of parallel developments occurring at the same time in the UN and in the wider world. No understanding of the Committee's work is possible without close attention to the text of the Convention as a legally binding document, yet there is still some disagreement, even among specialists, about the criteria by which racial discrimination is to be defined. To try to clear up some of the obscurities, I stopped work on this book for a while in order to write an introduction to the concept; this was published in 1994 by the Open University Press under the title *Discrimination*. Readers who wish to follow up the legal features of the Convention may consult the book by Natan Lerner (1980) and another by Warwick McKean (1983) which is concerned with its place in international law.

Some of the text has had to be written not in ordinary English but in that special idiom which is sometimes called 'UN-ese'. If documents are to be acceptable to international bodies, they have to be written in a flat gutless style that translates between Arabic, Chinese, English, French, Russian, and Spanish, which guards against unintentional value judgements, and which reduces the possibility of misunderstanding on the part of readers whose mother tongue is none of the five listed. Direct speech is not always considered tactful. For example, I recall a discussion in which one member was proposing that the Committee say that a report represented 'a step backwards'; another member demurred. I passed him a note about some of the ways in which the report, when compared to its predecessor, was a retrogression. He replied 'retrogression is a better word than step backwards'. When I asked why, he said 'because you don't have to look up "step backwards" in a dictionary'! This may seem petty, but my colleague knew from experience how his fellow-diplomats could react. If there are some leaden passages in my text, the reader must therefore understand that they may reflect the original wording, and that there may be practical reasons for the somewhat technical language that has been developed to handle some acutely sensitive issues.

To make reading easier, I have kept references to the minimum and inserted them in the text rather than burden it with a mass of footnotes. When lawyers write on these matters, they have to quote the words of every relevant text and to cite every authority. Believing that this can discourage the general reader, and that there are many general readers who ought to take an interest in the subject of this book, I have compromised in ways that will not satisfy everyone. For example, when describing the UN General Assembly debate prior to the adoption of the Convention, I have not furnished references to the dates and paragraphs of delegates' speeches, because anyone who looks up the published record will be able to find them fairly easily. On the other hand, I have included references to passages in the Committee's annual reports and to the summary records of its proceedings, because these are much less easily checked without references.

By the time this book appears on the shelves international action against racial discrimination will have moved further, yet 1995 is a convenient year in which to try to sum up the successes and failures of the legal dimension to this activity. Following upon the UN's Vienna Declaration of 1993, the prospects of achieving universal ratification of the Convention have improved. In October 1994, twenty-eight years after it signed the Convention, the USA deposited an instrument of accession. In the same year a new democratic government assumed office in South Africa. Members of the CERD have long looked forward to political change in South Africa. When the International Day for the Elimination of Racial Discrimination was commemorated at UN headquarters in 1990, Mr George Lamptey, a former Chairman of the Committee, addressed the gathering:

If we meet under auspicious circumstances today, it is partly because the worthy enterprise in which we have been engaged for so long is now yielding some fruits. It is beholden to all to ensure that our progress is sustained. We can then look forward to the day when a free and non-racial South Africa would join the International Convention on the Elimination of All Forms of Racial Discrimination, and when the whites who had so long dominated and mistreated their fellow black countrymen and women, on the basis of race, would find in the Convention's provisions added security on the international level that they in turn would not be subject to bestial treatment by the black majority. When that day dawns then we can truly say that the martyred of Sharpville did not pay the supreme sacrifice in vain.

The transformation of the political scene in South Africa means that delegates who deliver speeches to international bodies will no longer be able to confine their contributions to the condemnation of apartheid as the most heinous form of racial discrimination, or to a rehearsal of the well-publicized evidence of the discrimination suffered by labour migrants to the industrial regions of Western Europe and North America. Everyone needs now to acknowledge that discrimination is a universal feature of social life and to take better account of the ethnic dimension to conflicts such as those in the former Yugoslavia, in the Caucasus, Sri Lanka, Indochina, Tibet, and, of course, in the desperate tragedies of Rwanda and Burundi. Wherever there are encounters between persons who differ in respect of race, colour, descent, ethnic or national origin, there is a potential for racial discrimination contrary to international law. The Convention offers protections to all of them, even to those who have earlier benefited from the practice of racial discrimination.

Michael Banton

*September 1995*

# CONTENTS

*List of Tables*     xiv
*Abbreviations and References*     xv

1. Extending the Rule of Law     1

2. Crimes Against Humanity     11

3. The United Nations     21

4. The Racial Convention     50

5. The Committee's Inheritance     74

6. Laying the Foundations     99

7. The Last of the Cold War     123

8. Seizing the Initiative     142

9. Dialogue with European States     182

10. Dialogue with American States     224

11. Dialogue with African States     249

12. Dialogue with Asian States     276

13. States Parties     305

Appendices
  I. Text of the International Convention on the Elimination
     of All Forms of Racial Discrimination     319
 II. Selected General Recommendations     333
III. Elections to the Committee     338
IV. Legal and Educational Measures Against Racial
     Discrimination     341

*References*     346
*Index of States*     351
*Index of Persons*     355
*Index of Subjects*     358

# LIST OF TABLES

1. Growth in UN membership, by regional group                27
2. Dialogue with selected European states                    172
3. Dialogue with selected American states                    175
4. Dialogue with selected African states                     177
5. Dialogue with selected Asian states                       180

# ABBREVIATIONS AND REFERENCES

| | |
|---|---|
| ARIS | Anti-Racism Information Service |
| CEDAW | Committee on the Elimination of Discrimination Against Women |
| CERD | Committee on the Elimination of Racial Discrimination |
| CSCE | Conference on Security and Cooperation in Europe |
| EC | European Community |
| ECOSOC | Economic and Social Council [of UN] |
| EU | European Union |
| FAO | Food and Agriculture Organization [of UN] |
| FRG | Federal Republic of Germany |
| FPR | Front Patriotique Rwandais |
| HCI | Haut Conseil à L'Intégration |
| ICCPR | International Covenant on Civil and Political Rights |
| ICERD | International Convention on the Elimination of All Forms of Racial Discrimination |
| ILO | International Labour Organization |
| MRND | Mouvement Républicain Nationale pour la Démocratie et le Développement |
| NGO | non-governmental organization |
| OAU | Organization of African Unity |
| OSCE | Organization for Security and Cooperation in Europe |
| PLO | Palestine Liberation Organization |
| RPF | Rwandan Patriotic Front/Front Patriotique Rwandais |
| UDHR | Universal Declaration of Human Rights |
| UN | United Nations |
| UNESCO | United Nations Educational, Scientific, and Cultural Organization |
| UNHCR | United Nations High Commission for Refugees |
| WEOG | Western European and Other Group |
| WHO | World Health Organization |

## REFERENCE NUMBERS TO UN DOCUMENTS

General Assembly document reference numbers relating to plenary sessions consist of three components: A/session number/ sequential number. The verbatim records of plenary meetings are then A/session number/PV./sequential number, but prior to the changes made around 1978 they started A/PV. The reports of CERD to the General Assembly began in 1970 with the reference A/8027; since 1976 they have followed the style A/31/18, in which the 31 designates the number of the UN session and the 18 that it is the report of CERD. The summary record of the proceedings of the General Assembly's Third Committee are identified by the reference A/C.3/session number/SR followed by the number of the meeting.

Documents of the Economic and Social Council are identified by reference numbers starting with E; those of the Human Rights Commission have reference numbers beginning E/CN.4/ followed by the year and the sequential number, while documents of its Sub-Commission on Prevention of Discrimination and Protection of Minorities now have an entry like /Sub.2/ before the year.

The documents of treaty bodies are identified by their initials (thus, CERD, CCPR). The summary records of the CERD are designated CERD/C/SR.957, etc., the last numeral being the number of the meeting (as opposed to the session). In this book the references have been abbreviated to SR. Periodic reports of states are given references like CERD/C/192/Add.3, though in this book they have been identified as initial, second, or third periodic reports, etc. References for documents relating to the human rights instruments in general start with HRI, thus HRI/GEN/1/Rev.1 is the Compilation of General Comments and General Recommendations adopted by Human Rights Treaty Bodies; the first section of state party reports is common to reports submitted to all relevant treaty bodies, and therefore starts HRI/CORE, while, for example, HRI/MC/1994/2 denoted a report of the Secretary-General submitted to the Fifth Meeting of Chairpersons of Treaty Bodies.

# 1

# Extending the Rule of Law

THE story of international action against racial discrimination, as of international action against many other evils, is that of the struggle to extend the rule of law. It is a highly political struggle, because it is about cajoling states to give up a little of their sovereignty. They are reluctant to do this unless they can get something in exchange. By acceding to a convention they may be able to contribute to a cause they think important, to improve their image in the diplomatic world, or to put pressure on some other state of whose policies they disapprove. In democratic countries people are accustomed to seeing their governments criticized daily in many of the morning newspapers, but when a foreign official criticizes the same government, reactions are different. People ask whether circumstances in the foreigner's country are such that he or she is entitled to complain. Diplomats, in particular, are trained to defend their countries' honour, and they can be very prickly. They are on the look-out lest the rules of international relations are applied unfairly to their countries' disadvantage. As an example of the sort of little struggle that can result, consider the scene as it was in Salle XI at the Palais des Nations in Geneva on 9 August 1989.

## THE COMMITTEE AT WORK

Sixteen of the eighteen members of the Committee on the Elimination of Racial Discrimination (CERD) were sitting, well spread out along the sides of two long tables. They had just completed their consideration of the ninth periodic report of Iceland, submitted in accordance with the International Convention on the Elimination of All Forms of Racial Discrimination (ICERD). The Chairman, Mr George Lamptey (who was Ghana's ambassador to Rome), announced at 11.00 hours that the Committee would next consider the ninth periodic report of Venezuela. Mr Rudolfo

Taylhardat, Venezuela's ambassador to the UN at Geneva, took his place at the table. Introducing his government's report, Mr Taylhardat said that Venezuela's regular compliance with its reporting obligations reflected the serious view it took of its responsibilities and its clear commitment to equality and fundamental freedoms for all individuals. Racial discrimination did not exist in Venezuela and was totally alien to Venezuelans, who were egalitarian by nature and abhorred all forms of discrimination. He then recapitulated the position set out in paragraphs 14–16 of his country's report, as follows:

The Government of Venezuela ventures to dissent from the Committee's interpretation of the reports to be submitted in compliance with article 9 of the Convention. . . . The questions raised by the Committee in paragraphs 561, 564 and 566 of the report of the Committee on the Elimination of Racial Discrimination for 1985 (A/40/18) and submitted to the General Assembly at its fortieth session, underscore the interest shown in the preceding paragraphs [concerning the guaranteeing of the equal rights of the Venezuelan indigenous peoples]. Venezuela, as a sovereign State, considers that the questions raised relate to its implementation of the internal legal standards in respect of rights and obligations *vis-à-vis* nationals or aliens, since the fact that racial discrimination was abolished by the provisions of the Constitution is well known and has been explained at some length, especially in the eighth report. Consequently, Venezuela does not belong to the category of State which is required to comply with articles 2, paragraph 1 (*a*), (*b*), (*c*) and (*d*), 5 and 7 of the Convention. However, in its ninth report, Venezuela will endeavour to reply to the questions put by the Committee about its policies in respect of the indigenous population, and its achievements in respect of the provisions of articles 3 to 7 of the Convention, in order to reaffirm the principles of equality and non-discrimination guaranteed in its internal legislation and as a supplement to the detailed information provided in the eighth report.

Mr Taylhardat spoke, in Spanish, for about half an hour. Most of the persons present, around the Committee tables or in the public gallery, listened through little plastic earphones to the simultaneous interpretation. (In small cubicles round the room, fronted by glass panels, sit the persons who interpret into, and out of, Chinese, English, French, Russian, and Spanish. At a long table down the centre sit the précis-writers, the press officers, the conference room officer, and any observers from UN specialized agencies. Behind members' chairs are places sometimes occupied by staff from the diplomatic missions.)

The Chairman then called on Mr Mario Yutzis, who, at the previous session, had been the Committee member designated 'country rapporteur' and given the task of opening the discussion. Mr Yutzis was Professor of Philosophical Anthropology at the Buenos Aires Higher Evangelical Institute for Theological Education, in Argentina. He commended Venezuela's report but drew attention to the fundamental difference of opinion between the Committee and the reporting state. It was difficult to accept that subtle forms of racial discrimination did not exist in Venezuela as in the rest of the world. Indigenous groups, and migrants to the cities, were very vulnerable. Venezuela had not complied with its obligation under article 4 of the Convention to declare incitement to racial hatred and discrimination offences punishable by law. A recent decision of the Venezuelan Supreme Court had stated that it was not easy for the Court to decide a case of discrimination because of the unfortunate absence of a law on the subject. Mr Yutzis could not accept the statement in paragraph 8 of the report that 'it is necessary to stress that when the Venezuelan State ratified the Convention, it did so out of solidarity and in order to reaffirm Venezuela's existing legal position on racial discrimination'. Any state acceding to a convention must comply with its provisions unless it has entered specific reservations acceptable to the other states parties; the nature of the obligations was clearly defined in the Vienna Convention on the Law of Treaties. He congratulated Venezuela on its policies towards indigenous communities, but posed a series of questions about the consequences for some of these about oil-drilling in one region, about reports of torture in one locality, about a particular development project, about some groups' loss of land, and about the dubious practices of some transnational religious groups which forced the indigenous peoples to forgo their traditional lifestyles and symbols.

Mr Yutzis's speech took twenty-four minutes. Since it covered the central issues, the speeches of other members could be briefer. The first was from Mr Mahmoud Aboul-Nasr, then Egypt's ambassador to Madrid. He recorded his complete disagreement with the suggestion that Venezuela was not bound by the Convention's obligations. The Committee's task was to engage in a constructive, mutually informative dialogue on the situation in a given reporting state and on issues requiring clarification. These same points were reiterated by other members. Mr Ferrero Costa (Dean of the Faculty of International Law in the Catholic University of Peru) said that the sovereignty of Venezuela was not in question; it had expressed its sovereignty by voluntarily accepting and ratifying the Convention. Mr Karl Joseph Partsch (formerly Professor of Public Law in the University of Bonn), concurring, asked about the requirement that citizens must understand Spanish to be registered as electors. Mr Banton (the present author) enquired about action taken on a petition from an indigenous group who claimed that their land was being taken by a colonist. Then the Chairman, speaking as a member of the Committee, associated himself with the criticism of Venezuela's position.

In reply, Mr Taylhardat said that Mr Yutzis's charge that Venezuela had not complied with article 4 was serious and should be brought 'through the proper channel'. He referred to the provisions of article 11. Mr Aboul-Nasr had not understood Venezuela's position, which was that, since there was no discrimination in the country, it did not have to provide certain kinds of information. Some of the questions asked by Committee members related to matters on which Venezuela was not obliged under the Convention to supply information.

After the lunch interval (which lasted from 13.05 to 15.20) Mr Yutzis asked for the floor again. Among other things, he explained, for Mr Taylhardat's benefit, that members of the Committee served in their personal capacity (as provided in article 8.1). Article 11 was for the use of a state party which wished to complain about another state party. Mr Partsch supported him and explained the sorts of action necessary if a state was to comply with the requirements of article 4. Mr Aga Shahi (formerly Pakistan's ambassador to the UN in New York and sometime foreign minister) observed that, by acceding to the Convention, the Venezuelan government had empowered the Committee to question it on all those aspects of its domestic policy which the latter deemed to fall within its competence. It was the Committee's duty to question the reporting state on the implementation in practice of its legislation concerning indigenous populations. Mr Aboul-Nasr added that, even if a state claimed that racial discrimination did not exist within its borders, in ratifying the Convention it undertook to take measures to prevent any cases of discrimination arising in the future (this had been clarified in 1972 by the Committee's general recommendation II). Mr André Braunschweig (formerly president of the criminal division of the French Court of Appeal) stated that the reasons for ratifying an international instrument mattered little; what was important were the obligations deriving from accession. Mr Rhenan Segura (a legal adviser to the government of Costa Rica) remarked that Venezuela had always played a leading role in UN human-rights bodies, which made the difference of opinion the more regrettable. Mr Song Shuhua (Vice-President, Central Institute of Nationalities, Beijing) asked whether there was a contradiction in the report in that it referred both to the assimilation of minorities and to the preservation of their identity. The Chairman then expressed the hope that the Venezuelan government would consider carefully the views expressed in the Committee.

In response, Mr Taylhardat maintained many of his previous positions, insisting that, since his state's policy towards its indigenous population was in no way discriminatory, it did not have to answer questions about it. This might then have been the end of the exchange, but Mr Ferrero Costa used the opportunity to offer four comments on legal aspects of a state party's obligations which he wished Venezuela to take into account when preparing its next report. Mr Yuri Rechetov (an international lawyer also, and deputy chief of the Division for Humanitarian Issues in the USSR's ministry of foreign affairs) then added that the reporting state's reference to ratification out of solidarity should not be taken as implying that Venezuela had not intended to implement it. Mr Taylhardat responded, again describing as 'a very serious accusation' the statement that his country had not fulfilled its obligations under article 4. (This combativeness was not at all in tune with the conciliatory way in which members of the Committee had spoken. Mr Aboul-Nasr, for example, had earlier observed that other states parties, including his own country of Egypt, had not met all their obligations in this respect.) The Chairman commented to similar effect, and thanked Mr Taylhardat for responding to members of the Committee. Mr Aboul-Nasr spoke once more, referring to the apparent deadlock and raising the possibility that the Committee might make a formal suggestion to the state concerned in accordance with article 9.2 of the Convention. The Chairman thought that the expression of views as reflected in the summary record would suffice, and was supported in this by Mr Ferrero Costa. So, at 16.45 hours, the Chairman declared that the Committee had concluded its consideration of the ninth periodic report of Venezuela and brought down his gavel.

Taking account of a query raised by Mrs Sadiq Ali (of India), eleven members of the Committee had expressed views or asked questions; five members had not spoken, and two were absent (one of them sick). This was not a typical occasion because, though many other states fail to meet all their obligations and do not answer questions, it is most unusual for a state to argue so explicitly that important provisions in the Convention do not apply to its circumstances.

## CONSIDERATION OF REPORTS

The time taken for consideration of state reports varies greatly. Some are very brief. To take just the session at which the Venezuelan report was considered, the report from Luxembourg occupied little more than half an hour of the Committee's time, since there was very little new to report about action taken during the previous two years. Iceland's report took very little longer. But the report from the Libyan Arab Jamahiriya (another brief document) was also out of the ordinary. Libya acceded to the Convention in 1968. Its fifth report had been considered in 1979. No representative of the state had then been present to introduce it. Members had observed that the report lacked substance; the Committee had invited the state to submit another report of direct relevance to the Committee's work, for consideration at the next session. None was received, but in 1987 the state submitted a report which constituted in one document the sixth, seventh, eighth, ninth, and tenth reports. It still failed to specify how the state was meeting treaty obligations. This time a representative attended. He emphasized the importance Libya attached to the noble cause which the Committee defended and stated that he would listen carefully to comments which would be taken into account in the next report. Only one member of the Committee spoke. This was the designated country rapporteur, Mr Isi Foighel (Professor of International Law in Copenhagen, a former minister in the Danish government, and a judge in the European Court of Human Rights). He observed that the report did not fully comply with the Committee's guidelines. It did not supply information about the composition of the population. With regard to article 4, he asked what the victims of racial discrimination could do if attacked? What measures had been taken to implement subparagraphs (*a*), (*b*) and (*c*) of that article? The information provided raised more questions than it answered and might not do justice to the country's efforts to combat discrimination. The Chairman declared that the silence of other members must indicate that they shared the views expressed by Mr Foighel. Mr Omar, the Libyan representative, then acknowledged that his country's report was in some respects deficient. He had taken careful note of Mr Foighel's comments; the replies would be given in the next report, if necessary after consultation with the secretariat. By contrast to the dialogue with Venezuela, the whole tone of this exchange was restrained and cooperative. Most discussions lie somewhere between these two extremes.

Consideration of the Libyan report took just over an hour and a quarter, whereas those at the same session from Colombia, the FRG, the Philippines, and Sweden took around three hours each. There was much interest in the Swedish report. Many members wished to speak, and when many questions are asked a state representative may take a long time to reply to them all. Sometimes a representative returns to reply the following day, having been in touch with his or her government during the interim. The proportion of time taken by Committee members' comments relative to the time taken by the state representative varied at this session between 13 and 75 per cent of the total time. There had been occasions at previous sessions when some state reports (e.g. from Chile and Israel) had been received with hostility. Some representatives adopt a defensive style, often, but not necessarily, because their governments are vulnerable to criticism. Some representatives do not argue back but say simply that they will transmit to their governments a record of the views expressed. Others elaborate, sometimes at tedious length, about their countries' philosophy regarding group relations. Some states have complex reports to present. For example, Australia brings a report from the Commonwealth government subsuming reports from the seven constituent states. Similarly, the Canadian report contains separate sections about the eight provinces. Some states send a single representative, others a delegation consisting of various specialists who take the questions relating to their areas of expertise. A representative may appear of a reporting state which, because of some crisis, is in no position to take effective action about racial discrimination—as when a representative of Democratic Kampuchea explained that his government could control only a small part of the state's territory. Few members commented on this report. If much depends on the reporting state, so does the length and character of a discussion depend upon the interests of the Committee members. Reports about the occupation of territory have occasioned some lengthy discussions leading to resolutions transmitted to the General Assembly. The reports of small states can attract as much attention as those of big states. Many members may, for example, have something to say about a report from the Holy See—which is a party to the Convention although it is not a UN member state.

## THE COMMITTEE'S ACHIEVEMENTS

Since its first meeting in 1970, the Committee has altered in many ways as a result of changes in the world situation, the kinds of persons elected to it, and the development of the Committee's procedures and accumulated experience. States parties now, in general, have much better laws against racial discrimination than they did in 1970. The Committee has established itself as an autonomous body, master of its own procedures, exercising powers given to it under the Convention. It is not a court, nor a debating society, but a treaty body which in certain circumstances (e.g. in dealing with individual petitions) functions judicially and not politically. As later chapters will suggest, political influences sometimes enter into the Committee's work, but the key question is whether, seen over more than two decades, there has been a trend for the Committee's character as a legal body to develop, and, if so, in what respects.

An answer has to be subjective, because there is so much material that might be considered and it is so diverse. Nor is all the documentation easily accessible. The Committee reports annually to the UN General Assembly, and those reports are not difficult to locate. In 1977 it was decided that Committee documents, including reports from states parties, should be publicly available. Since 1975 a summary record has been published which provides, in a condensed form, a near-verbatim account of everything said. These documents are available in English, French, Russian, and Spanish, which are the working languages of the Committee. (Working languages are to be distinguished from official languages. The official languages are the four just mentioned, plus Chinese. Documents are made available in the working languages only.) Interpretation into and out of official languages (and others on occasion) is provided by the UN. In 1987 the states parties considered a proposal, from Iraq, to make Arabic an official language for the Committee—as it is for some other committees. At current prices this would have added $1,600 per meeting day to the costs. Morocco and China proposed that Arabic and Chinese be made working languages. This would have cost about $13,600 more per session. (None of these proposals has yet been implemented.) The present study is based on reports to the General Assembly from 1970, the summary records, and published commentaries upon the Committee's work.

The Committee convened first at a time when many states were pressing hard at the UN upon what they saw as the completion of a process of decolonization. The responsibilities of the former imperial powers for racial discrimination were much emphasized. Diplomats brought the arguments of the General Assembly into meetings of the Committee. With the accumulation of state reports, attention shifted to dialogue with the states in order to improve standards of compliance. The so-called 'Cold War' came to an end. The UN's budgetary crisis from the end of 1985 (which arose because the US government, irritated by many UN policies, started to withhold parts of its financial assessment) meant the cancellation of many sessions. The cancellations stimulated some improvements in the Committee's working methods. Progress has been steady rather than dramatic, but, because it is the outcome of many little struggles within the administrative and diplomatic framework, several chapters are needed to state the case for an optimistic evaluation of it.

It is also essential to interpret the history of the Committee as part of the world-wide growth in human-rights law since the confrontation with the Hitler regime in the early 1940s. The movement for human rights is, to a significant extent, an attempt to discipline governments, getting them to accept the rule of law; that is, to acknowledge restrictions upon their freedom of action and their accountability for observing the legal obligations that constitute the laws of the international community. These are products in part of custom and in part of treaties. This body of law has grown in response to dangers, and to the conviction that certain disasters, like the rise of fascism, must never be allowed to recur. That particular disaster became one of the spurs to international action in defence of human rights. Just how it did so is the subject of the next chapter.

# 2

# Crimes Against Humanity

WELL before the Second World War was over, the allied powers started to consider what they would do if Hitler or any of his close associates were to fall into their hands in the event of victory. Should they be shot or tried? If they were to be tried, with what offences should they be charged? There is a well-recognized principle deriving from Roman Law that *nullum crimen sine lege*. No person can be held to have broken a law unless that law was in force at the time of the offending action. What law had Hitler broken? Putting such doubts aside, in 1943 seventeen of the allied nations established the UN War Crimes Commission to be responsible for the detection, trial, and punishment of persons accused of war crimes.

## THE NATURE OF LAW

Properly to appreciate the difficulties in the Commission's path, it is necessary to reflect, even if only briefly, on the long history of debate about the nature of law. Is it any more than the implementation of the decisions of a sovereign prince or a sovereign parliament? Can there be any source of right other than the acknowledged law of a particular jurisdiction? These are questions of political philosophy, and the best way to explain the arguments is to trace their history. This brief exposition draws upon that of R. J. Vincent (1986: 19–36).

The English word *law* combines two concepts which are distinguished in other European languages. In Latin the word *ius* signified law in the abstract, as opposed to *lex*, the concrete law of a statute or a precedent. In French, *droit* is opposed to *loi*; in German, *Recht* to *Gesetz*; in Italian, *diritto* to *lege*; in Swedish, *rätt* to *lag*, etc. In its abstract sense, people speak of the law of England or the law of libel, or they refer to the criminal law as something more than the sum of the separate laws against particular crimes. The Romans divided their law into the *ius naturale*, a set of laws imposed upon humanity by nature, or, some would say, by God, or by reason. It is more general than the *ius gentium*, or law of peoples, which should apply irrespective of ethnicity, and the *ius civile*, or that law which applies within the jurisdiction of the state. Medieval political theory took its inspiration from a belief that the law expressed the organic unity of humankind. Church and state were separate, but at a higher level the Pope was overlord of both the spiritual and temporal domains. With the pressure from rulers who sought political independence, a plurality of states emerged and the medieval synthesis crumbled. Natural law had to be based on the individual. So the 'fundamental fact' at the close of the Middle Ages, according to Vincent, was the obliteration of all groups intermediate between the individual and the state, 'and it is in the contest between the victors that the western theory of human rights is worked out'.

The primacy of the individual as a source of natural rights was proclaimed at the end of the eighteenth century in the French and American revolutions. The preamble to the former's Declaration of the Rights of Man and of the Citizen asserted that 'ignorance, neglect, or contempt of human rights, are the sole causes of public misfortunes and corruptions of Government'. There was no mention of original sin. Humans were naturally good and evil came about only as a result of the faulty organization of society. The US Declaration of Independence maintained: 'We hold these rights to be self-evident, that all men are created equal, that they are endowed by their Creator with certain unalienable Rights, that among these are Life, Liberty, and the pursuit of Happiness. That to secure these rights, Governments are instituted among Men . . .'—an unambiguous statement that individual rights come first and that governments are a means to an end. The reference to 'unalienable rights' is also notable, because these rights are held to be more important than democratic decisions. A democratically elected legislature acting in accordance with the country's constitution can still not deprive anyone of unalienable (or inalienable) rights, nor can the holder of such a right divest himself or herself of them (as by selling himself or herself into slavery). To do so would be to breach a higher principle. The arguments of the US Declaration reflect those of John Locke, who taught that it was from natural law that humans derived rights which those who governed were bound to respect. Anyone, whether ruler or subject, who infringed such rights threatened the constitution and was therefore guilty of the greatest of crimes. Such a person was to be treated as the common enemy of humankind. In opposition to prevailing political theory, this implied a right of rebellion. Charles I had good grounds in the law of his time to maintain that 'a king cannot be tried by any superior jurisdiction on earth', but his argument was unavailing. He was executed in 1649 for treason and 'other high crimes against the realm of England'. The reasons given may have been but excuses, yet some justification was required and events themselves reinforced the argument that there was a law even kings had to obey.

There was a subsidiary theme in the debate which stressed group rights. The French Declaration described the nation as 'essentially the source of all sovereignty; nor can any individual, or any body of men, be entitled to any authority which is not expressly derived from it'. Where eighteenth-century thinkers placed liberty at the beginning of the historical process, Hegel and some other nineteenth-century thinkers, seeking to recapture the importance of community, pictured it as a goal of historical movements seeking the realization of collective rights. From a very different stand-point, Edmund Burke contended that humans acquire rights only as members of particular societies. Natural rights reflect the evolution of the nations in which people happen to live. Jeremy Bentham was equally insistent upon the priority of *lex* over *ius*, declaring in a famous passage that 'Right is the child of law; from real laws come real rights, but from imaginary law, from "laws of nature", come imaginary rights . . . Natural rights is simple nonsense, natural and imprescriptible rights rhetorical nonsense, nonsense upon stilts.' Karl Marx was no kinder to the claims of natural law. From his perspective the theory of natural rights was but the special language of a group defending its shared interests; freedom was possible only through community.

Nineteenth-century socialists reacted against the inequalities they saw around them and demanded that governments actively inter-vene to redress social and economic injustices. Their successors in Eastern Europe saw the state as the source of rights conferred upon individuals. Governments came before rights. Thus one Soviet lawyer explained: 'the individual has no rights so long as the State

has not fulfilled its obligation to grant them. The State acts as a
necessary channel of transformation of its obligations into individual rights.' According to the Soviet view up to the 1980s,
international law was a body of norms established between states.
It was states that were the subjects of international law, not
individuals (Bloed and Van Hoof 1985: 43–6). This introduces
another dimension. Whether or not states are bound to observe any
principles of natural law, they are certainly bound to observe any
treaties or contracts they make with other states and to observe
customary international law. So, when states that went to war with
one another sent their enemies' ambassadors home with promises
of safe conduct and expected their enemies to do likewise, this
became a custom that new states were also expected to observe. An
important part of international law has grown from the recognition
of such customary practices.

## THE FIRST WORLD WAR

For several centuries also it had been recognized that the existence
of a state of war did not excuse actions of a criminal character,
such as the mistreatment of prisoners and the murder of civilians.
After the First World War the preliminary peace conference created
a commission to inquire into 'the responsibilities relating to the
war'. This body recommended war-crimes trials before national
courts (those of the victors) and, where appropriate, before a
tribunal representing the victorious states collectively. It contemplated trials for violations of the laws and customs of war (of
which it listed thirty-two categories) and for crimes against
humanity. Special measures were to be taken against those
responsible for starting the war and for violating the neutrality of
Belgium and Luxembourg. But the victors disagreed about the
proposal that heads of states should be held criminally liable for
political actions. The treaty of Versailles contained no provision for
trying defendants for crimes against humanity, and only indirectly,
as to the former Kaiser, was there provision for a trial for an
alleged crime against peace. Partly because of German reluctance to
surrender those accused, the victors ultimately agreed to permit the
cases to be tried by the Supreme Court of Leipzig. The *Encyclo-
paedia Britannica* describes the result as ineffective: 'The great

majority of those tried were acquitted, despite strong evidence of guilt; those convicted received grossly inadequate sentences (and, in several instances, were quickly permitted to escape from prison); and all were treated as heroes by the German press and public' (cf. Taylor 1993: 14–18).

In 1918 the US President, Woodrow Wilson, made a historic speech listing his country's war aims in the form of fourteen points. He alluded to self-determination, and then a month later clarified his conception of such a principle as a foremost goal of US foreign policy. The idea caught the attention of minorities in many regions of the world, including countries like Japan and China which resented the prejudice against their nationals shown in the USA. So Japan solicited Wilson's support for the inclusion of a statement on racial equality in the covenant of the League of Nations:

The equality of nations being a basic principle of the League of Nations, the High Contracting Parties agree to accord, as soon as possible, to all alien nationals of States members of the League equal and just treatment in every respect, making no distinction, in law or in fact, on account of their race or nationality.

The US and the colonial powers were suspicious or opposed to this proposal, so the Japanese pared it down to the very minimum, asking for recognition of 'the principle of equality of nations and the just treatment of their nationals'. On a vote in the League Commission, eleven out of seventeen voted in favour, but Wilson, who was chairman, ruled that such a proposal would require unanimity; no more was heard of it until a similar dispute occurred a generation later in the drafting of the Charter of the United Nations (DeConde 1992: 88–92; Lauren 1988: 79–96).

To reduce the risks of another terrible war it was necessary as far as possible to accommodate national aspirations by redrawing several boundaries. This led to the creation of the new states of Czechoslovakia and Yugoslavia. Under the Ottoman and Austro-Hungarian empires ethnic minorities had become established in regions far away from their heartlands and they were left exposed when those empires crumbled. In the wake of wars and boundary changes, groups have found that they have been made citizens of different states, with new requirements about language, schooling, land rights, military service, nationality laws, and so on, and that their new rulers have been suspicious of their loyalties to the state of which they have newly become citizens. The relationship can be very uneasy. After 1918 the victorious powers bound the defeated states of Austria, Bulgaria, Hungary, and Turkey to Minorities Treaties to be supervised by the League of Nations. They created similar treaties to bind the new states of Czechoslovakia and Yugoslavia and those with altered boundaries: Greece, Poland, and Romania. They made special provisions for the Åland Islands, Danzig, the Memel Territory, and Upper Silesia. The Bulgarian constitution already contained guarantees for its Greek and Turkish minorities. The effect of the new treaties was to give members of many national minorities collective rights analogous to constitutional rights because internationally supervised. The treaties were not altogether successful, partly because the victorious states were not subject to similar obligations. Although Italy gained territory with a resident German-speaking population, its policies towards that new minority were unconstrained by international oversight. Gilbert Murray, who was involved in these negotiations, concluded: 'It was an error of principle in the Peace Treaties to impose the clauses for the due protection of Minorities upon the new nations alone. The same obligations should have been accepted by the Great Powers, and made part of the common law of Europe' (quoted in Mair 1928: p. vii).

It is highly unusual for state boundaries to be changed in peacetime. If, after a war, a state acquires new territory with a resident minority, it is likely that discontented members of that minority will turn for sympathy to their own people across the border. If an international procedure is set up for protecting their rights, there is a danger that any initiative will come from the government of the adjoining state, and the move will develop into an interstate dispute rather than as the concern of an international treaty body. In such circumstances states are understandably anxious that the new citizens acknowledge an obligation of loyalty to the state. Thus the governments of India and Pakistan in 1950 reached an agreement in which it was stated: 'Both governments wish to emphasize that the allegiance and loyalty of the minorities is to the State of which they are citizens, and that it is to the Government of their own state that they should look for redress of their grievances.'

In 1928 sixty-three states (including Germany) signed the Pact of Paris (or the Kellogg–Briand Pact as it is sometimes called), according to which they renounced war as an instrument of national policy for the solution of disputes. Some regarded this as little more than another pious hope. They thought that the Pact did not have the character of law because it did not provide a clear definition of aggression, specify how offenders would be tried, or indicate how they were to be punished. The alternative view was that a legal right was not lost because it was not used, and that law could develop through court decisions as well as by statute. What better moment could there be for moving towards international law than after a period of lawlessness when there appeared to be an international consensus that action was necessary?

## THE SECOND WORLD WAR

Such arguments were revived early in the Second World War. What were the allies to do if, at its end, the Nazi leaders were taken prisoner? There was a widespread conviction that the enemy's leaders constituted a criminal regime, that the atrocities were part of a deliberate plan, and that those most responsible were the Nazi leaders themselves. So the punishment of war crimes became one of the stated aims of the allied governments and led to the creation, in 1943, of the War Crimes Commission mentioned at the beginning of this chapter (Tusa and Tusa 1983: 20–2, 58–60).

The judge appointed by the USA to lead the prosecution team believed that the 'crime which comprehends all lesser crimes is the crime of making unjustifiable war'. Other lawyers insisted on the principle of *nullum crimen sine lege*. At the time the Nazis planned their aggressions their action might have been contrary to *ius* but was not clearly contrary to *lex*. Were the actions of the allies to be assessed by the same criteria? Had not the USSR in Finland, Poland, the Baltic states, and elsewhere also 'entered into a common plan or enterprise aimed at domination over other nations' which involved 'atrocities, persecutions and deportations' on a colossal scale? What of the bombing of Dresden and Hiroshima? When the allies drew up a charter establishing an International Military Tribunal and detailing the kinds of charges that could be brought, they were open to the accusations that the court would administer only 'victors' justice', and that the supposed offences were formulated after the event and were designed to fit a special case. The charges eventually brought were (1) the pursuit of a common plan or conspiracy; (2) crimes against peace, e.g. waging aggressive war; (3) war crimes, so defined as to make rulers and commanders liable as well as their subordinates; (4) crimes against humanity, covering the persecution of racial and religious groups (Tusa and Tusa 1983: 56, 72, 85–7, 415). The Nuremberg Tribunal consisted of two judges from each of France, the USSR, the UK, and the USA, and there were four prosecution teams from the same countries. The lawyers were accustomed to different procedures and held contrasting ideas about criminal liability, especially the crime of conspiracy and the proposal that the Tribunal declare illegal organizations like the leadership corps of the Nazi Party, the Gestapo, the SS, the SA, the Reich Cabinet, and the General Staff and High Command of the German Armed Forces. Nevertheless, twenty-four men were arraigned and twenty-two survived to hear the verdicts. Three were found not guilty of the charges against them. Twelve of the remaining nineteen were sentenced to death by hanging. The first three of the named organizations were found to have been criminal. The judgment expressed the judges' unanimous opinion that aggressive war was a crime, and well established as such in international law. When the defendants invaded peaceful countries, broke international treaties, and violated the Hague and Geneva Conventions on the customs of war, they had known that they were doing wrong. These were not technical offences which depended on the way a law was drafted at a particular time. So the whole process could be seen as confirming the existence in human affairs of natural law, while the manner in which, over a period of ten months, the proceedings were conducted, led nearly all observers to conclude that it had indeed been a court of justice.

Another war-crimes trial was held in Tokyo. Twenty-eight Japanese were indicted on fifty-five counts, similar in character to those brought at Nuremberg. The trial, before eleven judges from the various countries that had been at war with Japan, lasted two and a half years. By the time the war had ended on the Chinese mainland, six million civilians had been killed by the Japanese. The Rape of Nanking, the Bataan Death March, the Siam–Burma Railway, the Rape of Manila, and other atrocities in the Philippines, Vietnam, and New Guinea testified to a pattern in which the Japanese treated non-Japanese in a way they would never have treated Japanese. Of the twenty-five defendants at the time of sentence, seven were sentenced to death by hanging (Brackman 1987: 17, 185–96, 267–75, 365, 463–9).

One of the judges at Nuremberg wrote that what sustained him in difficult circumstances was

the knowledge that this trial can be a very great landmark in the history of International Law. There will be a precedent for all successive generations, and aggressor nations, great or small, will embark on war with the certain knowledge that if they fail they will be called to grim account.

His optimism was justified and the qualification 'if they fail' could some day be unnecessary. One of the distinguishing characteristics of the new offence of crimes against humanity was that charges could be brought without limitation as to time. Public opinion in the FRG was so strong in 1965 that the criminal law there was extended to permit such offences to be still prosecuted despite the lapse of time.

In 1950 the International Law Commission, as directed by the UN General Assembly, formulated the principles of international law recognized at Nuremberg defining crimes against peace, war crimes, and crimes against humanity: these last were listed as

murder, extermination, enslavement, deportation and other inhuman acts done against any civilian population, or persecutions on political, racial or religious grounds, when such acts are done or such persecutions are carried on in execution of or in connection with any crime against peace or any war crime.

The General Assembly instructed the International Law Commission to prepare a draft code of offences against the peace and security of mankind, considering various drafts and seeking the observations of governments. Progress has been steady (see UN 1994: 294–301).

## CONTINUING CONTROVERSY

Since 1990 hostilities in the Middle East and the Balkans, and genocide in Rwanda, have given a new interest and urgency to the question of proceedings under international law for the abuse of human rights. An international tribunal has been established to try crimes committed in the break-up of Yugoslavia and in Rwanda but proposals for a permanent international criminal court have not been able to overcome the suspicion that such a court would be too much influenced by the most powerful states. Too many recent events suggest that the UN Security Council employs double standards in the action it takes against certain states while ignoring violations by others.

Later chapters will seek to differentiate preventive action against racial discrimination from remedial action. A state which accedes to a human-rights convention binds itself to provide protections which should reduce the chances that remedial action will ever be necessary. It is more important to try to prevent crimes against humanity than to punish those who have been responsible for such crimes.

# 3

# The United Nations

THE men and women who founded the United Nations were more ambitious than those who drafted the Covenant of the League of Nations. The Covenant opened with the words: 'The High Contracting Parties, in order to promote international co-operation . . . agree to this Covenant'. It was to be a league of governments. The Charter of the United Nations aimed higher, for it begins:

We the peoples of the United Nations determined

to save succeeding generations from the threat of war . . .

to reaffirm faith in fundamental human rights, in the dignity and worth of the human person, in the equal rights of men and women and of nations large and small, and

to establish conditions under which justice and respect for the obligations arising from treaties and other sources of international law can be maintained, and

to promote social progress . . .

The UN sought to represent the peoples of the world organized as nations, but in practice it has been an organization of states as these are represented by governments and those who take decisions on their behalf.

## UN BODIES CONCERNED WITH RACIAL DISCRIMINATION

The main source of authority for international action against discrimination is to be found in the Charter, which declares in article 55 that the UN shall promote 'universal respect for, and observance of, human rights and fundamental freedoms for all without distinction as to race, sex, language or religion' (Partsch 1994). In article 56, member states pledge themselves to take joint and separate action for the achievement of those purposes. China had proposed that the Charter include the statement 'the principle of equality of all states and all races shall be upheld'. This proposal was unacceptable lest such a reference to races authorize interference in the internal affairs of states; to restrict any such possibility, article 2.7 was inserted. It affirms that nothing in the Charter 'shall authorize the United Nations to intervene in matters which are essentially within the domestic jurisdiction of any state'.

The UN organization includes a variety of bodies with separate but sometimes overlapping functions with respect to human rights: the General Assembly, the Security Council, the Economic and Social Council, the Trusteeship Council, the treaty-monitoring bodies, and the specialized agencies, including the International Labour Organization (ILO) (an autonomous organization founded in 1919) and the UN Educational, Scientific and Cultural Organization (UNESCO). This chapter seeks to provide sufficient information about these institutions for the reader to understand the context within which CERD works.

At the first session of the General Assembly a proposal was put forward (by Panama) that there should be a Declaration on Fundamental Human Rights and the Rights and Duties of Nations. This was later expanded into a proposal for an international bill of human rights to be prepared by the Commission on Human Rights (a subsidiary of the Economic and Social Council). The Commission decided in favour of a bill containing three parts: a declaration containing general principles (realized in the Universal Declaration of Human Rights (UDHR) of 1948); a covenant or covenants embodying these principles in the form of a treaty so that they would be binding on any state which adhered to the treaty, and 'measures of implementation'.

Two covenants—one on economic, social, and cultural rights, the other on civil and political rights—were approved in 1966 and entered into force ten years later after their ratification by the minimum of thirty-five member states. The covenants are implemented by an obligation upon states to submit periodic reports which were to be considered in the one case by the Economic and Social Council and in the other by the Human Rights Committee under provisions set out in the civil covenant. In the case of the latter instrument there is a further method of implementation, the first Optional Protocol to the covenant, which empowers the

Human Rights Committee to receive and consider communications (or petitions) from individuals claiming to be victims of violations of any of the rights set forth in the Covenant, provided that the state to whose jurisdiction they are subject has ratified that protocol. In addition to the International Bill there are three regional conventions, the European Convention for the Protection of Human Rights and Fundamental Freedoms, the American Convention on Human Rights, and the African Charter on Human and Peoples' Rights. Proposals for a regional convention on human rights in the Asia–Pacific region are under discussion. The covenants and regional conventions all specify that the rights in question are to be secured without discrimination.

The Commission on Human Rights is composed of fifty-three elected states. It examines allegations of gross violations of human rights both in public sessions and under a confidential procedure authorized by resolution 1503 (on which see UN 1994: 311–14). It appoints special rapporteurs to visit selected countries and investigate; they are not always allowed into the states concerned, though the legitimacy of their work is gradually coming to be accepted. Meetings of the Commission are very different in character from those of CERD as described in Chapter 1. They are held in a large auditorium with five rows of concentric tables each forming about two-thirds of a circle. The first rows seat the fifty-three delegations, usually two seats at the table with three behind for additional delegation staff. In the outer circles, tables and seats are allocated to non-governmental organizations (NGOs) to whom the UN has accorded consultative status (such as, say, Amnesty International). To hear the speaker, a microphone is essential, because delegates and observers walk about constantly and hold consultations in the auditorium.

At its sessions in the early 1990s it was usual for the Commission to consider alleged violations of human rights in some thirty countries. In 1992 it held two emergency sessions on the situation in the former republic of Yugoslavia, and in 1994 one such session on Rwanda (emergency sessions may last no more than three days). The Commission has also, from time to time, set up working groups to consider situations in which rights are threatened, including the working group on Southern Africa and the working group on the draft Declaration on the Rights of Persons Belonging to National, Ethnic, Religious and Linguistic Minorities.

Much of the Commission's work on racial discrimination is carried out through its main subsidiary, the Sub-Commission on Prevention of Discrimination and Protection of Minorities. This was established in 1947. It consists of twenty-six elected experts who serve in their personal capacities and not as the representatives of states. Sessions of the Sub-Commission (which meets for four weeks per year) are also held in a large auditorium and are attended, in addition to members and alternates, by observers from states, from international agencies, and from recognized NGOs. At the outset, the Economic and Social Council requested the Secretary-General to organize studies and prepare analyses that would help the Sub-Commission in its work. Among these were two publications. *The Main Types and Causes of Discrimination* (1949) and *Definition and Classification of Minorities* (1950), both of which have stood the test of time very well. The Sub-Commission has in turn set up working groups, including groups on: communications (i.e. allegations of consistent patterns of gross and reliably attested violations of human rights); indigenous populations; and contemporary forms of slavery. It has regularly commissioned studies to be carried out by a member in the capacity of special rapporteur.

In 1948 the Economic and Social Council suggested 'that UNESCO consider the desirability of initiating and recommending the general adoption of a programme of disseminating scientific facts designed to remove what is commonly known as racial prejudice'. In response, UNESCO in 1950 called upon a group of experts to set out in simple terms the outcome of scientific enquiry into the nature of racial differences and to indicate what were the implications for social relations. They prepared a 'statement on race' (1950), which was followed by meetings of other groups leading to the 'statement on the nature of race and race differences' of 1951, the 'proposals on the biological aspects of race' of 1964, and the 'statement on race and racial prejudice' of 1967. In 1960 the General Conference of UNESCO adopted a Convention against Discrimination in Education which sets standards and binds to its terms any state acceding to it, but provides no specific measures of implementation. The same can be said of UNESCO's Declaration on Race and Racial Prejudice (1978), which, 'bearing in mind the four statements on the race question adopted by experts convened by UNESCO', declares, *inter alia*, that all human beings belong to a single species . . . all individuals and groups have the right to be different . . . any theory which involves the claim that racial or ethnic groups are inherently superior . . . has no scientific foundation and is contrary to the moral and ethical principles of humanity . . . any form of racial discrimination practised by a State constitutes a violation of international law . . .

and so on. This Declaration brought to a conclusion the long campaign against the misunderstanding of racial and ethnic groups as the product of biological processes. UNESCO has a continuing major programme concerned with the elimination of prejudice, intolerance, and racism.

The ILO has, from its beginning, been concerned with equality of opportunity and treatment. In 1954 it was asked, by the Economic and Social Council, to undertake a study of discrimination in employment and occupation. The ILO has subsequently adopted a variety of conventions and recommendations which bear upon areas of possible discrimination, but the centrepiece is the Discrimination (Employment and Occupation) Convention (no. 111) of 1958. By 1988, 108 states had ratified it and many of those which had not done so (like Japan, Nigeria, the UK and the USA) were nevertheless willing to submit reports on the position in their countries with respect to the implementation of the Convention's standards. These reports have been brought together in the ILO's published survey, *Equality in Employment and Occupation* (1988).

Among the general studies on racial discrimination that have been prepared under UN auspices should be mentioned one on the economic and social consequences of racially discriminatory practices which was originally presented to the Economic Commission for Africa. Its character and findings have been partly overtaken by subsequent UN actions against apartheid and by political change in southern Africa. Another, published in 1971 as *Racial Discrimination*, and in 1976 in a revised version, dealt with the political, economic, social, and cultural fields. Such studies have provided a basis for resolutions in the Economic and Social Council and in the General Assembly, exhorting states to improve the conditions of those suffering from the effects of past and present policies of racial discrimination.

The UN General Assembly was in 1946 asked by the Indian delegation to consider racially discriminatory measures enforced by the Union of South Africa against Indians resident there. These measures were said to be in violation of the Charter's human-rights provisions and the Capetown agreements of 1927 and 1932 concluded between the two governments. The South African government denied the General Assembly's competence to deal with the complaint, claiming that it concerned a matter 'essentially within the jurisdiction' of the Union and therefore exempted by article 2.7 of the UN Charter. South Africa proposed that the question be referred to the International Court of Justice. The General Assembly decided that it should consider the practice of discrimination because it impaired friendly relations between two member states. Having earlier appointed a commission to consider the matter, in 1954 it noted the commission's conviction that '*apartheid* constitutes a grave threat to the peaceful relations between ethnic groups in the world'. South Africa then recalled its delegation, maintaining token representation for a further three years.

The question of apartheid came before the Security Council in 1960 in consequence of the shooting of demonstrators in Sharpeville; a growing number of UN bodies, such as the Human Rights Commission, became increasingly involved. The priorities of the General Assembly started to alter with changes in its composition. At the end of 1959 there were nine African member states; another sixteen were admitted in the year 1960 alone and, as can be seen from Table 1, a further sixteen took their seats before the decade was over. One priority shared by all the African states, and for which there was much support elsewhere, was action against apartheid and racial discrimination in southern Africa.

An International Convention on the Suppression and Punishment of the Crime of *Apartheid*, adopted in 1973, was followed twelve years later by a convention against apartheid in sports. Few western states have ratified these conventions, since they are not satisfied with the definition of apartheid as a crime. In 1974 and 1979 the UN rejected the credentials of delegations sent by South Africa. In its 1976 Programme of Action the General Assembly summed up what it had been doing. Apartheid, it said, must be eradicated, because it is a crime against humanity, an affront to human dignity, and a grave threat to international peace and security. In its Declaration on South Africa of 1979 the

TABLE 1. *Growth in UN membership, by regional group*

| Date | Group | | | | | |
| --- | African | Asian | East European | Latin American | Western European and Other | No group |
| --- | --- | --- | --- | --- | --- | --- |
| Orignal members (24 Oct. 1945) | 1 | 6 | 6 | 9 | 6 | 1 |
| 1945–9 | 4 | 7 | 2 | 12 | 8 | 1 |
| 1950–9 | 6 | 8 | 2 | | 6 | |
| 1960–9 | 32 | 5 | | 5 | 1 | |
| 1970–9 | 8 | 11 | | 5 | 1 | |
| 1980–9 | 1 | 2 | | 3 | | |
| 1990–5 | 2 | 5 | 17 | | 4 | |
| TOTAL | 53 | 45 | 27 | 33 | 26 | 2 |

*Note*: This table is based on the 185 member states of the UN at 30 September 1995 and records the period in which they became members. It may be noted that Australia, Canada, and New Zealand are members of the Western European and Other Group (WEOG). Israel is not and at one time South Africa was not a member of any group. The USA is not a member of any group but attends meetings of the WEOG as an observer and is considered to be a member of that group for electoral purposes.

Assembly affirmed that all states should recognize the right of the oppressed people of South Africa to choose their means of struggle. It approved measures against apartheid to be funded from the regular UN budget which were estimated, eight years later, to provide employment for more than 200 staff and to cost $US45m. per annum. By this stage it was conventional to refer to 'the racist regime of South Africa' or 'the racist and colonialist regime', terminology which could be justified but which is notable for its rhetorical character. As indignation about apartheid increased, so the words used to describe it became even stronger. This reflected the change in sentiment but also accelerated the change. It had rhetorical value in promoting political ends. Throughout the UN there is great stress upon reaching decisions by consensus, and an acute concern with procedural propriety. Business is expedited if resolutions or drafts can be adopted by consensus, so it can be important to use wording that has proved acceptable on previous occasions. Any changes in wording which imply a different, per-haps more critical, political stance will not be easily agreed. Rhetoric is therefore not a decoration, but a vital element in the construction of international alliances and the building of shared sentiment. It is an indicator of priority which commits those who have agreed to it—even if only by silence.

Revulsion from apartheid was possibly the main motive force behind the adoption in 1965 of ICERD and many of the decisions of the International Conference on Human Rights in Tehran in 1968. The Final Act of that conference contains resolutions on occupied territories, action against nazism and racial intolerance, apartheid, racist regimes, non-discrimination in employment, action against racial discrimination, decolonization, women's rights, and armed conflicts.

## DECADES TO COMBAT RACISM

In 1966, as part of a General Assembly resolution calling for ratification of ICERD, a clause was included to proclaim 21 March (the anniversary of the Sharpeville shootings) as International Day for the Elimination of Racial Discrimination. Shortly afterwards, as proposed by the USSR, 1971 was designated International Year to Combat Racism and Racial Discrimination, and a programme of action was drawn up. The Secretary-General was requested to collect information from governments and international bodies on measures and activities in this sphere. After considering the replies, the Assembly designated 'the ten-year period beginning on 10 December 1973 as the Decade for Action to Combat Racism and Racial Discrimination'. The programme for the Decade included the convening of two world conferences, in 1978 and 1983.

In 1975 a set of proposals about implementing the programme and convening the first conference came through the Third Committee to the General Assembly. To it, in resolution 3379, was added the declaration which 'determines that Zionism is a form of racism and racial discrimination'. The principal speaker for this resolution was a member of the Kuwaiti delegation who was also the rapporteur of CERD. For him, as for very many others, racism and racial discrimination were synonymous. As evidence for his thesis he referred to the Israeli Law of the Return, permitting a Jew who had never been in Palestine to 'return' when Palestinians were prevented from returning to their actual homes. This was a practice which had 'the effect of excluding some people on the basis of their being non-Jews and including others on the basis of their being Jews—Jewishness being decided officially by Zionism as an ethnic and not strictly a religious definition'. He contended that the resolution was not directed against Judaism. US delegates spoke strongly against it, but the resolution was carried by 72 votes to 35. In an Explanation of Vote immediately afterwards (A/PV.2400: 152–65), Daniel Patrick Moynihan, then US ambassador to the UN, recalled that in the course of a discussion about the drafting of a resolution in 1968:

The distinguished representative of Tunisia argued that 'racism' should go first because, he said, Nazism was a form of racism. Not so, said the no less distinguished representative of the Union of Soviet Socialist Republics, for, he explained, Nazism contained all the main elements of racism within its ambit, and should be mentioned first. That is to say that racism is merely a form of Nazism . . .

Moynihan continued:

If, as the distinguished representative declared, racism is a form of Nazism, and if, as this resolution declares, Zionism is a form of racism, then we have step by step taken ourselves to the point of proclaiming—the United Nations is solemnly proclaiming—that Zionism is a form of Nazism.

The resolution was pure rhetoric, but rhetoric can be very important. The resolution was enormously influential in many countries and international assemblies. It is notable, for example, that a preambular paragraph of the African Charter on Human and Peoples' Rights rehearses an undertaking to 'eliminate colonialism, neo-colonialism, apartheid, zionism, and to dismantle aggressive foreign military bases . . .'. On 16 December 1991 the General Assembly revoked resolution 3,379 by 111 votes to 25.

Delegates to the first World Conference to Combat Racism and Racial Discrimination in 1978 were presented on the final day with a draft declaration that apparently had the support of a majority of states but contained elements which were unacceptable to some of them. Representatives of the nine member states of the European Community (Belgium, Denmark, France, the FRG, Ireland, Italy, Luxembourg, the Netherlands, and the UK) together with the representatives of Australia, Canada, and New Zealand, stated that they could not associate themselves with the results or any longer participate in the proceedings. Their reservations centred on a passage which 'condemned the existing and increasing relations between the zionist State of Israel and the racist regime of South Africa', and on one that

recalled with regret the cruel tragedy which had befallen the Palestinian people 30 years before, preventing their right to self-determination and resulting in the dispersal of hundreds of thousands of them, the establishment of settlers from abroad in their homeland and the practice of racial discrimination inimical to their human rights.

It was said that these passages introduced elements extraneous to the purposes of the Decade and the work of the Conference.

When the agenda for the second conference in 1983 was submitted to it, the General Assembly removed items relating to the Middle East. The African group at the UN took the initiative in making proposals about the Decade. At the conference its delegations revised their draft declaration to meet Arab wishes by including (as paragraph 20) an expression of regret concerning 'the practices of racial discrimination against the Palestinians'. By 101 votes to 12 with 3 abstentions, the conference adopted a declaration composed of twenty-eight paragraphs. The first five concerned racial equality; nine were directed against South Africa and apartheid (including support for national liberation

movements); three set out what governments should do; separate
paragraphs concerned neo-Nazi and fascist organizations, racial
discrimination against Palestinians in Arab territories occupied
by Israel, the protection of minorities, the rights of indigenous
populations; double discrimination against women, the effects of
discrimination upon children; the problems of refugees, migrant
workers, the realization of the Decade's goals, and the launching of
a Second Decade. The Conference also adopted a Programme of
Action comprising ten chapters: on education, the mass media,
minorities, recourse procedures, ICERD, apartheid, national legislation, seminars, NGOs, and international cooperation.

When it comes to voting on such resolutions, the manœuvring
can be complex. For example, when the African group brought
to the General Assembly the declaration from this conference,
including the proposal for a Second Decade, it resisted any amendments (which might have come from the Soviet bloc or from Arab
states as well as from Western states) and insisted on their
resolution being accepted as a whole, without voting on separate
paragraphs. A delegation which objected to one or two paragraphs,
and forced a vote on them, might therefore in the end be held
responsible for the failure of a resolution which was, on the whole,
reasonable. This would weaken its position when next it wanted
the support of those it had offended. Such a delegation might vote
in favour of the resolution but protect its position by making an
Explanation of Vote afterwards. To press too hard can sometimes
be counter-productive. Nor is it easy to calculate whether more will
be gained or lost by withdrawing from an organization that reaches
unwelcome decisions—as the USA withdrew from the first Decade
after the 1975 vote, and as both the USA and the UK withdrew
from UNESCO.

The General Assembly instituted a Second Decade from 1983 to
1993. After reviewing the report from the second world conference
it noted with concern that, despite the effort of the international
community, the principal objectives of the first Decade had not
been attained, and that millions of humans continued to be the
victims of various forms of racism, racial discrimination, and
apartheid. It approved a programme of action for a Second Decade
which has entailed correspondence between the Secretary-General
and member states and international organizations with a view
to encouraging action in accordance with the objectives of the

Decade; preparing model legislation; and conducting a series of seminars, studies, and training courses to improve the recourse procedures available to victims of racial discrimination. There has also been a seminar of cultural dialogue between the countries of origin and the host countries of migrant workers. The Decade's objectives have been featured in the UN's World Public Information Campaign on Human Rights. Implementation of parts of this campaign has been financially dependent on voluntary contributions by states to a UN trust fund. There was little response to appeals for contributions to this fund.

In 1989 a 'Study on the Achievements Made and Obstacles Encountered during the Decade to Combat Racism and Racial Discrimination' was prepared for the Sub-Commission on Prevention of Discrimination and Protection of Minorities by one of its members, Mr Asbjørn Eide, a Norwegian professor. It was later presented to the General Assembly (A/45/525). A document of ninety-six pages, this report lists in sequence the various decisions of UN bodies and associated institutions (like UNESCO, ILO, World Health Organization (WHO), Food and Agriculture Organization (FAO)), stressing that 'practically all United Nations bodies have been involved, in one way or another, in the effort to bring *apartheid* and similar racist policies to an end'. Action against apartheid takes up much of the report's space, but it also underlines 'the disintegration of racist mythology'; it notes that 'indigenous peoples were not given much attention in 1973' but that their problems had become an international concern; likewise 'migrant workers were only very briefly referred to in 1973' but they and their families were about to receive the protections of a convention; more effort was being devoted to information campaigns, while work continued in order to improve the protection of ethnic minorities. The report closed with recommendations mostly designed to reinforce and extend existing UN policies but including a recommendation that, in order to concentrate upon fundamental questions, the forty-year-long attempt to define a minority be abandoned. The UN was recommended to consider the protection of linguistic rights, including the right of everyone to use his or her mother tongue; it should formulate rules concerning the right of a person to his or her culture, including the protection of the material base of that culture; it should examine the possibility of partial autonomy for minorities and the relevance to them of the right to development proclaimed in 1986.

As part of the Second Decade, the UN published in 1991 a *Global Compilation of National Legislation Against Racial Discrimination* (UN 1991a). The Secretary-General had requested from member states information about their legislation. Replies were received from forty-four. The *Compilation* set out, in 200 pages, the legislation then prevailing. Classified regionally, the states in question were:

Africa: Ghana, Malawi, Mauritius, Nigeria

Asia: China, Cyprus, India, Iran, Pakistan, Qatar, Tuvalu, United Arab Emirates

Eastern Europe: Bulgaria, Byelorussian SSR, Czechoslovakia, Hungary, Poland, Ukrainian SSR, USSR

Latin America: Bahamas, Brazil, Colombia, Cuba, Dominica, Ecuador, El Salvador, Mexico, Panama, Trinidad & Tobago, Venezuela

Western European and Other: Australia, Austria, Canada, Denmark, Finland, France, FRG, Netherlands, New Zealand, Norway, Portugal, Spain, Turkey, UK

The information supplied casts light upon what some states understood by racial discrimination. For example, Qatar supplied details of four decrees: two halted the export of petrol and severed economic, trade, and commercial relations with South Africa, Portugal, and Rhodesia; two later ones exempted Portugal from these decrees and cancelled the boycott of Southern Rhodesia. The view held in Qatar in 1980 about domestic legislation was reflected in the statement of its representative when he told CERD 'that racial discrimination was forbidden by the law of God in an Islamic society and therefore no further legal provisions were considered necessary' (A/35/18, para. 281).

The Second Decade came to an end in December 1993 and has been followed by a third. Its programme of action acknowledges that the biggest contribution to the elimination of racial discrimination will be that which results from the actions of states within their own territories. It includes measures to ensure a peaceful transition from apartheid to a democratic, non-racial regime in South Africa, measures to remedy the legacy of apartheid, action at the international, regional, and national levels, basic research, and improved coordination and reporting. It asks 'have there been any successful national models to eliminate racism and racial prejudices that could be recommended to States, for example, for educating children, or principles of equality to tackle racism against migrant workers, ethnic minorities or indigenous peoples?' If it can identify any such models, they can be publicized under the programme.

Observance of the International Day for the Elimination of Racial Discrimination was until 1994 arranged within the UN's New York headquarters by the Special Committee against *Apartheid*, which met on that day in a big hall so that the many diplomats attending could listen to addresses from the president of the General Assembly, the Secretary-General, the president of the Security Council, the chairman of the Special Committee on the Situation with Regard to the Implementation of the Declaration on the Granting of Independence to Colonial Countries and Peoples, the chairman of the Committee of Trustees of the UN Trust Fund for South Africa, and, on occasion, the chairman of CERD. The meeting was also addressed by special guests, by representatives of the regional groups of member states, and by representatives of national liberation movements, including the Palestine Liberation Organization (who have emphasized the parallels between the struggles of Palestinians and black South Africans). After the installation of a new democratic government, South Africa on 23 June 1994 resumed its seat in the UN and the mandate of the Special Committee against *Apartheid* was terminated. Observance of the International Day should henceforward become more truly international and less preoccupied with the affairs of one country. A critically minded visitor watching the proceedings in one of the years before 1994 might have calculated the costs of staging such an event and doubted whether they brought any proportionate benefit to black South Africans, but the occasion cast its own light on the nature of the UN as an organization.

## THE PROTECTION OF MINORITIES

From the beginning of the UN, international action against racial discrimination has been linked with moves to protect minorities (Thornberry 1991). In 1946 Egypt submitted to the General Assembly a draft resolution relating to 'religious and so-called racial persecution and discrimination'. It stated that in several states of Central Europe citizens belonging to religious minorities were persecuted. The references to Central Europe occasioned objections and were removed. A resolution in general terms was approved. Two years later, when the final text of the UDHR was being prepared, several delegations wished to include in it an article about positive measures for the protection of minorities. There were objections. It was thought impossible in a single article to effect a compromise between the views of the New World, which in general wished to assimilate minorities, and the Old World, in which racial and national minorities wanted protection. In addition, one representative argued that the rights of all minorities would be protected by other articles; thus article 18 guaranteed them freedom of religion, article 19 freedom of opinion and expression, article 20 freedom of assembly, article 26 the choice of education, and article 27 the right to participate in cultural life; in addition, article 2, on non-discrimination, expressly protected all minorities.

Eventually the General Assembly referred to the Economic and Social Council proposals on minority rights submitted by Denmark, Yugoslavia, and the USSR. The problem ended up with the Sub-Commission, which has struggled with it ever since, though not without several successes. In 1951 it prepared what was to become article 27 of the International Covenant on Civil and Political Rights (ICCPR):

In those States in which ethnic, religious or linguistic minorities exist, persons belonging to such minorities shall not be denied the right, in community with other members of their group, to enjoy their own culture, to profess and practice their own religion, or to use their own language.

For many years this stood almost alone as an acknowledgement of minority rights. The Sub-Commission persisted, but its drafts were referred back. As a special rapporteur, Mr Francisco Capotorti in 1977 formulated a definition of 'minority' drawn up solely with the application of article 27 of the ICCPR in mind:

A group numerically inferior to the rest of the population of a State, in a non-dominant position, whose members—being nationals of the State—possess ethnic, religious or linguistic characteristics differing from those of the rest of the population and show, if only implicitly, a sense of solidarity, directed towards preserving their culture, traditions, religion or language.

The Commission on Human Rights in 1978 established an informal working group to consider the drafting of a declaration on the rights of minorities within the framework of article 27. Yugoslavia submitted a draft. At one point in the discussions the Commission requested one of its members, Mr Jules Deschenes, to prepare guidelines, and in 1985 he submitted a study which concluded with another proposed definition of a minority:

A group of citizens of a State, constituting a numerical minority and in a non-dominant position in that State, endowed with ethnic, religious or linguistic characteristics which differ from those of the majority of the population, having a sense of solidarity with one another, motivated, if only implicitly, by a collective will to survive and whose aim is to achieve equality with the majority in fact and in law.

This proposal failed to command general approval in the Commission.

The continuing dispute about minority claims is reflected in the declaration of the French government, entered when acceding to the ICCPR, that 'article 27 is not applicable so far as the Republic is concerned'—that is, that no such minorities exist in France. This prompted the FRG to send to the UN Secretary-General a declaration that

The Federal Government refers to the declaration on article 27 made by the French Government and stresses in this context the great importance attaching to the rights guaranteed by article 27. It interprets the French declaration as meaning that the Constitution of the French Republic already fully guarantees the individual rights protected by article 27.

In May 1991 the French Constitutional Council reaffirmed that there is one indivisible French people without distinction of origin, race, or religion. Reinforcing the long-standing refusal to recognize national minorities, the Council held that the legislature could not identify the Corsican people as a part of the French nation because this would admit a distinction necessarily based upon ethnic origin.

Neither the French nor the German interpretation would satisfy some Bretons, who regard the 1532 treaty between Brittany and France as a continuing guarantee of their collective rights. The FRG's own position has also been questioned. In its third periodic report under the ICCPR, it stated that for its purposes only a group of citizens of the same origin and living in the same area is considered a minority. Only the Danish minority fulfilled the three criteria, and not Jews—despite the specific reference to religion in the article.

In the eyes of the French and German governments, the question of whether a particular group constitutes a minority is a question of law, to be answered in the terms of their constitutions. In the eyes of many members of such groups, the question is one of fact: do they have the attributes of a minority, whether or not national law recognizes this fact? The Human Rights Committee in 1993 adopted a General Comment on article 27 of the Covenant in which it stated that 'The existence of an ethnic, religious or linguistic minority in a given State party requires to be established by objective criteria and not by a unilateral decision by the State party.' This statement could be important for groups which are not recognized as minorities by governments, such as the German group in Poland and the Korean group in Japan.

It is sometimes held that article 27 was not meant to protect indigenous populations (or peoples). They do not consider themselves to be minorities. Definitions of their rights have been formulated in the draft Universal Declaration on Indigenous Rights drawn up by a working group of the Sub-Commission. Other developments are possible. Nineteen indigenous groups of Canada have signed a Treaty of Defensive Alliance following the NATO model. Taking note of the precedent set by the League of Nations resolution of the dispute between Sweden and Finland over the status of the Åland Islands, which gave the islanders a degree of autonomy, questions are now raised about the possibility of a similar arrangement for the Saami (Lapp) population of the Nordic countries.

In opposition to the view that article 27 is intended to protect territorial minorities (and perhaps Gypsies), it can be argued that, if new minorities appear as a result of immigration or of the interaction between an indigenous group and other persons, these minorities are entitled to benefit from the same protections. There is also a dispute about the scope of the protections themselves. The article says only that members of minorities 'shall not be denied the right', but the rights in question are (with the possible exception of language) already covered by other articles in the covenants. In accordance with the principle of efficacity in the reading of international instruments, the article must be presumed to add something to the rest of the text. On one view, therefore, the article lays an obligation upon states to assist their minorities to maintain their culture, language, and religion at a level equivalent to that of the majority population.

In December 1992 the General Assembly adopted a Declaration on the Rights of Persons Belonging to National, Ethnic, Religious and Linguistic Minorities. This proclaims that states shall protect the existence and the national or ethnic, cultural, religious, and linguistic identity of minorities within their respective territories and shall encourage conditions for the promotion of that identity. Many problems remain, concerning the definition of minorities and whether rights are individual or collective in character.

Developments in the UN may be pushed forward by proposals before other fora. Under the Conference on Security and Co-operation in Europe (CSCE), which has since become the Organization for Security and Cooperation in Europe (OSCE), states accepted an obligation to 'create conditions for the promotion of ethnic, cultural, linguistic and religious identities of national minorities on their territory' (paragraph 19 of the Vienna concluding document). The Parliamentary Assembly of the Council of Europe in 1990 adopted recommendation 1134 on the rights of minorities, which is primarily concerned with national minorities, while the Committee of Ministers of the Council of Europe in 1992 adopted a recommendation to member states advising them to adopt explicit policies on community-relations questions. The heads of state and government of the member states of the Council of Europe, meeting in Vienna in October 1993, adopted a Declaration and Plan of Action on combating racism, xenophobia, anti-Semitism, and intolerance. The European Union has also taken action in this field. A Committee of Inquiry into Racism and Fascism in Europe reported in 1985 and 1991. The European Parliament in 1993 expressed support for a Directive that might be issued by the Council of Ministers to try to bring EU protections against racial discrimination to the same level as those against discrimination on grounds of sex. National minorities in Europe see the creation of super-national political structures such as the OSCE, the Council of Europe, and the EU as offering them possible guarantees for their collective identities. National minorities may be the pace-makers for other kinds of minority.

## TREATY BODIES

In the process of protecting human rights, the first stage is the declaration of rights which sets the standards acknowledged by the states in question. The second stage is that whereby states assume the obligations of membership in an organization such as the UN or as set out in a convention. Thus the UN Commission on Human Rights works under the authority of the UN Charter and can put pressure on all UN member states, whereas a covenant or a convention imposes treaty obligations only upon the states which have chosen to accede to it. The third stage is that whereby states permit international bodies to check up on whether they are keeping their promises, by questioning reports they have submitted or by conducting investigations. A further, and very important check is put in place when a state permits individuals within its territory who believe they have not received the promised protection to take their case (or 'communication') to an international tribunal. This improves very greatly the implementation of the treaty's provisions.

For examples of individual communications, it can be interesting to turn to decisions of the Human Rights Committee on cases brought under article 27 of the ICCPR, since these come closest to issues of racial discrimination. In a Canadian case, a registered Maliseet Indian called Sandra Lovelace lost her status as an Indian when she married a non-Indian, and could not get it back when the marriage ended. She nevertheless returned to live on the reserve. Threatened with eviction, she was able to petition under the ICCPR, since Canada is a party to the Optional Protocol. The Human Rights Committee inquired into her communication (considering the state's reply to the complaint) and found that Canadian legislation violated her rights under article 27, so Canada amended the legislation.

Another case was that brought by a Saami living in northern Sweden who was not entitled to membership in a Saami village community since Swedish legislation limited membership to persons who had reindeer husbandry as their primary source of income. Since Ivan Kitok was a Saami for whom it was only a subsidiary source of income, he maintained that the legislation made him a 'half-Saami', and denied him the right to enjoy the culture of the Saami. The Committee did not uphold his complaint, but expressed 'grave doubts as to whether certain provisions of the

Reindeer Husbandry Act, and their application to the author, are compatible with article 27 of the Covenant'. The Committee questioned whether the outcome had been proportionate to the legitimate ends sought by the legislation. They noted that, as in the Lovelace case, there could be a conflict between the protection of the rights of the minority as a whole and the rights of an individual member. A restriction on the rights of an individual member of a minority must be shown to have a reasonable and objective justification and to be necessary for the continued viability and welfare of the minority as a whole. Case law on minority rights and racial discrimination will gradually be developed in response to such petitions and to similar petitions submitted under article 14 of ICERD. The first such communications are described later.

The number of human-rights treaty monitoring bodies has increased in line with the number of treaties. The first such body was CERD, followed by the Group of Three under the Convention on the Suppression and Punishment of the Crime of Apartheid and the Human Rights Committee. Then came the Committee on the Elimination of Discrimination Against Women (CEDAW) in 1982, the Committee on Economic, Social, and Cultural Rights (1987), the Committee Against Torture (1988), and the Committee on the Rights of the Child (1992); they may soon be joined by a committee established under the Convention on the Protection of the Rights of All Migrant Workers and their Families. Thus UN action respecting human rights now includes two systems: that of the Charter-based organs (primarily the Commission on Human Rights and its Sub-Commission, described earlier) and the treaty-based system.

The General Assembly has sought to coordinate the activities of the treaty bodies. In 1984 it convened a first meeting of persons chairing these bodies to consider problems with states' reporting obligations. Successive meetings in 1988 thereafter have reviewed a wider range of matters. The 1990 meeting considered a study prepared, on the recommendation of the General Assembly, to review possible long-term approaches to enhancing the effective operation of existing and prospective treaty bodies; it was the work of an independent expert, Mr Philip Alston. The meeting made suggestions, *inter alia*, for improving liaison between treaty bodies, and, very significantly, considered the long-term rationalization of the existing system of treaty bodies. Having heard from the representatives of some committees how much they had been helped by information provided by NGOs (a matter on which CERD has displayed greater caution than some others), it concluded that each committee should decide in the light of its own circumstances the extent and form of the cooperation with NGOs.

There is some overlap between the matters considered by different human-rights conventions, and some further overlap between the treaty bodies and the activities of the Commission on Human Rights. The Commission has appointed a special rapporteur on torture who, since he works under the authority of the Charter, can report on allegations of torture in all UN member states irrespective of whether they have acceded to the Convention Against Torture and submit reports to the treaty body that monitors implementation of that Convention. In 1993, on the recommendation of its Sub-Commission, the Commission also appointed a special rapporteur on racism and xenophobia. CERD was not consulted at any stage. Since there was no suggestion that the special rapporteur should cover states that were not submitting reports under the ICERD, the need for such a post was not evident. *The Times* newspaper on 12 December 1994 told its readers that the appointment stemmed from

the resentment many Third World countries felt at what they saw as the 'disproportionate' focus on abuse in the developing world, and the relative silence over race relations in richer, industrialized countries. Turkey, especially, was piqued at the focus on its treatment of Kurds, and wanted more publicity for the treatment of Turkish migrant workers in Germany.[1]

In 1994 the Commission requested the special rapporteur, Mr Maurice Glélé-Ahanhanzo, of Benin,

to examine according to his mandate incidents of contemporary forms of racism, racial discrimination, any form of discrimination against Blacks, Arabs and Muslims, xenophobia, negrophobia, anti-Semitism and related intolerance, as well as governmental measures to overcome them, and to report on these matters to the Commission at its fifty-first session [i.e. twelve months later].

---

[1] In 1994 the government of Turkey submitted to the European Commission against Racism and Intolerance a preliminary draft convention against racism. Though Turkey has signed ICERD, it has never ratified it and accepted the obligations that ensue.

The list of possible victims of discrimination is an indication of the various groups involved and their interests in the appointment.

Some private institutions have taken an interest in the more effective operation of the system for the protection of human rights. In 1988 the Fletcher School of Law and Diplomacy, with funding from the Ford Foundation, held a workshop to review human-rights procedures. In the same year the Minister for Foreign Affairs of the Netherlands sent the UN Secretary-General an advisory report of the Netherlands Human Rights and Foreign Policy Advisory Committee on the functioning of the human-rights conventions under UN auspices. These activities and those of international NGOs demonstrate that there now exists a body of persons, both in governmental and non-governmental service, who have expectations of the human-rights system as a whole and of the treaty bodies as a very important part of it. They judge the performance of any one such body by comparison with what the others are achieving. This is a new development for those members of CERD who formed their views of how the Committee should operate in the years before the other treaty bodies started. As one illustration of the tension, it may be noted that, at the 1991 session of CERD, reference was made to a briefing document of the International League for Human Rights which, discussing the failure of some states parties to meet their financial obligations, observed:

Some have questioned whether it makes any difference if CERD meets less often, or perhaps not at all. Why, they ask, should the UN general budget support a body set up under a separate treaty, and especially, why support one like CERD, whose reputation is not the strongest of the human rights bodies in the UN?

Within the Committee, Mr Lamptey described this criticism as unfair. He maintained that some NGOs would like to change the composition and terms of reference of the Committee and have it act politically, as if it were an entity like themselves. The League might have replied to him that other treaty bodies had been more active than CERD in adopting general comments and developing the potential of the instruments under which they operated; there was a period, from about 1979 to 1987, when CERD was scarcely creative. As the 1990s come to a close, CERD has to meet the expectations of a larger and more vocal body of onlookers.

The General Assembly was accustomed for many years to debate the annual report of CERD together with an agenda item on decolonization. In 1989 and recent years this debate has been followed by another on 'Effective Implementation of United Nations Instruments on Human Rights and Effective Functioning of Bodies Established Pursuant to such Instruments', which provides a framework for considering the work of CERD in relation to the human-rights system as a whole. It is notable that this second debate is of a higher quality. Many delegations have used the racial-discrimination debate as a forum for speeches to further their foreign policies. Only rarely could it be inferred that any speaker had read any part of CERD's report other than that relating to his or her own state or some state which the speaker's government wished to criticize. The new debate is becoming a vehicle for the expression of new and authoritative expectations of the Convention and the Committee.

## CONSOLIDATING THE GAINS

Since the various treaties were prepared to deal with different sorts of problem, their character and means of implementation differ, but some of the variations—for example, in the manner of funding—are difficult to defend. The ICERD was the first, and when it was being drafted those responsible were conscious that the monitoring body would be reporting not to the states parties but to the General Assembly, where states which had not ratified the treaty could take part in the debate and might want to influence events for their own political ends. So a dual system of funding was devised to reflect the difference between the responsibilities of the states parties and those of the General Assembly. Under article 10.3 'The secretariat of the Committee shall be provided by the Secretary-General of the United Nations.' The general budget of the UN finances the expenses of the meeting-place, the staff, including the interpreters, and all the correspondence and preparation of documents. Under article 8.6 'States Parties shall be responsible for the expenses of the members of the Committee while they are in performance of Committee duties.' They are assessed according to a UN scale which takes account of differences in national wealth, so that, for example, the Netherlands is assessed to pay more than four times as much as either Bangladesh or the Sudan. Some states parties have failed, from early years, to pay their assessments. Up to 1985 the deficiency was made good by advances from the Secretary-General. After 1985 these were no longer forthcoming and this led to the cancellation or abbreviation of many sessions. Some of the other treaty bodies are funded to a greater extent from the UN budget, some less so. Most states concluded that human-rights issues were so important that it might be better were they all put on the UN budget. Australia proposed this in 1991. The amendments are set out below, pp. 167–8.

ICERD article 9 requires states to report within one year of the assumption of their obligations, and thereafter 'every two years and whenever the Committee so requests'. The interval was kept at two years so that the Committee might watch developments in states which were not taking their responsibilities sufficiently seriously, but the time gap was too short for states with no racial minorities and nothing new to report. It also imposed a burden on states, particularly upon the poorer and smaller states with smaller numbers of civil servants. As the number of treaties has grown, so has the burden. Some monitoring bodies ask for similar information, so in 1990 consolidated guidelines were introduced whereby the initial part of a state report under any of the human-rights conventions consists of a 'core document' common to all human-rights treaty reports. It is to begin with a section covering 'land and people, general legal framework, information and publicity'. This eases the burden only slightly, but the UN has started a training programme for officials likely to be given the task of preparing such reports which is designed to help them and their governments.

The increase in the number of treaties, plus the increase in the number of states acceding to each treaty, plus increases in the activities of the committees themselves, create extra work for those who have to study their reports and make it all the more important that the committees liaise with one another. It has been calculated that, during the 1990s, the annual reports of the eight committees will reach 1,000 pages. The pages in question are dense, each containing about 600 words on matters which governments often see as sensitive because of their bearing upon national honour. Mr Alston's report was updated to keep track of this growing problem, which is the more worrying because of the limited ability of many states to cope with its implications. Since many governments have difficulty remaining in power, or are caught up in regional conflicts, they cannot give a very high priority to the improvement of the UN human-rights system.

In 1988 it was suggested in Geneva that the time was ripe for a second international conference to reinforce the framework for the protection of human rights. So the World Conference on Human Rights was held in Vienna on 14–25 June 1993. It was a conference of states, with many NGOs represented by observers. These observers, and the representatives of the treaty bodies, were dissatisfied that the states did not allow them to play a more active part in the proceedings. Many states are sensitive to the pressure these organizations and bodies exert. Many states are vulnerable to criticism.

The central activity at conferences of this kind is the drafting of declarations and resolutions, which to some readers will appear mere words when action is needed. This betrays a failure to understand the importance of rhetoric in international relations. The drafting of resolutions on these occasions follows the principle of the ratchet, a kind of wheel that cannot ordinarily be turned backwards. A formulation that has been used in a previous resolution can be repeated; the parties are unlikely to object, even if the wording no longer reflects present circumstances, because they earlier accepted it and now have more pressing objectives to pursue. To accept a particular formulation is therefore to make a commitment. States may also attempt to strengthen formulations used on a previous occasion. An example of this steplike process can be seen in the sequence of UN resolutions that started as condemnations of racial discrimination and led to the 1975 General Assembly determination already mentioned 'that Zionism is a form of racism and racial discrimination'. The condemnation was rhetorical, mere words, but became a powerful counter in moves (often Arab-inspired) against those who could be labelled Zionist. The rhetoric of human-rights resolutions is important because it can be used as a basis for decisions which, if approved by the General Assembly, create obligations for all member states, even if they are not of themselves legally enforceable. Declarations may later be used as a basis for the preparation of conventions which are legally binding upon those states which choose to accede to them.

In the preparations for the conference it began to look as if the ending of east–west bipolarity was being replaced by a north–south bipolarity, with the less developed states of the south objecting to the human-rights priorities of the richer industrialized states. In particular, it was suggested that the northerners were over-emphasizing the importance of civil rights relative to economic rights, and that they had too individualistic a conception of civil rights. Preparatory committee meetings in Geneva failed to agree the agenda for the conference.

Three regional groupings also held preparatory meetings. The African group, meeting in Tunis, reaffirmed the indivisibility and universality of human rights, but also declared that 'no ready-made model can be prescribed at the universal level since the historical and cultural realities of each nation and the traditions, standards and values of each people cannot be disregarded'. The Latin American and Caribbean group, meeting in Costa Rica, agreed that no rights might be denied on the grounds that the full enjoyment of other rights had not yet been achieved. They called attention to many obstacles (some new) to such achievement, and expressed hesitations about the 'right of interference for humanitarian purposes'. The group of Asian states had difficulty agreeing its preparations for the meeting eventually held in Bangkok. Its declaration, which highlighted the right to development, was not as serious a challenge to the universality of rights as some had feared. It declared that the states would 'discourage any attempt to use human rights as a condition for extending development assistance'.

The conference therefore opened in an apprehensive mood, over-shadowed by reports of atrocities not far away in the former Yugoslavia which the West Europeans had failed to prevent. Though it did not realize all the original hopes, the Vienna Declaration and Programme of Action showed that the conference was successful in reinforcing the existing international framework for the protection of human rights. The Declaration strengthened international commitments on some new problems, as can be seen by comparing its thirty-nine operative paragraphs with the nineteen paragraphs of the Proclamation of Tehran twenty-five years earlier. The Declaration included two paragraphs on the right to development 'as a universal and inalienable right and an integral part of fundamental human rights', and others on debt, poverty, terrorism, minorities, indigenous peoples, children, the disabled, the right to asylum, migrant workers, torture, NGOs, and the mass media.

The accompanying Programme of Action added specific recommendations. It called on the Commission of Human Rights to take further steps in connection with the recent Declaration on the Rights of Persons belonging to National or Ethnic, Religious and Linguistic Minorities. It called for completion of the draft declaration on the rights of indigenous people and recommended the proclamation of an international decade of the world's indigenous people to begin from January 1994. It called for the adoption of the draft declaration on violence against women. It urged reconsideration of the reservations entered by many states when they acceded to the CEDAW convention and the drafting of an additional protocol to permit individual petition under this convention. It stressed women's rights to health care and family-planning services, and encouraged the increased employment of women within the UN system. The Programme of Action urged reconsideration of reservations to the Convention on the Rights of the Child also, supporting proposals for a special study of the protection of children in armed conflicts and recognizing the important role played by NGOs in this field. It supported an optional protocol to the torture convention to establish a preventive system of regular visits to places of detention. It recalled the General Assembly's programme of action concerning disabled persons and called upon it to adopt the draft standard rules on the equalization of opportunities for persons with disabilities.

The World Conference also recommended that the General Assembly create a post of High Commissioner for Human Rights. The recommendation was implemented and is already proving a significant development, since the holder of this post has wider powers to take initiatives (for example, in Rwanda) than the holders of lesser UN offices.

With the ending of bipolarity, new burdens were thrown upon the Security Council. People throughout the world looked to the UN to stop the killings in so many regions. The Secretary-General produced an important report entitled *An Agenda for Peace* which distinguished a sequence of phases in the process. Preventive diplomacy embodied confidence-building, fact-finding, early warning, preventive deployment of observers or forces, and the creation of demilitarized zones. Peace-making could involve recourse to the

International Court of Justice, international assistance, sanctions, and the use of military force. Peace-keeping makes substantial demands upon member states to furnish military, police, and civilian personnel. Post-conflict peace-building could then follow. As events have demonstrated, the Security Council cannot handle all the demands made upon it and it needs the assistance of regional organizations.

## A POSSIBLE CONCLUSION

Few targets are as easy to attack as the UN. It is frequently blamed for the failures of its member states. Political considerations enter at every stage into the positions that they take up. Thus it was for political reasons, apparently, that the Commission on Human Rights appointed a special rapporteur on racism and xenophobia. Equally, the World Conference on Human Rights of 1993 would not have taken place had some states not seen it as an opportunity for them to pursue concerns of their own. Thus, according to the Director of the International Service for Human Rights (Zoller 1993: 2):

The idea of convening a great world conference on the subject of human rights was first aired unofficially at the UN in Geneva in 1988. Not long afterwards, its promoters were confronted with the events of 1989. They paid little attention to the way in which the Moroccan delegation, eager to improve the image of its regime following revelations about detention centres, took possession of the initiative. Though other States showed little real enthusiasm, none of them opposed the idea, which gathered momentum as it progressed through the various levels of the UN system . . .

To try to exclude politics from human rights would be to misunderstand the relation between politics and law. In politics, a discussion which simply repeats a previous discussion must be a failure. If a discussion leads to a conclusion such that the next discussion starts from the position reached on the previous occasion, then some progress has been made. At the UN such a conclusion is usually expressed in the form of a resolution, which can sometimes move on to a General Assembly declaration and eventually to a convention. States that accede to a convention bind themselves in ways that prevent their going back to the starting-point. Law has structured the debate, removing some matters from the agenda and impelling the parties to move on. Sometimes, perhaps, the assembled representatives of states know what they are doing when they take a step forward. On other occasions, or so the next chapter will conclude, they have different ideas about what they are doing, and progress is providential.

# 4

# The Racial Convention

LIKE Plato's *Republic*, the Convention is founded upon a noble lie. Plato maintained that it would be easier for the guardians to rule his ideal republic if the citizens believed they had different capacities. He recalled a myth that, when God made men, into some he put gold to make them capable of ruling; into the auxiliaries he put silver; into the farmers and craftsmen, iron and copper. If the citizens believed their abilities to be predetermined, this would lower their aspirations and there would be less discontent. Some English versions of *The Republic* have translated a reference to the use of this myth as a noble lie.

The International Convention is founded upon the lie that racial discrimination, *as defined in ICERD article 1.1*, can be *eliminated*. There is no question that it can be reduced, and maybe if it was defined in some other way it could be eliminated, but to aim for the elimination of the conduct defined in article 1.1 is another matter. The belief that racial discrimination *could* be eliminated was a nobler lie than Plato's, because it mobilized governments in pursuit of a higher objective and because without it they would never have committed themselves as they did.

In retrospect, the decision taken in the General Assembly on 21 December 1965 was an astonishing event. Many of the states voting in favour subsequently ratified the Convention but failed to keep their promises to submit reports and to pay their share of the expenses. Many of those which have kept these promises have nevertheless failed to fulfil all their obligations to legislate and have sometimes disputed the nature of these obligations. If they were so half-hearted, how did they come to be swept into the steady movement of accession? How did the General Assembly come to accept that, by action of the kind proposed, racial discrimination could be eliminated? These are complicated questions which are best considered chronologically, so far as this is possible.

## PRELIMINARY STEPS

To begin with, it should be noted that the word 'discrimination' was not used in the UN Charter or in the Universal Declaration of Human Rights. So the Secretary-General's memorandum on *The Main Types and Causes of Discrimination* of 1949 had to explain a concept that was still unfamiliar to most readers. It began with the view of the Sub-Commission on Prevention of Discrimination and Protection of Minorities: 'Prevention of discrimination is the prevention of any action which denies to individuals or groups of people equality of treatment which they may wish.' It maintained that the prevention of discrimination must be based on two guiding principles (individual freedom, and equality of all human beings before the law) and on knowledge of actual social conditions. That knowledge

must be based on sociological analyses of the facts involving discrimination, their causes, how they function, and their effects. From such analyses it should be possible to ascertain: (*a*) those discriminatory practices which may be directly prevented by legal action; (*b*) those practices which may be curtailed or restricted by administrative actions; and (*c*) those practices which, although harmful, cannot be effectively controlled except through long-term educational programmes. (para. 16)

The memorandum went on to distinguish moral and juridical equality from material equality, acknowledging that industriousness deserved reward, but moral and juridical equality excluded any differentiation on such grounds as colour, race, sex, language, and so on. It continued:

Discriminatory practices are those detrimental distinctions which do not take account of the particular characteristics of an individual as such, but take into account only collective qualifications deriving from his membership in a certain social or other group . . .

Thus, discrimination might be defined as a detrimental distinction based on grounds which may not be attributed to the individual and which have no justified consequences in social, political, or legal relations (colour, race, sex, etc.), or on grounds of membership in social categories (cultural, language, religious, political or other opinion, national circle, social origin, social class, property, birth, or other status).

Acts of discrimination assume three forms:

(*a*) Inequality in treatment which takes the form of imposing disabilities;

(*b*) Inequality in treatment which takes the form of granting privileges; and

(*c*) Inequality of treatment which takes the form of imposing odious obligations. (paras. 87–9)

It discussed public discrimination in the form of disabilities, privileges, and the imposition of duties, before listing forms of discrimination by private persons. Possible legal measures and educational principles for the prevention of discrimination were then reviewed.

The key concept in this early formulation came to be called that of *grounds*. One man may treat another differently because he believes him to be of a particular race. That is discriminatory, whether or not the other man actually belongs to the race in question. If Jones were persuaded by Smith that there was a race of Danireans who represented a threat to their interests, and that Robinson was a Danirean, and if, as a result, Jones treated Robinson less favourably, that would be discrimination even though there is no race of Danireans. This way of defining racial discrimination made possible a solution to what was otherwise an intractable problem. Racial discrimination was thought to be based on an erroneous nineteenth-century doctrine that every human belonged in some racial category, membership of which exercised a determining influence upon his or her abilities and social position. Any method of combating discrimination which made use of a racial classification would legitimize a view of human differences that had been used to justify the denial of human rights. By defining discrimination as action on the grounds of race, sex, language, and religion (distinctions which the UN Charter declared incompatible with its objective of promoting respect for human rights and fundamental freedoms), it was possible to bypass any arguments about the nature of these differences in themselves. However, if discrimination was to be detrimental by its very definition, then it would be necessary to consider the possibility of making exceptions, so that certain sorts of action with a laudable purpose might be excluded from its scope (on this, see Banton 1994).

Within the system of international institutions the first definition of racial discrimination was that adopted by the ILO for its Discrimination (Employment and Occupation) Convention (No. 111) of 1958. Discrimination was said to include 'any distinction, exclusion or preference made on the basis of race, colour, sex, religion, political opinion, national extraction or social origin, which has the effect of nullifying or impairing equality of opportunity or treatment in employment or occupation'. The Convention against Discrimination in Education, adopted by the General Conference of UNESCO in 1960, contained a very similar definition but extended it to cover any distinction, etc., which had *the purpose or effect* of nullifying . . . etc.

As was mentioned in the previous chapter, the Sub-Commission on Prevention of Discrimination and Protection of Minorities happened to be in session in January 1960 at the time of the attacks on synagogues and Jewish burial grounds in what was then West Germany, and which were copied in some other countries. The Sub-Commission adopted a resolution to say that it was

deeply concerned by the manifestations of anti-Semitism and other forms of racial and national hatred and religious and racial prejudices of a similar nature, which have occurred in various countries, reminiscent of the crimes and outrages committed by the Nazis prior to and during the Second World War.

It will be argued later in this chapter that the decision of the Sub-Commission to describe the attacks as manifestations of prejudice was to use an approach different from, and inconsistent with, the approach used in the ILO Convention. To describe them as manifestations was to liken them to a sickness, whereas the ILO approach was to declare acts of discrimination unlawful and to liken them to crimes. The description of racial attacks as manifestations or forms of some unobservable force or condition of society exemplifies what Sir Karl Popper called 'the spell of Plato'. If observable behaviour is the outward form of some inward condition, how can one be certain about the nature of that condition? In medicine there are objective techniques for defining such conditions. To liken societies to social organisms and apply to them medical metaphors can be dangerous when there are no comparable techniques for identifying social pathologies. The 1975 General Assembly resolution that 'Zionism is a form of racism and racial discrimination' is an example of what is at stake. Whether or not Zionism is a form of racism depends upon the way in which the two terms are defined, and they have both been seen in highly political ways. To argue that something is a form of something else is quite different from a decision that, if someone acts in a particular way, he is to be punished. It is unusual for anyone to talk of the 'forms' of crime, because actions are defined as criminal by the statement of their prohibition or of the penalty they may evoke. The 'forms' of burglary may be the differentiation of the burglary of a dwelling-house from the burglary of commercial premises, the burglary of a dwelling-house at night when someone is likely to be asleep there from the burglary of an empty house during the day-time, and so on.

The Sub-Commission condemned the manifestations in question as violations of human rights. Among other things, it urged that the UN Secretary-General assemble more information about these manifestations, about counter-measures, and the views of states concerning their 'deep-lying causes and motivations'. Since its recommendations were well received, the Sub-Commission was in a position in the following year to recommend the preparation of an international convention against religious and racial discrimination, which would impose specific legal obligations on the states that chose to accede to it.

In the General Assembly a number of African states, later joined by others, argued for a convention against racial discrimination. Some delegations favoured the preparation of a declaration instead. Though some states wished the action to be directed against both religious and racial discrimination, the Third Committee (which deals with Social, Humanitarian, and Cultural matters) in November 1962 eventually decided in favour of a declaration on racial discrimination to be followed by a convention, and then a separate declaration and convention on religious discrimination. Opposition to combining the two came from some of the Arab delegations and reflected the Arab–Israeli conflict. Many delegations, particularly those from Eastern Europe, considered questions of religion to be less urgent than those of race.

On the agenda of the Third Committee was an item entitled 'Manifestations of Racial Prejudice and National and Religious Intolerance'. A resolution was submitted by a group of francophone West African states (Central African Republic, Chad, Dahomey, Guinea, Ivory Coast, Mali, Mauretania, and Upper Volta) calling for 'the preparation of an International Convention on the Elimination of All Forms of Racial Discrimination'. There is nothing in the records of the committee to suggest that this proposal on the crucial question of a name for the convention gave rise to any controversy. There were no alternative proposals. At this stage the proponents were asking for improved educational measures, the repeal of discriminatory laws, the adoption where necessary of legislation against discrimination, and action to discourage the dissemination of prejudice and intolerance. This can be seen from the text of the draft resolution it recommended to the General Assembly. It read:

The General Assembly . . .

1. *Invites* the Governments of all States . . . to continue to make sustained efforts to educate public opinion with a view to the eradication of racial prejudice . . .
2. *Calls upon* the Governments of all States to take all necessary steps to rescind discriminatory laws . . . to adopt legislation if necessary for prohibiting such discrimination if necessary . . .
3. *Recommends* to the Governments of all States to discourage actively, through education and all information media, the creation, propagation and dissemination of such prejudice and intolerance in any form whatever . . .

The first fruit of the Assembly's acceptance of this recommendation was the adoption, in 1963, of a Declaration on the Elimination of All Forms of Racial Discrimination which, in its fourth preambular paragraph, referred to the Declaration on the Granting of Independence to Colonial Countries and Peoples and the necessity to bring colonialism to a speedy end; it then noted that any doctrine of racial differentiation or superiority was scientifically false, morally condemnable, and socially dangerous. In its first substantive paragraph it described racial discrimination as an offence to human dignity and an obstacle to friendly relations between peoples, but did not define it. There followed a list of prescriptions about what states and UN bodies should and should not do. As a strategy for combating racial discrimination, it was state-centred, with little concern for the private sector.

This Declaration provided guidance to the Sub-Commission, which, in the following year, set about drafting a convention. For this purpose the members had before them the texts of the earlier conventions, the General Assembly declaration, and proposals submitted by six governments. Some members were not satisfied with the Declaration and argued that any convention should represent 'a further progress' while others held that they should not try to impose upon states obligations greater than those arising out of the principles proclaimed in the Declaration. The summary record (E/CN.4/873, para. 29) continues:

Certain members urged that the question of the elimination of racial discrimination should be examined in the context of recent historical developments and, in particular, in the light of the emergence of new States from colonialism and the struggle of various groups for equality and dignity. They felt that the convention should recognize the intimate relationship between manifestations of colonialism, which continue to affect millions of people, and racial discrimination. They expressed the hope that the convention would become an effective and practical instrument for eradicating fascism and racism as well as racial discrimination. Other members pointed out that manifestations of racial hatred and discrimination had not always been linked, in the past, to the existence of colonial territories.

This summary suggests, and in this it would be in line with other evidence, that there were three main positions. The Western states had been forced on the defensive by the pressure for decolonization which brought the Soviet group into alliance with the Afro-Asian group at the UN and gave them a big majority when it came to voting. The Western countries have long seen human rights as individual rights which could be exercised against the state. Those who spoke for the Soviet position maintained that in the West these rights were in practice enjoyed by only a minority and in the colonies by just a small élite. Political action was needed to create a just state. It was then the state which conferred rights upon citizens. The desires of individuals could not constitute a good starting-point because they had been conditioned by the societies in which they had been brought up. States came first. Politicians and diplomats from newly independent ex-colonial states could sympathize with the Soviet outlook. They were trying to hold together fissiparous societies and build up popular legitimacy for new forms of rule. Two campaigns on which the East European and African groups could unite, and to which, as individuals, many were genuinely committed, were the criticism of the continuing influence of the former colonial powers and the attack on the policies of southern African governments. Such differences in the interests of states seeking political advantage in the negotiations at the UN, and in their view of the world, were bound to generate conflicts between their views of what a convention against racial discrimination should look like.

These differences could be reflected both in the preambular paragraphs introducing a convention, and in its substantive sections. Preambular paragraphs set out the rationale for the whole document, and they can be important in interpreting later articles when questions arise about their application. Differences in views about the use of law and of political approach were indeed soon evident. The Sub-Commission member from the UK proposed a very brief set of preambular paragraphs totalling no more than forty-nine words, whereas the members from the USSR and Poland proposed four paragraphs which recalled the 1960 Declaration on decolonization and that part of the 1963 Declaration which referred to the falsity of racial doctrines. By the time the Convention was finally adopted this preambular section had grown to twelve paragraphs. The Sub-Commission's draft was eventually elaborated and extended in several respects, but it is notable that the crucial question of how to define racial discrimination was answered quickly and that the definition was subject to very little subsequent modification. The chosen definition was based closely on that which featured in the ILO and UNESCO Conventions. These definitions, like that in the Secretary-General's memorandum of 1949, were capable of application to interpersonal behaviour and differed from the Sub-Commission's concern with the manifestations of racial and national hatred. A feature that deserves particular emphasis is that the chosen definition represented racial discrimination as resembling criminal behaviour rather than as the manifestation of some underlying sickness. It seems as if no one remarked on this during the drafting stage, though the difference is vital: people are held individually responsible for criminal behaviour but rarely for falling sick. Yet when, in the General Assembly debate, speakers referred to the forms of racial discrimination, very many seem to have envisaged something that resembled a sickness.

The draft convention as proposed by the Sub-Commission, and modified somewhat in the Commission on Human Rights, came before the General Assembly's Third Committee in 1965. Some additional proposals from governments and papers from the UN Secretary-General accompanied the text, which was debated in that committee almost continuously from 11 October to 15 December before going to the General Assembly's plenary meetings on 20–1 December.

## ADOPTION BY THE GENERAL ASSEMBLY

Many of the speakers in the General Assembly debates spoke about racial discrimination as they knew it, rather than about racial discrimination *as defined in article 1*. All the participants thought they knew what racial discrimination was, though they had different things in mind. Many proclaimed their peoples' abhorrence of racial discrimination, or declared that it was not practised in their countries, or recalled how their peoples had suffered from racial discrimination at the hands of others. Underlying the positions taken in that discussion were differing conceptions of the nature of racial discrimination itself.

The representative of the USSR had the most comprehensive and coherent conception. For him, racial discrimination was a 'revolting and monstrous anachronism' and a 'shameful aberration'. He remarked that 'So long as the economic and social conditions that gave rise to racism persisted in certain States, manifestations of racial discrimination were only to be expected.' The preparation of the Convention was 'an aspect of the struggle conducted by the peoples within the United Nations against the colonial régimes . . . In any event, colonialism, and its corollary, racism, were destined to disappear as a consequence of an unavoidable process.' The Soviet Union 'would have no difficulty in ratifying the Convention because, since 1917, it had eliminated all forms of subjection, imperialism and colonialism'. Some other speakers placed more emphasis upon the dissemination of erroneous beliefs; for example, the Chilean representative observed that 'racial discrimination was a very ancient phenomenon, the survival of which was due to the perpetuation of the false doctrine that certain races were superior to others'. The Cameroonian representative maintained that 'ideas and doctrines of that nature had fostered the emergence of apartheid policies'.

Statements such as 'colonialism is the most terrible form of racial discrimination' (from the Sudanese representative) and 'the most serious forms of racial discrimination are connected with colonialism' (from Mauretania's representative) passed unchallenged. The nature of the alleged connection was not clarified, other than by the Tanzanian representative, who declared that 'colonialism . . . was based on the idea of national and racial superiority and it therefore necessarily entailed discrimination'. A delegate from the

United Arab Republic averred that 'To the Arabs, Zionism was synonymous with racial discrimination and nazism . . . colonialism was responsible for all the cases of discrimination he had mentioned, except that of the United States.'

The Western delegations were ill prepared to counter these thrusts. They denied the implication that racism and colonialism were in some way associated. Speaking for the UK, Lady Gaitskill maintained that racial discrimination was an extremely complex problem and doubted whether legislation alone was a sufficient response: 'using legislation by itself was like cutting down a noxious weed above the ground and leaving the roots intact.' She said that, unlike other representatives, she did not deny that there was racial discrimination in her country, where it had been aggravated by a large influx of new immigrants. The British press made no attempt to hide that fact. Other delegates were more concerned about discrimination in the colonies than in Britain, and when, in the Third Committee, amendments were proposed that would enable the inhabitants of Trust and Non-Self-Governing Territories to petition the UN concerning racial discrimination by administering powers, the Western delegations could muster few votes in opposition.

The nature of the disagreement can be better understood by contrasting two conceptions. According to the first, racial discrimination is like a living organism: the delegate from the Ukraine asserted that 'nazism had not died with the ending of the Second World War. It was alive today in South Africa and Southern Rhodesia, and various forms of nazism had developed in West Germany . . .'. In this view, racial discrimination was an outward form or manifestation of a pathological internal condition produced by a certain kind of social structure. It was restricted to particular historical and geographical circumstances, and therefore could be eliminated. According to the second conception, racial discrimination was a normal characteristic of social relations, one that could be found, either currently or potentially, wherever and whenever people differentiated themselves in terms of race, colour, descent, or national or ethnic origin. Official action could reduce it, as such action has discouraged people from driving a car after drinking alcohol, or without using a seatbelt, or riding a motor cycle without a crash helmet, but it would not eliminate discrimination any more than it has eliminated motoring offences.

Even those who object to the first conception can be pleased that it was so widespread at the time, because otherwise it would almost certainly have been impossible to muster sufficient enthusiasm to secure adoption of the Convention. Most of those who supported the proposal seem to have believed that racial discrimination was something practised in a few pariah countries, but not in their own. They appear not to have appreciated the scope of the definition in article 1, and the way it comprehended relations between individuals within the private sector as well as the actions of governments.

None of the drafts of the Convention attempted to enumerate or specify the forms of racial discrimination, and there might have been no discussion of the forms had not Brazil and the USA proposed in the Third Committee to insert into the draft a new article:

States Parties condemn anti-Semitism and shall take action as appropriate for its speedy eradication in the territories subject to their jurisdiction.

This provoked a counter-proposal from the USSR:

States Parties condemn anti-Semitism, Zionism, nazism, neo-nazism and all other forms of the policy and ideology of colonialism, national and race hatred and exclusiveness and shall take action as appropriate for the speedy eradication of those inhuman ideas and practices in the territories subject to their jurisdiction.

Poland wanted a reference to 'nazist and similar practices' and Czechoslovakia to the 'dissemination of racial, fascist, nazi or other ideas and doctrines based on racial superiority or hatred'.

The Polish representative wanted this reference in the preambular paragraph because 'nazism . . . was the most flagrant manifestation of racial discrimination'. Yugoslavia could not understand why there should not be 'a reference to something which had caused the extermination of millions of human beings . . . more than one million Yugoslavs had died fighting nazism . . .'. The Soviet representative

appealed to all delegations to understand his country's concern at the possibility of a repetition of the horrors of nazism. Either the draft Convention must confine itself to a general prohibition and condemnation of all forms and manifestations of racial discrimination, or it must enumerate the various forms; even if one other form of racial discrimination was mentioned, his delegation must insist most forcefully that reference should also be made to nazism and neo-nazism.

In his view, all forms were equally dangerous; 'nazism and fascism were quite as dangerous as apartheid, and Zionism as anti-Semitism.' The Mongolian representative concurred, while Jordan proposed the insertion of the words 'fascist, colonial, tribal, Zionist and similar practices'. The speaker from the Sudan maintained that anti-Semitism was alien to the Moslem world: 'Indeed, when anti-Semitism had arisen and intensified in Europe, it was in the Moslem countries that Jews had often sought and found refuge.' The current dispute over Israel was neither religious nor racial but political. 'For the Arabs, Israel was what South Africa was to the African nationalists and Zionism was the equivalent of apartheid.'

The representative of Saudi Arabia opposed reference to any forms

because there were countless 'isms' which would have to be enumerated if any one was. For example, while the greatest recent affliction of Europe had been nazism, for the rest of the world it had no doubt been colonialism, and it could be convincingly argued that colonialism was a cause of racial discrimination. In addition, Arabs had suffered owing to a certain 'ism' . . .

He asked if anti-Semitism applied 'to persons of Semitic ethnic origin, of whom 95 per cent were Arabs?' Later he argued that anti-Semitism should more correctly be called anti-Judaism, and that it was an exclusively European phenomenon. Other countries, like Nigeria and India, joined in opposing any reference to particular forms, contending that the convention 'should be formulated in quite general terms so that it would be applicable to the entire world'. The delegates of Malawi, Iraq, and the Sudan concurred, cautioning that no one could foresee what new forms of racism might arise in the future. Like others, their conception of a 'form' assumed that racial discrimination was a social pathology.

The course of the debate was then changed by an announcement from the Moroccan delegate 'that the Afro-Asian group had decided to reject all new proposals and to vote in favour of the original text'. Brazil and the USA were unwilling to withdraw their proposed amendment but the balance of opinion was swinging strongly against them. Greece and Hungary proposed a resolution directed against 'any reference to specific forms of racial discrimination'. The Philippines moved adjournment of the debate. The Chairman asked for a vote on whether the Greek and Hungarian motion should have priority; the Committee agreed that it should, by 80 votes to 7, with 18 abstentions. Thus, on a procedural motion, the Committee decided that there should be no reference to specific forms. In an explanation of vote, the Belgian delegate said that he had voted against the resolution in the belief that it was inconsistent with article 3 of the draft convention, adopted three days earlier, which by condemning 'segregation and *apartheid*' had already included a reference to a specific form of racial discrimination. But this was to no avail, and the reference in question was subsequently defended by Nigeria on the grounds that apartheid was different in being 'the official policy of a State Member of the United Nations'.

This decision narrowed the area of contention, and thereafter the debate proceeded more smoothly. The main remaining area of contention centred upon article 4 with its requirement that states should (*a*) make all dissemination of ideas based on racial superiority punishable by law; and (*b*) prohibit organizations which incite discrimination and make participation in them punishable by law. Some West European States were anxious that any resulting legislation might be in conflict with rights to freedom of expression and association, but chose not to delay the drafting process because they would have an opportunity to make reservations covering these points at later stages.

## THE STRUCTURE OF THE CONVENTION

The Convention as it was eventually adopted consists of three parts. Part I (articles 1–7) specifies the substantive obligations of states parties. In article 1 the term 'racial discrimination' is defined and the limits of the scope and applicability of the Convention are demarcated. Articles 2–6 list what states parties have to do in order to eliminate racial discrimination. Implementation of the Convention's anti-discrimination provisions is the responsibility of the states. What most differentiates a Convention from a Declaration is that the list of obligations is followed in Part II by provisions for the international scrutiny and review of the way states fulfil their obligations. There is, firstly, an obligatory reporting procedure (article 9); secondly, a discretionary procedure whereby one state party may complain about another state party's non-fulfilment of its obligations (articles 11–13 and 16) (since no state has shown any interest in utilizing this provision, questions can be asked about why it was thought worth including it); thirdly, an optional procedure for the adjudication of complaints from individuals (article 14); and, fourthly, an advisory responsibility regarding racial discrimination in colonial territories. This scrutiny and review is to be carried out by a Committee (CERD); its election, mandate, and meetings are specified in articles 8–10. Part III of the Convention (articles 17–25) governs such matters as signature, ratification, accession, denunciation, entry into force, reservations, revision, and settlement of disputes over the interpretation or application of the Convention.

The documentary record does not tell the whole story of the drafting process. There may be much behind-the-scenes consultation before a proposal is brought forward. A case in point concerns what became article 14, the procedure by which a state party may allow individual complainants to petition the Committee. In 1965 the USSR was strongly opposed to such procedures and when ratifying this and other conventions it entered reservations to prevent its becoming subject, without its consent, to the jurisdiction of the International Court of Justice. The author has been told that, when Mr Lamptey told the Soviet delegation that his president, Kwame Nkrumah, supported the inclusion of such a provision in the Convention, they agreed not to oppose it. If true, that reflects the politics of the mid-1960s.

The practice of states regarding treaty-making varies. Some will first sign and later proceed to ratification according to the provisions of their domestic law. Other states accede directly. A treaty may come into force once a certain number of states have acceded. When a state ceases to exist (perhaps because it divides into two or more states), the successor states may declare that they continue to be bound by obligations assumed by their predecessors. To give effect to their assumption of obligations, some states are able to incorporate a treaty into their domestic law, so that the treaty can be invoked before, and be enforced by, its domestic courts, tribunals, or administrative authorities. For example, Tunisia, in its twelfth periodic report under the Convention, stated that in Tunisia conventions are one of the sources of law.

By the act of ratification alone, they are immediately included in national law. No higher authority is necessary to decide beforehand whether the national law is in conformity with these treaties or not. Nor is it necessary for the provisions of those treaties to be transposed into national laws in order to be applicable. Tunisia has opted for the monist concept according to which the national order and the international order are compatible with one another.

Other states, with different kinds of constitution, have to give effect to their obligations by way of internal laws or administrative regulations. This mode of implementation is sometimes said to exemplify dualism, according to which the rules of international law and domestic law exist separately. If a state fails to implement domestically all its treaty obligations, the remedy has to lie in the international field and is in the hands of the other states parties to the treaty.

Many of the Convention's articles have occasioned general recommendations formulated by CERD. The most relevant ones are set out in Appendix II. Nevertheless, it may be helpful to draw attention at this point to certain features of the Convention's definition of racial discrimination. It should be noted that when a state legislates against discrimination it creates a *protected class*. The definition of racial discrimination in ICERD article 1.1 creates such a class divided into five subclasses: race, colour, descent, national origin, and ethnic origin. This differentiation will be discussed in greater detail later in connection with the laws of particular states. For the present, it is important to remark that the Convention does not prohibit discrimination in private relations such as the choice of marriage partners, in decisions about which shops to patronize, or in the making of bequests to charities intended for the benefit of persons belonging to a particular ethnic group. Discrimination is prohibited in what may be called *protected fields*—those of human rights and fundamental freedoms, including equality before the law, the right to security, political and civil rights, and economic, social, and cultural rights (the latter two sets paralleling the two covenants). The right of states to distinguish between citizens and noncitizens is explicitly excepted from the protected fields. Another exception, set out in article 2.2, permits preferential measures on behalf of disadvantaged groups. Some states, like the UK, make further exceptions in their domestic legislation with the objective of overcoming disadvantage.

ICERD prohibits distinctions which have the 'purpose or effect' of impairing the rights of persons in the protected classes. The addition of the words 'or effect' extends and complicates the definition of discrimination. It is surely proper to interpret the word 'purpose' in article 1.1 as denoting action motivated by a belief that the other person belongs to a particular race. Motivation is a concept similar to, but wider than, that of intention. Actions are intended to secure particular goals; they are forms of conscious behaviour. Whatever their intentions in performing particular actions, actors are also motivated by ambition, avarice, jealousy, loyalty, pride, and other preoccupations of which they are not necessarily conscious. Racial prejudice may be a motivation without being an intention. In many systems of criminal law a conviction requires evidence to satisfy the condition *actus non facit reum, nisi mens sit rea* (there can be no crime without a guilty mind). A court may listen to evidence about, say, the behaviour of someone who left a store without paying for goods placed in the pocket or the bag of the accused. The court compares the description of the accused's behaviour with his or her explanation of it to determine whether, at the time in question, the action sprang from a guilty mind. The law against discrimination prohibits certain kinds of motivation in certain circumstances. Someone influenced by one of them may be found to have had a guilty mind.

By adding the words 'or effect' ICERD went much further and declared that an action performed with a laudable intention could still be unlawful if it had a discriminatory effect. That effect could be one that could not have been foreseen at the relevant time. It complicates the law, because to a certain extent it detaches the concept of discrimination from that of unlawful grounds.

It is insufficient for a court to find that an action has sprung from a guilty mind. It has to relate that finding to a particular prohibition if it is to declare that a law has been broken. If one man treats another less favourably because he is a Jew, is that discrimination on grounds of race, ethnic origin, or religion? If, in Northern Ireland, a Protestant shows favour to another Protestant, is that on grounds of religion or political identification? If a Serb treats a Croat, or an Armenian treats an Azeri, less favourably, is that on grounds of ethnic or national origin? If an ethnic minority seeks to secede from a state and is prevented from so doing, is that prevention of ethnic discrimination? There are many such questions that arise from the concept of grounds, and which at present are either difficult or impossible to answer. A court can only review the evidence before it and decide whether the particular action of a particular accused sprang from a particular prohibited motivation. A state may be in breach of the Convention but not an individual. To comply with the Convention a state has to enact laws prohibiting both actions with a discriminatory purpose (direct discrimination) and actions with a discriminatory effect (indirect discrimination). They may provide different penalties to deal with indirect discrimination because it does not spring from a guilty mind (if it did, then the action would be direct discrimination). Individuals and corporations can be in breach of those laws. A state could be found in breach of the Convention if it acted in contravention of its provisions.

The adoption of the Convention was a major achievement, the greater because it was adopted on a unanimous vote.[1] Those states which ratified it would be subjecting themselves to a new form of international supervision for which there was no corresponding provision in, for example, the Genocide Convention. They would be undertaking to report on the discharge of their obligations to an independent committee which would in turn be reporting to the General Assembly on the outcome of its examination of state reports. There were other provisions whereby the Committee might consider interstate disputes and individual petitions, again of a relatively novel character. After the vote, the floor was given to the Ghanaian delegate (Mr Lamptey), who had played the leading role in negotiations. He explained that some representatives would have liked a stronger convention; he hoped that the present one might in a few years be replaced by a more effective instrument. Yet he could add that: 'when the story of the twentieth session of the General Assembly comes to be told, it can well be said, as it was said by a great war leader: This was its finest hour.' Fourteen years later, when the then Director of the UN's division of human rights (Mr Theo van Boven) addressed a meeting of the Committee, he recalled the opinion of the official who had had the administrative responsibility for the drafting of the Convention (Mr Egon

---

[1] There was one minor drama. The representative of Mexico abstained from voting on the adoption of the Convention. At a further session of the Assembly later the same day he announced that he had obtained new instructions from his foreign ministry and asked that his vote be changed to an affirmative one.

Schwelb) that Mr Lamptey 'proved how, under certain favourable conditions, one person can have a major impact on an important branch of the work of the United Nations'. Adoption of the Convention opened the way to the adoption of the two Covenants which are so much wider in scope (SR 407).

## RACIAL DISCRIMINATION AS SOCIAL PATHOLOGY

Subsequent chapters will maintain that the delegates in 1965 launched a bigger enterprise than they realized, and that Mr Lamptey had no cause for disappointment. This may, however, be the point at which to return to the unanswered questions about what are the various forms of racial discrimination, and how a new form might be identified. As has already been indicated, the ways in which the delegates spoke suggested a philosophical polarity between two conceptions of racial discrimination. According to the first of these, no distinction could be drawn between the forms and the manifestations of racial discrimination, all of which could be traced back to historical movements. The causes of racial discrimination, which were not distinguished from its forms, were thought to lie in the structure of the society, and this might offer to its members few alternative ways of behaving. Since states differed in their social structures, any struggle against racial discrimination had in some measure to be a matter of foreign policy. The persistence of this conception may explain why the states parties have so often nominated diplomats for election to the Committee. According to the second conception, racial discrimination presented a complex problem to be tackled in the same ways as other social problems with which governments were confronted. As with other domestic problems, much could be learnt about causes from the examination of individual behaviour and it was of only limited value to try to enumerate forms.

Those who pictured racial discrimination as pathological seem to have drawn (consciously or unconsciously) upon the prescriptions of philosophical realism. They wanted their definition to grasp the single underlying cause of discrimination that produced the observable kinds of behaviour. This cause had psychological, socio-economic, and ideological components which varied in their relative importance as circumstances changed. Hence any diagnosis had to be historical and to start with the collective phenomena that influenced individual conduct. Thus, for the Soviet representative, the most important social conditions producing racial discrimination were state policies (imperialism, colonialism, Zionism, nazism) and political movements (neo-nazism, fascism, and anti-Semitism). These conditions came together in particular historical constellations, so for him, as for the Yugoslav delegate, it would not have been unreasonable to picture nazism as an agent which caused the death of millions. If racial discrimination (or racism) was like a sickness, it was like an epidemic rather than an individual malady. This was the reality that had to be grasped by a definition.

There will, however, always be different ideas about what is socially pathological. To recall Lady Gaitskill's metaphor, who says that the plant is a weed? Could it not be a useful plant that has been prevented from bearing fruit by some form of mildew borne in the atmosphere? The roots may still be healthy. Botanists have objective methods for determining the pathological, sociologists do not. Nor have any clear criteria been suggested for deciding just what is a form of racial discrimination, and it was their absence which left the way open to proclamations such as that of the General Assembly resolution which 'determines that Zionism is a form of racism and racial discrimination'.

The presumption that racial discrimination is pathological was not challenged in the UN debate, because the alternative view was never advanced. Since human nature and social organization are not perfect, there is a normal expectation that some individuals will at times be motivated by prejudices (just as some individuals will commit crimes), some socio-economic structures will at times heighten conflicts of group interest, and some belief systems will disseminate false forms of consciousness. Quite apart from such considerations, all individuals have preferences about the kinds of people with whom they wish to associate, and differences in outward appearance may be one factor among many in their preferences. For such reasons, the potential causes of racial discrimination are multitudinous. Just as it is said that 'every man has his price', so there are circumstances in which any person will discriminate. Some discrimination may be morally justifiable (like that described in article 2.2 of the Convention). According to such a view, the definition of racial discrimination should follow the prescription of philosophical nominalism, conceiving of racial discrimination as simply those actions which were named in the Convention in the sense that they fell within the scope of article 1's definition. Such a prescription generates 'how' questions rather than 'why' questions. The origins of discriminatory structures and of racial doctrines may repay historical examination, but historical analysis is not essential; action against racial discrimination is to be devised in the here-and-now. Social conditioning may be important, but its effects have first to be identified in individuals before working up to their sources at the level of collective life. Seen from this standpoint, to describe racial discrimination as a social sickness is to evade the conclusion that for every act of unlawful discrimination someone is responsible and should be brought to account.

The philosophical polarity between the two ways of defining racial discrimination is paralleled by another contrast, which depends upon whether the emphasis is placed on the first word or the second. Statements are sometimes made to CERD about the racial composition of a country's population which derive from the conceptions of race that were current in the anthropology of the 1930s rather than from the manner in which anthropologists study human variation in the 1990s. To emphasize race is to start on the wrong foot. The alternative emphasis begins from the general nature of discrimination and looks for common causes underlying racial, sex, religious, and other forms of discrimination. Many countries have found it simplest to create a common legal framework for measures to prevent and prohibit discrimination of all kinds. Their laws may make it possible to assess individual responsibility for the denial of admission to restaurants or dance halls, of access to employment, education, housing, and so on. This leads to a more practical understanding of racial discrimination and of ways to combat it.

It can be more difficult to assess responsibility on the political level. Governments often share collective responsibility for their decisions; they may act in a questionable manner in the present from a belief that by doing so they may achieve a better result in the longer term. It is then difficult to apply the criteria of criminal responsibility. Nevertheless, under international law a head of state can now be held responsible for an action that is a crime under international law. The International Convention on the Suppression and Punishment of the Crime of *Apartheid* presents apartheid as a crime for which responsibility is shared by a very large group indeed. The conception of crime has been expanded.

At the time the Convention was adopted, all parties were agreed that racial discrimination was an evil, but their ideas about the nature of that evil derived from different experiences and beliefs. In the General Assembly the delegate of the United Arab Republic (which at that time combined Egypt and Syria) referred to racial discrimination in the USA, South Africa, and Southern Rhodesia. He added 'To the Arabs, Zionism was synonymous with racial discrimination and nazism', and went on: 'colonialism was responsible for all the cases of discrimination he had mentioned, except that of the United States.' The underlying thesis was that colonialism involved contact between unequally developed societies; to secure its position of advantage the colonizing group had to maintain a united front, reserving certain positions for its own members, and in this way introducing occupational and residential segregation. This represented colonialism as a constitutional form within which racial discrimination developed or was encouraged.

Even when seen from the Soviet standpoint, colonialism was a progressive phase in world history in that it extended the international network of economic relations, and, by bringing small political units within larger ones, helped create states comparable in size to those of states in other world regions. Racial discrimination was not a prime mover of colonial expansion but an outcome that varied in importance from place to place. The preoccupation with the decolonization process in the General Assembly at the time distracted attention from the ways in which unequal development leads to racial discrimination even without colonialism. The unequal development of states or of regions within states can encourage discrimination, while unequal development is also a major factor in the plight of indigenous peoples. Within industrialized societies, immigrant minorities are often at a disadvantage in employment, housing, education, and health. An employer may be right to believe that members of a given minority are on average less well qualified for a certain kind of position, but quite wrong to assume that a particular job applicant from that minority is *therefore* inadequately qualified. This is the way in which inequality, or disadvantage, causes discrimination, and it is

the more serious because in so many societies inequality is transmitted from one generation to the next. The children of the rich
start with an advantage, and the children of the poor with a
handicap. Discrimination based on race, colour, descent, and
national or ethnic origin is more persistent when these differences
are associated with economic differences.

While there may be political advantages in describing colonialism as a form or as a cause of racial discrimination, there seem
to be no advantages for social science. Nor can much be derived
from the Convention itself. Article 1.1 identifies four kinds of
behaviour—distinctions, exclusions, restrictions, and preferences—
each of which can be based on five different grounds, and each of
which can have a discriminatory purpose or effect. Multiplying,
this could distinguish forty possible forms, but nothing would be
gained from the exercise. The analogy with criminal behaviour
might suggest instead an analysis of the *legal* forms of *prohibition*
of discrimination. Here the most important distinction is that
between the prohibition of behaviour which is discriminatory in
purpose or in effect. In the search for the causes of *purposefully*
discriminatory behaviour, evidence about the acceptance of racial
ideologies and about individual psychology will attract attention.
In the search for the causes of behaviour that is discriminatory
in *effect*, assumptions deriving from social inequality or unequal
development will be to the forefront.

When the Convention was being drafted, it was customary to
speak of racial discrimination rather than racism. At that time the
word racism was used to denote a particular kind of doctrine, but
later it came to be used in a much wider sense, so that the General
Assembly in 1969 designated the year 1971 as 'International Year
for Action to Combat Racism and Racial Discrimination'. The
Assembly did not explain why it chose to add the word *racism*, but
it must be assumed that by doing so it meant to extend the scope
of the action proposed. In all probability those involved were not
crystal clear as to any differentiation of meaning between the two
words, and it falls to their successors to try to clarify their best
usage. A possible solution might be to use *racial discrimination* for
those forms which are crime-like, and *racism* for those which are
sickness-like. Two particular difficulties with any such suggestion
are that the alleged sickness has not been sufficiently well diag-
nosed and that the word *racism* (especially in its adjectival form

*racist*) so strongly implies a moral condemnation. For example, there have been animated debates in Britain about whether the action of Idi Amin in expelling Asians from Uganda was a form of racism. If racism is defined as a historical force for the exploitation of blacks, can blacks be racist? Anti-Semitism has sometimes been described as a historical force for the expulsion or extermination of Jews. It suggests that one kind of prejudice is to be defined by the identity of its victims rather than by its causes. There can be similar disputes about whether or not ethnic conflicts, like those between Serbs and Croats, qualify as instances. Are they manifestations of the same kind of sickness? Whether or not Zionism is racist, blacks can be racist, or racism depends upon differences of colour are matters of definition, but since in ordinary life there is often little time for such niceties, the power to define what is pathological can be a source of peril.

It may sometimes be worthwhile running this risk. In 1990 the Sub-Commission on Prevention of Discrimination and Protection of Minorities adopted a resolution in which it expressed concern that the scourges of racism and racial discrimination were continually assuming new forms, requiring a periodic re-examination of the methods used to combat them. It is probable that in the forefront of members' minds when they spoke of 'new forms' were the attacks on immigrants in West European countries. But to describe such attacks as the appearance of racial discrimination in a new form is to imply that within members of the public, or a proportion of them, a racial hatred has reappeared, and that this explains what has happened. It takes no account of the influence of state policies concerning immigration and of changing circumstances. Nor does it allow sufficiently for changes in motivation. When the Convention was being drafted there was a particular concern with the prohibition of doctrines of racial superiority. Some of the new anti-immigration doctrines in Europe maintain that foreigners from other regions should be excluded not because they are inferior but because they are different. It is argued that the attempt to create multiracial societies has been a failure. Muslims cannot compromise their faith. People of different ethnic origin cannot coexist peacefully, and therefore they are best kept separate. It is possible to maintain that these arguments are new forms of racism, but such a conclusion requires a careful examination of a whole set of assumptions; the purpose of such an interpretation is usually one of political rhetoric and it does not advance the socio-logical analysis of trends in those societies in which such arguments gain greater public acceptance.

It is the duty of the academic to comment on the language in which political bodies express themselves. In this way the academic can draw the attention of decision-takers to aspects they may have overlooked, which may be particularly important in UN bodies where many people speak in a language other than their mother tongue. It can be relevant to suggest that metaphorical references to racism as a scourge are popular because this word (which denotes a mode of punishment for a crime but is often used for a pestilence) covers up the distinction between a crime and a sickness.

## THE HAND OF PROVIDENCE

One implication of this chapter's arguments is that the Convention was misnamed, and that it should have been entitled a convention for the reduction of racial discrimination. Yet without the political myth that racial discrimination was a social sickness that could be eliminated by political action, would the UN's member states have invested so much energy in legislating? Surely not. The use of such a metaphor may have its drawbacks, but it proved to have great rhetorical power, mobilizing opposition to apartheid, stigmatizing discrimination, and persuading more than three-quarters of states to accede to the Convention. Intellectual argument free from the sorts of emotion displayed in the debate about the forms of racial discrimination could never have brought the same results. To describe discrimination as a sickness, or a noxious weed, may be a way of recruiting a majority to vote for legislation which can then be phrased in terms of the alternative view of discrimination as crime-like.

The claim that all forms of racial discrimination could be elim-inated was only one of the errors in the Convention adopted in 1965, but it proved to be of positive value. If the hand of Providence can be discerned in some of these misconceptions, then it suggests that the key in 1965 was not any lack of clarity but the presence of political will. The rhetoric then employed was crucial to the creation of that will.

# 5

# The Committee's Inheritance

IT is understandable that when the delegates to the General Assembly in 1965 debated the proposed Convention, much of what they said should have been based upon their own experiences and knowledge of racial discrimination. No one knows what is happening in every corner of the world. Diplomats concentrate upon the situations that concern their governments. So politics influences both perceptions and priorities within the UN.

## THE SUB-COMMISSION'S CONCEPTION OF THE PROBLEM

An observer seeking a picture of racial discrimination around the world at the time of the debate, or the time, shortly afterwards, when CERD started work, could well have turned to a UN study published in 1971 and entitled *Racial Discrimination*. It was prepared by Hernán Santa Cruz, a special rapporteur who explained in his Foreword that he had 'prepared this study in strict conformity with the guidelines and resolutions of the Sub-Commission, both with respect to the information that could be used and regarding the scope and purposes of the study'. He explained that he 'did not have the intellectual and political freedom that a scientist writing without any restraints or limitations might enjoy'. Had Hernán Santa Cruz enjoyed such freedom, 'the situations that are described in the study would have been compared with other existing situations that could not be dealt with by the author under his terms of reference'. The restraints on the author's freedom (as on the authors of other UN reports) were considerable. He had to present a sequence of drafts for the approval of the Commission on Human Rights and to utilize UN materials. He had to begin by preparing summaries of the material dealing with each UN member state and these had to be forwarded to the governments concerned for 'comment and supplementary data'. While the report was in preparation the rapporteur was requested 'to add material on the revival of nazism in its present-day forms' and he had to take note of a resolution condemning organizations which profess racist ideologies and promote 'the criminal policy of *apartheid*, colonialism, and racial intolerance'. In its representation of the nature and causes of racial discrimination the study perpetuated some of the biases evident in the 1965 General Assembly debate.

This chapter, which aims to present a baseline for assessing what the Convention has achieved, is not subject to the constraints upon UN studies. It outlines the character of ethnic relations in most of the major states at the end of the 1960s, so that the reader can have a better understanding of the starting-point from which the dialogue between the states parties and the Committee developed. Since there are so many states, any attempt to describe their reporting one-by-one would run into too much detail. A regional approach should make it possible to consider together states which share similar problems. Yet the drawing of regional boundaries can be politically contentious, and the regional grouping recognized by the UN has its peculiarities. As was mentioned in connection with Table 1, the Asian group includes Cyprus, while the Western European and Other Group (WEOG) includes Turkey, Australia, Canada and New Zealand. The former USSR was the dominant state within the East European group, but it included many republics which are Asian in character. The East European states have more recently been strengthening their relations with Western Europe and joining European political and economic institutions. So for the purposes of this book it seems better to use a simple geographical grouping which treats Europe from the Atlantic to the Urals as one group, the Americas (including Canada) as a second, followed by Africa as a third, and then finally Asia, including in this group the Pacific states such as Australia and New Zealand.

A further question arises as to the order in which these four regions should be considered. It has sometimes been argued that racist ideologies originated in Europe and then were transmitted, like a sickness, to other regions, so that an account of the situation in the late twentieth century should start historically, beginning in Europe and considering other regions in the order in which they were affected. This argument can draw strength from the evidence of Nazi atrocities assembled in the Nuremberg trial. Could men have been brought to slaughter their fellow human beings with such brutality and in such numbers had they not been indoctrinated to believe that these others belonged to inferior and dangerous races? It seems unlikely. Yet the numbers who were ready to carry this ideology to its logical conclusions were relatively small. Moreover, these extreme cases are not representative of the extensive range of racially discriminatory practice. To start from racist ideologies would therefore not be true to the Convention's definition of racial discrimination; it would imply acceptance of a particular diagnosis and an associated recommendation about the best remedy. To give an illustration, towards the end of his study (UN 1971: 298) Hernán Santa Cruz proposed that the UN should try to place a copy of the 1967 UNESCO statement on Race and Racial Discrimination 'in the hands of every literate person in the world with a view to eradicating, once and for all, false racist beliefs based upon a lack of scientific knowledge'. Such a proposal implies that racist beliefs are the main cause of racial discrimination.

## CONCEPTIONS OF RACE

This chapter, by contrast, assumes neither that racist beliefs are the prime cause of racial discrimination, nor that they can be eradicated by the spread of scientific knowledge. The historical record suggests that, throughout the world, wherever previously separate peoples have come into contact with others they have regarded them as different and have, at times, behaved towards them in ways that fall within the definition of racial discrimination set out in ICERD article 1.1. The practice of racial discrimination has been universal. What originated in Europe was an idiom of race as a way of defining this otherness. At times the idiom incorporated and rationalized a belief in white racial superiority, but this was only part of a more complex development. Ideas of race shaped a special group self-consciousness in opposition to other groups identified by race. Notions of identity and entitlements which had previously been implicit and taken for granted were made explicit and were articulated in racial vocabulary. So too, around the world in 1970, there were many situations of inter-group relations which the parties did not see as being in any way racial. They thought of the interacting groups in terms of their unique characteristics, rather than of any features which they might share with other groups elsewhere. Usually they knew little of inter-group situations in other countries or regions which displayed similar characteristics. As people became better educated about the life of other societies this was bound to change, but people on the other side of the world were not obliged to adopt the European idiom of race in order to conceptualize the group contacts that were becoming important to them. A less misleading way could certainly have been found.

The reality, however, was that the European idiom had been reinforced by developments in North America and that it was carried thence in potent forms to other regions. Many governments in Latin America and Asia associated racial discrimination with a particular phase of European thought, and with the imperialism of European powers. Yet in 1965 they accepted a definition of racial discrimination which was of very much greater reach. The sequence in which regions are considered in this chapter therefore shows a superficial resemblance to the image of a spreading sickness but is actually quite different. What was spread was a European way of classifying others (some would call it a false consciousness, since the system of classification did not have the significance those who used it believed it to have). How peoples treated one another depended on economic, political, and cultural factors which combined with the mode of classification to create a particular consciousness of group difference.

The nature of racial consciousness can be better appreciated by comparing it with the consciousness of other kinds of difference, notably those of caste, class, ethnicity, gender, and nation (to list these in alphabetical order). In considering the ways in which societies have developed structures of social differentiation, a parallel can be drawn with the processes of socialization, in particular with the development of a child's consciousness of group differences. Such structures have been highly elaborated in Hindu caste. A child who grows up in a Hindu village may learn, first, that 'We take food from the As but not the Bs; the Cs will take food from us, but the Ds will not.' The names As, Bs, and Cs are proper names that identify groups but do not say what sorts of group they are. Secondly, the child may learn that the As, Bs, Cs, and Ds are *jatis*. Thirdly, he or she may come to appreciate that *jatis* fit together as parts of a comprehensive social system and cosmology. If consciousness of caste is defined subjectively, by reference to a person's thought, it cannot be said that there is a full consciousness of caste until the third stage has been reached. This is to describe an actor's (or participant's) model of the Hindu social structure, which is necessary to explain who will eat with or marry whom. Sociologists seek first to understand how actors interpret the social systems in which they have to pursue their lives, and then to uncover underlying principles of which the actors may be unaware. They try to formulate an observer's model of the social structure which may seek, among other things, to explain why it is that the actors see their situations in the ways that they do. In an observer model the awareness that there are group differences in the taking and receiving of food (that is, at the second stage or level in the process described above) might be held sufficient evidence of caste consciousness.

With respect to gender, a child will learn that he or she is a boy or a girl, that there are children of the other gender, that the genders of children correspond to those of adults, and that in some circumstances social roles and cultural constructions are founded upon gender. In the case of both caste and gender, an individual may come later to believe that such differences constitute unjustified inequalities which should be resisted and removed. An observer may also conclude that a shared consciousness may not correspond with an objective reality, and that therefore there can be a false consciousness.

In Western industrial societies individuals learn varied models of class relations. Class differentiation may be seen either as a continuous differentiation of status, or as a discontinuous differentiation into two, three, or more categories; the differentiation may be seen as founded upon income, property, power, or lifestyle. From the statistical study of social mobility, from the analysis of sequences of historical change, and in other ways, observers have inferred patterns of class differentiation of which the actors are unaware, and have built these into observer models.

These remarks are preliminaries to two important theses. First, the consciousness of social inequalities is not directly related to the degree of inequality in question. Great inequalities can be accepted when they are taken for granted, whereas in other times and places

smaller inequalities can occasion strong resentment. In this connection it is necessary to distinguish between objective inequality and
the justification of inequality. The pay of a steward on an aircraft
is not equal to that of the pilot. To attract people with the skills
required of pilots it may be necessary to pay them more. There is
therefore an objective inequality, but whether the particular
differential being observed by employers is justifiable either
economically or morally is a matter of judgement. People can
sometimes be persuaded that something they have never previously
questioned is unjustifiable. They can only be so persuaded if they
have become conscious that the differentiation is not natural but
social, and therefore changeable. Consciousness of caste, class,
ethnic, gender, national, and racial differentiation is a consciousness of social constructs.

A second important thesis is that much of the confusion
concerning the nature of racial and ethnic relations derives from a
failure to distinguish sufficiently carefully between the social align-
ments that are observed or experienced and the names that are
given to them. Names belong in the realm of human consciousness,
and this varies in time and space. It is, therefore, important to
distinguish three levels of increasing complexity: first, that of the
actual relations between individuals and the names they use to
describe those whom they encounter; secondly, the task of deciding
whether those relations are to be classed as racial, ethnic, religious,
national, or perhaps a combination of two or more; thirdly, the
problem of accounting for features of the observed relations, like
discrimination.

In Latin American and Francophone countries the relations
between individuals of different physical appearance have often
reflected a continuous pattern of differentiation in which education
and wealth could be more important than skin colour. People have
described those of different colour not so much as members of
groups but as individuals with individual attributes. Racial discrimination in these countries may be in some respects less severe
but in other respects more difficult to recognize.

One way of comparing patterns of racial discrimination in
different regions of the world is to study the use of race as a social
sign. Physical differences between groups do not directly influence
the relations between the people assigned to different groups. They
exercise an influence only indirectly when the differences are given

a social significance. When a man is of an unusual skin colour, this may signify that he has come from another region, or that some of his ancestors did. In some countries a lighter skin colour may signify a probability that the person is relatively rich or of a higher social status. In racially divided societies skin colour may lead one section of the local people to conclude that a man is 'one of us', and the other section to presume that he is 'one of them'. So if 'racial' differences are differences in outward appearance, it can be inferred that they signify different things in different regions. Similar principles govern the significance attributed to differences of culture and language, so, for the purposes of eliminating racial discrimination as defined in ICERD, racial differences include differences of ethnic origin.

In those parts of Europe with which Chapter 9 is concerned, 'race' is mostly the badge distinguishing minorities resulting from relatively recent immigration in response to the demand for labour resulting from industrialization. In many of the American societies to be discussed in Chapter 10, racial signs differentiate the population of indigenous origin from the larger population that derives from European settlement over several centuries, and differentiates both of them from smaller populations deriving from African and Asian settlement. In Africa, racial signs have likewise differentiated groups deriving from intercontinental migration, but, taken together with ethnic differences of culture and language, they have a wider significance. Many contemporary countries attained recognition as independent states in the relatively recent era of decolonization. Many of their citizens define themselves by membership in ethnic groups ('tribes'), and this can undermine institutions of democratic government. Historical differences between ethnic groups can then be important politically. In many parts of East and South Asia the picture is different yet again, because their political institutions are different; nor in this region, apart from certain Pacific countries (including Australia and New Zealand), is there any big gap between an indigenous population and the descendants of later settlers. In Asia, differences of racial or ethnic origin are often compounded with differences of religion. The importance of this connection in the Middle East needs no emphasis here.

Just as a European conception of race was exported to other regions, so was a European conception of the nation-state. It is easier to define a state than a nation or a national group. Any political unit that is recognized as a state by other states is a state. The English language permits references to multinational states, such as the USSR, the former Yugoslavia, or the UK. In the Middle East, however, reference is made to an Arab nation, the members of which are citizens of different states. So a nation may be either smaller than the population of a state, equivalent to that population, or larger than it. In many black African states there are ethnic groups which the English have called 'tribes', but in Sierra Leone at the end of the colonial period—and doubtless in some other countries too—a questioner in the local pidgin dialect would ask 'What nation you?' There is no clear rule to state that a group like the Mende or the Temne may not be classified as a nation, and, indeed, some African countries (perhaps taking a hint from Soviet practice) have designated these groups 'nationalities'. What matters is the feeling of constituting a political community, not the name observers give to a particular kind of political community.

In European history there were some countries in which a state was formed round about the same time as the inhabitants came to feel themselves a political community; England and Sweden may be examples. There are other countries where a state was formed first and then had to set about creating a nation to sustain the new institution; France is usually thought to have created such a state in 1789 at a time when the nation existed only in embryo. There are yet other countries in which people shared a feeling of constituting a nation before they had their own state; Germany, Norway, Finland, and perhaps Poland are examples. In many other parts of the world also, the states came first and their governments found themselves expected to develop institutions corresponding to the European idea of a nation-state. The routes through which peoples have become the citizens of nation-states have influenced the kinds of nationalism that have characterized the states.

Since the late nineteenth century most Europeans have belonged in nation-states with a predominant ethnicity, and have projected onto the rest of the world their assumption that political rule should be based on the nation-state. They have taken the lead in establishing, as a basis for global relations, a League of *Nations* and a United *Nations*. These were the organizations, not of nations, but of states, though the assumed equivalence of nation with state made the distinction between the two seem unimportant. The

European model did not allow satisfactorily for the presence within the state of ethnic minorities. The consequences of this failure have been serious in Europe but quite disastrous in black Africa.

According to Islamic and some versions of Christian belief, the state exists to serve religious ends, but twentieth-century practice has been to regard the state as sovereign and accountable only to itself. In theory, the sole and recent constraint has been the development of the natural-law tradition to create the concept of inalienable human rights. Even a unanimous vote of a democratically elected legislature cannot remove from anyone his or her inalienable rights. In practice, there have been many constraints deriving from the economic and political relations between states, notably the creation of areas of free trade and of defence. All these affect the interaction between law and politics in the application of human-rights conventions.

An observer surveying the patterns of racial and ethnic discrimination in Europe, America, Africa, and Asia in 1970 (i.e. of racial discrimination as defined in ICERD) could separate the patterns involving indigenous peoples from those involving national groups and those involving immigrant minorities. Yet, while the category of indigenous peoples is relatively unimportant in Europe, it is crucial in the Americas. In Africa and Asia there are forest peoples who continue a traditional way of life on the fringes of the national societies but they are not necessarily more 'indigenous' than other peoples. The relations between national groups are important in Europe, Africa, and Asia, but less so in the Americas. Relations with immigrant minorities are important in the regions of economic growth which have attracted workers from far away (primarily in Western Europe, North America, South Africa, the Middle East, and Japan), and they have implications for the people in the regions where these workers originated. There must therefore be changes in emphasis as any survey moves from one region to another.

## EUROPE IN 1970

When, in the sixteenth century, Europeans penetrated further into other regions of the world and came into contact with their peoples, they thought of themselves as Christians and usually conceptualized the differences between the groups in religious terms. They saw themselves as the subjects of particular monarchs and therefore also as Dutch, English, French, Portuguese, and Spanish. Racial classification came later. It started in eighteenth-century Britain and North America within a cosmological framework provided by the Bible's account of creation. When humans were described as belonging to races, they were assigned to groups constituted by descent. Their differences were explained genealogically by tracing them back in a speculative manner to the different sons of Adam, to the groups formed after Noah's flood or after the fall of the tower of Babel. So consciousness of belonging to a race could be consciousness of belonging to a group with a special destiny within God's plan (comparable to the third level of understanding of Hindu caste). Since the Bible had not prepared Europeans for the discovery of peoples in the New World, some daring writers were led to conclude that God might have created other races not mentioned in the Bible.

The meaning given to the word *race* started to expand at the end of the eighteenth century. French writers described their country's history as resulting from the interaction between two races, the Franks and the Gauls. English writers described the Norman conquest of their land as having entailed the rule of the Norman race over the Saxon race. Some maintained that Irish resistance to English rule derived from a racial incompatibility. Two of the most prominent expositors of what came to be called scientific racism, Arthur de Gobineau in France and Robert Knox the Scottish anatomist, were both inspired to write by the uprisings in Europe in 1848. The present generation regards these as having been politically motivated revolutions and attempted revolutions. Gobineau and Knox thought them evidence of the wars of races; they then extended to other regions their theory for explaining intra-European differences and conflicts. Races were for them permanent types with distinctive capacities to create new civilizations. Each type by descent transmitted different physical and cultural attributes. Consciousness of race became a way of understanding the limits within which nature had confined a group's future (with nature replacing God as the author of the plan). Among a wider public at that time, *race* became a synonym for *nation*, a large group of persons sharing a common language who wished to be governed as a single political unit.

The discovery of natural selection and of the way in which this process modified the inheritance of physical characters, revived the conception of races as constituted by descent but gave a new meaning to that definition. For some at least, consciousness of race became a way of learning that a group could have a brighter future if it observed the principles of eugenics and cultivated a racial team spirit. But most scholars concluded that socio-cultural evolution had to be explained in a different way from biological evolution. Groups which shared a common culture and usually a common territory were to be recognized as ethnic rather than as racial; consciousness of belonging to such a group was to be understood as a political consciousness.

Political tensions arose because in many areas ethnic boundaries failed to coincide with political boundaries. Under the Hapsburg, Ottoman, and Russian empires ethnic groups had moved, or been moved, into new territories and were left exposed when the imperial power retreated (as happened to the ethnic Hungarians in Romania and the ethnic Turks in Bulgaria). In the Balkans the collapse of the Ottoman empire had left a congeries of peoples held together in the multinational state of Yugoslavia, which to a certain degree resembled the plural societies of South-East Asia in which peoples mixed but did not combine. Further east there were latent tensions between many groups in Transcaucasia. In 1970 these resentments were suppressed so that they made little impact on world diplomacy, but with the collapse of Communism in 1989 many of what had been Soviet republics declared their independence. Fighting broke out between Armenia and Azerbaijan, primarily on account of Armenian minorities within Azerbaijan. Ethnic civil war erupted in Georgia.

No one in the 1965 debate mentioned the Gypsies as victims of racial discrimination, but the decline of the old order led to more trouble for the Gypsies in Romania, while in Poland—a country which since the genocide of the early 1940s has had only a diminutive Jewish population—new political parties maintained that it was vital to solve 'the Jewish problem'.

In 1970 racial discrimination appeared to be a problem for Western but not Eastern Europe. The former imperial powers were reducing their links with former colonies and moving into closer economic and political relations with neighbouring states. Great Britain had received significant numbers of new workers from the

West Indies, India, and Pakistan, most of whom had voting rights as Commonwealth citizens so that the question of citizenship—so important elsewhere—did not arise. France had drawn in workers from North Africa but their relations with the French were profoundly affected by the war of Algerian independence which ended in 1962. Belgium and the Netherlands also engaged workers from North Africa, but the latter took many from its former colonies, notably Suriname. Sweden recruited substantially from Yugoslavia. The labour force in the FRG was augmented by new workers from the Eastern *Länder*, and particularly from Turkey. They were called *Gastarbeiter*, implying that one day they would be going back to their home countries. Their marginality to the national society has given rise to what is sometimes called 'the new racism'. Whether it is actually new is a matter for dispute. An important dimension is that of citizenship, or a set of ideas that there are different kinds of people with different entitlements in their dealings with others. The actors themselves may in everyday speech designate the groups as simply 'those people'; in more formal settings they will use national or ethnic names rather than racial ones and they may not use the vocabulary of race when describing the relations between groups. Nevertheless, observers often maintain that a racial categorization lies behind expressions which make no use of racial terms.

## AMERICA IN 1970

The problems of racial discrimination in the American continent are twofold. There are, first, those involving the relations between the indigenous peoples and the immigrant peoples. Secondly, there are those stemming from the relations between different immigrant groups, as when one such group has acquired a dominant position and is accused of discriminating against more recent arrivals, or when, as in Canada, there were initially two immigrant groups, one English- and the other French-speaking. There are also major differences between the social systems in different parts of the continent, with Canada and the USA sharing certain commonalities by comparison with Latin America, from Mexico to southernmost Chile, and distinct again from the islands of the Caribbean.

The states of North and South America were all the products

of the European colonization that started from the end of the fifteenth century. From the seventeenth to the nineteenth centuries Africans were imported to replace the Amerindian slave labour force. Throughout the Americas, the European settlers showed a lively concern for their political liberties *vis-à-vis* the governments of the countries from which they originated, but only a few of them thought the same principles should apply in their dealings with the indigenous or imported groups. In the images which the settlers built up of themselves and their societies there was, for several generations, no place for the indigenous peoples. They had to become like their conquerors or disappear.

The populations that resulted from the bringing-together of previously separate peoples divided themselves in terms of appearance, socio-cultural status, and ancestry. In the Spanish and Portuguese territories complex classifications developed for naming persons of varying degrees of Amerindian, European, and African origin. Where the indigenous peoples maintained a distinct community life, the various groups were distinguished both by their social life and their cultures (notably their languages and religions). In the USA the cleavage between blacks and whites became so deep as to create a two-category system; whether an individual belonged in the one category or the other depended upon his or her ancestry (Banton 1983: 15–31). By the twentieth century there was a sharp contrast between North and South America, both in the patterns of relations and in the ways in which these relations were described and experienced. While a North American might perceive relations between two individuals as the interaction between someone who is white and someone who is black, the Brazilian might see them more in terms of the individuals' social status.

Though the creation of European colonies in the Caribbean goes back to the early sixteenth century, it was the development of sugar production in the late eighteenth century that brought them to prominence. Slaves were purchased in West Africa and transported to produce the sugar for which there was so much demand. Slavery was abolished in British possessions in 1834, at a time when the demand for sugar was declining; since then the market has fallen further and the islands have been left with an oversupply of labour. In Jamaica there was a black plantation workforce, but elsewhere Indian contract workers were also imported; in Guyana they came to outnumber those of African descent, while in Trinidad and Suriname their number rose to be more than one-third of the population. Parallels can be drawn with the other sugar colonies of Mauritius (in the African regional group), where those of Indian origin rose to over two-thirds, and with Fiji (in the Pacific—see below), where the Indian population rose to equal that of the native Fijians. Further parallels can be drawn with countries in South-East Asia, like Malaysia, where under colonial rule a Chinese workforce was introduced and this gave rise to racial tensions.

The colonization of Latin America was based upon conquest. It was not preceded, as in North America, by a phase of treaty-making. No leader of an indigenous people in Latin America could borrow the words of a Canadian counterpart when he explained 'we have lived up to our side of the treaties, but the rights promised to us have been neglected . . . To us a treaty is an international document signed by two nations' (Oreskov 1989: 159). It is not now seen in that way in international law, which does not challenge the conclusion of the US Supreme Court in 1831 that the indigenous peoples of Georgia were 'domestic dependent nations . . . living in a state of pupilage. Their relationship to the United States resembles that of wards to guardian . . .'. Put briefly, indigenous peoples are objects but not subjects of international law. They cannot enter into treaty relationships with sovereign states. Nevertheless the existence of these treaties has given the indigenous peoples of some countries the basis for a form of nationalism independent of that of the state in which they reside.

The European groups which settled in Canada and the USA entered into treaties with the indigenous peoples which they did not always honour subsequently. The constitution of Canada has had to be altered to recognize the rights of the 'first nations' and to provide a legal basis for the distinctiveness of the French-speaking section of the population. Official documents have to be prepared in both English and French. Already in 1970 Canada had started down the path of 'multiculturalism'.

The USA in 1970 had just undergone a 'second reconstruction'. White society was still reeling from the effects of the Black Power movement, which taught 'Black Pride' and a new assertiveness. Whereas the idea of 'race' had previously been used as part of a white consciousness of black subordination, in the context of affirmative action programmes it became the basis for minority claims to forms of preferment that would otherwise not have been available to them. Independently of the international movements which led to the adoption of the Convention, in the USA the concept of race was already acquiring an additional and protective quality.


## AFRICA IN 1970

In South Africa the National Party came to power in 1948 and set about implementing its dream of apartheid, or separateness. The plan could not be reconciled with the pressures generated by a capitalist economic system, with the expectations of international opinion, or with the growing power of the black majority. In 1960 the shooting of sixty-nine Africans in Sharpeville caused an outcry. South Africa became an international pariah. By the end of 1969 Nationalist politicians were beginning to seek compromises. White people throughout the southern part of the continent could read the signs of the times, though in what was to become Zimbabwe the whites had in 1965 proclaimed an unlawful declaration of independence and were subject to UN-ordered sanctions. Meantime there were other territories that had not yet obtained independence. The larger ones included Angola, Namibia, and Mozambique; the smaller ones were Cape Verde, Comoros, Djibouti, Guinea-Bissau, Sao Tome and Principe, and the Seychelles.

A black government had assumed power in Kenya, where there was an important group of white farmers. The difference in colour might have led some observers to detect racial or ethnic tensions of a different character from those between groups who were of the same colour—such as, say, Kikuyu and Luo. In 1965 no one remarked that the prohibition of discrimination based upon descent or ethnic origin covered the relations between tribal groups. The expression *tribalism* has long been disliked by many Africans because it is a word used to identify ethnic differences among black Africans only; it carries an implication that Africans are less modern than the peoples of other regions, and more primitive. Ethnic divisions in black Africa appeared to be distinctive only because of the pace of change. In cities and mining compounds men from different cultural groups were thrust into a new way of life in which they had to turn for support to those who spoke their mother tongue and whom they could more readily trust. As decolonization approached, the competition between ethnic groups increased. In many of the new states the largest ethnic group mustered the most votes and became the successor to the colonial power, claiming a more than proportionate share of important posts. Much political activity centred upon competition for new schools, hospitals, roads, and other resources at the disposal of politicians. Where the competing regions were ethnically distinctive, this reinforced the political significance of ethnic differences.

The decolonization of Burundi and Rwanda was bound to bring into question the way in which the Hutu group in these two countries had for some three centuries been subordinated to the Tutsi group. Theirs were not colonial boundaries, though elsewhere it was a different story. In recent years colonial rule has often had to serve as a scapegoat for the weaknesses of others, but in no respect has the colonialists' responsibility been heavier than in the cavalier way in which they drew boundaries between what were to become states. They ignored the way that along the upper range of black Africa there is an ethnic fault-line marking off the Arabic-speaking North. Chad has been described (Brogan 1989: 19–21) as wracked by hatred between the peoples of the Arab North and the Christian and animist South, and by the rivalries between the northern tribes. The French and Italian colonial powers demarcated their political frontiers without regard to the ethnic frontiers. The successor states have had to bear the consequences of these decisions. A similar complaint can be made about the frontiers of what was Spanish Sahara, now known as Western Sahara and claimed by Morocco. Further East in the Sudan, territorially the largest country in Africa, there is a comparable scenario. Two-thirds of the Sudan's population of fourteen million live in the North and are Muslims by religion and Arabs by culture. The South has quite a different environment and is inhabited by peoples who are either Christian or followers of traditional religion, and who have more in common with the peoples of northern Uganda. The Egyptians ruled the Sudan from 1819 until the British conquest in the 1870s and the establishment of an Anglo-Egyptian regime. The country became independent in 1956, but by then the southern corps of the army had mutinied and ethnic disputes had begun. It might have been better had the colonial power shown more respect for the ethnic frontier.

Boundary problems in the Horn of Africa have been less acute, but the competing claims to the Ogaden Desert of Somalia and Ethiopia led to a terrible war. Ethiopia was traditionally a mini-empire of the Amharic peoples; more recently it has been rent by ethnic disputes and described as 'one of the states least likely to survive' (Brogan 1989: 27).

The states of North Africa had less cause for concern over ethnic tensions. Algeria had achieved independence from France in 1962 after an eight-year armed struggle of increasing barbarity. To its Arab neighbours it became known as 'the country of a million martyrs'. The states of this region were facing mounting problems, but ethnic differences were less troubling than in other parts of the continent.


## ASIA IN 1970

Until quite recently there was very little consideration of racial discrimination in Asia other than as a consequence of European colonization. A summary review of the main features of ethnic relations in the region at the time the Convention came into effect may therefore help indicate the problems of applying the Convention in this large and heterogeneous region. It will start in the Pacific, and move through East Asia towards the Middle East,

European settlement in Australia commenced in 1788. No treaties were made with the indigenous people, and, whatever may have been the policies of the Colonial Office in London, the idea took hold that legally the land was *terra nullius*, no man's land, available for the taking. Six states were established and in 1900 they came together to create a federation. The states ceded powers to the Commonwealth, but they have remained jealous of their relative autonomy. The Aboriginal people were denied citizenship or voting rights until after a referendum in 1967 by which the vast majority of the voters approved a constitutional amendment making it possible for the Commonwealth Parliament to make laws for Aboriginal people throughout the country. In 1970 Aboriginals had but a feeble voice in Australian politics. Mention of 'race' was as likely to evoke debate about the 'white Australia' policy which had sought to encourage immigration from Western Europe and to keep out would-be Asian immigrants.

The Maori name for the country they settled about a thousand years ago is Aotearoa. The rest of the world know it as New Zealand. European trading vessels started to call there in the late eighteenth century. Then in 1840 a British official concluded with the Maori the Treaty of Waitangi, by which the British sovereign assumed the government of the land and gave its people the rights and duties of British citizenship. Settlement by the British (called *Pakeha* in Maori) was not peaceful. Lands were confiscated in violation of the treaty. During the 1950s and 1960s many Maori moved to the cities. Racial inequality started to feature as a problem and Maori protests became more organized.

European missionaries arrived in Fiji in the 1830s. Sugar plantations were established a little later. In 1874, responding to an invitation from the Fijian chiefs, the British government declared Fiji a colony and sent Sir Arthur Gordon as Governor. He introduced indentured labourers from India while at the same time legislating to prevent any further alienation of native land. Gordon sought to make Fijian society conform to what contemporary anthropologists thought must have been its original structure! In the twentieth century, as the Indian population grew towards numerical equality, its representatives demanded equal rights. The Fijians insisted that, as they were the people who had ceded authority to the British in 1874, the country must be returned to them basically as it had been before. So the independence constitution of 1970 protected their special status. It sought, with only limited success, to balance two conflicting rights: those of historical possession and those of the equality of citizens.

Few of the colonies in the Pacific had attained independence by 1970. The tiny island of Nauru (population 8,600), the Cook Islands (16,000), Tonga (104,000) and Western Samoa (159,000) were among them. The biggest, Papua New Guinea (3,350,000), was then administered by Australia. The peoples of some of the smaller islands had been affected by the extraction of minerals and by nuclear testing, which, since they were the work of the Western states, had a racial aspect. Potential trouble signs could also be detected in New Caledonia, where the population of French settlers was increasing and by 1970 almost equalled that of the indigenous Kanaks.

The populations of both Japan and Korea are relatively homogeneous in their composition and outward appearance. Yet Japanese society is notable for the extent to which *gaijin*, or 'outside persons', are socially excluded. Possibly three million persons are accounted Burakumin, a classification that derives from a partial caste system of the seventeenth century. If an examination of the birth registers of the Buraku settlements shows that someone is descended from a person born in one of these, he or she is identified as Buraku. Agencies have compiled lists of persons of Buraku descent and these lists have been used by employers who wanted not to employ Buraku. In the early 1970s it was estimated that 70 per cent of Japanese parents employed private investigators to check that a prospective son- or daughter-in-law was not of Buraku or Korean descent. The Buraku campaigned vigorously in the 1970s about such practices when they became public knowledge. Those members of the smaller Korean minority who immigrated after 1945, or descend from such immigrants, have difficulty obtaining Japanese citizenship. As aliens they are subject to finger-printing and experience much discrimination. There are about a million residents from the Okinawan islands, and persons of mixed Japanese and outside parentage who also have only a marginal status. The Ainu minority in the North (some 20,000) are an indigenous people who are regarded by the ethnic majority as being of low status. In the Japanese language there are three words which may be used to translate 'race': *shu*, corresponding to 'species', *henshu* for 'subspecies', and *jinshu* for a division of the human species such as that between Caucasians, Mongolians, and Ethiopians. In the written form all these words share the character for 'seed'. There is no affinity between them and *kokka*, which is used to translate 'nation'. Nor is there any linguistic affinity with *gaijin*, but members of Japan's ethnic majority are so averse from contacts with all kinds of 'outside persons' that Westerners regard the processes of exclusion as being as racist as anything in Europe or North America.

Whether there is racism in China is a more difficult question to answer, and much will depend upon the criteria employed. Most Chinese are of Han ethnicity, and this will be translated into English as a 'nationality'. The People's Republic of China deplores 'Han chauvinism' and seeks to ensure equal rights for all citizens irrespective of nationality. In Chinese, 'race' can be translated by *Renzhong*, which, when written, combines two characters, one for 'human' and the other for 'species' or 'type'. Another possible translation is *Zhongzu*, which combines the second character of

*Renzhong* with one representing a group with common characteristics, or, on its own, race or nationality. So 'race' and 'nation'
may be closer in Chinese than they are in Japanese. It is probable
that the Chinese words do not have the sense of a hierarchical
distinction that 'race' once had for many Europeans, but the
meanings are close enough to translate the sense of the Convention.

If, in the late 1960s, some critic had wished to maintain that
racial discrimination was a serious problem in China which the
Convention had to regulate, he or she might well have focused
upon Tibet. All Chinese governments have for a long time regarded
Tibet as part of China, though there have been periods in which
central control has been weak and Tibetans have enjoyed a *de facto*
independence. The Chinese People's Liberation Army moved into
Tibet in 1950, in order, as they saw it, to liberate the people from
the oppression of the manorial lords and the monasteries. In 1956
some Tibetans revolted, and after a further revolt in 1959 the
Dalai Lama fled to India. Following that revolt the International
Commission of Jurists issued a report which discussed whether
the systematic violation of Tibetan human rights had constituted
genocide. Several hundred thousand Tibetans had lost their lives.
Seven years later the Cultural Revolution started in China. Young
Red Guards, many of them Tibetans, started to destroy religious
objects. The number of monasteries, which had once exceeded
3,000, was then reduced to less than twenty. Later the Chinese
government was to acknowledge that a mistake had been made: by
widening the class struggle they had failed to show due respect to
the minorities' right to autonomy. By 1970 a Chinese military
presence had been established, together with an administration of
Han officials and technicians. They did not learn local languages
or respect local customs. There were significant inequalities between Chinese and Tibetans in their rights to housing, freedom of
movement, education, employment, and health care. The degree of
segregation resembled that which had operated in many European
colonies.

Viet Nam was conquered in the mid-nineteenth century and
made part of French Indochina, together with Laos and Cambodia.
After the Japanese attack during the Second World War, the
French were unable to re-establish their rule. Viet Nam was
partitioned and the USA tried in vain to support the South;
many of the troops it brought in were black. In the early 1960s

relations between China and the USSR became tense, with the latter supporting Viet Nam. The conflict spilled over into Laos and Cambodia, crossing a cultural frontier, for, while Viet Nam is a product of Chinese Confucianism, the cultures of Laos, Cambodia, and Thailand stem from Buddhist India. These were bitter and murderous conflicts which often had a racial aspect even if their origins were primarily political.

Europeans first reached Indonesia in the early sixteenth century. By the middle of the next century the Dutch had driven out most of their rivals and were creating a trading empire based upon Java. There (like the British in Burma), they created what J. S. Furnival called a 'plural society', associating a medley of peoples— European, Chinese, Indian, and various indigenous groups:

They mix but do not combine. Each group holds by its own religion, its own culture and language, its own ideas and ways. As individuals they meet, but only in the marketplace, in buying and selling. There is a plural society with different sections of the community living side by side, but separately, within the same political unit. Even in the economic sphere there is a division of labour along racial lines. (Furnival 1948: 304)

The Indonesian nationalists collaborated with the Japanese when they occupied Indonesia in 1942 and then annexed it in the following year. When the US army closed in on them, they accepted the principle of independence. A new state was envisaged including Portuguese Timor, Malaya, Singapore, and British Borneo. The Dutch accepted the independence only of Java, but had to agree to the transfer of their sovereignty over the remaining territory at the end of 1949. By 1965 the Communist Party, with three million members, was seen as a threat to the new state of Indonesia. Anti-Communist demonstrations were followed by massacres in which at least 400,000 people were killed, many of them Chinese. Again, it is difficult to decide how many of the killings were racially motivated.

The Spaniards came to the Philippines in 1521. They used Manila as a trading station until 1898, when the territory was ceded to the USA. The Filipinos resisted Japanese rule during the Second World War and lost one million people in the struggle. They were rewarded with independence in 1946, but the Philippines remained a state with many deep ethnic and religious divisions.

After the humiliating defeat of the British by the Japanese, communism appeared more attractive to the Malayan Chinese. In 1948 communist terrorists began their attacks on government posts and forces. The insurgent movement was steadily overcome during the 1950s, and Malaya became independent in 1957. Six years later, Singapore, Sarawak, and Sabah joined with Malaya to form the federation of Malaysia. On the Malayan peninsula the proportion of persons of Chinese origin (who were concentrated in the towns and cities) increased until they could challenge Malay political supremacy. The management of the ethnic balance became difficult, so that in 1965 Singapore was forced to withdraw from the federation. Then, after the election results of May 1969, some Chinese in Kuala Lumpur held a victory celebration which touched off a serious riot. Malay political supremacy was reasserted and a new economic policy introduced to promote Malay interests and to secure parity in economic matters.

In 1947 the British abandoned their attempts to control India and departed, leaving behind two states, one of which (Pakistan) was Muslim, and the other (India) nominally secular but mainly Hindu. The partitioning of the territory was a brutal process in which twelve million people fled their homes. Trainloads of refugees passing from one side of the new frontier to the other were stopped and everyone on board murdered. Not far short of one million people lost their lives. In the far north, the Maharajah of the predominantly Muslim state of Kashmir hoped for independence also, but when the government of Pakistan sent in irregular forces to seize power he signed a treaty of accession to India. There followed the first of three wars between India and Pakistan, all of which concluded to India's advantage, unlike its failure in the 1962 border war with China; this brought about a pro-Moscow realignment in Indian foreign policy.

Both India and Pakistan were to experience internal conflicts. In India, many of these have centred upon the caste system. The building blocks of this are the occupational monopolies called *jatis*, which are arranged in a hierarchy that in the eyes of its beneficiaries is legitimated by the Hindu religion. Groups lower down often dispute this and many of their members have converted to other faiths to escape their ritual degradation. The Indian government has denied that discrimination based upon caste is covered by the Convention. The government has also had to contend with demands for the recognition of new states within India, often based upon language. None of these has been fiercer than that of the Sikhs in the Punjab, but their insurgency did not come into the open until 1981.

Within Pakistan as it is in 1995 there are ethnic differences between the mountain people (Baluchis and Pathans) and those of the plains. Because of the 1948 partition, there are also ethnic differences within the population of Karachi. In the period leading up to the 1971 secession of Bangladesh (which was aided by India), the Bengalis in East Pakistan claimed that their part of the country did not receive a fair share of the resources, which may have been a sign of ethnic tension.

Ceylon became independent in 1948 and changed its name to Sri Lanka in 1972. Some 18 per cent of the population were Tamils, originating in south-eastern India. Like some other minority groups, they turned to education as a path of advancement and their consequent success excited resentment. After 1956 the government exploited Sinhalese nationalism by imposing quotas upon the Tamils and encouraging discrimination against them. Tensions of a racial character were building up during the 1960s.

Afghanistan, like many other countries in the world, is an artificial creation. It has been seen as a buffer zone between the peoples of Pakistan, Persia, and Uzbekistan, and between the British and Russian spheres of influence. Afghanistan is inhabited by peoples of differing ethnic origin, language, and religion, who have fought one another for most of their history. When, in 1979, the USSR increased its influence in Afghanistan's affairs, and new weapons became available, these tensions acquired additional savagery.

In the 1960s opposition in Iran to the rule of the Shah was expressed through a movement for Islamic reform, but there were significant ethnic minorities like the Baluchis and the Turkomans. The major ethnic conflict of the region, however, centred on the Kurds, a people numbering some 16–17 million. Over eight million of them lived in Turkey, over three million in Iran, over three million in Iraq, and smaller numbers in Syria and the USSR. A significant number were becoming migrant workers in Western Europe. In 1920, after the break-up of the Ottoman empire, the British contemplated the establishment of a separate Kurdish nation-state, but then abandoned the idea. After the 1923 Treaty of Lausanne most Kurds found that they were subject to a secular government that insisted that they were not Kurds but Turks, while others were subject to British and Arab rule from Baghdad. The first of many Kurdish revolts ensued. A war was fought in Iraq between 1961 and 1970 which resulted in some 50,000 deaths.

Arab sentiments about the creation, in 1948, of the state of Israel were forcefully voiced in the General Assembly debate of 1965. Two years later the new government of Syria provoked what became the Six Day War, in which Israeli troops captured the Golan Heights and advanced to the Suez Canal. This conflict had a destabilizing effect upon Lebanon, a multiethnic state with a constitution designed to give each group a proportionate political influence. Historically, Lebanon has been part of Syria, but Syria was a French mandated territory from 1920 to 1943, and France made Lebanon a separate political unit. There was a Maronite president, a Sunni prime minister, and a Shiite president of the chamber of deputies. This did nothing to encourage or allow for any nationalist sentiment. Many Palestinian refugees resided in Lebanon, and when it became a base for guerrillas of the Palestinian Liberation Organization (PLO) Israel attacked them.

In detailing the ethnic conflicts of the Middle East in the 1960s, some mention should be made of the many migrant workers attracted to the oil-rich states of the Gulf Cooperation Council (Bahrain, Kuwait, Oman, Qatar, Saudi Arabia, United Arab Emirates). An indication of the pace of change is seen in the population expansion of Kuwait: from 70,000 in 1944 to 206,000 in 1957 and 467,000 in 1965. Many of the immigrant workers were Arabs, but later workers were drawn from Pakistan, India, Bangladesh, the Philippines, Korea, Thailand, and Turkey. Their status was that of guest workers, admitted for a limited period subject to a contract. Naturalization was very restricted.

In considering the possible application of the Convention in the Middle East it is well to remember the problems that can arise when European language words for 'race' are translated into languages that have no exact equivalent. Arabic has a word *unsur* which corresponds to race in the sense of lineage, but there is also the word *jins* which is closer to the concept of variety. A verse of the Qur'an may be quoted: 'We created you male and female and divided you into peoples and tribes so that you may know each other.' Consciousness of belonging to a people or tribe is, in this scheme, comparable with a consciousness of belonging to a race that is part of God's purpose for the world. Of the four senses of the word race in European history it may be this first one that has most equivalents in other regions.

## UNIVERSAL APPLICATION

The International Convention is a universal instrument applicable all over the world, but the forces behind its adoption were not universal. The Convention identified racial discrimination as the product of colonialism and the dissemination of ideas of racial superiority. Many of the states involved in its preparation had already agreed to the ILO Convention prohibiting racial discrimination in the workplace and had their own reasons for action to prevent any recurrence of nazism. The application of the Convention to most countries in Europe, America, and Africa therefore appeared straightforward (even if some of the Latin American and newly independent African states did not see all the ways in which it bore upon their affairs). Because of uncertainties about what was 'racial', application of the Convention to the circumstances of many Asian states was much more problematic. It has always to be remembered that implementation of the Convention is for the states themselves, so, if their ministers and officials do not fully understand their obligations, patience may be necessary.

This was one of the long-term challenges facing CERD when it started work. It was not a pressing priority, because the Committee had first to get the system of reporting established. This is one of the subjects of Chapter 6.

# 6

# Laying the Foundations

INTRODUCING an account of the drafting history of the Convention, an author who had himself been involved in the drafting process cautioned against over-optimism. 'It remains to be seen', he wrote, 'whether the enthusiasm expressed in these and other speeches will also be demonstrated by depositing instruments of ratification' (Schwelb 1966: 997). At this time it was not thought that many states would ratify, but, to the contrary, ICERD quickly became the most widely accepted of the human-rights conventions and remained so up to 1993, when it was overtaken by the Convention on the Rights of the Child.

In some countries the government has itself the power to enter into treaties; in others it has to seek the consent of the legislature either to ratify or to approve any amendment to a treaty. Treaty-making powers vary. The government of Switzerland had, by means of a referendum, to secure its citizens' approval of a law against racial discrimination before it could contemplate accession to the Convention. Such differences in the legal powers of governments affected the rate at which ratifications were deposited. The Convention came into force in January 1969 after receipt of the twenty-seventh ratification; the parties to the Convention then consisted of seven states in the Asian Group, seven in the Latin American, six in the African, five in the East European, and two in the West European (Iceland and Spain). Thereafter the number of states parties grew steadily. In five-yearly intervals, the number was: 1970, 41; 1975, 84; 1980, 107; 1985, 124; 1990, 129; 1995, 143.

## WHY RATIFY?

It seems that most states saw accession to the Convention as a matter of foreign policy. Many perceived it as a way of establishing their anti-apartheid credentials with but few implications for their internal affairs. It is difficult otherwise to interpret statements such as that of Venezuela, which in successive reports has explained: 'it is necessary to state that when the Venezuelan State ratified the Convention, it did so out of solidarity . . .'; in its initial report Luxembourg also stated that it had become a party to the Convention in order to engage in an act of solidarity (A/36/18, para. 112). Unless states are seen as primarily concerned with their own special problems and objectives, it is difficult to understand how it is that many have failed to meet the financial and reporting obligations they assumed on accession; or to understand why they have not been subject to sanctions by other states parties, since their failure to meet financial obligations caused many of the Committee's scheduled sessions to be cancelled.

States parties' expectations of the Convention have been reflected in whom they have chosen to nominate and elect as members of CERD. When it first assembled, the Committee consisted of ten diplomats, one recently retired diplomat, four law professors, and three judges. Three of the professors were from Czechoslovakia, Poland, and Yugoslavia and did not enjoy the same independence as professors from some other regions. Five of the members were nationals of states in the Asian Group, four were from Africa, two from Latin America, five from Eastern Europe and two from Western Europe. (On elections, see Appendix III.) It has since been agreed that the 'equitable geographical distribution' required by article 8.1 is met by having four Asian, four African, three Latin American, three East European, and four 'Western European and Other' seats on the Committee.

After election, or re-election, to the Committee, a member makes a declaration: 'I solemnly declare that I will perform my duties and exercise my powers as a member of the Committee on the Elimination of Racial Discrimination honourably, faithfully, impartially and conscientiously.' Members serve 'in their personal capacity'. Nevertheless, governmental influence over them has often been evident, most notably with respect to East European states in the early years. Thus in 1972 the Committee was notified by the USSR that N. K. Tarassov had been 'transferred to other work' (he had actually been named as ambassador to Brazil) and that V. S. Safronchuk had been nominated in his place. The Committee objected that it could recognize a vacancy only after receiving directly from the member concerned a written notice of his or her resignation. It was also proposed, again from the USSR, that if a member was unable to attend, he might, subject to Committee approval, appoint an alternate. This also evoked opposition. (One member of the Committee has said in private that he has noticed that when substitution is permitted, and when a country's national interests are affected, the member has appointed his or her ambassador as alternate and has retired to the public gallery.) In addition, it has been said, unofficially, that there was an occasion on which a member from the USSR failed to state his government's position on an issue and, as a result, was obliged to resign from the Committee and, as a punishment, found his professorship transferred from a high-status university to a low-status one.

In 1974 the states parties queried the Committee's practice of holding two three-week sessions per year and suggested instead one meeting of five weeks. Committee members objected that the Convention entrusted to states parties only one power, that of electing members. The Chairman then ruled that the states parties' suggestion was not a decision, a ruling described by Mr Safronchuk as 'in violation of the Convention' since 'meetings of the States Parties constituted the highest organ established under the Convention'. He got little support. The great majority agreed that the Committee was master of its own procedure and constituted an autonomous body within the UN system (A/9618, paras. 266–7). Their view was confirmed in 1976, when the UN's Committee on Conferences requested and received a legal opinion from the Office of Legal Affairs that 'the Committee was not a subsidiary body of the General Assembly and that the resolutions of the General Assembly did not override the provisions of the Convention' (A/31/18, para. 300).

A reading of the records suggests that initially many of the diplomats saw their membership of CERD as one duty to be accommodated with others in their personal timetables. By 1971 the first indications had already appeared that it was sometimes difficult to assemble the quorum needed for a meeting (the rules provide that: 'A majority of the members of the Committee shall constitute a quorum. The presence of two thirds of the members of the Committee is, however, required for a decision to be taken.').

## THE FIRST SESSIONS

The new Committee's first task was to elect its officers: a chairman, three vice-chairmen, and a rapporteur. Together, these constitute the Committee's 'bureau', a kind of organizing subcommittee. There are five offices, to reflect the five regional groupings. Elections are held every two years and each group has to be represented in the Bureau. The Committee's second task was to agree what would become its Rules of Procedure. The third preliminary task was to adopt a communication to states parties setting out general guidelines to be followed in the preparation of periodic reports submitted under article 9 of ICERD.

From the very first day there were signs of political tension (Partsch 1994: 105). Some of the most important differences of opinion centred upon the Committee's role and powers, as was seen in the debate about which sources members could use in their consideration of state reports. It was prompted by the very first report to be tabled, that from Argentina. It consisted of a single sentence:

No racial discrimination in any form exists or has ever existed in the Argentine Republic, either in the laws or in the practical application thereof, and the constitutional and legal provisions both at the national and the provincial levels affirm the absolute equality of all inhabitants; the enjoyment of the rights of citizenship is not based on discrimination of this kind either.

The reaction of Mr Sayegh, a member of the Kuwaiti diplomatic corps, was to say that

the Committee was not called upon to compare the report with the actual situation; its only sources of information were the reports from states parties, and under the Convention members of the Committee were not empowered to say that, as individuals, they had information which contradicted that given in the reports. (SR 29)

Mr Ingles, a judge from the Philippines, was challenged when he referred to the Argentine constitution, on the grounds that this was not part of the state's report. He replied that the Argentine government had supplied the details of its constitution to the UN, which had printed it in one of its human-rights yearbooks; it was therefore a permissible source. Mr Sayegh conceded this point, but held that it would still not have been permissible, for example, to refer to the report on racial discrimination prepared for the Sub-Commission by Mr Santa Cruz, since this was not a document officially submitted by a state party. The knowledge which members possessed as experts could not constitute a basis for suggestions and general recommendations in terms of article 9. Mr Aboul-Nasr insisted that members were under no obligation to consult UN documents. He supported the view of Mr Tarassov that 'the legislation of sovereign States was a matter exclusively within their competence; all the Committee could do was to detect an incompatibility between the domestic laws of a country and a specific provision of the Convention'. The Committee could not recommend new legislation (SR 29).

Mr Sayegh then revised his views to contend that the range of permissible sources depended on the Committee's four obligations and rights under article 9: (*a*) it had to consider the reports; here there should be as little restriction as possible upon the sources that could be used; (*b*) it had a right to request further information; the exercise of this right must be based on a wide range of background material; (*c*) it could make suggestions and general recommendations; in so doing the Committee was limited to documents provided by the state party concerned, either to the Committee or to another UN organ; (*d*) it had to report to the General Assembly on its activities; the record does not indicate what sources he considered permissible in this connection, presumably because the text of the Convention provides no guidance.

Although it was eventually agreed that the Committee would allow members 'to use any information they might have as experts', the debate about permissible sources continued intermittently for twenty years, with some members expressing anxiety about other members' basing their comments upon unsubstantiated press reports or upon information supplied by NGOs (see UN 1991*c*: paras. 121–30). These members took a restricted view of the Committee's mandate. For example, Mr Aboul-Nasr maintained that 'it was not for the Committee to judge whether a State party had discharged its obligations under the Convention; that was a role conferred upon States parties by article 11 [the procedure for inter-State disputes]' (SR 91, p. 7). Mr Safronchuk also insisted that 'interpretation of the Convention was the exclusive prerogative of the States parties' (SR 140). Nor, according to this view, could the Committee cast doubt upon the authenticity of the information supplied by a State party (SR 68). Members from other regions supported the view that it was not for the Committee to interpret the Convention, and it was indeed the member from Argentina who appealed to the maxim *ejus est interpretari, cujus est condere* (interpretation is for those who entered into the treaty).

On the other hand, the Committee had a mandate, and if it was to discharge its duties, it had, for its own purposes, to reach certain understandings. By 1979 there was sufficient agreement on this point for the Chairman to be able to state that the very work of the Committee implied interpretation of the Convention. If there happened to be a consensus on how a particular article was to be interpreted, then that could be taken as the Committee's position. If one member disagreed, the Committee's competence was not thereby impaired (SR 427, para. 33). Writing in the UN *Manual on Human Rights Reporting* (UN 1991*b*), Mr Valencia Rodriguez (who has three times been Chairman of CERD), stated:

One author [Meron 1985: 285] has rightly pointed out that 'While the Committee has not been given general competence to interpret the Convention, as a treaty organ, the Committee may be competent to interpret the Convention insofar as is required for the performance of the Committee's functions. Such an interpretation *per se* is not binding on States parties, but it affects their reporting obligations and their internal and external behaviour.'

Thus, a state party can still disagree with the Committee's interpretation, and, if two states parties dispute such a matter, then, under article 22, one of them can refer it to the International Court of Justice for decision. The Committee has no power to refer a matter to the Court.

A second area of disagreement within the Committee concerned the nature of racial discrimination. The fourth preambular paragraph of the Convention recalls the UN's condemnation of colonialism and all practices of segregation and discrimination associated therewith. It mentions no other cause of racial discrimination. Committee members from Eastern Europe initially took the view that certain kinds of economic and social structure, being the products of class interest, generated ideologies which encouraged racial discrimination. Political reorganization could prevent this completely. Thus in 1971 it was recorded that 'Mr Tomko felt that the praise addressed at a previous meeting to the Soviet Union for having been the first State to achieve not only theoretical but also practical elimination of all forms of racial discrimination even before ratifying the Convention could also be bestowed upon the Ukrainian SSR' (SR 42). Mr Tomko was from Czechoslovakia. This outlook became the more important after the General Assembly declared 1973–83 a Decade for Action to Combat Racism and Racial Discrimination, and invited the Committee to contribute to it. Thereby Committee members were given an opening towards states which were not parties to the Convention, but most members insisted that they could not properly go beyond the provisions of the Convention. The Committee's 1974 report to the General Assembly notes 'most members stressed that racial discrimination, being a consequence of colonialism, could be found in areas under foreign occupation' (A/6918, para. 47). In the following year the Committee adopted a resolution on the thirtieth anniversary of the defeat of nazism and fascism as 'ideologies based essentially on racism and racial discrimination' and reminded states parties of their obligations to put 'an end to racism and to the vestiges or manifestations of such ideologies' (A/10018, p. 69). Mr Safronchuk maintained that

Fascism, as an ideology and a practice, constituted an extreme form of racism and had cost tens of millions of lives . . . the peoples of Asia had had to suffer racism in the form of Japanese militarism and the militarism of various imperialist groups . . . fascism was one manifestation of racism and was also the militaristic form of imperialism. Fascism and imperialism in general were manifestations of one and the same phenomenon. (SR 242)

Assertions about the absence of racial discrimination were voiced not only with respect East European and Asian societies, but also, and with equal force, concerning Latin America. Mr Ortiz Martin (Costa Rica) assured his colleagues on the Committee that in Bolivia and other countries of the region 'industrial development had brought into the towns Indians, whites and mestizos alike. Racial integration in those societies was perfect' (SR 201). Mr Valencia Rodriguez (Ecuador) confirmed this view of Bolivia (SR 270). Mr Brin Martinez (Panama)

reiterated that the report of a Latin American country could not be considered in the same manner as the report of a European country or a developed country in another part of the world. He would like the

Committee to study more specifically the situation that prevailed in those countries in which racial discrimination persisted, ones where colonialism and imperialism were still rife. (SR 302)

When a Russian member spoke of the impressions he had gained on a visit to Libya, Mr Partsch reminded him that, when he had wanted to inform the Committee of the impressions he had gained during his stay in a country, the report of which was being discussed, he had been interrupted on a point of order, on the grounds that the Committee should limit itself exclusively to information supplied by states parties (SR 302).

States parties had their own views about the nature of racial discrimination, made evident when the Committee's rapporteur summarized the picture of racial discrimination portrayed in the initial reports from the first forty-five states. Considerably more than half, he said, had proclaimed in the most emphatic language that their territories were totally free of racial discrimination. Twenty-eight had declared that such discrimination was unthinkable or inconceivable in their territories, while, as has already been noted, one had stressed that it had adhered to the Convention not out of domestic necessity but as a gesture of international solidarity. Only five had admitted that discrimination existed in their territories, two of these—Panama and Syria—explaining that it was being practised by another state. Swaziland had attributed the existence of racial discrimination to vestiges of a previous era, while the UK attributed it to a new phenomenon, that of significant demographic change. The last of these five countries was Finland, which coupled its admission of discrimination (against Gypsies) with an assurance that an effort was being made to eliminate it. Apart from these five, the Committee was dealing with states which considered that they had unblemished records. Apparently, states which had ratified the Convention did not need it, whereas those which did need it had not chosen to ratify. (Later it became more common for some states to refer to racial discrimination as part of their inheritance from the colonial era.)

Equally interesting, according to Mr Sayegh, were the reasons given to support the astonishing claim that racial discrimination did not exist in so many countries. Ten attributed it to their respective national traditions or outlooks, four referred to Islam, five to socialism, while two spoke uninformatively of an absence of the social conditions conducive to racial discrimination. Twenty-one of the twenty-eight states had thus even given reasons to explain their purity. Most of the reporting states mentioned either implicitly or explicitly that they had found no need to take legislative, judicial, administrative, or other measures to give effect to the Convention, and, by implication, that they saw no need to report on such measures. What should the Committee do when it received a report denying the existence of racial discrimination but members read in the press about racial problems in the territory in question (SR 92, 93; also A/8718, paras. 43–50)? That raised questions about the most appropriate working methods for the Committee. Yet underlying Mr Sayegh's heavy ironies was an alternative view of racial discrimination, as something of which members themselves had experience, either personally or vicariously through their friends and fellow-countrymen. The alternative view, that discrimination could occur in any society, was to be endorsed ever more strongly as the years passed. When in 1972 the Committee issued General Recommendation II advising states parties that they had undertaken to report periodically 'whether or not racial discrimination exists in their respective territories', the UK sent a formal response doubting whether there were any states on whose territory racial discrimination did not exist (A/8718, p. 68).

This was probably still a minority view among states parties. When, in 1978, Bolivia was told that there was nothing in its fourth report that could truly be called a report, the representative complained that this

was simply the same dialogue of the deaf that was taking place in various UN bodies between the representatives of cultures which had filled the world with laws which had never been implemented, and representatives of the new thinking in the developing countries, which had succeeded in rejecting in time the prejudices that others had sought to bequeath to them. (SR 368)

Since so many states parties saw the Convention as intended for other states than their own, it was not surprising that many of their reports failed to supply the information the Committee needed to do its work. One of the Committee's first actions was to draw up guidelines for states to follow when preparing their reports. It also used its power to request from states additional information. To take one case, the Committee was not satisfied with the initial report from Madagascar and sent the government a request for additional information with a copy of the guidelines. This was not sufficient, so the request was repeated. A reply came back to say that 'the Malagasy Government considers that the detailed questionnaire in the aforementioned communication is intended for countries in which either *de facto* or *de jure* racial discrimination exists'. Some Committee members objected that acceptance of such a position 'would have the effect of dividing states parties into two groups—those which were required to meet the obligations set forth in the Convention and those which were exempt from so doing'. So the Committee in 1972 repeated its request for the necessary information, obtaining later in the year a second report with a supplement which it examined in 1973 and declared satisfactory. (The Committee had by then adopted the practice of classifying reports as satisfactory or unsatisfactory on the basis of whether or not they were complete. It was intended to be a formal classification of the topics covered in the information supplied and not a substantive evaluation of whether it demonstrated that the state had complied with its obligations. As the Committee's work progressed, and it became more involved with the substance of reports, it abandoned this classification (see UN 1991*c*: paras. 103–4)). Deficiencies in reports led CERD in 1972 to adopt its first and second general recommendations, drawing attention to the obligation to legislate in fulfilment of obligations deriving from article 4, and the obligation to report irrespective of whether a government thought that there was or was not racial discrimination in its territory. From his review of the early years, Buergenthal (1977: 189) concluded that states had misconceived the enforcement potential of the reporting requirement.

## INTERSTATE DISPUTES

The tension between politics and law has also been evident in the views members have expressed about the Convention itself. Those who stressed its relationship to the political objectives of the UN, and who have often seen racial discrimination as a consequence of colonialism, have also tended to interpret the Convention teleologically as an instrument of international policy elaborating and applying universal norms. Mr Tomko, for example, maintained that racial discrimination was an international crime which did not fall essentially within the domestic jurisdiction of a state, within the meaning of article 2.7 of the UN Charter. Therefore the Committee could combat racism even if it occurred in the territory of a state which was not a party to the Convention (SR 89). Though members who felt like this wished to appeal to General Assembly resolutions, and to the UN connection in general, in order to combat racial discrimination in colonial territories, on other points they often maintained that the Convention was a treaty like other treaties, so that the Committee was at the disposal only of the states which had created it.

Underlying some of the arguments of the East European members about the nature of the Convention were the socialist doctrines that only states are subjects of international law, and that it is states which confer rights, and, possibly, the fear that if the Committee were to behave more like a court this could be to their countries' disadvantage. This was one reason why the question of permissible sources remained a live issue. The East Europeans and their allies tended to a narrow interpretation of the Committee's duties under article 9.2 in its relations with states parties. In 1974 the members from the USSR, Czechoslovakia, Egypt, Yugoslavia, and India spoke against a proposal made by the member from the Netherlands. He suggested that a resolution in connection with the Decade for Action to Combat Racism and Racial Discrimination should include a clause drawing attention to article 14 as one means for promoting the effectiveness of the Convention. These members objected that, were the Committee to draw attention to 'a very controversial article', this might discourage further ratifications (A/9618, paras. 46, 49). The same members nevertheless took an expansive view of their duties under article 3, directed against apartheid, and under article 15, dealing with non-self-governing territories.

When it was proposed in the Committee that states should be invited to send representatives to present reports and answer questions on them, these proposals were twice rejected. When two states asked that their representatives might appear before the Committee to present their government's comments on matters before the Committee, these requests were also rejected on the grounds that there was no provision for this in the Convention. Some members disliked the possibility that state representatives might be subjected to 'cross-examination by individual Committee members'. Yet, when the General Assembly supported the idea, the

Committee changed its mind (Partsch 1994: 106–8), and this innovation has proven of the greatest value.

The broad construction of article 3 was illustrated in 1972 when the Committee recalled that in the tenth preambular paragraph states parties had resolved 'to build an international community free from all forms of racial segregation and racial discrimination', noted article 3's reference to apartheid, and went on to express the view that 'measures adopted on the national level to give effect to the provisions of the Convention are interrelated with the measures taken on the international level to encourage respect everywhere for the principles of the Convention'. Therefore they welcomed inclusion in state reports of information regarding the state's 'diplomatic, economic and other relations with the racist regimes in southern Africa'. By decision 2(XI) in 1975 the Committee went further to declare that policies which have the effect of sustaining racist regimes are irreconcilable with the commitment to the cause of the elimination of racial discrimination inherent in ratification of the Convention. They called on states parties to reconsider any relations they might have with such regimes and commented on the General Assembly's exclusion of the delegation from South Africa—all of which sat ill with arguments that CERD should take no action that was not required by the Convention.

The Committee was diverted from its main tasks in the early years by what have been called disguised interstate disputes. To quote Buergenthal (1977: 211): 'Resorting to some imaginative lawyering, Panama and Syria used their article 9 reports as a vehicle to charge the United States and Israel, both non-member states, with racial discrimination. Cyprus adopted a similar approach after the island was invaded by Turkey, another non-member state.' Panama claimed that, while it was in all respects complying with the Convention, in that part of 'Panamanian territory' known as the Panama Canal Zone the USA was violating it by operating racially discriminatory salary scales. (On these disputes, see UN 1991c: paras. 133–42.) After Israel became a party to the Convention, other states could have invoked article 11 as a way of pursuing disputes about the Golan Heights, the West bank of the River Jordan, and the Sinai peninsula, but they did not do so. The issues raised by the complaining states were very complex; they served only to generate publicity for the complainants, and no opinion was reached on which practices of the kind complained of constituted racial discrimination within the terms of the Convention.

The disguised interstate reports brought out some of the political tensions within CERD. When Mr Partsch proposed that the Committee take no action on one of them, Mr Tarassov said that he would regard this 'as an encouragement to aggressors, colonialists and racists' (SR 89). Another dispute which opened up similar divisions and occupied quite a lot of the Committee's time occurred after the military *coup* in Chile. When in 1975 a report from that country was tabled, a member of the Committee argued that it should not be considered because it was not submitted by the lawful government of the country. The Committee decided that it should at least invite the state representative to address the question of the extent to which the country's constitution was in force (A/10018, paras. 159–65). Many of the disagreements were reopened two years later (A/32/18, paras. 68–79). Some members of the Committee have regarded themselves as having an obligation to the people of a country, to see that as far as possible they benefit from the Convention's protections, irrespective of whether the government to which they are subject is legitimate.

The disguised interstate disputes also touched upon the question of equity as between states parties and other states. In 1972 the government of Kuwait sent the CERD a formal communication (possibly inspired by Mr Sayegh), stating that:

States who practise racial discrimination or who tolerate racial discrimination on their territory are reluctant to become parties to the Convention. It is precisely for this reason that the Committee on the Elimination of Racial Discrimination should address communications to these States. (A/8718, annex 4)

For the Committee to be able to criticize a state party, but to be unable to take any action in the case of a non-state party, seemed to at least one member to be giving the latter preferential treatment (SR 67).

Another feature of the disguised interstate disputes has attracted less attention. Was it certain that the Israeli occupation of Arab territory, and the Turkish occupation of northern Cyprus were instances of racial discrimination? The parties could be distinguished in terms of national or ethnic origin, but the occupations appear to have been inspired by a political motivation rather than to have been 'based on race' in the sense of the Convention. Some of the invaders' actions subsequent to occupation, however, may well have been discriminatory in effect.

## DIALOGUE AS AN AID TO IMPLEMENTATION

The Committee gradually found that its role in relation to the states parties could usefully be summed up by reference to a concept that is nowhere mentioned in the Convention, that of dialogue. The first explicit reference to dialogue in the Committee's proceedings occurs in the report for 1973, when members commented upon how the report of Egypt responded to some of the questions that had been asked earlier (A/9018, para. 179). It was used again in the following year to describe similar responses from Iran and Ecuador, and by the end of the 1970s there were frequent references to beginning a dialogue with the Committee, to a desire to deepen a dialogue, to re-establish a dialogue, to continue a constructive dialogue, and so on.

Whether dialogue results in better implementation depends upon a complex chain of relationships, several of which were illustrated in Chapter 1's account of the Committee's consideration of the ninth periodic report of Venezuela. The relationships may be considered in sequence.

First it is necessary to consider what may have been the objects of a state in acceding to the Convention. This is not easy to establish. In speeches made by their representatives in the 1965 General Assembly debate, some states indicated their attitude towards the Convention, and some have since given hints in their periodic reports In all probability many states acceded on grounds of both altruism and self-interest. Ministers and their officials have often been morally affronted by the racial atrocities of the Nazis, by apartheid, and by some features of colonial regimes. Action against racial discrimination—like action against slavery and the abuse of women and children—has been seen as imperative in order to remove a stain from the conscience of the world. In considering their self-interest, states may have balanced the burden they were assuming against the diplomatic advantages they expected to gain. Their estimate of the burden will have depended upon their own circumstances, and on what officials in the relevant ministries understood of the nature and causes of racial discrimination (remembering that while the advantages accrue to the foreign ministry the burdens fall upon one of the interior ministries). A decision will have depended on ministers' willingness to introduce the necessary legislation. Some governments have to consider their chances of winning their next elections, and the likely electoral effects of introducing legislation which may be perceived as favouring minorities. Other governments may have calculated that, since the Convention was likely to be adopted, or was gaining adherents, they should support it in order to exert as much influence as possible upon its character or the manner of its operation.

With the increase in the number of UN member states, more diplomats found it advisable to use opportunities to publicize their governments' activities and to build up among their colleagues a good reputation for the countries they represented, and this may have affected their recommendations. Some states appear to have seen the submission of reports under the Convention as being in some measure a public-relations opportunity. They have on occasion drawn attention to their having been one of the first states to ratify, to the regularity with which they have reported, to special features in their national history, and so on. Some states enjoy a high reputation in diplomatic circles for their observance of human rights. This is based in part upon the formal assumption of legal obligations, and in part upon knowledge of the actuality that obtains in the country in question (the USA, for example, has a very poor record for accepting formal obligations but a relatively good one for its actual practice, and, since many diplomats will have been posted to New York or Washington, they have some personal knowledge of the latter). Factors such as these may have affected accession to the Convention and the assumptions underlying states' approach to dialogue with the Committee.

Secondly, for some states there may be a conflict between the theory and practice of reporting. In theory, states freely accede to a convention and then bring their domestic legislation into line with their new obligations. In the dialogue the state representative and the committee should then be equal partners concerned to ensure that the convention's requirements are applied in a manner appropriate to the state's circumstances. In practice, the legislation of many states is determined by the pressures of their domestic politics. The state then sends a representative to present its report, and he or she is expected to represent its policies as discharging the state's responsibilities under the convention. Thus some representatives believe that they appear before the CERD in order to defend the record of the state which employs them.

Thirdly, Committee members' individual objectives in their questioning has been influenced by their beliefs about the nature and causes of racial discrimination. Did they see racial discrimination as pathological or as a normal feature of social life? Committee members often shared with other members of the nations from which they originated assumptions about the nature of racial discrimination. Such beliefs formed part of shared political philosophies and affected the predispositions of committee members when considering state reports. This was noticeable in the early years in connection with reports from the former colonial powers and from Israel.

Fourthly, both Committee members and those responsible for state policies found that they had engaged upon a process in which they discovered more about the potential of the Convention. The text has its obscurities, but gradually, by a process of argument, Committee members have come close to a consensual view about how the various provisions are to be applied. In developing the dialogue the Committee has also followed its own priorities. Initially it set out to help states appreciate their main obligations, and in doing so the Committee was influenced by the priorities of the General Assembly during the 1970s. Subsequently the Committee has taken up previously neglected passages in the text and found in some of them new potential for better implementation.

Fifthly, members and those responsible for the implementation of state policies also found that they learnt more about the nature and causes of racial discrimination. It is possible to conclude that racial discrimination has pathological as well as normal features. Assuming that there is an objective truth about the determinants of racial discrimination, then it will be accepted that there is also ignorance of this truth, and that some of the ignorance can be attributed to distortion of the available knowledge by ideological pressures. It is this sort of ignorance, which is sometimes a political perversion, that may be accounted pathological. Extremist groups disseminating doctrines of racial superiority or of an inability of racial groups to live peacefully together may be considered socially pathological. So might the unwillingness of a government to acknowledge the reality of a problem confronting it, but any counterassertion about the true nature of that reality is bound to be highly political.

Sixthly, there is a sequence of exchanges when the Committee is in session. The state representative may come to the meeting with a combative or a conciliatory disposition. The representative may be subject to particular orders from his or her government. The kinds of question put to the representative, and the manner in which they are put, will depend not only upon the text of the report, but upon the occupational backgrounds and interests of the Committee members. A member who is a diplomat will put the sorts of question that a diplomat has been trained to raise, and may formulate them in a way that will be better appreciated by a state representative if that person is also a diplomat. Similar considerations apply if the member is a lawyer. Committee members become very familiar with the detail of the Convention. State representatives are much less familiar with it, so the effectiveness of communication depends in part upon the capacity, or willingness, of the representative to listen to other points of view.

Some states have entered into a dialogue in which committee members have succeeded in persuading states, through their representatives, that they need to undertake action of some kind if they are to fulfil their treaty obligations. Sometimes, too, a state representative persuades committee members that they have not properly understood circumstances in the reporting state, or that the actions they recommend would not have the results they seek. For an early example of a persuasive dialogue, the reader can turn to CERD's report for 1974 (A/9618, para. 116):

The Committee welcomed the announcement made by the representative of the Government of Greece . . . that, in the light of the previous year's discussion of the question by the Committee, the Ministry of Justice had instructed its legal drafting committee to prepare a draft legislative decree meeting the requirements of article 4 of the Convention.

Shortly afterwards satisfaction was expressed concerning a law prepared in Iran 'on the recommendation of the Committee' (A/33/18, para. 173). Several of the Latin American states notified the Committee that they were changing their laws as a result of observations made in the Committee. This confirms other impressions that several of the states in this group misunderstood the nature of the obligations embodied in the Convention but were nevertheless ready to stand by their promises. The Committee's review of state legislation relating to article 4 (UN 1986) contains sections describing legislation enacted in contemplation of adherence to the Convention, and of the enactment of new legislation after adherence. To bring such a review up to date, and to cover all the articles of the Convention, would now be a very arduous undertaking.

One result of the exchange of opinions can be that the Committee and the state party decide that they have irreconcilable views about the interpretation of the Convention. ICERD article 22 provides that, where two states parties dispute its interpretation, one of them may refer the dispute to the International Court of Justice for decision. No such references have yet occurred. The result is that on some matters (like the extent of obligations under article 4) the state party and the Committee may have to agree to differ.

In many instances, especially during the 1970s, there was no genuine dialogue between the Committee and the state party. Many states simply refrained from answering points put to them. In general dialogue is better when the reporting state sends from the capital an official who is familiar with the tasks of implementing policies in accordance with the Convention. Often, though, especially with the poorer states and those which believe that there is no racial discrimination in their countries, the report is of a skeletal character and is presented by a staff member from that country's diplomatic mission. At the end of committee member's questions, he or she may simply gather up the papers and explain that the questions will be referred to the government and will be answered in the next periodic report. In general, state reports have become increasingly informative and most questions have been answered, though sometimes it appears as if the state representative well understands the points advanced by Committee members but is restricted by the instructions received from the capital.

## THE REPORTING PROCESS

It was not easy for the Committee to deal with the blank incomprehension displayed in some reports. For example, the initial report of Peru consisted of the affirmation that, 'since there does not exist, nor has there ever existed, any racial discrimination in Peru, no legal provisions exist on the subject and obviously, no study or report is called for on racial discrimination in Peru'. In the Committee doubt was expressed whether this could be considered a report at all. The Committee therefore sent a special message to the government of Peru (A/9618, paras. 243–4, annex IV D). The government later submitted a much more informative report and the Committee took up with it, as with some other Latin American states, the question of whether a restriction of citizenship or voting rights to persons who were literate or were able to speak Spanish was in conformity with the Convention.

The Committee's 1976 report stated that the fourth periodic report of Venezuela 'added nothing new to the information contained in the preceding report and provided no replies to the enquiries made during the consideration of that report'. The state representative replied that it was difficult for his government to provide information on something which did not exist in his country. It

propagated the principles of the United Nations Charter but 'there was a risk that a specific mention of racial discrimination would create a problem that had not existed before . . . if by any chance a case of racial discrimination did occur, the police would intervene immediately . . . everyone would be greatly astonished if a new Penal Code included a special article declaring racial discrimination a punishable offence' . . . He would pass on to his Government the comments of the members of the Committee on the revision of the Venezuelan penal code but he 'could not guarantee that they would be taken into account in preparing that revision'. (A/31/18, para. 126).

Other cases have arisen, more particularly in the years following 1978, in which a state that has submitted several adequate reports falls behind and then submits a patently inadequate one, perhaps because trained staff are not available or because the responsible ministry does not give the matter sufficient priority. There have been instances in which the Committee has sent messages through the proper channels to the government but the foreign ministry has failed to communicate with the staff of its mission in Geneva. Administrative weaknesses can have as negative an effect upon dialogue as any official unwillingness to engage in a reasoned discussion of the meaning and application of the Convention's provisions.

Dialogue between the Committee and the state has had to take account of any reservations entered by the state at the time of accession. These have been various. Twenty-nine states have refused to be bound by any compulsory jurisdiction of the International Court of Justice. Some objected that articles 17 and 18 were discriminatory in the way they limited which states could accede to the Convention. Some Arab states indicated that accession did not imply any recognition of, or the establishment of treaty relations with, Israel. Several states made reservations concerning article 4, and others (Fiji, Tonga) concerning the alienation of indigenous land.

A basic feature which has its influence upon the process of dialogue is that a treaty body must treat all states equally, even though they are obviously very different in their size and the resources at their command. In the review of the Committee's progress over the years 1970–7, it was noted that

Over the years, members of the Committee have on many occasions noted non-compliance, or less than full compliance, by some States Parties with some of the anti-discrimination provisions of articles 2–7 of the Convention. But the Committee as such has not formally pronounced itself to that effect with reference to any particular State Party. (UN 1991c: para. 114)

The Committee could make formal use of this power as a sanction, but it would be difficult to use it in a manner compatible with the fiction of the sovereign equality of states. Consider the situation of Tonga, a small Pacific island state that is not a UN member state but which acceded to the Convention in 1972, and has regularly submitted reports even though it has not been able to send a representative to attend for the examination of these reports. Tonga has not complied fully with its obligations, but it is unlikely that in its day-to-day life there are many instances of racial discrimination. What purpose would be served by a declaration of non-compliance? Or consider the circumstances of a small state belonging to the Gulf Cooperation Council, rich with oil revenues, but with an alien immigrant population outnumbering the indigenous population, only a small number of officials with the relevant legal skills, and a legal order founded on the Islamic Shariah. To report formally to the General Assembly that such a state was not in compliance would evoke vigorous protests from other Islamic states, which would consider such a step highly unjust in view of what was happening elsewhere in the world. The requirement that states be treated equally even when their circumstances are so different can be a significant constraint. Within UN bodies certain states have been regarded as pariahs, like South Africa from 1974 to 1993, Israel for a long period, and Chile under the Pinochet regime, and these could be vilified with impunity; but otherwise criticism has had to be qualified, especially by an acknowledgement that the same criticism could be made of other states that were not being mentioned. Diplomats in particular have often been ready to defend states belonging to their own regional groups, either because they suspected the motivation of the criticism or because they believed that the same criticism could equally well have been directed towards others.

As part of the first Decade, and as mentioned in the previous chapter, a World Conference to Combat Racism and Racial Discrimination was convened in 1978. CERD was invited to participate. It agreed a six-page statement for its Chairman to present (see A/33/18). This stated, *inter alia*, that

In the nine-year experience of the Committee on the Elimination of Racial Discrimination, one aspect of the universality of the abhorrence of racism has manifested itself with remarkable constancy, and it has had an exhilarating effect upon the Committee . . . States parties have in large numbers declared that racism and racial discrimination are inconsistent with the most basic persuasions which animate their respective societies and social systems—notwithstanding the diversity of the traditions of those societies . . . nations . . . have found in their common commitment to the goal of eliminating racial discrimination a rare occasion for unanimity.

The statement went on to say that the Committee attached special importance to the application of articles 4 and 7 of the Convention, as being needed to prevent the dissemination of racist ideas and incitement, and to add that

The final requisite for an adequate national policy . . . is largely implicit in the Convention. It pertains to the foreign relations of a State party . . . a State's condemnation of racial discrimination and its formal undertaking to eliminate it within its own frontiers [cannot] be compatible with its indifference to the practice of racial discrimination outside those frontiers . . .

The political tensions within the Committee probably contributed to the care with which the members investigated the legal authority for their every action. For example, to determine whether they could report a general recommendation to the General Assembly straight away, or had first to await observations from states parties, they studied the *travaux préparatoires*, such as the views expressed by delegates to the General Assembly debate (see Gomez del Prado 1985: 504–6). Their comments upon state reports were always tactful. For example, a report of 1974 on whether Romania's penal code covered racist propaganda said that

Members of the Committee did not all agree that the word 'fascism' was synonymous with the word 'racism', or that the use of the former word in penal legislation without an interpretation of its precise connotation would serve the purposes of the legislation. (A/9618, para. 113)

Every year the Committee considered with care the observations made about its work in the General Assembly debate, and sought guidance from the delegates while maintaining its own independence. Because the Committee was to start both with caution in its dealings with states and in tune with opinion in the Assembly (which was then strongly anti-colonialist), the initial resistance of states was steadily overcome. Sometimes its links with the General Assembly seemed too close, because some members of the Committee occasionally served in their national delegations to the Assembly and spoke on behalf of their governments when CERD's annual report was debated. Mr Partsch appealed to them to try to avoid serving in this other capacity lest it call into question their independence as members of the Committee. Mr Bahnev (Bulgaria) maintained to the contrary that there were advantages to the Committee (A/32/18, para. 25; see also the observations in Partsch 1992*a*). In recent years it has been less common for CERD members to serve on these delegations. In 1995, in private conversations, some members maintained that, as a result, General Assembly delegates were less well informed about the Committee's work.

It was the practice of the General Assembly at the conclusion of its debate to adopt a resolution on the report from CERD. In several years this resolution referred approvingly to the Committee's request for information on a state's relations with South Africa. Clauses to this effect had regularly to be put to the vote, since some states maintained that this was not within the Convention. The objections were voted down, enabling the Committee to infer that the propriety of its action had been confirmed. Perhaps it was because the Committee was in accord with the majority opinion in the General Assembly that the director of the division of human rights in the UN could in 1977 tell CERD that he 'considered it one of the most effective bodies working within the framework of the UN system' (SR 336).

## SUCCESSES

It may be concluded that implementation of the Convention improved greatly during the years 1970–8. Many states parties introduced new legislative, judicial, and administrative measures against racial discrimination, often at the prompting of a Committee which they themselves had set up and whose membership they had determined. That Committee's priorities were threefold: to persuade states parties to discharge their reporting obligations; to point out respects in which they had failed to introduce measures to fulfil their obligations, especially the mandatory obligation to legislate against incitement to racial hatred; and to press them to act against racist regimes in southern Africa.

In all three respects it was successful. As Buergenthal (1977: 218) has written, the Committee won some important battles. It succeeded in gradually dispelling the expectation of many states that the Committee would never be more than a timid depository of their self-serving reports. By its restraint and patience, the Committee persuaded states to follow its reporting guidelines, to supply the texts of their laws so that members could see whether they actually met the requirements, and to provide demographic information concerning ethnic differences in their population. It brought them to a better understanding of the commitments they had accepted and dispelled the assumption that racial discrimination was something that occurred only in a minority of states. It won recognition for its independence (see UN 1991*c*: paras. 77–8) and established a foundation on which more ambitious future action might be based. These achievements were the more notable in the light of the turnover in Committee membership: forty-three members occupied the eighteen seats during the nine-year period. The members of the Committee were not paid for their services and had no clerical or research assistance, but, more importantly, they had the support of a substantial body of opinion which regarded action against racial discrimination as one of the priorities of international politics. So the rule of law with respect to its prohibition was progressively expanded at the expense of unilateral political action.

# 7

# The Last of the Cold War

THE year 1978 is a convenient point to make a division between the period covered in the previous chapter—one in which the states which had been formed as a result of the decolonization process were exercising their new-found influence in the UN—and a further period in which that influence was waning. Between 1979 and 1987 the conflict between the Eastern and Western blocs re-emerged as the overriding feature of the political framework within which CERD had to operate. Changes in that framework have had more influence upon the work of the Committee than any changes in its membership. Over the nine-year period there were forty-one members in the eighteen committee seats. As in the previous period, the turnover was only partly the result of elections. It happened quite frequently that a member resigned and was replaced by the government of the country to which the member belonged. Yet these changes in personnel did not occasion noticeable changes in the Committee's activities.

## POLITICAL PERSPECTIVES

During the years 1979–87 most of the earlier differences within the Committee persisted. The sharpest criticisms of some of the prevailing trends were voiced by Mr Dechezelles (France). He observed that he had attended the First World Conference to Combat Racism and Racial Discrimination and found it very much politicized. There had been many ideological speeches which bore little or no relation to racial discrimination. Instead they had focused on the political aspects of the struggle against racism to the detriment both of other aspects and of the means for campaigning against it. The impression he had gained was that one part of the world was putting the other part in the dock. The Conference had deviated from its prime objective, had become divided, and as a result it had been a partial failure (SR 493, 590). His criticisms extended also to most delegations in the Third Committee, since they seemed to attach far greater importance to the international aspect of the struggle against racism than to the purely national one (SR 521).

When, in 1979, a report of the Byelorussian SSR was being considered, Mr Dechezelles declared that he was 'sceptical of statements claiming that in whole continents, or in at least very large areas of the world, not a single case of racial discrimination had been brought before the courts because racial discrimination had completely disappeared among the population' (SR 417). Later in the same session, when commenting on the fourth report of Sweden, Mr Sviridov welcomed the accounts of court decisions regarding cases of racial discrimination, but added that 'such practices did not exist in socialist countries'. Mr Nettel (Austria) retorted that he drew a contrary conclusion: he assumed that, when there were no such accounts, it was because in the country in question the man in the street was discouraged from making use of the courts or did not understand how to use the legal system. Sweden did not fear to show that racial discrimination occurred and 'he preferred that attitude to the position taken by some who claimed that under their particular social or economic system there was no discrimination'. Mr Dechezelles then added that:

Mr Sviridov was not expressing the point of view generally held in the Committee. It was paradoxical that when a country identified incidents of racial discrimination, took specific measures to combat it and then provided the Committee with information on those measures, it was upbraided for the racism which it was trying to root out. In his view, it was sheer sophistry to suggest that a vast region of the world, spanning almost an entire continent, was free of racial discrimination owing to the social system adopted there.

Mr Sviridov replied that he 'could not agree . . . that racism was an inherent evil in every man. If that were true, the aims of the Convention could never be realized.' The Chairman brought this exchange to a close by stating that it was the Committee's 'generally held belief that racial discrimination existed almost everywhere' (SR 437). This indicates that there had been some change since Mr Sayegh commented on the views of states parties, but the difference of opinion between Mr Dechezelles and Mr Sviridov also suggests tensions between members of the committee.

These could reflect the East–West split or conflicts between neighbouring states (see, e.g., the exchanges between the members from Bulgaria and Yugoslavia in SR 296).

Mr Dechezelles disputed simplistic representations of the causes of racial discrimination. During the consideration of a report from Poland he insisted that, 'far from being unaware of the need to tackle one of the roots of that evil by opposing privilege and social and economic inequality, he stressed that racism, rooted as it was in human nature, had multiple causes which varied according to particular circumstances and countries . . .' (SR 491). As an indication of how some West Europeans felt at the beginning of the 1980s, it may also be relevant to note the first four words of one of Mr Dechezelles's observations on a report from a black African state: 'As a white man, he could only feel shame at hearing about the acts of segregation suffered by the people of Zaire in the past' (SR 486).

The Committee's discharge of its duties sometimes occasioned dissension within the General Assembly. Commenting on the reception of the Committee's report for 1982, the rapporteur, Mr Partsch, remarked that two controversial issues had prevented the Third Committee from adopting its resolution by consensus. One arose from the consideration of the report of Israel. Controversy had arisen because the opinions of some Committee members had been wrongly attributed to the Committee as a whole. The second centred upon whether the Committee was authorized to request information on the foreign policy of states parties towards the racist regime of South Africa. It had been argued that the obligations of states parties were laid down by the Convention and that neither the Committee nor the General Assembly could extend these obligations for political reasons. The rapporteur referred to this as 'the unsolved problem of the interpretation of article 3' (SR 621).

Further dissension arose in 1985 in connection with the Committee's consideration of a report from Morocco. Although CERD's report did not refer to the territory covered by Morocco's report, Algeria objected that the Committee had considered a report 'one chapter of which was devoted to measures taken by the State party in a territory it occupied by force. That decision was a serious breach of the Committee's terms of reference and of article 15 of the Convention' (A/C.3/40/SR 15).

Algeria's objection was reflected in the General Assembly's draft resolution on CERD's report, paragraph 4 of which read:

*Considers* that the Committee should not take into consideration information on territories to which General Assembly resolution 1514(XV) applies unless such information is communicated by the competent United Nations bodies in conformity with article 15 of the Convention.

The Moroccan delegate raised several queries: was this view of ICERD's article 15 compatible with articles 3 and 9? could the General Assembly give CERD instructions on such matters? whose responsibility was it to interpret the provisions of the Convention? and what effect might adoption of this resolution have upon the work of the Committee?

A representative of the UN Office of Legal Affairs replied that CERD

was not a subsidiary organ of the General Assembly but an autonomous treaty body . . . paragraph 4 . . . if adopted, would constitute a recommendation to the Committee and not a binding instruction. Furthermore, the right to give authoritative interpretations of the Convention, and the powers of the Committee thereunder, rested not with the General Assembly but, in the first instance, with CERD itself, as the body responsible for monitoring compliance with the Convention, and ultimately with the States parties. Hence, were paragraph 4 to be adopted, it would be the responsibility of CERD to determine the extent to which it could be given effect . . . (A/C.3/40/SR 46)

Delegates then held private discussions to see if an amended text could be agreed, but a separate vote had to be taken. Paragraph 4 was adopted by 82 votes to 9 with 36 abstentions. EC states voted against on the grounds that the General Assembly was not empowered to instruct the Committee. A separate vote had also to be taken on a reference in another paragraph to apartheid as 'a crime against humanity', with Western states abstaining and the USA opposing on the grounds that the reference was not directly relevant and was 'known to cause legal difficulties for many delegations'.

The tension between the political campaign against apartheid and the wording of article 3 was to be seen in 1979 in connection with the third report of Belgium. With respect to this article the state reported that there was 'no connection of any kind with such a system under Belgian legislation. There therefore appears to be no point in adopting measures at a national level to condemn a non-existing practice . . . segregation, as practised in certain countries, is regularly denounced and stigmatized.' The state representative maintained that questions about Belgium's relations with the regimes in southern Africa were highly political in nature and therefore fell rather within the competence of the General Assembly and the Security Council (A/34/18, paras. 225, 231). This did not satisfy all members of CERD.

The priority given to the condemnation of South Africa could affect the consideration of other state reports, such as that of Lesotho in 1983. Mr Karasimeonov (Bulgaria) used the occasion 'to express his personal solidarity with the people of Lesotho in their struggle against the racist regime of South Africa'. Mr Dechezelles said that it was more important for Lesotho to have come before the Committee seeking sympathy than for it to have submitted a report. Mr Devetak (Yugoslavia) proposed to draw the attention of the General Assembly to the fact that a whole valiant country was under the pressure of discrimination and apartheid as a victim of the aggressive policy of South Africa. Mr Lamptey won the public support of only one of his colleagues when he protested that CERD was not a political committee. Its only task was to ensure the compliance of all states parties with the Convention; and in considering the various reports it could not make different demands on different states. The Committee must not allow its legitimate sympathy to blunt its view of what was basic to its work. Lesotho should consider the Committee's comments carefully and try to correct lacunae, as other countries were doing; that had nothing to do with Lesotho's front-line or land-locked situation (SR 608).

As in the preceding period, members insisted that action against apartheid had to be one of their highest priorities. Yet all they could do as a committee was to question states about their relations with the South African government, and to pass resolutions. Thus in 1985, when possible contributions to the Second Decade to Combat Racism and Racial Discrimination were discussed, CERD adopted decision 1(XXXII) to condemn the regime and appeal to states parties to implement a Security Council resolution. The Chairman made a long statement which was published in the annual report to the General Assembly (A/40/18, annex IV). No Committee member opposed these proposals, though some must have thought that political action against apartheid was better left to other organs of the UN and that a committee which was called an expert body might have concentrated upon aspects of the Decade's programme which were related to its expertise.

## TROUBLESOME REPORTS

Disguised interstate disputes continued to trouble the Committee. In 1981, in connection with its sixth report, the Syrian Arab Republic lodged a formal protest over its inability to exercise its responsibilities in the Golan Heights. On ratification Syria had entered a reservation stating that its accession 'shall in no way signify recognition of Israel or enter into a relationship with it regarding any matter regulated by the said Convention'. So Syria was appealing to the members' sense of justice and inviting them to study an illegal situation without placing the victim and the aggressor on the same footing. Mr Partsch proposed that this be regarded as an article 11 notification (Israel having become a state party two years earlier); on his reading of this article, it was for the Committee, and not the state party, to decide whether or not the article applied. The reservation entered by Syria could not prevent this, since, under article 20.2, no reservation was allowed which would inhibit the operation of any of the bodies established by the Convention. However, the Committee would not be able to pass on to the establishment of a Conciliation Commission under article 12.1 because of the reservation. Other members disagreed. The Chairman then ruled that the relevant section of the Syrian report did not constitute a communication under article 11 on the following grounds: (*a*) that the representative had expressly stated that his country was not invoking it; (*b*) that states parties had not objected to the reservation; and (*c*) that the reporting state had simply requested the Committee to study the conclusions of a special committee appointed by the UN. This ruling was maintained by a vote of 11 to 2, with one abstention. The state representative later said that he had expected a less juridical and more humanitarian response to his appeal (see A/36/18, paras. 170–3; SR 507–8, 519).

The Turkish occupation of part of the island has been the subject of regular protests on the submission of periodic reports from Cyprus, as in 1983, when it resulted in the adoption of decision 1(XXVII). Mr Lamptey and Mr Shahi declined to join the consensus as they considered that one of the operative paragraphs fell outside the scope of the Committee's competence (A/38/18, para. 96). In 1989, on the ninth report of Cyprus, reference was made to this (SR 847), but by then it was considered inappropriate to do more than report expressions of concern.

Just as in 1975 the submission of a report from Chile had given rise to a preliminary discussion about whether the Committee should receive the report, so in 1980 submission of the initial report of Israel occasioned a preliminary procedural discussion. One member believed that the report implied that the West Bank, Gaza, Sinai, Golan, and East Jerusalem were part of the territory of Israel, and therefore expressed concern lest consideration of it should imply recognition of the illegal occupation of Arab lands. Other members felt that Israel's denial of the rights of the Palestinian people constituted a breach of the Convention and that the Committee should therefore reject the report. After CERD had agreed that consideration of the report should not be interpreted as implying the recognition of any title, the representative of Israel was invited to present the report. He replied that, in listening to the statements made by members of the Committee, he had found it hard to believe that it was a debate of experts, elected in their personal capacity. Given the biased discussion which had already taken place and which had prejudged the Israeli report, he would take no further part in the proceedings (SR 483). The Committee decided to postpone consideration of the report until the following session (A/35/18, paras. 330–4).

By that time Israel had revised its report, omitting references to occupied territory. Some members stressed that the Committee could nevertheless not disregard the fact of such occupation as conflicting with both the letter and the spirit of the Convention. They also considered that the discretion allowed to the Supreme Court amounted 'to a limitation on generally recognized law that formed part of *jus cogens*, under which the struggle against racial discrimination was being waged'. Regarding the demographic information in the report, one member considered that its division into Jews and non-Jews constituted racial discrimination (A/36/18, paras. 89, 91). After consideration of the report, the Committee held a separate discussion on the question of whether or not Israel should report on the implementation of the Convention in the occupied territories. Some members who were opposed argued that the situation itself was a violation of the right to self-determination and was thus clear evidence of the existence of a form of discrimination which might be classified as racial. But to ask the occupying power to report would be to recognize its rights over such territories. On the other hand, the Committee would not be able to seek that information from the neighbouring states since they were prevented from exercising their jurisdiction. Members who took the other view pointed out that the Convention was universal in scope and applied to every person irrespective of whether the jurisdiction was legitimate. Since there was no consensus in the Committee, further discussion had to be postponed (A/36/18, paras. 107–10). The issue was reopened, though at less length, during consideration of Israel's combined second and third reports (A/37/18, para. 332; A/40/18, para. 203).

The politics of the Middle East sometimes appeared to affect the consideration of reports from other regions too. Commenting on the ninth periodic report of the USSR, Mr Banton (UK) asked about facilities for studying in Yiddish and the decline in the number of Jewish students admitted to universities, especially the evidence of discrimination for admission to study mathematics. Mr Aboul-Nasr then

asked why so much fuss was made about Jews in all issues relating to human rights . . . Jews in the Soviet Union seemed to be privileged compared with other nationalities . . . the question therefore arose as to why the Soviet Union was treating Jews better than other groups. Was it perhaps because the Jewish lobby was stronger? (SR 779)

The question of whether it was more difficult for Jews than other Soviet citizens to obtain permission to leave the country led on to a question about where they would go if they left, and upon whose land they would settle.

One argument for refusing to receive a report from the government of Chile was that it emanated from an illegal government installed by a military seizure of power in 1973. In the case of Israel, however, Syria and some other states refused to recognize the existence of the state itself. The recognition of a new government is quite different from the recognition of a new state and poses other problems. Their nature can be sensed from the decision of the UK in 1980 that it would no longer accord recognition to governments as distinct from states, because the recognition of governments was often taken to imply approval. This could be embarrassing when a government was violating human rights but nevertheless exercised effective control of the territory and could not be ignored. There is the further question of whether doubts about the recognition of a government should affect the operation of the Convention when the state is a party to it. (Apparently there were occasions in the early years of the Committee when diplomat members absented themselves during the consideration of a report from states which were not recognized by their governments.) The same question was raised in a different form with respect to Yugoslavia at the meeting of states parties in January 1994 (see the discussion in Chapter 8).

Governments change. The government of the Philippines submitted a periodic report in 1985 during the presidency of Ferdinand Marcos. The new government of President Aquino, which came into power the following year, withdrew that report and submitted a different one in 1989. In other cases (for example, that of Chile after the restoration of democratic rule) new governments have distanced themselves from the statements of their predecessors or have contradicted them. Should members of the Committee have taken the reports of the previous governments at face value if they had reason to think that they were not telling the whole truth and were likely to be replaced by governments which would give a different account of the situation? To discuss this question is to distinguish the legitimacy of governments as opposed to their legality. All governments seek to establish their rule as legitimate—that is, as morally justifiable—in the eyes of their own subjects and those of observers from other countries (see Beetham 1991). But whereas governments are adjudged to be either legal or illegal, legitimacy is a matter of degree. A lawful government can gradually lose legitimacy in the eyes of some of its electors, who then vote in a new government when they have the opportunity. A government can be regarded as legitimate by those who belong to the ethnic minority but be seen as illegitimate by members of a minority. This is one of the points at which law and politics continually interact.

The question of permissible sources was reopened by Mr Dechezelles in 1983. He referred to a document which he and other members of the Committee had received from the International League for Human Rights which he wished to transmit, through the Bureau, to the government of Poland and to ask them in their next report to comment on any of the statements in it which they felt to deserve comment. Mr Devetak objected that there was no provision for this in the Rules of Procedure. He and others said that Mr Dechezelles should himself ask any questions he wanted answering, but the Chairman agreed to Mr Dechezelles's request. Later Mr Staruschenko (USSR) protested at the distribution of papers from 'an unknown non-governmental organization' and asked who had authorized their circulation. The representative of the UN Secretary-General replied that the Secretariat had authorized no distribution. The representative of Poland said that he would reply only to the questions of Committee members (see SR 600).

A similar incident occurred in the following year in connection with Uganda. Mr Staruschenko insisted that

the Committee worked only with documents submitted by Governments, and it was not entitled to refer to material circulated by non-governmental organizations . . . to consider material from unofficial sources would be tantamount to expressing a lack of confidence in the Government. The fact that a non-governmental organization had managed to gain access to the conference room and to distribute copies of a document was regrettable. Why had that particular organization been permitted to circulate its documents, and not others? The Secretariat ought to take more effective measures to prevent the distribution of unofficial documentation.

Mr Partsch suggested that, as the relevant information might be available from the UN High Commission for Refugees (UNHCR), consideration of the report could be suspended. Mr Karasimeonov thought this would be a dangerous precedent. Mr Čičanovic (Yugoslavia) said that he had received three envelopes but had not read their contents since they had been distributed illegally. It was not clear to him what rule of procedure could justify the suspension proposed by Mr Partsch. Mr Staruschenko objected that, after Uganda had submitted its report, other documents had been submitted by certain parties interested in compromising Uganda, which had responded by submitting a revised report. Yet again:

a compromising document had been received and had inspired the proposal before the Committee that it should for the first time defer consideration of a report in order to consider a document from an organization hostile to the reporting country. To do so would imply mistrust . . . Accessions to the Convention would be discouraged.

Mr Staruschenko and Mr Karasimeonov later deferred to the Chairman's wish to allow a postponement on the understanding that this would not set a precedent (SR 680).

At a subsequent meeting Mr Partsch said that he had found a legitimate source of information in a UNHCR press release concerning the circumstances of the refugees. He proposed that the Committee make a formal request to the government of Uganda referring to passages in its report and enquiring

Whether the manifestations of 'ethnic antipathy' mentioned therein concern the movements, in October 1982, of thousands of refugees and displaced persons which caused special appeals of the UNHCR to the Head of State in the interest of securing guarantees for the safety of the affected persons; if this should be the case, why and to what extent 'enforcement measures to ensure security and tranquillity for all' were necessary in order to control these movements.

Mr Staruschenko thought it would be singularly inappropriate

for the Committee to employ a special procedure in regard to Uganda at a time when that country's misfortunes had been heightened by the decision of the Government of the United States of America to suspend all aid to it, a decision announced only one day before the date of Uganda's initial report. (SR 687)

The Committee decided to make a request for the information in question in its annual report (A/39/18, para. 383) instead of formally requesting it under article 9.1.

Political influences could be discerned in connection with European states also, as with the fifth periodic report of the FRG. Mr Nettel then observed that 'when certain reports were being considered the usually quiet and placid atmosphere of the Committee was ruffled by a political breeze' (SR 440). A notable example of political influence was furnished when the Committee discussed the rapporteur's draft for that section of the 1982 annual report which dealt with the USSR. Mr Staruschenko maintained that the summary was one-sided. One of the changes he sought was a congratulatory reference to the sixtieth anniversary of the founding of the Soviet Union. He was supported by Mr Bahnev, but others thought this propaganda. A compromise was reached whereby the report read 'Members of the Committee congratulated the Soviet Union for having taken steps during the previous sixty years to eliminate racial discrimination . . .' (see SR 597; A/37/18, para. 421).

## FORCED ASSIMILATION IN BULGARIA

What could, in retrospect, be seen as one of the last clashes of the Cold War occurred in March 1986, when CERD considered the eighth periodic report of Bulgaria. That report had originally been submitted in October 1984 and circulated to Committee members. It had then been withdrawn and a new version substituted in January 1986. Behind the change, apparently, was the state's introduction in December 1984 of a policy designed to achieve the assimilation by force of the country's Turkish minority. The 1984 report had stated 'Also living in our country are Bulgarian citizens of Turkish, Gipsy, Armenian, Jewish, Greek and other origins'; and that 'all Bulgarian citizens have the right to declare their national affiliation and this gives them the right to study and speak their native tongue, develop their national culture, maintain their traditions, etc.'. No passages of this kind appeared in the 1986 report. Committee members had also heard, from press reports, Amnesty International, the Bulgarian Turks of America, Turkish diplomatic missions, and other sources, that the Bulgarian government had started forcing Bulgarian Turks to change their names to Bulgarian names. Amnesty International had received the names of over 100 ethnic Turks alleged to have been killed by the security forces during the implementation of the campaign. Expecting a public dispute, many diplomats from missions in New York had come to the conference chamber to hear the exchanges.

Introducing his government's report, the Bulgarian state representative said, among other things, that a violent anti-Bulgarian campaign was being waged regarding the situation of Bulgarian Muslims. To understand what had been happening, it was essential to remember that during Ottoman rule Bulgarians had been under pressure to adopt Turkish culture and the Islamic religion. Since achieving independence, Bulgaria had been liberal in allowing Bulgarians with a strong Turkish national identity to migrate to Turkey. The others, Muslims and unbelievers with Turkicized names, had chosen to belong to the Bulgarian people and in recent times, particularly with the issuing of new identity documents, had availed themselves of the opportunity to change their names. This could also be seen as a reaction on the part of Bulgarian Muslims to Turkish claims concerning them. For good reason, Turkey was not a party to the Convention and its government could scarcely be less qualified to say how it should be implemented in view of the human-rights abuses for which it was responsible (A/42/18, paras. 199–226; SR 761–2).

The first speaker on the report was Mr de Pierola y Balta (Peru), a member who was often supportive of the position taken by East European states. He said it would be useful to have more demographic information, but was not critical of the state's record. The Chairman, Mr Cremona (Malta), speaking as a member of the Committee, asked about the interaction of two legal provisions. Mr Aboul-Nasr said that, in view of previous references to an ethnic Turkish minority, he could not understand the statement that there was no longer such a minority. Mr Öberg (Sweden) spoke at greater length, drawing attention to discrepancies between the two official reports. Since reports of human-rights violations had caused great damage to Bulgaria's reputation, it would be in the government's interest to allow impartial observers to move freely and gather accurate first-hand information. Mr Shahi observed that the reports of forcible assimilation had caused great anguish in the Islamic Conference and throughout the Muslim world. He sought reassurance concerning the reported closure of more than 1,000 mosques and of restrictions on the observance of Muslim religious rites. Mrs Sadiq Ali also queried the conclusion that Bulgaria was an ethnically homogeneous state.

Mr Čičanovic reviewed the references to minorities in successive reports from Bulgaria, drawing attention to the 'disappearance' of the Macedonian minority. He asked for additional information on any contemplated measures to ensure that such groups could exercise their rights under article 1 of the Convention. Mr Yutzis maintained that it was unlikely that a relatively large group of people would suddenly decide to change their names, since names are important to cultural identity. Mr Braunschweig enquired whether it would be possible for a group of observers representing the Committee to visit Bulgaria in order to obtain objective information on the situation; the Committee was currently in no position to draw any conclusions. Mr Partsch opined that there was admissible evidence that the Muslim minority in Bulgaria was being subjected to a coercive assimilation campaign in violation of their minority rights. He recalled that the General Secretary of the Bulgarian Communist Party had claimed that the Bulgarian Muslims were in reality Bulgarians who had been forced to adopt

Islam when the country was under Ottoman rule. He supported Mr Braunschweig's view and insisted that the Committee must act. Mr Song had some further queries on the demographic aspects.

Mr Starushenko commented that the discussion had assumed a political character. The apparent problem was a consequence of five centuries of alien domination. He had studied Turkish and on frequent visits to Bulgaria had noticed a decline in the numbers who spoke that language. The decline could be explained by the ending of alien domination and the creation of an environment in which people did not need to believe in any god. There were no grounds for sending observers. Each state party used its own methods to solve its problems. Which method was best might be debated, and a country might not choose the best method, but only that country had the right to make that choice. Mr de Pierola y Balta then asked for the floor a second time to say that, if the problem of the Turkish minority was politicized, then it should be politicized within a world-wide framework. The peoples of Latin America, Africa, and Asia had been compelled to participate in the rivalry between two groups of developed countries. He wondered whether external pressure was being brought to bear on the government of Bulgaria. Mr Banton observed that the Committee had never formally reported non-compliance by a state party. A situation might occur in which this would be necessary. It was questionable whether Bulgaria was being candid with the Committee. If, as Mr Starushenko said, a state might not always choose the best methods of dealing with a problem, then a dialogue might be possible on that basis. A visit might be organized through the Islamic conference. Mr Sherifis (Cyprus) thought the Committee should exploit whatever possibilities there were for dialogue. Several other members then chose to explain points on which they thought they might have been misunderstood.

At this point the Chairman suggested that the ninth periodic report, which was already due, might include answers to the points raised. Mr Karasimeonov maintained that the Committee should follow its usual procedure. Mr Partsch suggested that the Committee should have a closed meeting in order to discuss proposals made in the current meeting. Mr Karasimeonov, Mr Starushenko, Mr de Pierola y Balta, and Mr Shahi spoke against this, so no more was heard of Mr Partsch's suggestion. Invited to respond to questions, the Bulgarian representative then elaborated upon some of his earlier observations. He promised that Bulgaria would always be very hospitable to visiting experts from the Committee as guests, but under no circumstances would the government agree to a commission of inquiry. Mr Yutzis gave reasons for finding the replies unpersuasive. Mr Shahi queried the kind of historical justification that had been advanced, remarking that, as a result of the British conquest of India, his country now had a large Christian population; to try to redress history by mistreating them would produce only chaos. Mr Čičanovic repeated that there were ethnic minorities in Bulgaria and if there were no figures about their size that was only because no effort had been made to collect them. Mr Öberg indicated his support for the three previous speakers' views, and then the Chairman announced that consideration of the reports had been completed, making it impossible to reopen the question of any further dialogue until the next report was received (which would not be until 1991).

Mr Banton thought it wrong that a member of the Committee should have tried to influence a decision concerning action on a report from the country of which he was a national, so he subsequently introduced a motion to amend the rules of procedure in this respect (A/42/18, para. 845). The proposal failed, partly because the members from Sweden and the Sudan had both vigorously criticized their own countries' reports (SR 768, paras. 27–9; 784, paras. 47–55). Since this also concerns a possible conflict of interest, it may be relevant to note that in 1987 and 1988, but not in 1993, the Chairman continued to preside over the Committee when his own state's report was under consideration (SR 755, 822, 971).

Reverting to the consideration of the 1986 Bulgarian report, and in the knowledge that there had, as alleged, been many serious human-rights abuses, the main conclusion must be that up to 1988 CERD was in no position to act against any but a pariah state. Chile and Israel found themselves in this position, and South Africa would have done had that country become a state party. There was insufficient trust within the Committee for it to take decisions other than by consensus, and this permitted any small minority to exercise a veto. Many members saw their obligations very much in diplomatic terms, and perhaps could do little else while the opposition between East and West hung over so many of the decisions that had to be taken.

Mr Öberg, a member of the Committee from 1984 to 1988, commented subsequently upon interpretations of the member's role in a booklet written in Swedish. He wrote:

Whether a representative or not, every member is influenced to some degree by the general values of his or her fellow citizens. It is unlikely that any government even in the most democratic of countries would nominate as a candidate someone who had already been critical of that government's discharge of its obligations under the Convention. Sweden might have faced that challenge but in the end it was not put to the test. During the consideration of Sweden's report in 1986 I advanced a sharp criticism of the government's neglect to prohibit racial discrimination in the workplace. Before my term of office expired in 1988 I notified the government that I would not be available for renomination. In accordance with an agreement between the Nordic states about rotation in the nomination of candidates for treaty bodies, these states then agreed to support a Danish candidate.

In 1985 Ecuador's report was considered. The member from that country, who had earlier been its foreign minister, was then CERD's chairman. He passed his gavel to a vice-chairman so that in his personal capacity he could comment on the report of a government composed of his party's opponents. When his term of office expired he was not re-nominated.

It should be noted, however, that the member from Ecuador did not use this opportunity to be very critical; he said that the report showed that in this field there were no ideological divergences between successive governments (SR 702, para. 14). That he was not renominated was probably due to a change in the political complexion of the government. Mr Öberg remarked on the solidarity shown by members from states of the East European group. When he was a member of the Committee he had himself commented on a remark of Mr Staruschenko that he spoke 'as the representative of a socialist country' in order to explain a difference of opinion between them (SR 792). He was not a member when a black African member referred to the black representative of a Caribbean reporting state as 'my sister'; had he been, he might have cited this as evidence of a solidarity based upon colour. Mr Öberg had the impression that Muslim members were like Western members in being inclined to look tolerantly upon the shortcomings of states in their own group. Diplomats, he said, were often obliged to take a placatory stance.

To take an actual example, one Committee member was at the time stationed in Belgrade and knew that he was soon to take up a new post as his country's ambassador to Moscow. Just how critical could one expect him to be in his comments on the reports of Yugoslavia and the USSR? The diplomat in question is of unusual charm and mild disposition. It was no surprise when at the next election to the Committee he received the largest number of votes of any candidate. (Öberg 1990: 11–13)

## CERD'S LOSS OF MOMENTUM

By way of conclusion to this chapter, it should be asked whether the years 1979–87 saw any improvements in the implementation of the Convention? The record shows that, while some states parties improved their application of it, others continued to have only a limited understanding of the obligations they had assumed. For example, the initial report of Gabon, considered in 1982, simply stated that

the Government of Gabon has not deemed it necessary to adopt any legislative, judicial, administrative or other measures relating to racial discrimination to give effect to the provisions of the relevant international convention, particularly because no discrimination exists between the different components of the Gabonese nation.

On another occasion Mr Nettel objected that the fifth report of Fiji was identical to its fourth with the exception of four lines relating to population figures. 'The submission of such a report was a waste of time and money for both the Committee and the Secretariat' (SR 629). Mr Braunschweig once regretted that state reports were 'frequently repetitious, incoherent and imprecise'; he thought that they should be more sharply focused (SR 808). Other states represented relations within their countries as idyllic. The representative of Uruguay admitted to the presence of 'what had been described as *angelismo*' in his country's seventh report (SR 579). Others might also have considered this possibility. For example, presenting its seventh report Brazil claimed that 'its harmonious racial and ethnic heritage . . . formed a unity and attested to the wholeness of the Brazilian nationality. The Indian, African, European and Asian elements had combined to form a single *ethnos*, which could be found in the personality of every Brazilian' (SR 612).

Some states had difficulty accepting the independence of committee members. Mr Ghoneim (Egypt) reported that his government had received a protest in relation to a statement he had made at the preceding session in connection with a state report. His government had responded in the appropriate manner, but such action could have a detrimental effect upon the Committee's work. Others agreed, so it was decided to publicize this view in the annual report (see A/38/18, paras. 78–9).

The Committee's contribution to the implementation of the Convention during this period failed to maintain the momentum of the years 1970–8. In 1983, presenting the report to the General Assembly, the director of the Centre for Human Rights cited the work of the Committee as a reason for the increase in the number of ratifications of the Convention (A/38/18, para. 19). But this was a charitable view, for in many respects the Committee had simply stood still. In particular, it tended to concentrate upon matters of foreign policy and on the texts of legislation without investigating the effectiveness with which the laws were applied. For example, Australia's second report, considered in 1979, included, as annexes, copies of reports from the Commissioner for Community Relations which have been described as

something of an embarrassment to the Government, not only for revealing the extent of the problems in the racial discrimination area that continue to exist in Australia, particularly at the level of defiance by State governments (notably Queensland), but also because they reveal weaknesses and the inadequacy of the resources made available . . . (Nettheim 1981: 135).

All periodic reports are translated into the Committee's official languages, but annexes are not usually translated or circulated. They are available for consultation in a file in the Committee's meeting-room. It would appear that on this occasion no Committee member read the reports of the Commissioner or made use of them in the examination of the government's report.

The Committee did not bear all the blame for the loss of momentum. Its ability to extend the rule of law and put pressure upon states parties to fulfil their obligations depended upon the kinds of person the states had elected, their ability to attend sessions, and the preparation they had undertaken. In 1985 there were further indications that the Committee sometimes had difficulty obtaining a quorum. According to the annual report,

some members had encountered difficulty in participating faithfully in the regular sessions . . . a member [Mr Yutzis] introduced orally a draft proposal recommending that States parties, in nominating and electing a candidate, should take into account the availability of that candidate to attend meetings regularly . . .

The Committee decided that the matter should be discussed at its next session (A/40/18, para. 10), but the proposal was overtaken by the UN's financial crisis. Since some states were not paying their assessments, the crisis led to the cancellation or abbreviation of many of CERD's sessions. The failure of the other states parties to take effective action against those of their number who contributed to this situation scarcely suggested much appreciation for the Committee's work.

In 1979–87 CERD built very little upon the foundations that had been laid in the earlier period. It extended to new states the principles established in that period (at the closing of the Committee's last session in 1978 there were 100 states parties; this had increased to 124 by the closing of the last session in 1987). The Committee reinforced the application of its earlier principles in its dialogue with all states parties, but it undertook no major initiatives to improve implementation of the Convention and was inclined to involve itself with the same political disputes as were being addressed in other UN organs.

# 8

## Seizing the Initiative

FOR many years the work of the Committee was primarily reactive, in responding to the periodic reports submitted by the states parties. Was this sufficient? With the ending of the Cold War, a change in mood became apparent. At the opening of the thirty-seventh session in 1989 Mr Aboul-Nasr reminded his fellow members of the Committee that, although the Convention had been in force for twenty years and the number of states parties was rising steadily, racial discrimination was increasing in its seriousness. Since 1945 there had been eighty-seven racially inspired wars, in which between fifteen million and thirty million people had been killed. Racial and religious conflict existed in every continent. The UN had made little or no practical progress in remedying a tragic situation (SR 832). Mr Aboul-Nasr has remarked that, whereas in the 1970s he had favoured a strict construction of the Committee's duties, subsequent events had led him to the view that the Committee should do more than merely react.

In the years that followed CERD was able to promote the implementation of the Convention more effectively because of the reduction in political tensions outside the Committee; because it enjoyed greater continuity of membership (between the years 1988 and 1995 there will have been just twenty-five members); and because the establishment of other treaty bodies has drawn CERD into a wider structure backed by pressure in the General Assembly for improving the implementation of all the human-rights instruments.

The ending of the Cold War had its effect after the 1988 elections to the committee. Prior to 1988 the member from the USSR was a professor who seemed faithfully to rehearse the official Soviet line on the countries under consideration. He was replaced by the head of the human-rights section of the department of foreign affairs in Moscow, a man who could say in public that his government no longer attempted to influence individuals who

were members of UN expert bodies (SR 883), and an independently minded personality. Prior to 1988 the Bulgarian member
had been a diplomat who made his contribution on almost every
state report that was presented even when he had little to add,
and who also appeared to be subject to instruction from his
foreign ministry. He was replaced by a man who had previously
been the Bulgarian ambassador to the UN and who, like his
Russian colleague, seemed to have greater freedom than his
predecessor.

The potential for change was evident, but it was slow in coming,
partly because of budgetary constraints. In 1986 CERD had been
enabled to meet for only three weeks instead of six. In 1987 it met
for four, in 1988 for two, in 1989 for four, in 1990 for three, in
1991 for six, in 1992 for two, and in 1993 for six weeks. The big
advances were made in 1991 and 1993, when more time was available for their consideration. In years like 1988 and 1992 it was all
the Committee could do to consider the reports that had come in
and to agree a report on them for the General Assembly. The
August session can be under particular pressure. The first two of
the three weeks have to concentrate upon the consideration of state
reports. A staff member will keep a record, in English or in French,
of the proceedings. This record has to be typed, edited, and
translated. Until 1995 it was used as a basis for a preparation, by
another staff member, of a summary of the proceedings, which was
then presented, with the provisional summary record, to the
committee rapporteur for checking and, as necessary, for amendment. It is the committee rapporteur's duty to present the draft
report to the Committee in the third week, for the Committee to go
through it and agree a text to be reported to the General Assembly.
The timetable is therefore very tight indeed. Since some state
reports are contentious, the standard of drafting has to be high and
discussion in the Committee is often animated.

While describing the length of sessions, it may be appropriate
also to consider their place. According to ICERD article 10.4 the
'meetings shall normally be held at the United Nations Headquarters' and this was taken to mean New York. After the transfer
to Geneva of the UN division of human rights, one of the
Committee's two sessions was held there in 1974, 1976, 1980–2,
and 1984–5. In 1977 one session was held in Vienna, and in 1976
one in Paris. The Committee has several times spoken in favour of

convening a session in a developing country, to help publicize its activities, but the greater costs have made this difficult. After 1974 a session in New York meant that several members of staff from the Geneva office had to be flown over, adding to the expense, so since 1986 all sessions have been in Geneva. Many of the smaller countries have diplomatic representation in New York and can participate in meetings held there, but have difficulty coming to Geneva. In 1991 the Committee adopted a decision recommending that its March sessions should be held in New York on this account, but to no avail. It is possible that sessions in Geneva are more removed from diplomatic pressures than meetings in New York.

## NEW METHODS OF WORK

The key to increased productivity in CERD, as in other institutions, has lain in the division of labour. From 1972 onwards, a series of proposals were advanced within the Committee with a view to the saving of time. They included: assigning a number of reports to each member, who would be principally responsible for their evaluation; dividing the Committee into small working groups to undertake preliminary reviews; and placing a time-limit on the statements made by any member on any one report (see UN 1991*c*: para. 153). In addition Mr Sayegh proposed that a comparative index be compiled, arranged in accordance with the articles of the Convention, and detailing everything known about the laws and provisions of each state party (SR 92; see also SR 199, 216). Some of these proposals were resuscitated from time to time—notably in 1981 (see A/36/18, para. 31) and in 1986, when a meeting was devoted to discussing them—but nothing came of any of these attempts.

From the outset the Committee divided into three working groups responsible for evaluating the information received from the UN about Trust and Non-Self-Governing Territories under ICERD article 15 (see UN 1991*c*: paras. 185–90). Why, if there was a pressure of work, should they not have agreed some similar practice for article 9 reports received from states parties? Why, more particularly, should they have been unwilling to designate a particular member to open the discussion of each report? This last practice—of designating a 'country rapporteur'—was eventually agreed in 1988, with no help from the then Chairman, and it has worked very well. Why did its adoption take so long?

From the time when, in 1972, the Committee first received a representative of the reporting state, it became the practice to draft its report to the General Assembly by summarizing, first, the observations of the state representative in presenting the report, then, article by article, the questions or observations of Committee members, followed by a summary of answers to their questions. From time to time the Committee reached a collective view on some point arising from consideration of a state report, but it reached no collective opinion on the extent to which a state was fulfilling its obligations. There were just the individual opinions of those members who chose to take part in the dialogue. Some members thought this fell short of the Committee's duty (e.g. Mr Videla Escalada (Argentina), as noted in SR 427). In 1991 the Committee agreed, however, to adopt such a collective opinion in the form of 'concluding observations' at the end of the summary of the dialogue with the state and its representative if one was present. That this change took so long to achieve seems to have been another aspect of the slowness of change affecting the other matters discussed.

Many people obtain their ideas of how committees ought to work from their experience of committees within a single institution (such as a university) or at the national level, when representatives of different government departments or interest groups are brought together to try to resolve problems of coordinated action. They do not think of bargaining sessions (as between an employer and trade-union representatives) as kinds of committee. But an international committee—even a treaty body—has some features of the latter kind of gathering. Diplomats are responsible to the governments that employ them and are rewarded for advancing their employers' interests. There cannot be the same trust between members of an international committee when there is the possibility that a decision may be to the disadvantage of one of the states concerned. Since some of the positions taken up by members of CERD in the first years were highly political, members were bound to be suspicious that the appointment of a country rapporteur could give a diplomatic advantage to a critic of the country whose report was being considered, and that this could be even greater if such an opportunity was given to a small working group. Equally, they were likely to fear the possibility that the adoption of a collective opinion would open a possibility for the Committee to behave more like a court (and it should be remembered that, when they ratified the Convention, many states, particularly from Eastern Europe, entered reservations to exclude the possibility that disputes involving them might be referred to the International Court of Justice under ICERD article 22).

CERD first agreed to appoint country rapporteurs in 1988 (A/43/18, para. 24(*b*) SR 823, 825, 827). The responsibility of anyone so appointed was to prepare 'a thorough study and evaluation of each state report, to prepare a comprehensive list of questions to put to the representatives of the reporting state and to lead the discussion in the Committee'. Several members doubted whether the procedure would save time (which was one ground on which it was proposed), and the objections of the Chairman, Mr Lamptey, were such as to occasion a sharp exchange between Mr Shahi and him (SR 827).

Later in 1988 there was a meeting of persons chairing treaty bodies which recommended that all treaty bodies should consider the appointment of such rapporteurs. In CERD their appointment has greatly facilitated the division of labour among committee members, because, when they know which of their colleagues is serving in this capacity, they can predict on which features of that report their colleague is mostly likely to concentrate and prepare their questions accordingly. A rapporteur can analyse a report in depth, checking back on the history of the dialogue with that state, while preparing less thoroughly his or her comments on the reports allocated to other members of CERD. Previously it was never possible for a member to prepare a full analysis of every report, and it sometimes happened that several members duplicated one another's efforts by preparing similar questions and comments. Under the new system rapporteurs prepare commentaries of a quality rarely achieved previously.

Since 1990 CERD's practice has been to invite members to volunteer to serve as country rapporteurs and for a list to be submitted for the Committee's approval. When further information is requested the country rapporteur continues in this office for the review of the information received, but otherwise the duty rotates, so that the same member does not normally serve as country rapporteur for the same state on the next occasion. Certain of the diplomat members do not volunteer to serve in this capacity.

The year 1991 saw an agreement (A/46/18, para. 31) that the relevant section of the committee report should contain: '(*d*) Concluding observations on the report and the comments made by the State party concerning the situation regarding racial discrimination in the country concerned.' The country rapporteur was made responsible for drafting concluding observations to be presented for the Committee's approval. Some difficulty was experienced in ensuring that these observations were even-handed as between different states, and securing agreement can be very time-consuming. So at its 983rd meeting in March 1993 the Committee decided to follow the practice of some other treaty bodies and ask for a member of the secretariat to prepare a fuller draft listing in turn the positive aspects revealed by the report, the Committee's principal subjects of concern, its suggestions and recommendations, and matters for further action. This has made possible the adoption of greatly improved observations and enabled the Committee in 1995 to decide that in future it could dispense with its summary of the dialogue. The securing of agreement on these observations remains very demanding on Committee time, and working from an English-language text puts some members at a disadvantage. Because of the pressures, members sometimes feel obliged to accept formulations they consider unsatisfactory, but so far the Committee has been able to obtain that agreement, apart from the observations on Bosnia in 1993, when Mr Aga Shahi was unable to join the consensus (see A/48/18, para. 464; SR 1012). A similar disagreement was expressed in 1995 in connection with the Committee's decision 2(47) on the situation in Bosnia-Herzegovina.

In 1991, 1992, and at the forty-second session in 1993, the concluding observations adopted were relatively brief, often being limited to emphasizing the mandatory nature of article 4, or to specifying information the Committee wished to receive in the next periodic report. In a few instances they touched upon matters of substance. For example, regarding the ninth and tenth reports of Iraq:

The Committee recorded that the Government of Iraq had undertaken to enter into a dialogue with the Committee and hoped that such an attitude would prevail. The Committee acknowledged that Iraq faced economic and political problems as a consequence of the recent events and that first steps had been initiated by it with a view to improving the human rights situation in general and, in particular, the situation of Kurds and other ethnic groups in Iraq. However, the Committee had not yet received the information which would enable it to assess the human rights situation in Iraq. The failure to address the treatment of ethnic groups in Iraq and, in particular, the treatment of citizens of Kuwait subsequent to 2 August 1990, since Iraq is under an obligation to respect and ensure to all individuals under its jurisdiction or control the rights recognized in the Convention, was a matter of grave concern to the Committee. The Committee called upon the Government of Iraq to include the requested information in its eleventh report, due in 1991, and to submit the eleventh report in time for the Committee to be able to discuss it at its next session. (A/46/18, para. 258)

(The report due in 1991 had not been received by mid-1995.)

Regarding the tenth and eleventh reports of the UK, the Committee observed:

The reports and annexes had provided very detailed and in-depth information on the situation with regard to racial discrimination in the United Kingdom. It was commendable that no attempt had been made to present the existing situation in the United Kingdom in a more favourable light than was warranted by the facts and that the Committee's attention had been drawn to areas where the United Kingdom Government still saw a need for improvement. The United Kingdom Government had done a great deal to strike a fair balance between the interests of the various components of its multi-ethnic society, and its efforts were fully in keeping with the objectives of the International Convention on the Elimination of All Forms of Racial Discrimination.

At the same time it was necessary for the United Kingdom to make increased efforts to improve the situation of members of ethnic minorities with regard to education, employment, housing and economic standing. Other steps, relating in particular to criminal prosecution, should also be taken to reduce significantly the number of incidents of incitement to racial hatred and racially motivated attacks. (A/46/18, paras. 208–9)

In the following General Assembly debate several delegations welcomed the Committee's approach to dialogue with states parties, and other features of its work, but none commented upon the adoption of concluding observations by consensus (see A/47/18, para. 16). Nor was there any comment the following year after the observations were expanded (A/48/18, para. 12). That the post-1993-style concluding observations made greater demands upon states can be seen from a comparison of the comments on the

UK reports quoted above with those on that country's subsequent report, as quoted in Chapter 9, or by considering, for example, the observations on the combined ninth to twelfth periodic reports of the Islamic Republic of Iran (A/48/18, paras. 271–7). They begin with an introductory paragraph which comments on the failure of the report to follow the guidelines, followed by two paragraphs of concern about the absence of information on the status of the Convention in domestic legislation, on the possibilities for individuals to evoke it directly before the courts, on the demographic composition of the population, and on the implementation of articles 4, 5, 6, and 7. The observations went on:

In that connection, the Committee wished to be informed about the treatment and the situation of ethnic, religious and linguistic minorities in the Islamic Republic of Iran. Reference was made, for example, to the situation of the Baha'i community, as well as of the Kurds and other ethnic minorities.

They continued with three paragraphs of 'suggestions and recommendations' about the implementation of the Convention, the desired content of the next report (particularly concerning the rights listed in article 5), and the request that the next report be submitted by the beginning of January 1994 (it was not).

The new-style concluding observations express significantly raised expectations of reporting states. If one state objects to the Committee's observations, much may depend upon the reactions of other states parties. At the same time some readers may find the observations unduly mild relative to the reported violations of human rights. They should remember that the Committee has to treat states parties equally. When some states fail to report as they have undertaken, and are not disciplined in any way by other states parties for this, then the Committee cannot be too critical of a state which observes its obligations to report, even when the content of the report is not reassuring.

Since the process of adopting concluding observations is politically sensitive, until 1996 the Committee discussed them in closed session. The summary records were then confidential. Committee members have responded differently when reports have been under review from states of which they themselves are nationals. Some never ask to speak on either the consideration of the report or the proposed concluding observations, though they may in private draw to the attention of a colleague some passage in the observations which they believe to be in need of amendment. Other members do not feel constrained by any conflict of interest.

## OVERDUE REPORTS

Many states have found the two-year reporting cycle under ICERD unduly burdensome. Acting on a recommendation from the eleventh meeting of states parties, the Committee in 1988 agreed as a general practice that, after the submission of initial comprehensive reports, states should submit further comprehensive reports at four-year intervals with brief updating reports during the interim. This did not dispose of the problem posed by states parties which had been neglecting to submit periodic reports for longer intervals, despite reminders, and despite appeals from the General Assembly. In 1990 Mr Banton proposed that the Committee should appoint country rapporteurs for such states, and consider their implementation of their obligations on the basis of information available through UN sources. Members of the Committee objected that this was not permissible because article 9.2 of ICERD states that 'The Committee shall report . . . based on the examination of the reports and information received from the States Parties.' While other members were stressing the objections, Mr Aboul-Nasr found a way round the obstacle: to review the implementation of the Convention in the defaulting states based upon the last report received and the consideration given to it by the Committee on the previous occasion (A/46/18, para. 27; SR 903). This enabled CERD to seize the initiative and take charge of the reporting process, instead of simply reacting to the submission of reports.

In 1991 letters were sent to thirteen states which were seriously overdue in the submission of their reports. A postponement was agreed in the case of a state which promised a report by a given date. Another sent a representative to take part in the proceedings. Eleven did not, although five of those had diplomatic missions in Geneva so it should not have been difficult for them to have participated in the review. In 1992 similar letters were sent to a further thirteen states. The Permanent Mission of Somalia to the UN at Geneva responded with a request that consideration be delayed until the situation in that country had been clarified.

The Committee would not agree to any indefinite postponement: 'After hearing from its country rapporteur about the situation in that country, and debating the issue in the absence of a representative of the State party, the Committee decided to defer for one year its consideration of the implementation of the Convention in Somalia.' It noted that the circumstances prevailing in Somalia included conflicts based on descent, which brought them within the Convention (A/47/18, paras. 225–6). Obviously it was difficult for the Committee to play a significant role in circumstances such as those in Somalia, but if states are to be treated equally the Committee should not close its eyes to such developments.

Later in 1992 the Committee brought a further twelve states parties into the review procedure; of these, three submitted reports, two sent delegations, and four requested postponements. In subsequent years further states parties were brought into the procedure, while in 1995 letters were sent to those states first reviewed in 1991 which had not resumed reporting, notifying them that they would again be reviewed in this way.

This new procedure, which has been continued in subsequent years, has caused some states to expedite preparation of reports and is progressively resolving much of the problem. The Committee has been commended in the General Assembly for its initiative, which has been copied by other treaty bodies.

A residual difficulty concerns states parties which have failed to submit an initial report several years after accession. For example, Guyana, Liberia, and Suriname, although they acceded to ICERD in 1977, 1976, and 1984 respectively, had not submitted their initial reports by 1994, so there was no legal basis on which the Committee could conduct an examination. The Committee wrote to the fifteenth meeting of states parties (1994) to draw this to their attention, but without result, so in 1995 it wrote directly to states parties which had not submitted initial reports advising them to avail themselves of the advisory services of the Centre for Human Rights. In 1995 CERD requested the Former Yugoslav Republic of Macedonia to expedite submission of its initial report and, by the time this book is published, it may have addressed similar requests to other states. It might be expected that the states parties themselves would have taken action against those of their number who have failed to discharge so basic an obligation (e.g. by suspending their right to vote in elections for members of the Committee), but such has not so far been the case.

The Fifth Meeting of Persons Chairing Human Rights Treaty Bodies therefore urged the states parties to deal with overdue and non-submitted reports at their regular meetings: 'These meetings should not only be devoted to elections of members of treaty bodies, but should consider general problems relating to the implementation of treaties' (A/49/537, para. 17). This recommendation was then endorsed by the General Assembly (resolution 49/178, para. 6) and by the Commission of Human Rights (resolution 1995/92, paras. 7, 9).

It has long been recognized that delays in the submission of reports, especially by the governments of developing countries, may stem from the shortage of personnel trained to do this work. The services of the UN Centre for Human Rights section of technical assistance are now available to states which ask for help, and the Committee in its general recommendation X recommended the further development of these services.

ICERD article 9.1 gives the Committee power to request further information from states parties. This power was utilized in the early years when periodic reports failed to supply the necessary information, but quite soon it gave way to the practice of asking that deficiencies be made good in the next periodic report. The power was next utilized explicitly in 1992, when the Committee, taking note of reports of ethnic conflict in Burundi and Rwanda, requested further information from those states, in particular concerning their implementation of article 5(b). Those reports should have been received in time for consideration in August 1993, and the Committee could have gone ahead without reports, but, because of a desire to accommodate the state representatives who had been inconvenienced by delays within the administration of the countries concerned, because of events in the interim, and because the Committee had to find time to formulate a response to the Secretary-General's *An Agenda for Peace* (UN 1992*a*), it postponed further consideration of implementation until March 1994 (see the discussion in Chapter 11). In 1992 also the Committee requested additional information from Papua New Guinea concerning reports of conflict in Bougainville (A/47/18, paras. 40, 266). Papua New Guinea had failed to submit the periodic report due in 1985, and, as the Committee reported to the

General Assembly, it did not supply this information either. Further information, requested in March 1993 from the governments of Bosnia-Herzegovina, Croatia, and Yugoslavia (Serbia and Montenegro), was supplied in time for consideration in August of that year. In the same year the Committee requested further information from Nigeria, for varied reasons, one of which was the political uncertainty in the country at the time of the Committee's session. This had prevented the attendance of the delegation from the capital. These and similar decisions were not reached easily, since members would have been unwilling to address such a request to one state if they had not made similar requests to other states in comparable circumstances, but they nevertheless mark an advance compared with the Committee's near paralysis over the allegations of violations made in 1986 in connection with the Bulgarian report.

Changes in committee membership entail changes in the character of the dialogue with state representatives. It is noticeable, if unsurprising, that (as already noted) lawyers tend to ask legal questions, diplomats diplomatic questions, and sociologists sociological questions. A new member may start a new line of questioning that may be taken up by others and may lead to the adoption of a committee decision or general recommendation. In the 1970s much of the questioning concentrated upon ICERD articles 3 and 4. Article 5 covers a great range of activity and its potential has as yet not been fully exploited, so there is plenty of scope for the development of dialogue on this, especially to ascertain how policy is adapted to changing circumstances.

Not the least of the achievements of the years following 1988 was that in 1991 the Committee laid to rest the vexed question of permissible sources. On the initiative of Mr Wolfrum, it adopted decision 1(XL), in which it stated that it will

continue to make its suggestions and general recommendations on the basis of the examination of the reports and information received from States parties . . . At the same time, in examining the reports of States parties, members of the Committee must have access, as independent experts, to all other available sources of information, governmental and non-governmental.

This understanding was important to the work of country rapporteurs and those members of the Committee who chose, in their questioning, to draw upon information other than that supplied by states. In the 1970s, when the Committee was concerned to get states to fulfil their reporting obligations, and when it spent time checking the texts of laws to see if they met the standards of the Convention, it was not necessary for members to undertake much work between sessions. Once the foundations for the Committee's work were laid, it could move into a new phase in which it assessed state reports against the background of more information about circumstances likely to encourage discrimination. At the same time it has to be remembered that most Committee members are in full-time employment and have other responsibilities. Nor have they as yet received any payment for their service on the Committee. They cannot be expected to be well informed about events in every part of the world. So the assistance available from NGOs can be valuable to them, even if the information originates from groups and persons who have an interest in publicizing a particular point of view.

Whenever the Committee has reviewed its methods of working, one issue that has often been raised is that of time-limits upon speeches. Committee time is expensive, particularly because of the costs of providing skilled interpretation. One calculation in 1994 estimated the costs at $US180,000 per day. (A visitor sitting in the public gallery might think that members are insufficiently conscious of these costs, for meetings regularly start at least ten minutes late; members may be engaged in informal discussions that help the subsequent meeting to go more smoothly, but the interpreters' services are not being utilized. A ten-minute delay in starting each of CERD's fifty-eight meetings during the year entails a cost of $US290,000.)

Sometimes state representatives speak at much greater length than is necessary, either in presenting a report or in answering questions (and some striking variations can be observed in Tables 2–5), but any request that they should have regard to the clock has to be expressed with courtesy. Sometimes one committee member, opening a discussion, takes time to thank the state representative for attending and expresses appreciation of the report, and then these courtesies are repeated, unnecessarily, by other committee members; questions may be repeated, be irrelevant, or be unlikely to evoke any response from the reporting state. A member who, as country rapporteur, is opening the discussion of a substantial state report (e.g. a state reporting both upon its domestic territory and upon implementation of the convention in a number of dependent territories) may need to speak at length, but there is room for doubt as to whether the length should stretch to 118 minutes, as on one recent occasion, or to sixty-three and fifty-two minutes as on two others. There are cultural variations, in that speakers from the Latin American region sometimes seem accustomed to more lengthy exposition, while those from the Nordic countries are sometimes so terse that the significance of the points they are making can be lost. (It may take a little longer to get the same point across speaking through an interpreter than in a face-to-face conversation in the mother tongue of both speakers.) Time limits could have a negative influence on occasions when a full statement is desirable; they could also encourage a speaker with little to say to use up all of his or her allowance! At committee meetings convened by a government department or in a university, if a speaker strays from the point, the chairman will call attention to this. In UN bodies the chairman is less interventionist, basically because of the sovereign equality of states. (CERD's *Rules* stipulate that 'In exercising his functions as Chairman, the Chairman shall remain under the authority of the Committee.') If it is suggested to a speaker that his remarks are irrelevant, he or she will almost always find some way of asserting the opposite. Many have concluded that, when formal procedures are proposed for saving time, they eventually consume more time than they save. Informal approaches have a better chance of success.

Though the number of periodic reports awaiting consideration increased as a result of the cancellation of sessions, the backlog was soon cleared. Some other treaty bodies convene pre-sessional working parties which give each reporting state prior notice of the main issues for discussion. CERD has concluded that in its case any advantages of such a procedure would not outweigh the extra delay and the inconvenience to members (SRs 1027 & 1029). Country rapporteurs, if they wish, may send an advance list of their questions for the secretariat to transmit to the reporting state.

This chapter has been much concerned with the sequence of procedural changes that started in 1988. The arguments for change were much more than procedural. The changes in the way in which the Committee went about its business enabled it to do things that previously had been very difficult. Since 1988 members have opened up new lines of questioning—especially in connection with articles 5 and 6. One of the main arguments of this book is that states, when they acceded to the Convention, rarely appreciated what they were letting themselves in for. What many of them have been finding, because of questioning by the Committee, is that racial discrimination as defined in ICERD article 1.1 is more complex than they had realized, and that their obligations to combat it are therefore much more extensive.

## INDIVIDUAL COMMUNICATIONS

An increasingly important component of the Committee's work has been the issuing of opinions on article 14 communications. The first one to come before the Committee was *1/1984, Yilmaz-Dogan* v. *The Netherlands*. When first considered in 1984 there were doubts about its admissibility. The case received further consideration in 1985 and would have done so again in 1986 had this not been prevented by the UN's financial crisis. The facts of the matter were that Mrs Yilmaz-Dogan was a Turkish national employed by a company in the textile sector. After she had become pregnant, her employer applied to the court for permission to terminate her contract of employment, stating

When a Netherlands girl marries and has a baby, she stops working. Our foreign women workers, on the other hand, take the child to neighbours or family and at the slightest set-back disappear on sick leave under the terms of the Sickness Act. They repeat that endlessly. Since we all must do our utmost to avoid going under, we cannot afford such goings-on.

The court granted the employer's application. Mrs Yilmaz-Dogan's lawyer sought unsuccessfully to have the decision overturned, but an appeal court held that it could not be determined that the employer intended to discriminate or that his actions resulted in racial discrimination. So he turned to CERD. After the Committee had declared the communication admissible in 1987, the state party denied that there had been any violation of the Convention, or that the court had accepted the employer's reasons. It maintained that the Convention did not oblige the state to interfere with the judgments of competent judicial authorities.

CERD's opinion stated that the freedom to prosecute—

commonly known as the expediency principle—had to be applied in the light of the guarantees laid down in the Convention. It found that the petitioner's right to work under article 5(e)(i) had not been protected from racial discrimination. It asked the state to take this opinion into account and provide Mrs Yilmaz-Dogan with such relief as might be considered equitable (A/43/18, annex IV).

The second such communication (*2/1989, Demba Talib Diop* v. *France*) was from a Senegalese lawyer, married to a French woman, who had been refused membership of the bar in Nice. Was this, as the applicant claimed, a violation of his rights to work, or, since he had been obliged to return to Dakar in order to practise his profession, was there a violation of his right to family life? CERD held that the facts did not disclose any violation. It noted

that the rights protected by article 5(e) are of programmatic character, subject to progressive implementation. It is not within the Committee's mandate to see to it that these rights are established; rather, it is the Committee's task to monitor the implementation of these rights, once they have been granted on equal terms. (A/46/18, annex VIII)

The third case (*4/1991, L.K.* v. *The Netherlands*) arose after L.K. had been offered municipal housing in Utrecht. Residents of the street in question threatened that, if he were to accept the offer, they would set fire to it and damage the car that he used as a partially disabled person. He complained to the police, who investigated. The prosecutor did not register any criminal case, on the grounds that it was uncertain that there had been any offence. An appeal to a court against this decision was dismissed. CERD found that there had been a violation of the Convention. This is discussed in Chapter 9.

In the fourth case (*3/1991, Narrainen* v. *Norway*) CERD had to consider a claim that the state was in breach of article 5(a) because a juror who had been overheard making a remark prejudicial to the defendant had not been disqualified. The Committee expressed the opinion that the remark might have been considered sufficient for her to be disqualified, but that, on the basis of the information available, it was unable to conclude that a breach had occurred. It went on:

The Committee recommends to the State party that every effort should be made to prevent any form of racial bias from entering into judicial proceedings which might result in adversely affecting the administration of justice on the basis of equality and non-discrimination. Consequently the Committee recommends that in criminal cases like the one it has examined, due attention be given to the impartiality of juries, in line with the principles underlying article 5(*a*) of the Convention. (A/49/18, annex IV)

A fifth communication (*5/1994, C.P.* v. *Denmark*) was declared inadmissible in 1995.

As will be seen, CERD, like other treaty bodies, addresses states in gentle tones. They are not yet accustomed to oversight from external bodies. The number of individual communications to CERD is likely to increase and this will reinforce other changes in the character and temper of the Committee.

Under article 15, the Committee has to examine material concerning non-self-governing territories, but the UN cannot supply it with the information necessary to fulfil this duty to the standard the Committee thinks appropriate. Since 1990 it has found no need to appoint working groups and has simply reported that it once again found itself unable to fulfil its functions, owing to 'the total absence of any copies of petitions . . . [and] no valid information concerning legislative, judicial, administrative or other measures directly related to the principles and objectives of this Convention . . .' (A/64/18, para. 422). This has been repeated in later years.

## COMMUNICATING WITH STATES PARTIES

CERD may make 'suggestions and general recommendations' based on its examination of reports. In its first twenty years it made seven such recommendations, all in the form of resolutions, concerning the mandatory nature of article 4 (on two occasions), claims about the absence of racial discrimination, relations with South Africa, the need for demographic data, the reporting obligation, and educational measures. In the six years that followed the Committee agreed twelve general recommendations and gave preliminary consideration to some further proposals.

The change in temper may be illustrated by reference to a different issue arising from the same power under ICERD article 9.2. In 1989 the review *The First Twenty Years* (UN 1991*c*) was in preparation; this was an updating of a document agreed eleven years earlier (UN 1979). Mr Banton proposed an amendment to insert the text of the 1985 legal opinion referred to in Chapter 7.

Mr Aboul-Nasr cautioned that 'the statement should not be quoted out of context, in so far as it indicated that it was for the Committee to interpret the Convention'. Mr Rechetov spoke to similar effect (the whole discussion in SR 856 is of interest, and shows that some members were uneasy about mentioning the possibility that the Committee might report non-compliance by a state, although this part of the text had appeared in the earlier version of the document).

At the next session in March 1990 CERD considered a report from Finland. Mr Aboul-Nasr compared the criteria used by the government for defining an ethnic group with the apparent unanimity in the Committee that the main criterion should be self-identification and not language use. He suggested that a general recommendation might be useful. Others supported this view. Later that session Mr Wolfrum submitted a draft general recommendation on this subject, accompanied by three others on other subjects. At the next session five draft general recommendations were tabled by Mr Banton and others were proposed by Mrs Sadiq Ali, Mr Shahi, Mr Rechetov, and Mr Diaconu.

In the course of their consideration Mr Aboul-Nasr reiterated his view that general recommendations were an interpretation of the Convention and should be adopted only to clarify a genuine point of disagreement between the Committee and one or more states parties. They had sometimes worked to limit the scope of the Convention even though they were not binding on states parties (SR 969). This is not the view taken by the Human Rights Committee or the Committee on Economic, Social, and Cultural Rights in their exercise of a similar power. The latter committee has explained:

The Committee endeavours, through its general comments, to make the experience gained so far through the examination of these reports available for the benefit of all States parties in order to assist and promote their further implementation of the Covenant; to draw the attention of the States parties to insufficiencies disclosed by a large number of reports; to suggest improvements in the reporting procedures and to stimulate the activities of the States parties, the international organizations and the specialized agencies concerned in achieving progressively and effectively the full realization of the rights recognized in the Covenant. Whenever necessary, the Committee may, in the light of the experience of the States parties and of the conclusions which it has drawn therefrom, revise and update its general comments. (HRI/GEN/1/Rev. 1)

Some members of CERD (more particularly the diplomats) sympathized with Mr Aboul-Nasr's caution, but the majority took the other view. Mr van Boven observed that the General Assembly had welcomed the adoption of general recommendations. Some treaty bodies had adopted them in what might be called a 'narrative form' rather than as resolutions (SR 967). Other members of CERD agreed that there were advantages in using a narrative form. The general recommendations adopted since March 1990 have been on the identification of racial or ethnic groups; on the importance of respecting the status of the Committee's members as independent experts (since some had been put under pressure from diplomats representing other countries); on technical assistance; on reporting on non-citizens; on successor states; on the training of law-enforcement officials; on discrimination in effect; on article 4 of the Convention; on not making references in article 9 reports to situations existing in other states; on the establishment of national institutions to facilitate implementation of the Convention; on the establishment of an international tribunal to prosecute crimes against humanity; and on article 3 of the Convention. Draft general recommendations awaiting consideration or further consideration concern article 5, reference to fields of public life, effectiveness, state policies, and the acceptance of amendments to ICERD.

The main problem in connection with successor states has arisen because some of the new states that used to be part of the USSR have deposited documents making themselves parties to the Convention, but others have not yet done so. CERD has encouraged them to confirm that they continue to be bound by the obligations contracted by the predecessor state. The Czech and Slovak Republics when they were a single state were a party to the Convention, but, having split, they had to deposit new instruments of accession.

In Belgrade there is a government which claims to be still the Federal Republic of Yugoslavia. In resolution 47/1 the General Assembly decided that this government should reapply for membership of the UN under the name 'Federal Republic of Yugoslavia (Serbia and Montenegro)', which it declined to do. So when representatives of the states parties to ICERD assembled for their meeting in January 1994, a representative of the Belgrade government sat behind a nameplate for 'Yugoslavia'. Since Bosnia, Croatia, and Slovenia were by then states parties to the Convention, there were objections to a situation in which former members of that same state were present in the room as independent parties to the Convention. Belgrade could no longer represent them; it was now the capital of a different state which did not include Bosnia, Croatia, and Slovenia. (Since Belgrade had recognized the government of Slovenia and negotiated with the government of Croatia, there was little legal justification for this complaint.) Other state representatives maintained that Belgrade had violated the basic principles of the Convention. Yet the man from Belgrade was there to represent his state under the name in which it had ratified the Convention. The meeting adjourned so that delegates could seek instructions from their capitals. When it reconvened, a motion was passed by 69 to 2 with 25 abstentions, deciding that the Federal Republic of Yugoslavia (Serbia and Montegnegro) 'shall not participate in the work of the fifteenth meeting of States parties'. The second contrary vote was from the representative of the Russian Federation, who opposed the removal of any state from participation in international agreements, since this could only weaken international legal regimes. Yugoslavia continues as a state party to the Convention, even if it was barred from the 1994 meeting.

## PREVENTIVE ACTION

The UN Secretary-General's document *An Agenda for Peace* was briefly described in Chapter 3. Mr Aga Shahi and Mr de Gouttes were impressed by its significance for the Committee's work and took the lead in drafting a working paper on early warning and urgent procedures (A/48/18, annex III). Two members of the Committee (Mr Song and Mr Diaconu) were unable to join the consensus in favour of this document, the main stumbling block being the suggestion that on occasion CERD might recommend to the Secretary-General that a situation be brought to the attention of the Security Council. The Committee's action in this connection was subsequently commended by the General Assembly. Since the Committee believes that preventive action should receive priority in its work, it has moved this item to the head of its agenda for sessions and altered the sequence of chapters in its annual report.

The working paper on prevention provided a basis for a new initiative in the same year, described in the part of the annual report entitled 'Federal Republic of Yugoslavia (Serbia and Montenegro)', para. 546:

Taking into account the wish expressed by the representative of the Government and the need to promote a dialogue between the Albanians in Kosovo and the Government, the Committee offered its good offices in the form of a mission of its members. The purpose of the mission would be to help promote a dialogue for a peaceful solution of issues concerning respect for human rights in Kosovo, in particular the elimination of all forms of racial discrimination and, wherever possible, to help parties concerned to arrive at such a solution. It was understood that such a mission should have every opportunity to inform itself of the situation directly, including full discussion with central and local authorities, as well as with individuals and organizations. In that connection, no one should be victimized for, or in any way have their rights or security impaired as a result of, cooperating with the mission.

A Good Offices Mission, comprised by Mr Ahmadu, Mr Rechetov, and Mr Wolfrum, visited Kosovo in November 1993. The continuation of the Mission was then called into question by the action of the states parties two months later in excluding the representative of the Yugoslav government from their meeting; the government objected to what it regarded as unequal treatment. Believing that it has a duty to the people intended to be protected by the Convention, the Committee has tried to persevere with its good offices.

The Committee also offered the services of one of its members to undertake a mission to Croatia under the advisory services and technical assistance programme (A/48/18, paras. 487, 507). Mr Yutzis travelled there and a report on his mission was received at CERD's forty-fifth session. In 1995, following the request of the state, Mr Yutzis was designated to undertake a mission to Guatemala to advise on implementation of the Convention.

In March 1994, after hearing about current circumstances in Rwanda and Burundi, CERD adopted its general recommendation XVIII (already mentioned), in which, *inter alia*, it said that, after having examined various reports submitted by states parties to the ICERD, it

Considers it urgent to establish an international tribunal with general jurisdiction to prosecute genocide, crimes against humanity, including murder, extermination, enslavement, deportation, imprisonment, torture, rape, persecutions on political, racial and religious grounds and other inhumane acts directed against any civilian population and grave breaches of the Geneva Conventions of 1949, and the Additional Protocols thereto . . .

Also in March 1994, the Committee responded to reports of the shooting of worshippers in the Abraham Mosque in Hebron on 25 February 1994 by adopting a proposal from Mr Aboul-Nasr to call for further information from the government of Israel 'on measures taken to guarantee the safety and protection of the Palestinian civilians in the occupied Palestinian territory'. This action evoked a protest from 'United Nations Watch' that Israel was being 'put in the dock . . . accused under the same line item as countries such as Rwanda and Burundi'. Israel's response is described in Chapter 12. For present purposes it is important to note that the decision about Hebron opened the door to other resolutions upon possibly similar events. It was as a result of a discussion on this point that CERD took its decision 3(45) on Racist Acts of Terrorism, condemning the attacks on Jewish organizations in Buenos Aires on 18 July and in London on 26 and 27 July 1994; it invited the governments of Argentina and the UK to expedite their periodic reports, providing pertinent information on measures they have taken in fulfilment of the Convention.

If such action was appropriate in these cases, why not also in respect of the 1993 uprising in Chiapas, Mexico, and the murders of foreigners in Algeria and Egypt? Proposals were advanced in 1994 to call for further information from Mexico and to urge the government of Algeria 'to continue to do its utmost to guarantee the safety of all'. On the one hand, it was argued that the Committee must treat all reports of ethnic conflict equally, and that a request for information was not an accusation. On the other hand, it was contended that the conflict in Chiapas was political, not ethnic, that no useful purpose was served by such decisions, and that the Committee should not react like a fire brigade. Divisions of opinion within the Committee at that time followed regional lines, but sentiments had changed by the next session in spring 1995 because of events in Chechnya. The Committee agreed, without a vote, to express alarm over the disproportionate use of force in Chechnya and to request the government of the Russian Federation to expedite its overdue periodic reports so as to permit consideration of the situation in Chechnya at the following session. Was this within its competence? The government was entitled to act against an attempted secession, so was not this a political matter? The Committee decided that only when it had received information from a government would it be in a position to consider whether a conflict had an ethnic dimension. For similar reasons it requested the government of Algeria to expedite its overdue periodic reports, and asked Mexico to submit further information on the situation in Chiapas in time for consideration together with its recently submitted periodic reports. It asked the government of the Former Yugoslav Republic of Macedonia to expedite its initial report in order to facilitate consideration at the same session.

The Committee's decision on Chechnya called for 'an immediate cessation of the fighting and for a dialogue to achieve a peaceful solution while respecting the territorial integrity and the constitution of the Russian Federation'. CERD did not wish to encourage any bid for secession, and, to make this clear to others, started to draft a decision on this subject. A proposal prepared by Mr Wolfrum attracted support but had not been adopted by the end of the forty-sixth session. It noted that the right to self-determination had internal and external aspects. According to the former, all peoples have the right freely to determine their political status and freely to pursue their economic, social, and cultural development. According to the latter, all peoples have the right freely to determine their place in the international community. The draft went on:

The Committee emphasized that, in accordance with the Declaration of the General Assembly on Friendly Relations and Cooperation among States, none of its actions shall be construed as authorizing or encouraging any action which would dismember or impair, totally or in part, the territorial integrity or political unity of sovereign independent states conducting themselves in compliance with the principle of equal right and self-determination of peoples and possessed of a government representing the whole people belonging to the territory without distinction as to race, creed or colour. In the view of the Committee international law has not recognized a right of peoples to unilaterally declare secession from a state. The Committee, in this respect, follows the principles as expressed in the *Agenda for Peace* (paras 17 *et seq.*), namely that any fragmentation of States would be detrimental to the protection of human rights as well as to the preservation of peace and security. This does not, however, exclude the possibility of arrangements reached by free agreement of all parties concerned.

A further innovation was the holding, in 1995, of discussions with two special rapporteurs appointed by the Commission on Human Rights: Mr Mazowiecki, the special rapporteur on the former Yugoslavia, and Mr Glélé-Ahanhanzo, the special rapporteur on racism. Mr Mazowiecki advised the Committee against following the reasoning of those who say that they cannot live in a pluralistic society, but CERD had already gone on record (A/48/18, paras. 468–9) as 'concerned that partition along ethnic lines in Bosnia and Herzegovina could encourage groups elsewhere who were unwilling to respect the territorial integrity of States. The Committee strongly supported the principle of multi-ethnic societies . . .'. If secession is to be discouraged, support for this principle is essential.

As already mentioned in Chapter 3, the Commission on Human Rights decided in 1993, on the recommendation of its Sub-Commission, to appoint a special rapporteur on contemporary forms of racism. Neither body consulted with CERD over this proposal, nor was proper consideration given to any possible overlap of functions. In this there was a parallel in the existence, side-by-side, of the Committee Against Torture, monitoring a convention, and the special rapporteur on torture. One rationale for such an arrangement would be for the special rapporteur to concentrate upon states which had not acceded to, or reported to, the relevant convention. Such seems not to have been the motivation behind the appointment of a special rapporteur on racism. In its resolution 1993/20 (preambular paragraphs 8 and 10) the Commission indicated that priority should be attached to manifestations of racism and xenophobia in developed countries and to their consequences for migrant workers and other vulnerable groups.

Another matter which has appeared as a regular item on the Committee's agenda is the Decade, first, second, or third, for Action to Combat Racism and Racial Discrimination. When the first Decade was conceived, the focus was on apartheid and on white discrimination against blacks. By 1993 the problems of South Africa were changing; ethnic violence in the former Yugoslavia and former parts of the USSR was seizing the headlines. CERD has supported the view that the Third Decade should be broadly conceived to cover all forms of ethnic as well as racial discrimination and has lent its support to proposals for the better development of social indicators designed to measure trends in this field. As part of the Second Decade, CERD produced the booklet *The First Twenty Years* (UN 1991c) about its own history; it commented upon the *Global Compilation of National Legislation Against Racial Discrimination* (UN 1991*b*), and upon a draft model statute for such legislation.

The work of the other treaty bodies has generated ideas that could have a bearing on CERD's work, but Committee members are conscious that some of these other bodies have to address very different problems. Action against racial discrimination requires both long-term policies and an ability to respond quickly to new developments, so they wish to retain the two-year reporting interval (with the understanding that states will, if circumstances permit, submit only brief updating reports on intermediate occasions) and have decided against the appointment of pre-sessional working parties to prepare the ground for the consideration of state reports. (For a view of the reporting process from the standpoint of the state party, see P. Thompson 1994.)

The new phase in the Committee's activities described in this chapter has been made possible because members can now trust one another to a greater degree than seems previously to have been practicable. Progress has been aided by the adoption of collective opinions on state reports, the use of country rapporteurs, the reviews of implementation in states whose reports are overdue, the agreement on permissible sources, the use of the power to request further information, the early warning and preventive measures, and the adoption of some new-style general recommendations.

The Convention can be better implemented when members of the Committee receive reliable information from international NGOs or organizations in the country concerned. The NGOs can supply members with information additional to that in the state reports. Publicity about CERD's reception of these reports can be used by NGOs to press states for better implementation measures. Until the 1990s it was unusual for NGOs to submit material for the use of Committee members; they have had to send it to the members as individuals, and the UN secretariat can play no part in the process. The year 1993 saw a major change with the establishment of the Anti-Racism Information Service (ARIS). This is an international NGO which serves a liaison function, helping national and other NGOs send in information, preparing independent commentaries on state reports, distributing these, and copying to interested parties the concluding observations on implementation of the Convention in particular states. Among the commentaries received from other bodies, special mention is due to those prepared by national sections of the International Commission of Jurists.

In 1993, for the first time, some members of the Committee held an informal meeting with representatives of an NGO in the country due for consideration on the following day. This concerned a situation where there was significant tension between the government of the state and an ethnic group which constituted the great majority of the population in the region in question, that is, the ethnic Albanians in Kosovo.

CERD has long recognized the importance of press publicity to its work. One regret over the transfer of meetings from New York to Geneva was that press coverage was better in New York. The Committee has held press conferences in Geneva but they have not attracted great attention. Occasionally the press in a particular state gets to hear that a report is to be considered and sends a representative to sit in the public benches and write something for publication in the journal concerned. The Committee has also taken steps to see that the texts of its concluding observations are made available to the press as soon as possible.

A comparison of present practice in CERD with that described in two articles on practice up to 1985 (Gomez del Prado 1985; Mahalic and Mahalic 1987) will surely help substantiate the claim made at the beginning of this chapter that in the years 1988–93 CERD was able to develop its work more rapidly than in the period 1979–87. More effective implementation has been made possible by the reduction in the political tensions outside the Committee; by its having more time to conduct its business; by its greater continuity of membership; and by its involvement in a structure of seven treaty bodies backed by pressure in the General Assembly for implementation of all the human-rights instruments.

The threat to CERD's work posed by the failure of states to meet their financial obligations has not yet disappeared, but it was eased by the decision of the states parties at their fourteenth meeting in 1992 to adopt two amendments to the Convention. Article 8 is amended in paragraph 6 to read: 'The Secretary-General of the United Nations shall provide the necessary staff and facilities for the effective performance of the functions of the Committee under the Convention', and in paragraph 7: 'The members of the Committee established under the present Convention shall, with the approval of the General Assembly, receive emoluments from United Nations resources on such terms and conditions as the General Assembly may decide.' In the General Assembly this addition to the UN budget was approved without a vote, though Japan and the USA indicated their opposition on the grounds that 'the user should pay' (A/C.3/46/SR 55). The amendments will enter into force when accepted by a two-thirds majority of states parties. By 31 July 1995 17 notifications of acceptance had been received from 143 states parties.

## REGIONAL VARIATIONS IN DIALOGUE

The next four chapters review the Committee's dialogue with states in the four regional Groups used for this book. They are based in part upon figures that the author started to keep in 1987 on the times taken for different phases in the consideration of states' reports. The figures are complete from the year 1990 onwards, but data are missing for many of the states whose reports were examined in 1987, and for some from the years 1988 and 1989. Tables 2–5 (which are gathered together at the end of this chapter) nevertheless serve to give an indication of how the Committee's time was utilized during this period, and provide an objective framework for discussing the nature of the dialogue. As can be seen from column 2 in each table, some states submit much longer reports than others. Column 6 lists the numbers of members taking part in the discussion. The number is higher when the reporting state has provided much interesting material, and when members are concerned about developments in the state in question. Sometimes consideration of a report raises a general issue affecting other states, or a procedural issue of concern to Committee members, and there may then be a discussion which has little relation to the report of the state which is formally under consideration at the time. For example, a larger number of members spoke on the report of Barbados listed in Table 3 because it gave rise to a discussion of what the Committee should do when a state was unable to send a representative to present its report. It can also be seen that sometimes state representatives utilize the occasion to talk at disproportionate length (e.g. Table 4 shows that the diplomat presenting Senegal's eighth report spoke for nine times as long as all the Committee members). When the fifth and sixth reports of Bangladesh were considered, the state representative chose to speak only briefly because he was offended by remarks made by two Committee members (see A/47/18, footnote to para. 126). Some variations in the use of time call for comment. The brevity of the consideration of the tenth report of Belarus can be attributed to its having followed immediately after a long consideration of the corresponding report from the USSR. The much greater length of time devoted to the eleventh and twelfth reports of the Holy See by comparison with the preceding report from that state can be related to the Committee's timetable. Because another state had requested a delay before its representative met the Committee, a space opened up in the timetable and the consideration of this report was allowed to continue for longer than would otherwise have been the case. The state representatives were pleased that their report could receive this extra attention. The total time given to a report varies very greatly, reflecting both the seriousness of the situation in the country concerned (e.g. Yugoslavia's response to a request for additional information, the tenth report of Iraq), the length of the report (e.g. the twelfth report of the UK and the eleventh and twelfth reports of Germany), and the pressure on the Committee's agenda. Since other Committee business sometimes intrudes during consideration of a report, the figure in the final column may exceed the sums of columns 3, 4, and 6.

A comparison of the four tables shows, firstly, that, while there is great variation in the length of state reports (from 2 to 104 pages), there is little variation between the regions in the average length of these reports. Secondly, that proportionately more African states were subject to the review procedure for states seriously overdue in reporting. Thirdly, relatively more European and relatively fewer American reports gave rise to long discussion in the Committee.

In the chapters that follow it has to be remembered that the dialogue is between the Committee and the government of the reporting state. The state representative can update and explain features of the report, but he or she is not empowered to negotiate in any way. States may now wish that in 1965 they had pressed for formulations in the Convention that would, in their eyes, be more appropriate to their present circumstances, but they are bound by the obligations they accepted earlier. Members of the Committee have considerable discretion as to the points on which they choose to concentrate, but they have to bear in mind state susceptibilities if they seek to persuade a government to address an issue that is difficult for it. A formal consideration of a state report in Geneva is therefore a very special sort of dialogue.

The character of the dialogue between the Committee and the reporting state is affected by the extent to which the state feels vulnerable to criticism. Criticism may originate from minorities within the state or from other quarters, such as neighbouring states which sympathize with the groups that complain. The more a question involves one state's relations with other states, or a state's international standing, the more it is seen as a matter of foreign rather than domestic policy and the more contentious it becomes. As has already been illustrated, anything which touches upon the relations between Jews and Palestinians, or between Israel and many of the Arab states, is likely to be seen in highly political terms. The Committee can exert relatively little influence upon states in which there is armed conflict, states subject to military rule, and states which have difficulty remaining viable. Its influence is limited when dealing with situations in which an ethnic minority is seen as supported by a neighbouring state. Similar considerations arise when a neighbouring state is suspected of encouraging malcontents. Political considerations can also influence the dialogue in the case of states which are criticized for failing to respect human rights generally, even if the ethnic dimension to the tensions is questionable.

Examination of state compliance with the Convention's legal requirements can be more dispassionate in the dialogue with most of the states of North and South America, Western Europe, those with a relatively homogeneous population (like Poland and Korea), and some of those of North Africa and Asia (such as Australia, India, New Zealand, Pakistan, and the Philippines). Nevertheless, when internal tensions result in ethnic disorders, or scandals are publicized in the world media, they reflect upon national reputation and become matters of foreign as well as domestic policy. In similar fashion, an assertion that a state is ignoring one of its obligations can be regarded as hurtful.

From what state representatives said in the 1965 General Assembly debate, and from the evidence discussed in Chapter 6, it may be inferred that most of the states that acceded to ICERD saw racial discrimination as a problem for states other than their own. The issues it raised were therefore matters for their foreign policy and it was appropriate for them to elect diplomats to membership of CERD. Such states, if they do not have to respond to criticism, may see the presentation of a report to CERD as a public-relations opportunity; they seek to explain to others the circumstances that prevail in their country and to improve Committee members' understanding of their countries achievements and difficulties. Other states may be more defensive.

In reading the discussion of the Committee's dialogue with states in the four chapters that follow, it may be helpful to bear in mind two tentative generalizations. First, that CERD can be most influential in circumstances in which it is possible for governments to act in ways that will prevent racial tensions escalating into open conflict. Once conflict has broken out only remedial action may be effective. This has to be the concern of the UN political organs, notably the Commission on Human Rights and the Security Council. Secondly, CERD's dialogue with a state is more likely to lead to improved implementation of the Convention when the reporting state sees the issues as matters of domestic policy. The concluding chapter of the book will maintain that the process of dialogue would be more effective if the Committee received more support from the states parties as a collectivity.

TABLE 2. *Dialogue with selected European states*

| State | Report | | State's report introduction (mins.) | Committee | | State's report reply (mins.) | Total (mins.) |
|---|---|---|---|---|---|---|---|
| | No. | pp. | | Mins. | No. of speakers | | |
| Austria | 7/8 | 13 | 3 | 25 | 7 | 34 | 62 |
| Belarus | 9/10 | 3 | 2 | 57 | 8 | 70 | 129 |
| | 10 | 9 | 11 | 13 | 1 | 13 | 37 |
| Belgium | 11/13 | 16 | 16 | 196 | 16 | 59 | 271 |
| Bosnia and Herzegovina | 5/8 | 46 | 21 | 106 | 13 | 116 | 243 |
| | FI | 6 | | 168 | 10 | | 168 |
| | FI | 7 | 16 | 203 | 15 | 27 | 246 |
| Bulgaria | 9/11 | 20 | 40 | 170 | 12 | 140 | 362 |
| Croatia | FI | 42 | 22 | 83 | 7 | 60 | 165 |
| | FI | 19 | 40 | 153 | 11 | 114 | 307 |
| Czech and Slovak Republic | 10 | 4 | 1 | 58 | 10 | 46 | 105 |
| Denmark | 8,9 | 10,5 | 9 | 150 | 13 | 65 | 224 |
| Finland | 9,10 | 12,7 | 8 | 75 | 10 | 20 | 103 |
| France | 9/11 | 20 | 56 | 213 | 11 | 81 | 350 |
| FRG | 9,10 | 11,15 | 38 | 78 | 9 | 42 | 158 |
| | 11/12 | 51 | 32 | 248 | 13 | 73 | 353 |
| Greece | 8/11 | 10 | 18 | 71 | 10 | 38 | 127 |
| Holy See | 10 | 5 | 14 | 37 | 5 | 44 | 95 |
| | 11/12 | 3 | 30 | 163 | 14 | 58 | 261 |

| | | | | | | | |
|---|---|---|---|---|---|---|---|
| Hungary | 9 | 12 | 15 | 115 | 11 | 90 | 231 |
| | 10 | 16 | 12 | 76 | 11 | 51 | 139 |
| Iceland | 10/12,13 | 17,3 | 17 | 57 | 10 | 32 | 108 |
| Italy | 5/6,7 | 10,8 | 16 | 51 | 6 | 53 | 122 |
| | 8/9 | 20 | 31 | 191 | 11 | 104 | 329 |
| Luxembourg | 5 | 9,7 | 2 | 18 | 6 | 16 | 36 |
| | 6/7,8 | 12 | 17 | 109 | 10 | 28 | 154 |
| Malta | 8/9 | 7 | 4 | 45 | 8 | 8 | 65 |
| Netherlands | 8,9 | 24,13 | 16 | 156 | 13 | 89 | 261 |
| Norway | 8,9 | 19,12 | 4 | 30 | 7 | 33 | 67 |
| | 10/11 | 14 | 10 | 186 | 14 | 56 | 252 |
| Poland | 9 | 13 | 13 | 35 | 8 | 44 | 92 |
| | 10/12 | 8 | 10 | 90 | 7 | 75 | 175 |
| Portugal | 2 | 33 | 17 | 59 | 9 | 38 | 114 |
| | 3/4 | 38 | 16 | 97 | 9 | 73 | 195 |
| | 7/8 | 16 | 15 | 88 | 11 | 34 | 137 |
| Romania | 9/11 | 30 | 20 | 158 | 14 | 126 | 306 |
| Russia/USSR | 10,11 | 14,18 | 22 | 120 | 12 | 94 | 236 |
| Spain | 9 | 21 | 13 | 27 | 7 | 30 | 70 |
| | 10/12 | 4 | 15 | 197 | 11 | 154 | 368 |
| Sweden | 8,9 | 28,3 | 24 | 135 | 12 | 51 | 210 |
| | 10 | 21 | 13 | 134 | 11 | 73 | 231 |
| | 11 | 13 | 10 | 177 | 13 | 40 | 227 |
| Ukraine | 9 | 32 | 10 | 84 | 12 | 45 | 151 |
| | 10 | 14 | 37 | 56 | 9 | 62 | 164 |
| | 11,12 | 9,31 | 44 | 145 | 10 | 109 | 298 |

TABLE 2. *(cont.)*

| State | Report No. | Report pp. | State's report introduction (mins.) | Committee Mins. | Committee No. of speakers | State's report reply (mins.) | Total (mins.) |
|---|---|---|---|---|---|---|---|
| UK | 9 | 39 | 13 | 177 | 14 | 30 | 220 |
| | 10,11 | 61,29 | 14 | 102 | 10 | 97 | 223 |
| | 12 | 104 | 30 | 337 | 16 | 67 | 434 |
| Yugoslavia | 9/10 | 4 | 27 | 65 | 8 | 86 | 178 |
| | FI | 17 | 31 | 379 | 15 | 152 | 562 |
| | FI | 29 | 0 | 122 | 14 | 0 | 122 |

*Note:* Column 1 lists the number of the state's report. If two separate reports were considered together, they are listed thus: 6,7. If the state has combined two or more periodic reports in a single document, this is listed thus: 6/7. FI indicates that the report was in response to the Committee's request for further information. R indicates a review conducted because a state's periodic report was seriously overdue. Occasions on which no state representative was present can be identified by the absence of figures from columns 3 and 6.

TABLE 3. *Dialogue with selected American states*

| State | Report | | State's report introduction (mins.) | Committee | | State's report reply (mins.) | Total (mins.) |
|---|---|---|---|---|---|---|---|
| | No. | pp. | | Mins. | No. of speakers | | |
| Argentina | 10 | 15 | 18 | 91 | 7 | 70 | 188 |
| Bahamas | R | | | 16 | 3 | | 16 |
| Barbados | 7 | 5 | 0 | 81 | 11 | | 81 |
| | R | | | 16 | 2 | | 16 |
| Canada | 9,10 | 39,23 | 89 | 166 | 13 | 98 | 367 |
| | 11,12 | 14,57 | 24 | 192 | 11 | 84 | 300 |
| Chile | 8 | 20 | 23 | 45 | 3 | 17 | 85 |
| | 9/10 | 15 | 14 | 68 | 7 | 30 | 112 |
| Colombia | 3,4 | 72,30 | 18 | 63 | 6 | 59 | 140 |
| | 5 | 27 | 25 | 88 | 8 | 29 | 184 |
| Costa Rica | 8,9 | 3,3 | 13 | 55 | 11 | 17 | 96 |
| | 10/11 | 45 | 19 | 79 | 8 | 70 | 168 |
| Cuba | 8 | 18 | 20 | 23 | 4 | 57 | 94 |
| | 9 | 15 | 9 | 57 | 10 | 51 | 129 |
| Dominican Republic | 1/3 | 4 | 1 | 16 | 5 | 0 | 17 |
| Ecuador | 9/10 | 7 | 17 | 82 | 9 | 40 | 135 |
| | 11,12 | 17,23 | 9 | 190 | 14 | 33 | 232 |
| El Salvador | R | | | 27 | 6 | | 27 |
| Guatemala | 3/8 | 12 | 47 | 162 | 13 | 35 | 244 |
| | 2/6 | 127 | 16 | 120 | 8 | 57 | 198 |

TABLE 3. *(cont.)*

| State | Report | | State's report introduction (mins.) | Committee | | State's report reply (mins.) | Total (mins.) |
|---|---|---|---|---|---|---|---|
| | No. | pp. | | Mins. | No. of speakers | | |
| Haiti | 7,8/9 | 13,13 | | 15 | 3 | | 15 |
| Jamaica | R | | 5 | 35 | 5 | 9 | 49 |
| Mexico | 7/8 | 38 | 14 | 99 | 9 | 51 | 164 |
| Nicaragua | 9/10 | 66 | 44 | 234 | 13 | 92 | 370 |
| Peru | 5/9 | 19 | 50 | 182 | 12 | 91 | 223 |
| | 10/12 | 26 | 25 | 179 | 11 | 77 | 281 |
| St Vincent | R | | | 1 | 1 | | 1 |
| Trinidad | 7/10 | 9 | 4 | 100 | 11 | 6 | 110 |
| Uruguay | 8/11 | 4 | 17 | 52 | 7 | 20 | 96 |
| Venezuela | R | | 8 | 7 | 7 | 0 | 15 |

*Note*: For explanation of columns, see Table 2.

TABLE 4. *Dialogue with selected African states*

| State | Report | | State's report introduction (mins.) | Committee | | State's report reply (mins.) | Total (mins.) |
| --- | --- | --- | --- | --- | --- | --- | --- |
| | No. | pp. | | Mins. | No. of speakers | | |
| Algeria | 8 | 34 | 18 | 56 | 10 | 47 | 131 |
| | 9/10 | 52 | 11 | 145 | 10 | 79 | 235 |
| | FI | | 13 | 79 | 10 | 21 | 130 |
| Botswana | R | | | 7 | 2 | | 7 |
| Burkina Faso | R | | | 12 | 1 | | 12 |
| Burundi | 3/5 | 4 | 22 | 49 | 5 | 34 | 105 |
| | 6 | 8 | 29 | 39 | 5 | 39 | 113 |
| | FI | | 6 | 194 | 13 | 23 | 223 |
| | FI | | | 141 | 14 | | 141 |
| | FI | | | 66 | 4 | | 66 |
| Cameroon | 7 | 19 | | 52 | 11 | | 52 |
| | 8/9 | 11 | 37 | 51 | 5 | 51 | 149 |
| Cape Verde | R | | | 14 | 2 | | 14 |
| Central African Republic | R | | | 35 | 6 | | 35 |
| Chad | R | | | 35 | 6 | | 35 |
| | 4 | 5 | 34 | 34 | 4 | 13 | 81 |
| | R | | | 27 | 2 | | 27 |
| Côte d'Ivoire | 5/9 | 3 | 51 | 71 | 6 | 23 | 149 |
| | R | | 14 | 28 | 3 | 18 | 63 |

TABLE 4. *(cont.)*

| State | Report | | State's report introduction (mins.) | Committee | | State's report reply (mins.) | Total (mins.) |
|---|---|---|---|---|---|---|---|
| | No. | pp. | | Mins. | No. of speakers | | |
| Egypt | 8/9,10 | 17,14 | 5 | 58 | 9 | 29 | 102 |
| | 11/12 | 30 | 20 | 162 | 13 | 64 | 246 |
| Ethiopia | 6 | 7 | 9 | 17 | 6 | 32 | 58 |
| Gabon | R | | | 20 | 6 | | 20 |
| Gambia | R | | | 5 | 1 | | 5 |
| Ghana | 9 | 3 | 10 | 50 | 11 | 10 | 70 |
| | 10/11 | 6 | 17 | 52 | 9 | 20 | 89 |
| Guinea | R | | | 13 | 3 | | 13 |
| Lesotho | R | | | 41 | 11 | | 41 |
| Libyan Arab Jamahiriya | 6/10 | 6 | 8 | 20 | 2 | 12 | 40 |
| Madagascar | R | | | 61 | 10 | | 61 |
| Mali | R | | | 19 | 6 | | 19 |
| Mauritius | R | | | 11 | 3 | | 11 |
| Morocco | 8 | 23 | 10 | 54 | 12 | 32 | 96 |
| | 9/11 | 11 | 7 | 224 | 13 | 103 | 334 |
| Mozambique | R | | | 29 | 4 | | 29 |
| Niger | 8/10 | 14 | | 30 | 5 | | 30 |
| Nigeria | 9 | 7 | 15 | 76 | 10 | 22 | 113 |
| | 10/12 | 8 | 15 | 104 | 12 | 82 | 211 |
| | 13,FI | 9,4 | 28 | 165 | 13 | 50 | 243 |

| | | | | | | | |
|---|---|---|---|---|---|---|---|
| Rwanda | 6,7 | 10,16 | 15 | 44 | 9 | 60 | 119 |
| | FI | | 4 | 26 | 5 | 25 | 55 |
| Senegal | 8 | 5 | 45 | 11 | 3 | 44 | 100 |
| | 9/10 | 22 | 10 | 85 | 11 | 84 | 179 |
| Sierra Leone | R | | | 11 | 5 | | 11 |
| | R | | | 32 | 8 | | 32 |
| Somalia | R | | | 44 | 9 | | 44 |
| | R | | | 45 | 10 | | 45 |
| Sudan | 8 | 15 | 4 | 182 | 14 | 160 | 346 |
| | FI | 9 | 24 | 158 | 12 | 129 | 311 |
| Swaziland | R | | | 33 | 11 | | 33 |
| Togo | R | | | 29 | 6 | | 29 |
| Tunisia | 9/12 | 51 | 15 | 173 | 14 | 57 | 245 |
| Uganda | R | | | 60 | 6 | | 60 |
| United Republic of Tanzania | R | | | 74 | 10 | 55 | 135 |
| Zaire | R | | | 26 | 6 | | 26 |
| Zambia | 7/11 | 6 | 17 | 77 | 8 | 29 | 123 |

*Note:* For explanation of columns, see Table 2.

TABLE 5. *Dialogue with selected Asian states*

| State | Report | | State's report introduction (mins.) | Committee | | State's report reply (mins.) | Total (mins.) |
|---|---|---|---|---|---|---|---|
| | No. | pp. | | Mins. | No. of speakers | | |
| Afghanistan | R | | | 32 | 6 | | 32 |
| Australia | 6,7/8 | 20,59 | 40 | 191 | 13 | 155 | 399 |
| | 9 | 51 | 72 | 168 | 16 | 77 | 317 |
| Bangladesh | 2/4 | 3 | 10 | 55 | 7 | 48 | 113 |
| | 5/6 | 16 | 7 | 106 | 14 | 2 | 115 |
| China | 3,4 | 17,13 | 16 | 184 | 12 | 92 | 292 |
| Cyprus | 9/10 | 21 | 16 | 42 | 8 | 23 | 81 |
| | 11/13 | 15 | 16 | 117 | 13 | 44 | 182 |
| Fiji | R | | | 75 | 9 | | 75 |
| India | 8/9 | 21 | 56 | 108 | 13 | 80 | 244 |
| Iran | 9/12 | 3 | 11 | 189 | 13 | 74 | 274 |
| Iraq | 9,10 | 13,20 | 10 | 125 | 10 | 91 | 226 |
| Israel | 5/6 | 13 | 18 | 198 | 14 | 44 | 260 |
| | FI | | | 170 | 11 | | 170 |
| Jordan | 6,7/8 | 8,29 | 14 | 57 | 11 | 21 | 92 |
| Korea | 5,6 | 7,8 | 2 | 37 | 6 | 24 | 63 |
| | 7 | 8 | 10 | 97 | 12 | 18 | 125 |
| Kuwait | 9 | 7 | 6 | 60 | 9 | 60 | 129 |
| | 10/12 | 21 | 23 | 135 | 10 | 56 | 214 |
| Lao People's Democratic Republic | R | | | 20 | 2 | | 20 |

|  | | | | | | | |
|---|---|---|---|---|---|---|---|
| Lebanon | R | | | 95 | 12 | | 95 |
| Maldives | 1/2 | 2 | | 10 | 1 | | 10 |
| | 3/4 | 2 | | 29 | 5 | | 29 |
| Mongolia | 9,10 | 9,6 | 12 | 44 | 7 | 31 | 84 |
| New Zealand | 8/9 | 60 | 15 | 88 | 5 | 47 | 150 |
| | 10/11 | 47 | 34 | 130 | 11 | 113 | 277 |
| Pakistan | 9 | 11 | 8 | 69 | 10 | 24 | 101 |
| Papua New Guinea | R | | | 25 | 3 | | 25 |
| | FI | | | 25 | 6 | | 25 |
| | FI | | | 49 | 7 | | 49 |
| | FI | | | 31 | 6 | | 31 |
| Philippines | 8/10 | 24 | 15 | 65 | 9 | 89 | 169 |
| Qatar | 5/6,7 | 18,6 | 34 | 41 | 6 | 9 | 84 |
| | 8 | 17 | 22 | 112 | 12 | 8 | 142 |
| Solomon Islands | R | | | 17 | 3 | | 17 |
| Sri Lanka | 3/6 | 13 | 14 | 146 | 9 | 124 | 284 |
| Syrian Arab Republic | 9/11 | 5 | 8 | 22 | 3 | 33 | 63 |
| Tonga | 8 | 4 | | 30 | 4 | | 30 |
| | 9/10 | 5 | | 16 | 2 | | 16 |
| United Arab Emirates | 6 | 14 | | 22 | 8 | | 22 |
| | R | | | | 15 | 1 | 15 |
| Viet Nam | 7/10 | 7 | 16 | 69 | 9 | 29 | 114 |
| | R | | 20 | 54 | 8 | 2 | 76 |
| Yemen | 2/5 | 14 | 18 | 130 | 10 | 95 | 243 |
| | 8/9 | 23,17 | 17 | 53 | 5 | 48 | 118 |

*Note:* For explanation of columns, see Table 2.

# 9

# Dialogue with European States

IN the 1950s and sixties the states of the East and West European blocs were profoundly suspicious of one another and, given the high spending on the arms race, they had cause for alarm. It may be conjectured that their reasons for ratifying or acceding to the Convention reflected these and other international tensions. Representatives of the Eastern states were accustomed to maintaining that the policies initiated by the USSR had solved 'the national problem' and eliminated racial discrimination, but they feared the possible revival of nazi ideologies in the West and were reluctant to confer powers upon international bodies lest this work to their disadvantage. To further their interests in international politics they sought to increase their influence with the recently decolonized states, and campaigning against apartheid gave them great opportunities. They ratified early to gain maximum influence in the new enterprise.

The states of Western Europe had already come together in the Council of Europe and had drawn up, in 1950, the European Convention on Human Rights and Fundamental Freedoms. This was testimony to their belief that the development of international human-rights law was important to future peace throughout the world. Most of them did not recognize that within their own societies there was any racial discrimination, or even any potential for it. Contemplating the UN convention, they had to calculate the balance of advantage to themselves. Ratification would give their critics opportunities to criticize their policies, but, since the Convention was coming into force and the treaty body was being established, it was to their advantage to take part in the process and use what influence they could acquire to see that the Convention was developed in the kinds of way they thought desirable. Indeed, it is notable that the UN official who oversaw the drafting of the Convention should have concluded his account of that process by remarking that it was in the interest of the Western Powers to become full participants, because 'Without such participation, there is the danger of the Committee on the Elimination of Racial Discrimination becoming an instrument for manoeuvers of one camp against the other, since the Committee will be a creation of the States Parties and not a subsidiary organ of the UN' (Schwelb 1966: 1058).

By 1983 all the European states admitted to membership of the UN had acceded to the Convention except Albania and Ireland (Albania acceded in 1994, by which time Ireland had decided to do likewise). Some states had legislated against racial discrimination before the Convention came into effect and might well have done so in any case, but others chose to legislate because they intended to ratify. State action in this field has usually been impelled by both internal and external pressure. Internally, groups within the majority population have sometimes been shocked by evidence of discrimination as incompatible with the moral standards they set for their countries. Externally, there have been diplomatic and moral reasons for accepting the obligations detailed in human-rights conventions. It is relatively easy to list those obligations and to note what laws obtain in states, but this sheds no light upon why compliance is almost always less than perfect. It is often difficult to find reasons why a state should have met certain obligations but not others; the answers may lie in the institutions of the state in question and in the political circumstances of particular periods.

Consider, for example, why it was that the UK introduced com-prehensive legislation earlier than other West European states. The political contexts of the three Acts of 1965, 1968, and 1976 were straightforward. The Labour government that assumed office in 1964 wished to maintain restrictions on immigration from countries of the New Commonwealth (primarily the West Indies and South Asia). They could satisfy their supporters only by making this part of a package; this had to provide protections for immigrants who were already settled in order to promote their inte-gration into the majority society. The protections enacted in 1965 were very limited. The man appointed to head the agency respon-sible for implementing them accepted the post only on condition that they would be reviewed after three years. An experimental study was then conducted which convincingly demonstrated that the incidence of racial discrimination in employment, housing, and the provision of services was far more extensive than anyone had believed. The findings shocked public opinion and created an atmosphere in which it was possible for the 1968 Act to extend the protections. Then in 1975 parliament passed an Act against discrimination on grounds of sex. The importance of the female vote was such that no party could oppose it. The following year a revised Act against racial discrimination was introduced in terms paralleling the Act against sex discrimination. Some Conservative members of parliament disliked it but nevertheless hesitated to oppose something so similar to the law they had enacted the previous year. This suggests that anyone seeking to secure the passage of reforming legislation needs to choose an opportune moment.

A comparable example is that of voting rights for settled immigrants. In Sweden they were enabled to vote in the local elections of 1976 and subsequently. Some eight years later a similar proposal was advanced in France, but failed for lack of public support. Then with the adoption of the Treaty of Maastricht a more limited right was accepted for citizens of states within the European Union. Parties at different points of the political spectrum seek support from different sections of the electorate and take up different positions. They have now to pay more attention to the policies of neighbouring states. Such influence as CERD can exert is subject to similar constraints. Its opinions weigh more heavily with some ministries and at some periods than with other ministries and at other periods.

Until the late 1980s membership of the Council of Europe was limited to the states of the West, but by 1993 membership had been extended to thirty-two states, many of them in the East. The Council has continued to be active in the promotion of human rights and in the prevention of racial discrimination and xenophobia. The European Community was created in 1969 by the amalgamation of three already existing regional communities, and after ratification of the Treaty of Maastricht it became, in 1993, the European Union. In 1975 thirty-five European and other states gave their political assent to the Final Act of the Conference on Security and Cooperation in Europe (the 'Helsinki Accord'), important sections of which set forth various human-rights obligations and which have since been built upon by further action, including the appointment of a High Commissioner on National Minorities. So it is relevant to note that European participation in ICERD has the support of a set of regional bodies. Some of these have encouraged their members to make the declaration under ICERD article 14 permitting individual petition, but so far with only limited success. It is equally important to note the strength of NGOs within most of these countries and their influence in campaigns for better implementation of international human-rights standards.

Table 2 is based on figures collected since 1987 (the table and relevant description can be found at the end of Chapter 8). It provides in a compressed form a great deal of information about the Committee's working methods and its interaction with states.

Before trying to decide to what extent the dialogue between states parties and the Committee has led to improved implementation of the Convention, it is necessary to note the influence of the political conditions governing the Committee's operation. As was shown in Chapters 6 and 7, in the work of CERD prior to 1988 there were what looked like political manœuvres by one camp against the other. The changes in Eastern Europe that started about that time have been reflected in the reports received from Moscow and in their reception.

## THE EASING OF POLITICAL CONSTRAINTS

In the 1970s some members of CERD were ready to heap praise on the USSR for having eradicated racial discrimination by the changes inaugurated at the revolution. A stress on general juridical principles continued to be a feature of Soviet reports up to the ninth one submitted in 1986. That began by saying that since the last report 'an event of enormous historical importance has taken place in the life of the peoples of the USSR'. This was the Twenty-Seventh Congress of the Communist Party of the Soviet Union, which had drawn up a programme for the further democratization of Soviet society. The Congress had been told that

national oppression and inequality of all types and forms have been done away with once and for all . . . The Soviet people is a qualitatively new social and international community, cemented by the same economic interests, ideology and political goals . . . Such development holds out the long term historical prospect of the complete unity of nations.

There was no information on the application of laws against racial discrimination, because such discrimination no longer occurred. People outside the USSR had heard accounts of African students being treated less favourably, especially when, for example, they became friendly with Russian girls, but it was difficult to use accounts of such a kind as a basis for criticizing the state's policies. The tenth report, of 1988, struck a very different note. It described the process of restructuring (*perestroika*) that had started. The eleventh report explained that that this process had given rise to national regeneration and national movements.

The democratic forces involved in these movements reflect the legitimate desires of citizens of all nationalities for self-determination and self-government, an improvement in living conditions and the protection and development of national cultures. The memory of historical injustices, the unsatisfactory pace of democratic changes, the fall in the standard of living, the crisis affecting the structures of power, the criminal exploitation of national sentiments for partizan and mercenary purposes have paved the way for an exacerbation of antagonisms between nationalities and of centrifugal tendencies.

It was scarcely necessary for Committee members to voice any suspicion that the Russians had not, after all, become a qualitatively new social community, or that they had all the weaknesses of peoples in other parts of the world and that their legislation was not furnishing the hoped-for protections.

Prior to 1988 any criticism of Soviet compliance was likely to be interpreted in political terms. Since that time, the Committee's ability to assess reports from Moscow, Minsk, and Kiev has been limited by the shortage of reliable information about events from sources independent of the governments. Such discrimination as occurs is likely to be on grounds of ethnic or national origin and may not always be as flagrant as that associated with differences of skin colour.

Reports from other East European states have also shown some significant changes. For example, the ninth to eleventh reports of Bulgaria were presented in 1991 by the state representative who had presented the reports which had occasioned controversy in 1986. According to him:

The repression of Muslims and Bulgarian Turks and the attempt to force them to assimilate, particularly during the last six years of the totalitarian regime, had been strongly condemned by the State and public opinion after the regime had collapsed. The episode represented a sad chapter of Bulgarian history, even if the number of the victims and the nature of the repression could not be compared to the ethnic strife with which a number of European countries were currently afflicted. In the previous two years a broad range of legislative and administrative measures had been introduced in order to restore rights violated during the attempted forced assimilation and to provide compensation for wrongs and injuries. In particular, the judicial procedure for the restoration of names forcibly changed had been replaced by a more streamlined administrative procedure with the amendment in November of the Citizens' Names Law, adopted in March of that year. By April 1991, some 600,000 applications for such restoration, mostly from Bulgarian Turks, Pomaks and Muslim Gypsies, had been approved. (SR 918).

The country rapporteur, Mr de Gouttes, commented on the many questions generated by the new reports; that 'the Committee should ask such questions and expect a reply—something which could scarcely have been hoped for in the past—was a tribute to the democratization of Bulgaria'.

Another set of events which brought out into the open some of the political constraints under which the Committee had been working was provided by the outbreak of ethnically based hostilities in Yugoslavia. In March 1993 CERD reviewed its previous considerations of Yugoslav reports. Members wondered whether they should have noticed impending trouble and either issued a warning or attempted some kind of preventive action. They noted wryly that some committee members had been full of praise for government policies. Mr Öberg had said that 'it was quite remarkable that a country like Yugoslavia could exist'; its viability could be attributed to its 'concerted policy of mutual respect for the various groups, languages, customs and religions present in the country' (SR 738). Mr Song had affirmed that 'racial discrimination did not exist in Yugoslavia', while Mr Staruschenko had thought it provided 'convincing demonstration of socialism's ability to resolve the nationality question'. Mr de Pierola had regarded Yugoslavia as 'an admirable model for the elimination of racial discrimination'.

The ninth and tenth reports were considered in 1990 (A/45/18, paras. 192–205; SR 874–5). Members asked why relations between Croats and Serbs had deteriorated and were told in reply that this was because the government of the Croatian republic had objected to demands for a referendum on the creation of an autonomous Serbian region within Croatia. Why was there tension in Kosovo? The state representative referred to 'the aspiration of a part of the national Albanian minority to make the province a republic and a sovereign state, and to declare what it considered the right of that minority to self-determination and secession'. This had led to the temporary suspension of the Assembly and Executive Council of Kosovo. Regarding the claim to self-determination, he stated that 'nowhere in the world did national minorities have that right . . . Kosovo formed part of Serbian territory and had never in history belonged to Albania'. Serbs had been forced to leave Kosovo 'partly as a result of intolerance by Albanian authorities but also because of the misguided attitude and policy of certain Serbian and Yugoslav politicians. The Albanians were not entirely to be blamed for the situation.'

If the Committee failed to assess properly Yugoslavia's compliance in 1990, that failure may be attributed in part to the insufficiency of accurate sources of information independent of the government's report. Readers may recollect the view of Mr Staruschenko, mentioned in Chapter 7, that the nature of the Convention is such that the Committee should normally trust governments to provide a truthful account of circumstances. They should also remember the need to treat all states equally. If Yugoslavia was deficient in 1990, were not some other states parties even more deficient?

The Committee decided that in August 1993 it would review the eighth and tenth reports of Yugoslavia considered in 1985 and 1990, and the Committee's consideration of them, to see whether any lessons could be learnt about the processes generating ethnic conflicts and about the ways in which the Committee could react to signs of increasing tension. That August it held a closed meeting to reflect upon its own record in this matter, and a sequence of four meetings in which it considered the updating information supplied by the government. In the course of a discussion of 'ethnic cleansing' one member suggested the following definition for the Committee's purposes: 'Ethnic cleansing is the expulsion or elimination from a given territory of persons who do not belong to the ethnic group responsible for such actions. It is an enforced segregation contrary to article 3 of the International Convention on the Elimination of Racial Discrimination' (SR 1003).

The government's report implied that the situation in Serbia and Montenegro was normal, leading the country rapporteur, Mr van Boven, to observe:

Although the oral statement by the government representative did come closer to reality, it was striking to note that blame was put either on the international community or on the minorities in the country itself which were said to have abused their rights. He appreciated the government's wish for a balanced view of the situation, but considered the government's presentation itself to be unbalanced. (SR 1003)

The Committee's concluding observations were extensive (A/48/18, paras. 530–47). It

considered that by not opposing extremism and ultranationalism on ethnic grounds, State authorities and political leaders incurred serious responsibility . . . links existed between the Federal Republic of Yugoslavia (Serbia and Montenegro) and Serbian militias and paramilitary groups responsible for massive, gross and systematic violations of human rights in Bosnia and Herzegovina and in Croatian territories controlled by Serbs . . . The Committee was deeply concerned by reports indicating that in Kosovo, as well as in Vojvodina and Sandzak, members of national minorities had been subject to a campaign of terror carried out by paramilitary organizations . . .

Among its other recommendations the Committee urged the government

to undertake all measures at its disposal with a view to bringing to an end the massive, gross and systematic human rights violations currently occurring in those areas of Croatia and Bosnia and Herzegovina controlled by Serbs. The Committee also urged the State party to assist efforts to arrest, bring to trial and punish all those responsible for crimes which would be covered by the terms of reference of the international tribunal established pursuant to Security Council resolution 808 (1993). (A/48/18, para. 545)

A similar recommendation was addressed to Croatia concerning those areas of Bosnia controlled by Croats. At subsequent sessions the Committee requested further information from the governments of Yugoslavia (Serbia and Montenegro), Bosnia and Herzegovina, Croatia, and the Former Yugoslav Republic of Macedonia. It continued to keep the situation in the region under review, though members differed in their opinions as to an appropriate role for the Committee in the prevailing circumstances.

To assess the extent to which a state meets its obligations under the Convention is much more difficult than looking through the books to see what laws exist on paper. A proper assessment requires first an appreciation of the circumstances in which suspicions of racial discrimination might arise in the state in question. Then, secondly, an understanding of the state's legal order including its provisions regarding discrimination. Thirdly, and no less important, is information about the extent to which the laws are effectively deployed to prevent discrimination or deal with its consequences. To assess the compliance of almost any country in the industrial world is therefore a research project in itself, and, given the number of European states, a task beyond the reach of this chapter. What it will attempt instead is to discuss the Committee's attempts, by dialogue, to improve implementation.

Chapters 10, 11, and 12 will review the Committee's dialogue with states in America, Africa, and Asia, taking states in an order similar to that employed in Chapter 5. This, as the first of the regional chapters, will pursue a different plan and follow the sequence given by the articles of the Convention, describing some of the occasions on which committee members have called attention to particular features of these. Proceeding in this manner will introduce some comments on the various articles which do not relate to the European states alone and could equally well have been associated with a review of dialogue with states in the American, African, or Asian groups. Since this chapter, therefore, does double duty, it has to be substantially longer than the other regional chapters, but this seems the best way to cope with the complexities of the material. Because one three-week committee session generates a summary record of some 300-odd closely typed pages, any account of the dialogue has to be highly selective. This account reflects the features and potentialities of the Convention which most interest the present author, quoting both from the summary record and the concluding observations. Other members of the Committee would doubtless wish to highlight different dimensions of the dialogue.

## ARTICLE 1

Two features of article 1.1 have recently attracted comment: the reference to distinctions *based* on race, and the question of whether they have either the *purpose* or the *effect* of nullifying rights.

The first of these concerns the test for what is 'based upon race'; it was raised in 1992, in connection with the ninth and tenth periodic reports of Austria (SR 947), when Mr Banton drew attention to article 1 of the Federal Constitutional Law of 3 July 1973. According to this law, the 'legislative and executive powers shall refrain from any discrimination on the sole ground of race, colour, descent or national or ethnic origin'. Since discriminatory actions may arise from multiple grounds, the restriction of the prohibition by the insertion of the word 'sole' must occasion further questions about the adequacy of the protection provided. He thought the Austrian government might find it of interest to consider the experience of Australia, where the legislation had been amended to

remove the requirements that racial discrimination be shown to be the dominant reason for an action in order for that action to be unlawful. This provision presented a significant range of complainants with problems of proof. The Act now provides that an action is unlawful if one of the reasons for the action constitutes racial discrimination, regardless of whether it is the dominant reason. (Australian eighth report, para. 46.)

In his response, the state representative noted that the 1973 law prohibited discrimination:

he wondered exactly what was meant by the term discrimination. Did it imply different treatment, or unjustified treatment? If the latter were the case, the restriction contained in the law would be open to criticism. He pointed out, however, that there did exist positive forms of discrimination . . .

This may have been on his part an interim response to a difficult question, and the next periodic report from Austria may include considered replies on these and other questions asked at the same time.

The Netherlands Equal Treatment Act of 1994 prohibits both direct and indirect discrimination but appears to render unlawful only those actions which are based on the *sole* grounds of political opinion, race, sex, nationality, heterosexual or homosexual orientation, or civil status. This will doubtless occasion questioning when that country's next periodic report is considered.

In Europe it is sometimes difficult to distinguish one ground of action from another. For example, the members of some religious groups hold views on abortion which lead them to take action that is political in character. They might maintain that it is not possible to separate the religious and political components in their motivation. Race, like religion, can be a shared attribute which leads to the formation of a group which displays a political character in some settings but not others. In other regions of the world membership of a racial group may be even more sharply coterminous with membership of a religious or political group. The concept of a ground of action as a part of the attempt to regulate behaviour by law will therefore necessitate much development in the future.

A second feature of article 1.1 is the distinction between purpose and effect (which is also known as that between direct and indirect discrimination, or between disparate treatment and disparate impact). Members of the Committee have raised this in connection with several state reports, and it was put to the Austrian representative, again with reference to Australian practice. Australia's report had continued:

The amendments make clear that unlawful racial discrimination under the Act includes 'indirect discrimination', that is where a rule or requirement not explicitly based on race none the less has a discriminatory effect. They further provide that employers are vicariously liable for acts of racial discrimination by employees in connection with their duties. This will assist complainants by reducing problems that have arisen in some cases of fixing responsibility for an act of discrimination on the appropriate person; it will also encourage employers to take measures to prevent racial discrimination in the workplace.

The Austrian representative thought that the effect of such legislation must be

to reverse the burden of proof; in his view, such a measure would only be justified in very specific cases, since if the right to a remedy was automatic, anyone could allege that he had been a victim of racial discrimination and it would then be for the accused party to prove the contrary . . . when there were four applicants for a post and only one was chosen, the others might claim that they had been rejected for reasons connected with their race, and might sue the employer for damages: how was the latter to prove that nothing of the kind had occurred?

Mr Banton replied that he thought these fears exaggerated; the problem did not arise in the same way in civil proceedings, and he asked Austria to take note of the remedies available in some other countries. Mr van Boven supported this, citing experience in the Netherlands.

Some European countries have prohibited only actions which are racially discriminatory in respect of their purpose. For example, Belgium told the Committee that in 1992 an amendment had been proposed to make the prohibition of racial discrimination more effective, but 'it should be noted that in all cases proof of racist intention must be adduced' (A/47/18, para. 62). The position in France is similar, so CERD in 1994 recommended 'that France strengthen its laws to prohibit actions which are discriminatory in effect'.

Article 1.2 excludes from the definition of racial discrimination distinctions made by a state between citizens and noncitizens. It shuts out any consideration of whether or not a state's immigration laws are 'racist', though it leaves open the possibility of considering whether such laws are implemented in a racially discriminatory manner. When the Convention was being drafted, the demand for labour in many European countries exceeded the supply, leading to immigration from outside Europe. In the early 1970s the balance changed. Then by the end of the 1980s even those countries which had traditionally been hospitable to asylum-seekers adopted restrictive immigration policies. These could not but clash with the inclusion of indirect discrimination within the definition in article 1.1 of racial discrimination since the excess labour supply was in countries with populations racially distinct from those in Europe. The exception in this subarticle has therefore been very important.

Some states have regarded the same subarticle as absolving them from any obligation to report upon measures to protect noncitizens from racial discrimination. This interpretation was first challenged in 1989 in connection with the eighth and ninth periodic reports of Germany. Mr Banton said that he could not accept the state's claim that the employment of ethnically distinctive foreign workers was not subject to compulsory reporting.

The exception created by article 1, paragraph 2, applies only to distinctions made by the state party, while article 2, paragraph 1(c) recognizes a state's obligation to eliminate racial barriers and divisions. So the Federal

Republic should tell us if there are patterns of foreign-worker segregation in work, housing, schooling, and so on, as a result of actions by employers, municipalities, private citizens or the workers themselves. (SR 844 para 63)

Mr Aboul-Nasr and Mr Rechetov expressed support for the German government's interpretation of article 1.2, whereas Mr Garvalov agreed with Mr Banton. The German representative replied that in his view the Convention was not intended to guarantee all the rights provided for in article 5 to citizens and aliens alike, as seemed obvious in the case of the right to vote.

In 1992 Mr Banton had put the same point to the Austrian representative, maintaining that ICERD article 1.2

recognizes the right of a State to decide who may be a citizen and the rights a citizen may enjoy, but it does not cover distinctions, exclusions, restrictions or preferences made by bodies other than the State (e.g. by private employers). There is therefore an obligation on the State to see that differences of race, colour, descent, and national or ethnic origin do not occasion less favourable treatment, and to report on action taken in discharge of that obligation.

The representative's response was to say 'That was an entirely new concept, which in his view was not in keeping with the spirit of the Convention.'

In March 1993 the Committee adopted a general recommendation which, while acknowledging that actions by a state party which differentiated between citizens and noncitizens were excepted from the Convention's definition of racial discrimination, affirmed that states were under an obligation to report fully upon legislation on foreigners and its implementation. By this time the German government had already prepared its twelfth period report, which included a restatement of their view that the Convention contained no obligation to report on such legislation. It remains to be seen whether this position will be maintained.

Among other features of article 1, it may be noted that discrimination on grounds of ethnic or national origin is prohibited. A man can change his nationality but not his national origin. Linking the prohibition to 'origin' has proven simpler than attempting to relate it to membership of an ethnic group, since 'membership' is in these circumstances difficult to define. Many individuals can claim multiple ethnic origins, and there may sometimes be room for argument about whether less favourable treatment has been based upon a particular ethnic origin. Since there is no prohibition of discrimination on grounds of religion, cases may arise in which someone complaining of discrimination belongs in a group defined by both religion and ethnic origin, like those of Jews and Sikhs. Since there are persons who regard themselves, and are regarded by others, as Jews and as Sikhs, but who do not practise the Jewish or Sikh religion, the ethnic group is larger than the religious one, and can be distinguished from it. The 'but-for' test approved by the courts in England in sex-discrimination cases could also be used in these circumstances. A court would have to decide whether the complainant would have been treated more favourably *but for* the presumption that he or she was of a certain ethnic origin. This test will work better when it is applied to the treatment of an individual than when it has to be applied to a group. It might not solve the problems presented by a possible mixture of motives in some of the cases that could arise in Africa, and which are outlined in Chapter 11.

The reference to 'public life' in article 1.1 was inserted to remove from the scope of the Convention discrimination within private relations. Queries as to the meaning of the restriction arose, not in dialogue with states parties, but in a committee discussion of the ways that in some countries schools and municipal services as well as social clubs have been removed, by privatization, from the scope of anti-discrimination legislation. The Committee appeared to agree that the effect of the phrase in article 1.1 was to define the political, economic, social, and cultural fields of life as fields of public life and to say that, if any other similar fields were ever recognized, they too would come within the scope of the definition of racial discrimination. The action of a state in permitting the privatization of schools is not sufficient to except them from the reach of the Convention. (SR 969)

## ARTICLE 2

States parties are allowed some discretion as to how they implement their obligations. In some states the act of ratification automatically makes the Convention part of domestic law, so that it is then self-executing. Greece and Spain offer examples of European states in which the Convention has been incorporated into domestic (or 'municipal') law. In some states international obligations take priority over domestic law if they come into conflict, but this is a technical subject which requires separate treatment by a specialist. Even when international treaties automatically become part of domestic law, further legislation would be needed in the case of ICERD to specify the punishment that would follow breach of the declaration under article 4(*a*), and to give particular tribunals jurisdiction. Other states may enact statutes either recapitulating the provisions of the Convention or amending existing statutes to ensure that the provisions of the Convention are covered. In these circumstances the Committee has quite often expressed doubt about whether all the provisions have been fully covered.

Many states have written provisions against discrimination into their constitutions. For example, in Germany, article 3.1 of the Basic Law embodies the equality of all people, while article 3.3 provides that no one may be prejudiced or favoured because of his or her sex, parentage, race, language, homeland, or origin. Any allegation of a violation by a public authority would be adjudicated in the constitutional court, whereas cases of discrimination by private persons can be taken to a civil court or a labour court.

Article 2.1 requires a state to pursue a policy for eliminating racial discrimination. The policies of some states are part of larger social policies, such as those promoting national integration. In 1990 France established a Haut Conseil à l'Intégration to help formulate this ideal. The Council has stated that

integration is evoking the active participation in society of all men and women who have decided to live permanently on our soil, accepting that there are cultural differences but putting the emphasis on similarities and convergencies in the equality of rights and duties needed to ensure the cohesion of our social tissue.

This is seen as very different from 'the logic of minorities' (HCI 1993: 8). The French policy is therefore teleological in conception, whereas the other West European countries which have tried to define their objectives have done so in more open-ended terms. The UK has declared that it is a fundamental objective of the government, acting in concert with other public and private agencies, to enable members of ethnic minorities 'to participate freely and fully in the economic, social and public life of the nation, with all the benefits and responsibilities which that entails, while still being able to maintain their own culture, traditions, language and values' (thirteenth periodic report). Sweden in 1975 declared that its actions should be based on the three principles of equality, freedom of choice, and partnership, while Norway stressed freedom of choice but said that it must be complemented by cooperation, reciprocity, and tolerance. What France calls a logic of minorities can be exemplified in the Netherlands, which has a minorities policy 'directed towards the achievement of a society in which the members of the minority groups living in the Netherlands are given an equal place in society and full opportunities for development, both as individuals and as members of groups'.

Sometimes state policies are primarily concerned with the public sector. The report from Austria prepared in 1986 explained that the state constitution prohibited any form of racial discrimination and put the legislative and executive powers under an obligation to refrain from any discrimination. The controls were comprehensive in that the state was liable for any injury; damages could be paid; there was an ombudsman, and legal aid was available. Provisions for preventing discrimination by private persons were to be found in penal legislation protecting public order. The right to work was set against the free contract of employment between the parties which was subject to civil law, but there was no indication of any remedies available by this means. No information was provided on the number of persons who had complained of racial discrimination. This was characteristic of the reports of many states. Their representatives often claim that the absence of cases proves the absence of discrimination, whereas the critic may suspect that the remedies are ineffective because the victim is unaware of them or has no confidence in them.

As was explained in Chapter 3 some states assume that whether or not a group constitutes a minority is a question of law rather than a question of fact. An interesting variation is to be found in Sweden. There the only reindeer-breeders are Saami. As will have been noted from a case mentioned in the same chapter, they enjoy special protections by virtue of their occupation but not on account of their ethnic distinctiveness. The power to define the nature of groups in this way can be of great significance. It has already been noted that one justification offered by Serbian nationalists for their denial of rights to ethnic Albanians in Kosovo—rights that they insist should be accorded to ethnic Serbs in Croatia—was that Serbs in Yugoslavia are a nation, whereas Albanians were only a national minority.

CERD is empowered under article 9.2 to 'make suggestions and general recommendations'. The former can be directed to particular states but according to *The First Twenty Years* (UN 1991*c*: para. 120) up to 1990 'No suggestions have been directed at or addressed to individual States parties, except for decisions requesting additional information.' The first such suggestion would therefore appear to be the one addressed to Greece in 1992 (A/47/18, para. 92):

Bearing in mind the provision of article 2(1)(*c*) of the Convention, the Committee called upon the Government of Greece to revise its Nationality Act as far as it differentiated between ethnic Greeks and non-ethnic Greeks, together with any legal or administrative practices which relied on such a distinction.

When the eleventh periodic report of Greece (a document incorporating the eighth, ninth, and tenth reports because the government had fallen behind with its reports) was considered by the Committee, the country rapporteur was Mr Wolfrum. He observed that under the 1955 Act a person of non-Greek origin who left Greece, not intending to return, could be declared to have lost Greek nationality. It was not clear how the authorities could establish such an intention. He was also concerned that such a decision could be made by a Minister of the Interior without a hearing, judicial review, or the right of appeal. He asked how many persons had lost their nationality under the provision (SR 940).

Mr Wolfrum posed further questions about charges brought against two particular individuals (with Turkish-sounding names) and why no action had been taken to punish those who had instigated riots against members of the Turkish minority in 1990. Mr Wolfrum asked for better demographic information concerning persons of Turkish ethnic origin in Thrace. Was it true that most Turkish associations in western Thrace had remained closed following a High Court decision in 1988 ordering their closure on the ground that the use of the term 'Turkish' to describe Greek Muslims endangered public order? Other members of the Committee also asked questions about ethnic minorities and about the government's practice of using the name of a religion to identify a group distinguished by its ethnic origin.

The state representative provided little information in response, and sought to evade certain of these questions. For example,

he wondered what exactly was meant by the term 'minority'. If no more than a few families scattered around the country could be so designated, then there was indeed an Albanian minority in Greece. However, it should be recalled that until the First World War a large part of Albanian territory was inhabited by Greeks under Ottoman administration and it was more appropriate to speak of a Greek minority in Albania. (SR 941)

Members of the Committee expressed disappointment that many questions had gone unanswered. In its concluding observations the Committee reported

an absence of information about judicial proceedings in which the respective provisions of the Greek criminal law had been invoked.

In order to determine whether the social differentiation of Muslims, Pomaks, Gypsies, Armenians and others, especially but not solely in western Thrace, had the effect of impairing the human rights and fundamental freedoms of members of those groups, the Committee called upon the Greek Government to include in its next periodic report information on the economic, social and cultural circumstances of these groups, bearing in mind the Committee's General Recommendation VIII regarding the criteria for the identification of ethnic groups, according to which the identification of individuals as members of a racial or ethnic group should be based upon self-identification by the individual concerned. (A/47/18, paras. 90–1)

Since 1992 the argument about whether there is a Macedonian nation, and its relation to the 2,260,000 Macedonian Greeks, has intensified. Some of this argument is between those who would deny ethnic distinctiveness to the inhabitants of the Former Yugoslav Republic of Macedonia on the grounds that they lack any long historical pedigree as a separate group, and those who maintain that, whatever happened earlier, the people in question developed a distinctive ethnic consciousness during the Tito era.

Article 2.1(*d*) is unqualified in its requirement that a state party bring to an end racial discrimination; it is not limited to the state sector or to governmental action or to the enactment of laws, but makes the state responsible for bringing to an end racial discrimination throughout the society. Article 2.1(*e*) is similarly extensive in requiring action against 'anything which tends to strengthen racial division' and in obliging the state to offer encouragement to non-state organizations.

## ARTICLE 3

As will have been apparent from Chapter 6, this article was always interpreted as being directed simply at apartheid until 1989, when Mr Banton, in connection with reports from the FRG and Sweden, contended that the reference to segregation was not limited to state-enforced segregation. In the FRG there were residential and other concentrations of foreign workers which would show up in any statistical analysis as patterns of separation or segregation. This might result from the wishes of the foreign workers themselves, and be a form of self-segregation. Nevertheless there was an obligation to report on it; the Committee should be told if segregation in work, housing, and schooling, as a result of actions by employers, municipalities, or private citizens, gave rise to any racial discrimination or fear of it (SR 844). In Stockholm, Sweden, there was a suburb where a few years earlier 65 per cent of the population had been of foreign descent and some 100 languages were spoken. The disadvantages of the first-generation settlers could be transmitted to their children and this possibility needed monitoring (SR 850). The Swedish representative said that his government was aware of the possible problems, but German representatives have hitherto been less forthcoming on these points.

In most European countries there are middle-class and working-class residential neighbourhoods, and the schools reflect the class composition of the areas from which their pupils are drawn. The negative consequences of such segregation are the greater when ethnic differences are added to those of class. In some countries parents can choose schools for their children within the state sector, and this is thought to improve standards by encouraging competition between schools. Parental choice may, however, increase the tendencies towards ethnic segregation. In its eighth periodic report in 1988 (para. 55), the Netherlands stated: 'A recent development is what has become popularly known as the "white/black school problem". The term has come about because there are schools where children from ethnic minorities are in a majority. There was a widespread fear that this might cause a deterioration in educational standards.' The government had concentrated on positive action to improve facilities at schools with a large proportion of ethnic minority pupils. Members of the

Committee indicated their concern about the implications of school segregation and returned to the issue in 1994 in connection with the report from France. They then expressed 'concern about social trends which result in segregation in areas of residence and in the school system'.

In March 1993 Mr Banton introduced a draft general recommendation on segregation (SR 969). The intention was to advise states that the scope of ICERD article 3 is not restricted to measures directed against apartheid, and that, while segregation can arise from state policy, it can arise from other sources also. He had circulated a memorandum recalling the drafting history of this article, and contending that, though a law might have been drafted with one object in mind, it might subsequently render illegal some form of conduct that was not in contemplation when the law was enacted. Article 3's reference to apartheid might have been directed exclusively to South Africa, but if the reference to segregation were also directed exclusively to one country, the article would not have required states in the plural to act 'in territories under their jurisdiction'. The article as a whole prohibited all forms of segregation. According to the text, states parties condemn *both* racial segregation *and* apartheid. Segregation is mentioned first, consistent with the view that apartheid is to be seen as *one* form of segregation. In view of the changes in South Africa, it could be timely for CERD to explain that the condemnation of segregation would remain, even if apartheid were completely eliminated.

Support for this interpretation could, he maintained, be drawn from other international instruments, from English-language dictionaries and practice, and from national laws. *The Oxford English Dictionary* listed the two first senses of the word 'segregation' as '1. The action of segregating . . .' and '2. The condition of being segregated . . .' When the tenth periodic report of Sweden was considered, there was a difference of opinion between two members of the Committee which centred upon whether segregation was to be defined only as 'the action of segregating' or also included 'the condition of being segregated'.

Since separation could be a cause of racial disadvantage and in turn give rise to discrimination, Mr Banton proposed that the Committee affirm that the condition of being racially segregated could arise from causes other than intentional action and have undesired consequences both for those who were segregated and for their descendants. In many societies in which there were no distinct barriers between races, economic and social segregation operated in such a way that there was a greater probability that persons of certain races would find themselves at a disadvantage relative to others. Therefore the Committee should invite states parties to review all practices which could give rise to racial segregation, intentional and unintentional, undertake preventive action, and notify the Committee of their progress in this respect in their periodic reports.

Since this proposal received support, Mr Banton was asked to redraft it and a recommendation was eventually agreed in 1995. In March 1993 the Committee had considered whether, as in the past, its general recommendations should be drafted in the form of resolutions or should follow the style of the Human Rights Committee and be written in what Mr van Boven called a 'narrative' form (SR 967). Some subsequent general recommendations have been drafted in this form, but a proposal to rewrite some of the earlier ones in this form so that they can all be consolidated has so far made little progress (see SR 1025). CERD seems to find it more difficult to secure agreement on general recommendations than the Human Rights Committee.


ARTICLE 4

In the 1965 General Assembly debate the delegate of the Netherlands said that he 'regarded article 4 as the key article of the Convention; it would make it a universal instrument'. It was indeed the key article for those who saw the dissemination of ideas based on racial superiority or hatred as the prime cause of racial discrimination, but other articles were equally universal. Article 4 was also taken by the Committee in the 1970s as a key article for its dialogue with states, because in their view it generated mandatory and uniform obligations to be discharged by all states.

It has also proven the most controversial article. As Mr Partsch has recalled (1992*b*: 24), the draft of the Convention prepared by the Commission of Human Rights and forwarded to the General Assembly proposed that 'all incitement to racial discrimination resulting in acts of violence or incitement to such acts' should be punished by law. This wording was close to that in article 20 of the ICCPR. In the Third Committee Czechoslovakia proposed an amendment to declare a punishable offence all 'dissemination of ideas and doctrines based on racial superiority or hatred' without requiring any connection with violence. Other amendments resuted in the final wording, which requires states to act: 'with due regard to the principles embodied in the Universal Declaration of Human Rights and the rights expressly set forth in article 5 of this Convention . . .'.

Mr Partsch (1992*b*: 24) has discussed three different views about the effect of the 'with-due-regard' clause upon the obligations of the states parties. The first is that states are not authorized to take any action which would in any way limit or impair the rights referred to in this clause (a position adopted by the USA). The second is that states parties must strike a balance between the fundamental freedoms and their duties under the Convention (a position adopted by Partsch himself). The third is that states may not invoke the protection of civil rights as a reason to avoid implementation of the Convention (a position regarded sympathetically by the author of CERD's study on article 4 (UN 1986)).

Committee members have had to address two general issues. One was that some states, primarily in western Europe, had entered reservations as to the effect of this article's provisions (as mentioned in Chapter 6). The other was that some states claimed that article 2.1(*d*) allowed them discretion as to whether or not they met their obligations by legislative or by other means.

A crucial issue is whether the dissemination of propaganda must have resulted in violence, incited hatred, or caused discrimination before it becomes punishable. Apart from this, it is very difficult to perceive any right protected by the reservations entered by Austria, France, and Italy, or by the UK's statement of interpretation, that is not covered by the due-regard clause, given that article 29.2 of the Universal Declaration states that the rights may be limited only for securing 'due recognition and respect for the rights and freedoms of others', while ICERD article 5(*d*)(viii) and (ix) lists the rights to freedom of opinion and expression and to peaceful assembly and association. Unless the reservations have some additional effect, they are redundant, and therefore incompatible with the spirit and purpose of the Convention. The Committee has therefore questioned these states about the justification for maintaining their reservations; the dialogue on this point in the early years is summarized in UN (1986).

Two countries, Norway and Sweden, considered entering reservations, but decided that this was not necessary, since they inferred that article 2.1(*d*) gave them discretion as to whether they fulfilled their obligations under article 4 by legislative means or by other means. (They might have done better to rely instead upon the 'due-regard' clause of article 4 and the second of the two positions described by Partsch.) Norway revised section 135 of its penal code to meet the requirements of article 4(*a*) but did not make any changes on account of article 4(*b*). In 1977 CERD reported to the General Assembly that, with regard to article 4(*b*),

the measures taken in Norway were directed not against the existence of certain organizations but against certain offences. While one member of the Committee thought that the situation was satisfactory, other members were of the view that the Committee required States parties to prohibit associations which promoted racial discrimination. (A/33/18, para. 185; quoted in UN 1986: para. 140)

CERD adopted the position that the obligations of article 4(*b*) were categoric and unconditional (cf. UN 1986: para. 143). It acknowledged that certain states had sought to retain a discretion in this connection by means of reservations, but went on: 'It has been said that this kind of reservation is incompatible with the object and purpose of the Convention and cannot be permitted under article 20, paragraph 2' (UN 1986: para. 222). According to E. Schwelb's article on the Convention's drafting history (1966: 1018) the qualification 'as required by circumstances' was inserted to make it clear that legislation was required if, and to the extent that, discriminatory practices occurred in the country in question. The Committee took a different view when (UN 1986: para. 221) it stated that 'Article 4 aims at prevention rather than cure'; a parallel reference to 'the preventive aspects of article 4' appears in general recommendation VII of 1985.

Reference was made to the phrase 'as required by circumstances' and its significance when, in 1986, the seventh periodic report of Sweden was considered. The report stated in paragraph 51 the government's view that article 2.1(*d*) allowed each state party a margin of appreciation. Members of the Committee disagreed. According to the annual report (A/42/18, para. 351),

They pointed out that the optional character of the use of legislative measures, among others, in pursuing the policy of eliminating racial discrimination under article 2 paragraph 1 (d) of the Convention did not override the precise mandatory character of the provision of article 4(*b*), which in relation to article 2 was a *lex specialis*.

This passage in the report was based on an observation of Mr Cremona, with which Mr de Pierola agreed, and the remark of Mr Partsch that article 2.1(*d*) conferred no latitude with respect to article 4 (SR 769, paras. 30, 31; 769 para. 1). Mr Partsch's view was that the discretion conferred by the reference to circumstances in article 2.1(*d*) was applicable 'except in so far as the Convention makes special provision in other articles . . .' (Partsch 1992*b*: 23).

The dialogue with Sweden on this point continued in 1994. Presenting his country's eleventh report, the state representative gave an account of a bill currently before the Riksdag which introduced new measures against racial attacks and defined racial motivation as an aggravating characteristic of an offence. The bill was based on the recommendations of a committee which had carefully considered the requirements of the Convention and the observations of Committee members. In his government's view the new law would fulfil Sweden's obligations under article 4, even though it did not make all dissemination of ideas based upon racial superiority a punishable offence in itself or prohibit organizations which promote racial discrimination. The country rapporteur, Mr Rechetov, rejected these claims. The freedoms of expression and association could not be used in order to denigrate ethnic groups. In his view there was no legal basis for the reservations some states had entered concerning this article. Other members of the Committee did not go so far, but they repeated their view that the wording of article 4 was so peremptory that it excluded this article from the discretion otherwise conferred in article 2.1(*d*), and disagreed that Sweden had fulfilled its obligations.

In the view of the Committee the discretion to employ appropriate means is overridden in the case of racial incitement by the wording of article 4(*a*) and (*b*). In saying that certain acts shall be punishable, the Convention requires sanctions under the criminal law. Actions prohibited under other articles of the Convention can be dealt with under other branches of law: administrative law, constitutional law, civil law, labour law, and so on, but not those to which articles 4(*a*) and (*b*) relate (Wolfrum 1990).

The dialogue with Norway on this point in 1994 led to CERD's concluding observation

that the State party has not implemented the provisions contained in article 4(*b*) of the Convention and has not provided information on the practical application of provisions of article 4. In that connection, it is noted that between 1982 and 1989 some 500 possible breaches of section 135(*a*) of the Penal Code were reported to the authorities and that very few led to any proceedings. The situation has not improved since 1989. It is regretted that no information has been provided by the State party on the existing case law.

Further to reports about the use of local radio to disseminate ideas which may be in breach of article 4(*a*) of the Convention, more detailed information is desired about the monitoring of transmissions and the implementation of procedures for receiving licenses to broadcast.

Addressing both Norway and Sweden in similar terms, the Committee stated:

paragraphs (*a*) and (*b*) are of a mandatory character . . . it notes that so far these provisions have not been fully implemented in Norway; therefore the Committee recommends that the State party should carry out each obligation . . . (A/49/18, paras. 254, 256, 261)

CERD's report for 1993 with respect to the report from the UK stated:

The Committee expressed concern that the State party was not implementing its obligations under article 4 of the Convention, which called for the adoption of specific penal legislation. By not prohibiting the British National Party and other groups and organizations of a racist nature, and by allowing them to pursue their activities, the State party was failing to implement article 4, which called for a condemnation of all organizations attempting to justify or promote racial hatred and discrimination. Additionally, the Committee considered that in the light of the increase in manifestation of racist ideas and of racially motivated attacks, the restrictive interpretation of article 4 violated the purpose and objective of the Convention and was incompatible with the general recommendation XV of the Committee.

The Committee encouraged the State party to review its interpretive statements and reservations, in particular, those with regard to articles 4 and 6 of the Convention, with a view to withdrawing them. (A/48/18, paras. 416, 422)

In its thirteenth periodic report (para. 36) the UK replied

robustly that the banning of groups like the British National Party would be counter-productive, leading to greater publicity and support for the groups in question; it would therefore run counter to the object and purpose of the Convention.

Mr Rechetov (1992) has elsewhere summarized the reports to CERD of states which have commented upon how they balance the prohibition of racial incitement with the obligation to protect freedom of speech, and has described the first case to come before a court in Russia in which K. V. Ostashvili was tried for incitement to hatred against Jews.

A case arose in Denmark which exemplifies the possible conflict between a state's obligation to implement article 4 and citizens' rights under article 19 of both the UDHR and the ICCPR. Two journalists had interviewed some young men who had been attacking immigrants and who justified their conduct on racial grounds. The young men (who called themselves 'Greenjackets') were convicted of offences, but the journalists were separately convicted for disseminating ideas based on racial superiority or hatred under legislation that had been enacted by Denmark to meet its obligations under ICERD. Did their conviction breach the journalists' rights to freedom of expression guaranteed by Denmark to meet article 10 of the European Convention on Human Rights? That article resembles article 19 of the two international instruments. It states:

1. Everyone shall have the right to freedom of expression. This right shall include freedom to hold opinions and to receive and impart information and ideas without interference by public authority and regardless of frontiers.
2. The exercise of these freedoms, since it carries with it duties and responsibilities, may be subject to such formalities, conditions, restrictions or penalties as are prescribed by law and are necessary in a democratic society . . . for the protection of the rights and reputation of others . . .

On a vote of 12 to 7, the European Court of Human Rights in 1994 concluded (*Jersild* v. *Denmark*, 36/1993/431/510) that the reasons advanced by the government were not sufficient to establish that the interference was 'necessary' or that the means employed were proportionate to the aim of protecting 'the rights and reputation of others'. There had therefore been a breach of the European Convention. The Danish legislation had been amended before the case reached the European Court, but the decision will be important to the future interpretation of ICERD article 4.

The same article was held to be relevant to the communication *L.K.* v. *The Netherlands*, which was described in Chapter 8. In that case CERD found

that the remarks and threats made on 8 and 9 August 1989 to L.K. constituted incitement to racial discrimination and to acts of violence against persons of another colour or ethnic origin, contrary to article 4(*a*) of the Convention, and the investigation into these incidents by the police and prosecution authorities was incomplete.

The Committee cannot accept any claim that the enactment of law making racial discrimination a criminal act in itself represents full compliance with the obligations of States parties under the Convention.

It added that the prosecutor's discretion, commonly known as the expediency principle,

should be applied in each case of alleged racial discrimination in the light of the guarantees laid down in the Convention.

When threats of racial violence are made, and especially when they are made in public and by a group, it is incumbent upon the State to investigate with due diligence and expedition. In the instant case, the State party failed to do this.

The Committee finds that in view of the inadequate response to the incidents, the police and judicial proceedings in this case did not afford the applicant effective protection and remedies within the meaning of article 6 of the Convention.

The Committee recommends that the State party review its policy and procedures concerning the decision to prosecute in cases of alleged racial discrimination, in the light of its obligations under article 4 of the Convention.

The Committee further recommends that the State party provide the applicant with relief commensurate with the moral damage he has suffered.

In August 1994 the representative of Canada was asked why her country had not so far made a declaration under article 14 of the ICERD when it had accepted the Optional Protocol of the ICCPR. She suggested that one reason for hesitation might be the scope of article 4, which conflicted with the Canadian view of the freedom of speech. Mr van Boven answered that any such concern might be misplaced. In his view, articles 2 and 4 dealt with policies to be pursued by states and were therefore unlikely to give rise to individual communications under article 14. Complainants were most likely to appeal to the rights secured by articles 5 and 6.

## ARTICLE 5

For those who believe that the main causes of racial discrimination are ideological and intentional, article 4 is the most important; but for those who believe that more racial discrimination springs from unconscious assumptions and the intergenerational transmission of inequality, it is article 5 that is the key article.

In 1973 CERD discussed the scope and implications of article 5 without being able to come to any agreement on several basic issues. That discussion, together with all the other relevant material available at the time, was reviewed in an article by Mr Partsch (1979). He concluded that the text and context of the provisions of article 5 appeared to give the right to equality before the law at least the same importance as the undertaking to prohibit and to eliminate racial discrimination. The drafting history tended to lay greater emphasis on the right to equality before the law. Reservations and interpretive statements also emphasized the right to equality before the law and supposed a mandatory character of the rights listed. Some members of the Committee, however, have taken the view that, if in a particular state a given right was not guaranteed by law, there could be no guarantee in respect of non-discrimination in its enjoyment. Mr Partsch maintained that a state fails to comply with this article only if a restriction upon one of the specified rights has been imposed as a result of a racial motivation or with the effect of impairing the full enjoyment of the right to equality before the law on grounds of race, colour, or national or ethnic origin. His article also discusses implementation up to 1978 of Article 5's subparagraphs (*a*)–(*d*). The Committee returned to this issue on several occasions between 1993 and 1995 in connection with a draft general recommendation proposed by Mr Wolfrum which enjoys wide support but had not been adopted by the end of the summer session of 1995. According to the draft:

Article 5 of the Convention, apart from the guarantee in the exercise of human rights to be free from racial discrimination, does not of itself create civil, political, economic, social or cultural rights, but presumes the existence of these rights. It obliges States to prohibit and eliminate racial discrimination in the enjoyment of human rights as they are guaranteed in the country concerned.

The rights and freedoms mentioned in article 5 do not address the same groups of persons. Some are related to all living in a given State, such as the right to equal treatment before tribunals; some are the rights of citizens, such as the rights to participate in elections, to vote and stand for election.

. . . Where the practices of private bodies influence the availability of opportunities, the State must ensure that the result has neither the purpose nor the effect of creating or perpetuating racial discrimination.

To give any account of the dialogue between the Committee and European states concerning implementation of article 5, it is necessary to call attention, if only briefly, to the five paragraphs and the many subparagraphs which comprise the article. The law relating to any one paragraph would be material enough for a whole book, so all that can be done here is to give an indication of the sorts of point that have been raised in connection with reports from European states.

Two preliminary points of different character should be borne in mind. The first is that the list of rights in the Convention follows those of the two covenants, but it is not exclusive. The opening paragraph concludes 'notably in the enjoyment of the following rights'; other, unspecified rights may be covered by it. The second preliminary point is to note that it may be impossible to ascertain whether or not there is equality before the law without quantitative data on the experience of persons of different race or ethnic origin. To collect such data individuals have to be classified, possibly by asking them to which ethnic group they assign themselves. There is considerable resistance to the collection of information on this basis. Some people, in many countries, refuse to assign themselves to such a category, believing the whole principle to be contrary to attempts to overcome the effects of racial differentiation. France in 1979 enacted Law 78-17 of 6 January 1978 on computer technology, files, and freedoms. This specifies that data on racial origins may not be stored electronically without the express agreement of the person concerned. Anyone who breaches the provisions of this act shall be imprisoned for a period between six months and five years or fined up to two million francs. The Centre Nationale d'Informatique et des Libertés monitors application of the Act. It has authorized exceptions in favour of official research projects into the social participation of young people who have received social assistance, and into the social and geographical mobility of immigrants and their children. It has also authorized the collection of data on racial origins for epidemiological research into cognitive ageing, risks of acquiring cancer, and for vaccines against human immunodeficiency virus (HIV). Applications for exceptions are carefully scrutinized. Many French people would contend that this protection of privacy is indispensable to the individual's dignity and the development of his or her personality.

In its concluding observations on the French report considered in 1994, CERD reported: 'concern is expressed lest the law on computer technology, files and freedoms impair the Government's readiness to ascertain whether victims of racial discrimination lack effective protection and remedies' (A/49/18, para. 148).

Paragraph 5(a) covers equality of treatment before organs administering justice. It has occasioned concluding observations regarding reports from several European states. In 1994 the Committee expressed the concern of members

that the implementation of [new laws of immigration and asylum] could have racially discriminatory consequences, particularly in connection with the imposition of limitations on the right of appeal to expulsion orders and the provision of preventive detention of foreigners at points of entry for excessively long periods. Concern is also expressed that these laws might generate or reinforce a xenophobic atmosphere in French society.

Concern is expressed over procedures concerning identity controls which confer on the police, for preventive reasons, broad discretion in checking the identity of foreigners in public, a measure which could encourage discrimination in actual practice. Concern is also expressed that the law enforcement services should reflect the ethnic diversity of the population and that adequate training with respect to racial discrimination be organized.

Concern was expressed in 1983 about the adequacy of sentences imposed for racially-motivated crimes; a new concern is added about whether the sentences for racially-motivated homicides are consistent, regardless of the ethnic background of the victims.

Among the suggestions and recommendations made by the Committee to the government were

that France strengthen its laws to prohibit actions which are discriminatory in effect, on grounds of race, ethnic or national origin, in accordance with its General Recommendation XIV(42), and in order to provide compensation to victims of such discrimination.

that the Government take further preventive measures to counter racist violence and to implement fully article 4 of the Convention, which obliges States parties to declare illegal and prohibit organizations which promote and incite racial discrimination.

that the training of law enforcement officials in human rights standards be strengthened and that their recruitment be broadened to include more members of differing ethnic backgrounds.

These were followed by two requests for information

on whether languages other than French (including Breton, Basque and German) may be used in official settings and in mass media publications.

on judicial decisions relating to racial discrimination, penalties applied and a payment of compensation. (A/49/18, paras. 144–57)

In its 1993 concluding observations on another state, the Committee said that it was

of the view that the German Government should guarantee equal protection to all minority groups living in Germany. In addition, the Government should consider reviewing certain restrictive provisions recently adopted with regard to asylum-seekers to ensure that they do not result in any discrimination in effect on grounds of ethnic origin. (A/48/18, para. 448)

The following year the Committee expressed its concern to Norway that

the exercise of discretion not to invoke criminal proceedings may result in an absence of effective remedies.

the arrangements for compiling lists from which juries are selected may not guarantee to qualified persons of minority ethnic or national origin an equal chance that their names will appear on the lists. [This should be read in conjunction with the opinion in respect of *Narrainen* v. *Norway* described in Chapter 8.]

insufficient information was provided on measures to ensure that persons of minority ethnic and national origin receive equal protection against acts of violence, and on measures to counteract their reported belief that it is futile for them to report such attacks to the authorities.

The 'suggestions and recommendations' made to Norway included:

that Norway both improve the training of public officials (including immigration officers) to avoid racial discrimination, and improve methods of supervision to ensure that there are effective controls upon their conduct.

that the State review its measures for guaranteeing the human rights of asylum-seekers, particularly women and children, and particularly their economic and social rights, to see whether there is room for improvement.

that the State review its measures for guaranteeing the economic and social rights of naturalized immigrants and resident aliens of minority ethnic or national origin, with particular reference to the rights to work and housing. (A/49/18, paras. 255–63)

In 1993 the United Kingdom was told that:

The Committee recommended that, in accordance with the proposal made by the Commission of Racial Equality, the State party should take adequate legislative and other measures, to better implement the provisions of the Convention. The State party should, in particular, consider amending the 1976 Race Relations Act. The Committee also recommended that the State party either adopt legislation relating to protection against racial discrimination in Northern Ireland, or extend the scope of the Race Relations Act to Northern Ireland. (A/48/18, para. 419)

The legislation in Spain has also been found insufficient. In 1994 CERD recommended that

necessary legislative measures should be taken in order to give effect to the provisions of article 4. In view of the fact that the draft new criminal Code will soon be submitted to the Parliament for approval, it is recommended that the requirements of article 4 be taken into account as well as the suggestions of the Committee in order to ensure full conformity of the new provisions of the Code with the Convention.

The Committee recommends that information be provided in the next periodic report on the implementation of the provisions of article 5 of the Convention. The State party is requested to provide detailed information on cases of complaints of racial discrimination brought before the courts and on remedies made available to victims of racism and xenophobia, according to the provisions of article 6 of the Convention. Information was also requested on the cases filed by the Defensor del Pueblo, together with the annual report he presents. (A/49/18, paras. 508–9)

As will be apparent, the adoption of concluding observations like these has greatly tightened the manner in which the Committee monitors implementation of the Convention. CERD's opinion in the case of *L.K.* v. *The Netherlands*, discussed in connection with article 4, also has a bearing upon article 5(a).

Paragraph 5(b) covers the right to security of person. It has entitled the Committee to request additional information from states in which ethnic conflict has been reported and enables it to review reports of racial attacks. Thus CERD told France of its

serious concern at the manifestations of racism and xenophobia which appeared to be on the increase in France, as well as in many countries in Europe and other continents. A particular concern is the high proportion of young people who, according to official statistics, were involved in actions of racial violence. It appears that an active extremist minority propagating nationalist and racist ideologies received increasing support in those sectors of society most affected by unemployment. (A/49/18, para. 143)

Likewise, in 1993 the Committee expressed to the government of Germany

serious concern at the manifestations of xenophobia, anti-semitism, racial discrimination and racial violence that had recently occurred in Germany. In spite of the Government's efforts to counteract and to prevent them, it appeared that these manifestations were increasing and that the German police system had in many instances failed to provide effective protection to victims and potential victims of xenophobia and racial discrimination, as required by the Convention. The Committee particularly held that all those who carried out functions in public and political life should in no way encourage sentiments of racism and xenophobia.

In view of the serious nature of the manifestations of xenophobia, racism and racial discrimination in Germany, the Committee recommended that practical measures should be strengthened with a view to preventing such manifestations, particularly acts of violence on an ethnic basis, and to punishing those who committed them. Measures should be taken, in that regard, against the organizations and groups involved.

While commending the Government of Germany for taking measures to prohibit extremist organizations disseminating ideas based on racial superiority or hatred, the Committee was of the view that appropriate measures should also be strictly applied against such organizations and especially against persons and groups who were implicated in racially motivated crimes.

In accordance with its General Recommendation XI, the Committee appealed to German Government to continue reporting fully upon legislation on foreigners and its implementation. (A/48/18, paras. 445–50)

After considering the twelfth report of the UK in 1993, the Committee stated that it

shared the concern of the State party about the rising number of racial attacks. However, it was of the opinion that not enough had been done to inquire into the causes of such attacks and the manifestations of racist ideas.

In addition, the Committee suggested that further effective legislative and other practical measures should be taken with a view to preventing incidents of incitement to racial hatred and racially motivated attacks; that, in particular, the causes of such attacks should be more accurately analysed; that current efforts to encourage recruitment into the police of members of ethnic minorities be reinforced; and that the activities of organizations of a racist nature be prohibited and the dissemination of ideas based on racial hatred declared punishable by law. (A/48/18, paras. 413, 421)

Paragraph 5(c), which covers political rights, particularly participation in elections, has not played any prominent part in the dialogue with European states. It is followed by paragraph (d) on 'other civil rights'—in particular, rights to freedom of movement, to leave a country, and to return to one's country. As has already been mentioned (see Chapter 7), the latter question was raised in CERD, though not with any force, in connection with the number of Jews who wished to leave the former USSR. When the number was allowed to increase, this then caused concern to Arab states because so many settled in Israel.

The right to nationality is affected by ICERD articles 1.2 and 1.3, which except from the definition of racial discrimination the actions of a state party in deciding who may be a national or citizen and what may be the rights of citizens, but these subparagraphs do not permit a state to discriminate racially between different classes of citizen. Many political rights, such as the rights to vote and to stand for election to the legislature, to take part in the conduct of public affairs, and to occupy certain kinds of position, are reserved to nationals of the state concerned. The right to own land may be similarly restricted. It is easy to understand a requirement that members of the police and armed services, and responsible officials of state institutions, shall be nationals, but the same argument may not justify a requirement that no one may be appointed to a position in the postal service delivering letters unless he or she is a national, so there is some scope for questioning the justifiability of restrictions that are widely drawn. This issue was raised in connection with the eleventh report of France in 1994 when in its concluding observations the Committee recommended 'that when France reviews its rules restricting occupations to French nationals, it ensures that none is discriminatory in effect' (A/49/18, para. 152).

In some countries there are large numbers of 'undocumented workers', 'illegals', or 'clandestines' who are liable to deportation and can more easily be exploited than workers who are nationals. Asylum-seekers need to be registered while their applications are under consideration so they are not equally vulnerable.

The question of nationality can therefore be important to discussions of racial discrimination. The 'New Commonwealth' immigrants in UK are entitled to vote, whereas (unless they have dual nationality) North Africans in France and Turks in Germany are not; this has a profound influence upon their relations with the societies in which they live. Nationality can be acquired in several ways: by birth in the national territory (the so-called *jus soli*); by virtue of a parent's nationality (the so-called *jus sanguinis*); by naturalization; and by marriage to a national. In Germany individuals seeking naturalization are obliged to abandon their previous nationality, but France is not opposed to dual nationality.

Not all nationals of a country may possess the same rights. The British Nationality Act, 1981, created three distinct classes: British citizenship; British Dependent Territories citizenship; and British Overseas citizenship. British citizens have a right of abode in the UK. British Dependent Territories citizens have a right of abode only in the territory from which they originate. There is a further category of Commonwealth citizens; persons in this category may, after perhaps two years' residence, be entitled to take part in elections in other Commonwealth countries.

Within the UK there has been much criticism of the 'primary purpose rule' under which the spouse of a British subject may be denied entry to the country if it is thought that the marriage was contracted with the primary purpose of securing a right of entry. This rule was criticized by CERD in 1993:

The Committee notes with concern that . . . the primary purpose rule regarding marriage under the immigration regulations may entail discrimination in effect on grounds of ethnic origin.

In the case of Hong Kong, in particular, the Committee expresses its concern at the discriminatory provisions of the British Nationality (Hong Kong) Act of 1990, according to which the authorities may register as British citizens only 50,000 'key people'. (A/48/18, paras. 417–18)

Other rights protected from discrimination under this paragraph include the rights to marriage, property, inheritance, freedom of thought, opinion, and association—the first three have not occasioned question, while the main issue concerning the remaining subparagraph has been covered in connection with article 4.

Paragraph (e) lists economic, social, and cultural rights, in particular subparagraph (i) the rights to work. After its consideration of Sweden's seventh report in 1986 the Committee reported that its members

observed with concern that, after 15 years of implementation of the Convention, no legislation had yet been adopted in Sweden to prohibit ethnic discrimination in the labour market. It was pointed out that the Swedish Commission on Ethnic Prejudice and Discrimination had found discrimination in hiring, promoting and training and concluded that legislation was needed in order to comply with the Convention; however, the Government had decided against such legislation because of the legal technicalities referred to in the report. It was further noted that, in the absence of any legal means, employers could, for instance, refuse to hire blacks and immigrants with impunity and that some cases of discrimination arose from agreements between managements and labour unions. (A/42/18, para. 353)

By 1994 the situation had changed. The Ethnic Discrimination Commission had re-examined the matter, taking careful account of views expressed in CERD, and the government had introduced a measure to provide remedies in civil law for those who had suffered ethnic discrimination in the workplace.

Like most European countries, Austria is behind Sweden in this respect. After considering its tenth report, CERD concluded:

'The Committee found it necessary to recall that under article 5(e)(i) of the Convention, everyone in Austria must be guaranteed the right, without distinction as to race, to equality before the law in the enjoyment of the right[s] to work. This guarantee must cover the private as well as the State sector. (A/47/18, para. 198).

Similar recommendations have been addressed to some other countries, including France:

that France introduce legislation to provide effective protection of the exercise, without discrimination, of the rights to work and to housing, in both the public and private sectors, and to provide compensation to victims of discrimination. (A/49/18, para. 155) and Germany:

taking into account that practices of racial discrimination in such areas as access to employment, housing and other rights referred to in article 5(*f*) of the Convention were not always effectively dealt with, the German authorities should give serious consideration to the enactment of a comprehensive anti-discrimination law. Such a law would constitute a clear reaffirmation by the German authorities that racial discrimination was absolutely unacceptable, detrimental to human rights and human dignity. Other preventive measures such as information campaigns, educational programmes and training programmes addressed particularly to law enforcement officials, in accordance with article 7 of the Convention and General Recommendation XIII of the Committee, would strengthen the effectiveness of legal provisions. (A/48/18, para. 447)

Norway was told that

insufficient information was provided on the implementation of provisions of article 5 of the Convention dealing with non-discrimination in respect of economic, social and cultural rights. (A/49/18, para. 259)

The UK was told that

The Committee noted with concern that in spite of various measures taken by the authorities the rate of unemployment affecting ethnic minorities remained very high . . . (A/48/18, para. 417)

Subparagraph (ii), on the right to form and join trade unions, has not attracted attention in dialogue with European states; nor has there been much questioning on (iii), the right to housing. In the last case it seems as if many European states are disinclined to try to regulate discrimination in the private housing sector, and the kind of information on its incidence which has been collected for many years in the UK has not been collected in other countries. The Committee members have not pursued this topic with any vigour, though in 1995 Italy was asked whether it was unlawful for the owner of a property to give discriminatory instructions to an agent selling it or advertising it for rent, or for a person to accept discriminatory instructions. The Committee was told that the new law now covered such circumstances (SR 1075–6).

Nor, hitherto, have members of CERD attached priority to subparagraph (iv) on the right to public health, medical care, social security, and social services. Mr Banton has raised this on occasion, as in a question addressed to Norway:

With respect to the right to health specified in article 5(*e*)(iv), it is relevant to recall that discrimination occurs if like things are treated differently, or if unlike things are treated in a manner that fails to recognize their differences. Research in Britain has found that persons of African and Caribbean ancestry experience higher rates of strokes, high blood pressure, accidents, maternal mortality and tuberculosis, but lower rates of bronchitis. Persons with origins in the Indian subcontinent experience higher rates of heart disease, diabetes, accidents, tuberculosis, but lower rates of bronchitis and certain cancers. One study also found that there was a longer time interval before Asian patients with heart disease were seen by hospital consultants, either because their general practitioners treated them less favourably or because the Asian patients took longer before they sought treatment. If all sections of the population are to be treated equally, those responsible need to monitor such processes. No doubt persons from ethnic minorities in Norway have distinctive health problems. Will the government report on equal treatment in this field?

Subparagraph (v) of article 5 requires that an individual shall be able to enjoy the right to education and training without distinction as to race. Discussing the ninth report of Italy, Mr de Gouttes commended the state's policy to integrate foreign pupils into Italian schools, but asked what happened in practice? Were some schools reluctant to take foreign pupils or, on the other hand, were there some areas where the majority of pupils were of foreign origin (SR 1075)? *De facto* segregation might, however, derive not from reluctance on the part of the schools but from the exercise of parental right to choose a school for their children, as has already been discussed in connection with Article 3.

Subparagraph (vi) provides that the right to equal participation in cultural activities shall be protected. Television programmes are very influential in the formation and transmission of images of ethnic groups. This has been recognized in France by the Haut Conseil à l'Intégration, which in its 1993 report *Intégration à la française* (HCI 1993: 127–33) commented on the under-representation of immigrants and immigrant-descended people in the media and its plans to open a dialogue with the responsible parties in this field. It was suggested that it would be helpful were the next periodic report from France to notify any progress in this field, as the Committee might well wish to prepare a general recommendation on this component of article 5. CERD has also noted the manner in which political controls upon television and radio in the former Yugoslavia and in Rwanda were utilized to aggravate racial hatreds. This poses a problem to which there is no ready solution.

Paragraph (*f*) lists the last of the rights to be specifically mentioned in article 5, namely those of access to services for the general public, such as transport, hotels, restaurants, cafés, theatres, and parks. In France there have been criminal prosecutions where restaurants, dance halls, and theatres have refused to serve persons on grounds of their race (in 1992 there were four convictions for offences of this character). Yet criminal prosecution is not necessarily the best or the most effective method of preventing discrimination in such establishments. In Europe they usually require a licence from the local municipality, and that licence may be withheld when they discriminate, which may bring the decision within the scope of administrative law. Several European states (including Germany and the Netherlands) prefer to rely on administrative measures to deal with these forms of discrimination.

## ARTICLE 6

While the criminal law may prevent discrimination, it is not necessarily the most effective means available to a government, and it needs supplementation if 'just and adequate reparation' for victims is to be provided in fulfilment of the terms of article 6. Experience in some countries suggests that remedies in civil law are often more effective than criminal prohibitions. Their advantages have been summarized as follows:

1. The standard of proof is different. In criminal proceedings the state, being so powerful, is required to prove its case beyond reasonable doubt. In civil proceedings, the plaintiff needs only to prove his or her case on the balance of probabilities.
2. In criminal proceedings the accused may have a right of silence, both in police custody and in court. He or she need not then testify and expose himself or herself to cross-examination, and no inference of guilt can be drawn from such silence. Under the British law on racial discrimination, if the respondent does not reply the tribunal can infer that the applicant's statement of the facts is reliable.
3. It is usually the police who initiate criminal proceedings, though the prosecutor takes the final decision. Victims or their relatives sometimes complain about a reluctance to prosecute or to prefer the most

serious charge. In racial discrimination cases the applicant has unhindered access to the tribunal.
4. Criminal proceedings have an all-or-nothing character (though the prosecutor sometimes accepts a guilty plea to a lesser charge instead of continuing with a contested hearing on a more serious charge). In racial discrimination cases the parties can settle privately without any admission of fault by the respondent. (Banton 1994: 56)

## ARTICLE 7

Most discussions of action to combat racial discrimination conclude that legal prohibitions need to be complemented by educational measures of the kind described in article 7. CERD has issued a general recommendation and published a study (UN 1985) on this obligation, but it remains one that is difficult for the Committee to monitor.

In 1992 CERD reported that

The Committee was disturbed to learn that in Austria, as in other parts of Europe, there were signs of an increase in racism, xenophobia and anti-Semitism, and readiness to ignore the rights of members of ethnic groups, including Jews. Since such hostile attitudes can be exploited by racist organizations, the Committee sought information about preventive and educational countermeasures. (A/47/18, para. 198)

Since educational measures are not necessarily effective, and Norway had been arguing that the Council of Europe should campaign to this end, her government was asked in 1994:

In view of the importance of measures in the fields of teaching, education and culture to combat prejudices which lead to racial discrimination, the Committee requests the State party to inform it on which measures it has found most effective, and which measures can reach those sections of the population most likely to engage in racist activities.

When replies are received from Austria, Norway, and Sweden (to whom a similar request was directed), the Committee may look for more specific ways in which to develop its responsibilities for the implementation of this article.

## ARTICLE 14

By 1995 Bulgaria, Denmark, Finland, France, Hungary, Iceland, Italy, the Netherlands, Norway, the Russian Federation, Sweden, and the Ukraine had made declarations recognizing the competence of the Committee to consider communications from individuals within their jurisdiction who claimed that their rights under the Convention had not been protected. Other European states have apparently decided not to do so for the time being but have not publicized their reasons.

When Lord Lester asked in the House of Lords (13 June 1994) whether the UK government would make such a declaration, the government referred to its having accepted the right of individual petition under the European Convention on Human Rights, adding:

The European system gives individuals access to a compensatory mechanism and it, therefore, affords a stronger form of redress than that under the International Convention on the Elimination of Racial Discrimination. In addition, domestic legislation allows for compensation to be sought through industrial tribunals. The Government do not consider that there is need for a further mechanism, but we will keep the position under review.

This repeats the answer given to CERD by a UK representative in 1994. It was not well received by the Committee, since it failed to acknowledge that there are many rights protected by ICERD (notably economic rights) which are not covered by the European Convention. The claim that the European system affords a stronger form of redress exaggerates the differences.

## CONCLUSION

From time to time the Committee learns that a state has modified its legislation to bring it into line with the Convention's standards. For example, in 1987 CERD was told by the UK that its new Public Order Act 1986 penalized conduct which was *either* intended to stir up racial hatred *or* likely to have that effect. Previously conduct had been penalized only if it had *both* such an intention *and* such an effect. In conversation shortly afterwards the author found that one of his colleagues attributed the change to the Committee's comments on earlier reports, whereas the author himself thought that it had been brought about by political pressure within the country. The Committee has no means of knowing how influential its dialogue is with the state when balanced against internal political considerations. It can only guess at the processes behind the submission of a periodic report or those which follow after consideration of it.

Sometimes it appears as if some of those within a state who should be implementing the Convention do not know of its existence, or pay it no attention because there is no pressure upon them to do otherwise. That may be because the Committee itself has not previously drawn attention to some shortcoming, or because domestic policies are insufficiently sensitive to international obligations. The reader should have learnt from this chapter that there are many passages in the Convention—particularly in article 5—which are relevant to circumstances in European states in ways that have not yet been fully examined in the reporting process.

Sweden is outstanding because it has attended so carefully to the Convention and because changes in its legislation have evidently been influenced by its dialogue with CERD. It is notable also because its has explicitly maintained a view of its obligations under article 4 which is at variance with the Committee's. Many other states have not yet prohibited discrimination in effect, have failed adequately to prohibit discrimination in the private sector, or have not allowed victims effective remedies and opportunities to obtain compensation.

The dialogue between the Committee and the states parties in Europe has, on the whole, been productive. This has been partly because, quite apart from the Convention, there is pressure within the Western states at least for improved action against racial discrimination. The state representatives have been open-minded in their exchanges (if occasionally irritated by observations from individual members), but their governments are still far from discharging all their obligations. Dialogue has been less intense with the states of Eastern Europe because the problems associated with immigration from the Third World have been less salient there. Some East European states have to contend with forms of discrimination resulting from the presence of national minorities which seek greater independence or which threaten the existing pattern of state boundaries. Accusations of racial discrimination then have a more political character and at present are less easily resolved by reference to the Convention.

# 10

# Dialogue with American States

IT is possible that there was more genuine idealism in the approach of American states towards the Convention than in other regions. States on the mainland, from Mexico southwards, believed that racial discrimination was a problem in other regions of the world, but not their own. Their representatives looked with hope towards the decolonization process and wished to lend their support. In the Caribbean there were ex-colonies with black populations which were ready to align themselves with the new African states. North of Mexico, Canada was among the states most committed to the UN. Unlike the USA, its policies were not constrained by any iso-lationist sentiment among its electorate. By contrast, in the USA, John Foster Dulles had declared that he would never bring any binding human-rights convention to the Senate for ratification (Lauren 1988: 226). In the event, the USA signed the Convention in 1966, accompanying its signature with a statement that nothing in it should be deemed to require legislation incompatible with the country's constitution. Not until Jimmy Carter became president was the Convention sent to the Senate. Since the USA ratified the Convention only in late 1994, its dialogue with the Committee had not started at the time this book was completed.

At the UN, the states of the Caribbean are part of the Latin American group; Canada is in the WEOG, and the USA is on its own. This chapter will consider the position of the Latin American states before that of Canada.

## LATIN AMERICA

Latin America experienced no form of nationalism comparable with those which stirred nineteenth- and early twentieth-century Europe. So Latin American diplomats did not after 1945 join the discussion of human rights at the UN with an equally urgent consciousness of ethnic divisions as a possible threat to world peace. When the UDHR was being drafted, there was a proposal to include in it a minorities article, providing that

persons belonging to such ethnic, religious or linguistic minorities shall have the right to establish and maintain, out of an equitable proportion of public funds for the purpose, their schools and cultural institutions, and to use their language before the courts and other authorities and organs of the State, and in the press and public assembly.

The successful attack on this and similar proposals was led by the representatives of Latin American states, arguing that minority problems were not universal but regional (Thornberry 1991: 135–6). No minorities clause was written into the American Declaration of the Rights and Duties of Man (1948) or the American Convention on Human Rights (1969). When the UN Covenant on Civil and Political Rights was under consideration, the representative of Brazil argued that the 'mere co-existence of different groups in a territory under the jurisdiction of a single State did not make them minorities in the legal sense'. Minorities resulted from 'conflicts of some length between nations, or from the transfer of a territory from the jurisdiction of one State to another'. Therefore Brazil and the other American states 'did not recognize the existence of minorities on the American continent'. It would seem as if, for Latin Americans, the sort of minority for which treaties were adopted at the end of the First World War and subsequently overseen by the League of Nations (Hannum 1990: 51–5) served as a paradigm case for their understanding of the nature of minorities. As Thornberry (1991: 154–5) adds, the constitution of Brazil prescribes the equality of individuals and the rule of non-discrimination without recognizing the possibility of groups intermediate between the state and the citizen. The denial of this possibility is crucial to any understanding of the outlook of so many of the governments in this region, though some of them have now provided for bilingual education and recognized national languages other than Spanish and Portuguese.

The UDHR has also been criticized for its failure to mention indigenous peoples and their rights. The Bolivian government had asked in 1948 for a sub-commission to study the problems of such groups. In 1953 the ILO published a study on indigenous peoples and in 1957 adopted Convention No. 107 and Recommendation

No. 104 on the Protection of Indigenous and Tribal Populations. Brazil regarded it as applying 'only to the forest-dwelling population', and some other Latin American governments have also taken a restricted view of its scope (Thornberry 1991: 338–41). Its emphasis was on protection and it was widely criticized for a paternalistic and assimilationist approach (Thornberry 1991: 369–71). The representatives of indigenous peoples did not like being referred to as indigenous populations, but many governments would agree to nothing else, because both the two UN covenants in their first article begin with the statement: 'All peoples have the right of self-determination. By virtue of that right they freely determine their political status and freely pursue their economic, social and cultural development.' The significance of this article is not yet agreed. To some it means that any people has the right to be sovereign and independent. To some it refers only to the decolonization process. To others it points to possible forms of autonomy that fall short of full independence. Until this has been clarified, states fear that to allow their internal groups to be called 'peoples' might be to make a rod for their own backs. They may be unduly apprehensive.

International pressure upon Latin American governments to protect the rights of indigenous peoples is a relatively recent development. In 1968 the International Work Group for Indigenous Affairs was established at a meeting in Copenhagen of the International Congress of Americanists (IWGIA 1989). In 1969 Survival International was founded in London, and led, in 1972, to the setting-up, in Cambridge, Massachusetts, of Cultural Survival (Benthall 1992). In 1980 several NGOs filed with the Inter-American Commission on Human Rights a complaint against Brazil's treatment of the Yanomani. In 1985 the Commission concluded that the government's failure earlier to take 'timely and effective measures' had led to violations of Yanomani rights (Hannum 1990: 414n.).

The pressure has not come only from outside. From early times there were persons within the population of European descent who sought to defend the rights of indigenous peoples. Latin American governments and individuals have played an important part in the formulation of the new international norms of human rights. The indigenous peoples are now a significant political force in many Latin American countries and able to press their own interests.

A new ILO Convention Concerning Indigenous and Tribal

Peoples in Independent Countries (No. 169) was adopted in 1989. It consists of forty-four articles, covering general policy, land, employment, social security, health, education, and contacts across borders. There were many draft proposals to choose between. The ILO is a tripartite body in which governments, employers and workers are represented. An account of the discussions (IWGIA 1989: 173–91) states that the workers' representatives were ready to table proposals drafted by a group of indigenous representatives and advisers. The employers were less sympathetic. The account continues (in what may have been a polemical vein):

Peru and Argentina joined Brazil and Venezuela in building a solid re-actionary block of South American countries. Battling against this were Colombia and Ecuador. Colombia, in particular, showed a principled and consistent position on indigenous rights . . . Asian countries, in the form of India and Japan, continued to lead the reactionary wing . . . From the Arab countries and Africa there was some concern at the reactionary nature of the meeting . . . Canada continued its political line of devaluing the Convention . . . The primary interest of all the governments, except for Portugal and Colombia, was to ensure that international standards remain well below the national legislation. (Gray 1990)

Some articles were revised by negotiation and then the meeting split down the middle with tied votes. As a result, compromise texts drafted by the secretariat were eventually adopted, with the result that some observers thought the new version to be no real improvement. When a clause was approved to state that 'the use of the term "peoples" in this Convention shall not be construed as having any implications which may attach to the term under international law', the indigenous representatives (present as observers) viewed this as setting up a two-tiered differentiation between 'ordinary peoples' and 'indigenous peoples'. They then withdrew from the meeting and adopted their own resolution condemning the ILO, calling for opposition to 'the racist revision', and urging states not to ratify it.

When the International Convention on the Elimination of All Forms of Racial Discrimination was finalized in the General Assembly, it had the enthusiastic support of nearly all the Latin American states. Most of them saw it as directed against apartheid and seem not to have been apprehensive that its comprehensive definition of racial discrimination would affect their policies *vis-à-vis* indigenous groups within their own frontiers. The one delegation to demur was Colombia, and that was over the use of criminal sanctions and not to do with indigenous peoples. The delegate wished to stress that 'ideas are fought with ideas and reasons; theories are refuted with arguments and not by resort to the scaffold, prison, exile, confiscation and fines' (A/PV/.1406, para. 70). Again a principled and consistent position!

The first reports submitted under the racial convention were considered in 1970, but before turning to them it may be well to note several related developments. One was work on drafting a Declaration on the Rights of Persons belonging to National or Ethnic, Religious and Linguistic Minorities, already mentioned in Chapter 3. Remarkably, the delegates of Latin American states which had earlier been so insistent that there were no minorities in their countries did not repeat these statements in the General Assembly debate on this declaration. In all probability they thought their position had been made clear and required no repetition.

That this is not absolutely certain can be seen from the responses of three of these states to a UN questionnaire. In 1989 the Sub-Commission on Prevention of Discrimination and Protection of Minorities appointed Mr Asbjørn Eide to report on national experiences regarding peaceful and constructive solutions of problems involving minorities—that is, 'nationalities, ethnic, linguistic or cultural groups which are significantly different from other groups within a sovereign State'. Bolivia, Colombia, and Venezuela chose to reply, saying that they counted indigenous groups as ethnically distinctive. They did not call them minorities, but implicitly they recognized the parallels.

Another important development started in 1970, when the Commission on Human Rights appointed a special rapporteur to prepare a study on the elimination of discrimination against indigenous populations. It was followed in 1989 by the initiation of a study of 'the potential utility of treaties, agreements and other constructive arrangements between indigenous peoples and states'. A draft Universal Declaration on Rights of Indigenous Peoples has been prepared by the Sub-Commission, but, when the Human Rights Commission in 1995 established a working party to elaborate a draft declaration for submission to the General Assembly, it was unwilling to stipulate that its working party should take the Sub-Commission's draft as a basis for its deliberations. One of the points that remains to be settled is whether certain of these rights are collective rights or shared individual rights. Representatives of indigenous peoples meet annually in Geneva as observers of the proceedings of the Sub-Commission's Working Group. They are now having a significant effect on the UN's work, but at least as important must be what they learn from one another and the growth of solidarity among indigenous movements in many regions (for a lively account of these occasions, see Gray 1993).

The indigenous peoples do not see themselves as minorities and some believe that, were they to be so described, the colonizers would have achieved their ultimate goal (Thornberry 1991: 331). Their members may benefit from the minorities declaration, and may be able to claim corresponding rights if that declaration is eventually succeeded by a convention, but some of their leaders would regard that as a betrayal of their cause. They insist that their rights are grounded upon their prior occupation of the territory.

The time which in recent years CERD has devoted to consideration of periodic reports from American states can be seen from Table 3 (which can be found at the end of Chapter 8). The account of the dialogue will begin by discussing official policies in relation to the indigenous peoples. It will have regard to the comparative study of nation-building, multiculturalism, and nationalism. Later the chapter will turn to the dialogue with Canada, which, as the table shows, has taken longer, as is only to be expected in view of the variety of ethnic groups in that country and the variations in responsibility of the federal and provincial governments.

Chapters 6 and 7 have already suggested that the dialogue between states parties and the Committee, over the years since 1970, has shown some sharpening of focus on the Convention's relevance to indigenous policy. They have acknowledged that this may have been caused in greater part by changes within the states and the general changes in opinion and outlook over the period.

Thirty-three states belong to the UN's Latin American regional group but not all need to be considered here. Paraguay has not yet acceded to the Convention, while Guyana and Suriname have yet to submit their initial reports (which were due in 1978 and 1985). Less attention need be paid to Uruguay because its indigenous population was exterminated. Of the remaining fourteen, Brazil is by far the biggest, with a population of over 112 million; Mexico has 81 million, while the population of all the others together adds to only a little more than that of Mexico (these are Argentina,

Bolivia, Chile, Colombia, Costa Rica, Ecuador, El Salvador, Guatemala, Nicaragua, Panama, and Venezuela). The indigenous population of some states (Argentina, Costa Rica, Venezuela) is less than 1 per cent of the total population, while that of some others, like Peru, reaches 50 per cent, depending to some extent upon the criteria used for its definition.

## INDIGENOUS PEOPLES

The Convention defines racial discrimination as covering any distinction based on race, colour, descent, or national or ethnic origin, and therefore clearly relates to differences between the indigenous peoples of Latin America and those descended or partly descended from European and African immigrants. As was explained in Chapter 6, those who in the 1970s prepared the reports from Latin American states were sometimes surprised to have this pointed out to them. Possibly they derived their conception of racial discrimination from the paradigm cases of the USA and South Africa. If they thought of racial discrimination as the legal or institutional establishment of differential rights, it is not astonishing if they could not see how socio-economic differentiation and the unequal development of culturally distinctive groups could occasion discrimination in the Convention's sense. With some states the reorientation has taken time. In 1989 the reports from Chile, Colombia, Mexico, and Venezuela were still asserting that there was no racial discrimination in their countries. The state representatives who presented them to the Committee, being diplomats with an experience of the world, could be ready to agree that these statements were misguided, but the officials in the capitals who prepared the reports often seem to have paid insufficient attention to the way racial discrimination is defined in the Convention. This can lead to an unwillingness to acknowledge legal obligations.

By 1976 Latin American states were being asked about their policies respecting their indigenous peoples. For example:

What was the philosophy underlying Mexico's policy relating to race? It was recalled in that connexion that some Latin American Governments had reported that their policy was based on the desire to create an amalgam of the various races in their respective countries, while other

Governments of Latin American countries were attempting to integrate all the ethnic groups into the body politic while preserving their respective ethnic characteristics. (A/31/18, para. 234)

Some more specific points were also made; for example:

Article 86 of the Peruvian Constitution appeared to introduce discrimination between Peruvian citizens by granting the right to vote only to citizens able to read and write; inasmuch as a large proportion of the Indian population in Peru did not meet that requirement, it was excluded from political life, contrary to the provisions of article 5 (para (*c*)) of the Convention. (A/31/18, para. 78)

Peru later amended its law regarding electoral rights to take account of this.

In this early period the Committee concentrated upon the relation between the legal obligations stemming from an international treaty and the country's internal legal order. Did the provisions of a treaty enter into effect automatically, or did the legislature have to adopt a law that gave effect to them? Had a state's laws been amended to meet all the requirements of the Convention? Did it appreciate that, while some articles allowed states discretion as to the manner of their implementation, article 4 on the prohibition of incitement to racial hatred was mandatory? Was the state furthering the objectives of the Convention by terminating diplomatic and commercial relations with racist regimes in southern Africa? Such questions were asked of all states, not just those of Latin America. By the 1980s a routine had been established and the reports of the Committee to the General Assembly increased in length, displaying a more detailed consideration of circumstances and an improved dialogue. It has already been noted that the early reports of Chile occasioned controversy because, following the military take-over, some members of the Committee doubted the legality and good faith of some of the claims made by the new government.

The question put to Mexico in 1976, about whether it was following a policy of the assimilation of ethnic groups or of protecting their culture, was addressed to other Latin American states as well. It is probable that members of the Committee themselves approached this question from different standpoints, with those from Eastern Europe being more favourable to assimilation. The reply of the Argentinian representative in 1982 is worth noting:

it was very difficult to promote development without integration and the danger was ever present of segregating people on the pretext of autonomy. He indicated that the indigenous reservations were not ghettos or prisons but farm unit areas provided with services to develop their potential. People from the reservations could attend school in any part of the country, and had the same right of travel as anyone else. As to the concern expressed about the participation of indigenous peoples in development projects which affected them, noteworthy progress had been achieved, as shown by the formation of associations on the part of communities, and the participation of their natural leaders (chiefs, mayors, teachers, and the like) in the different stages of project activities. Together with indigenous groups, immigration flows had long held the attention of the Argentine authorities. Argentina was now host to 5,000 Laotian families among other nationals. (A/37/18, para. 303)

In its concluding observations on the report from Argentina considered in 1991 the Committee stated: 'no information had been given regarding court decisions relating to racial discrimination, and no figures given to show the extent to which the indigenous population participated in Congress, the Administration or institutions dealing with indigenous affairs' (A/46/18, para. 64).

Brazil has been questioned about that country's conception of 'tutelage' for indigenous peoples. Panama was commended for its sincerity in acknowledging that previously there had been no realistic policy to tackle the way in which the indigenous people had been cut off from the life of the nation (A/34/18, para. 165).

The Committee was careful to treat all states parties equally as sovereign states, but the reader can discern differences in the kind of dialogue that was developing with the Latin American states that had so far acceded to the Convention. Ecuador and Panama were ready to respond to the Committee's concerns. Costa Rica was sympathetic, but slow to bring its legislation into line, though, like Ecuador, it had made the declaration under article 14 permitting those within its jurisdiction to petition the Committee if they had not received the promised protections. Peru has followed the example set by Costa Rica and Ecuador. However, the Bolivian government was uncomprehending in its belief that, since in its view there was no racial discrimination in its territory, it did not have to take any further action (A/33/18, para. 133). Venezuela's distinctive stance has already been described. In dialogue, its representative, like those of some other states, was sometimes unable to help the Committee and could explain only that the reports had been prepared in the capital by competent specialists (A/32/18, para. 301). In 1983 he said that he 'had the impression that certain Western European standards were being applied to Venezuela in cases where they were perhaps not appropriate. Since Venezuelans did not think in terms of special ethnic groups and minorities it was impossible to comply with some of the requests made by members of the Committee' (A/38/18, para. 216).

The year 1984 saw the consideration of the first reports from Colombia, El Salvador, and Guatemala. In 1988 Nicaragua described its Indigenous Peoples Autonomy Act of the previous year, drafted on the basis of consultations with their representatives, in which for the first time the country's multiethnic character was recognized. The languages of the indigenous peoples and communities of the Atlantic coast were recognized as national languages (A/43/18, para. 82). Significant changes had been initiated in Mexico, with a constitutional amendment to recognize the rights of the indigenous peoples. Official policy was based on respect for indigenous people and communities by guaranteeing equal access to the law and protecting and developing their cultures, social organizations, and resources (A/46/18, para. 348). Colombia was declared to be a multiracial society concerned to defend the cultural heritage of all indigenous communities; these had a significant number of representatives in the legislature (A/47/18, para. 47). In its eleventh report prepared in 1991 Ecuador for the first time stated that 'recognition of the fact that Ecuador is a multi-ethnic and multi-cultural society implies abandonment of the idea that it consists of a single culture'. This terminology is not being used by other states in the region and there seems to have been little consideration of its possible implications. The tenth periodic report from Chile was presented in 1992 by a representative of the new democratic government. It acknowledged the racial discrimination practised by the previous government and described policies of rectification. The Committee observed that it

welcomed the frankness with which the Government of Chile acknowledged the history of discrimination against the indigenous peoples. It took note of the measures being taken to improve the situation of indigenous peoples and expects that policy to be continued so as to improve the economic, social and educational status of those peoples and their enjoyment of human rights in accordance with article 5 of the Convention. (A/47/18, para. 220)

The government of Colombia has identified four periods in the history of its dealings with its indigenous peoples. There was a liquidationist period from 1810 to 1890, in which the state denied legal personality to indigenous political institutions and sought to undermine them. A statute of 1890 provided that 'the general legislation of the Republic shall not apply to savages who are being brought to civilised life by the Missions'. The government now observes that, 'In a kind of fetishistic cult of the written law, the legislators appeared to believe in the magical virtues of merely establishing rules intended to change an age-old social and political institution' (third periodic report, 1987, para. 9). During the same period the regional governments abolished the reservations established in the colonial era. New legislation in 1890 inaugurated the reductionist period, during which the indigenous peoples were permitted to reorganize and the state administrators gradually gained a better understanding of their outlook. The turning-point was in 1958, when a new act provided for a complex system of projects ranging from land redistribution to the introduction of new technological facilities. This integrationist period was therefore one which prioritized development in place of assimilation. It ran until 1982, a year which saw the beginning of the period of indigenous self-administration.

Misunderstandings of the scope of ICERD article 1.1 continue. It seems as if, when racial discrimination is mentioned, many Latin Americans think of the situations in the USA and South Africa, then, because the situation in their own countries is different, they infer that racial discrimination is absent from them. CERD attempts to correct this. In 1995 it said of Mexico:

Particular concern is expressed that the State Party does not seem to perceive that the pervasive discrimination being suffered by the 56 indigenous groups living in Mexico falls under the definition given to racial discrimination in article 1 of the Convention. The description of their plight merely as an unequal participation in social and economic development is inadequate.

With regard to El Salvador, the Committee insisted:

The assertion of the State party that, because there are no physical distinctions between the indigenous population and the population as a whole, and because the number of indigenous persons is insignificant, no racial discrimination exists in the State, is not acceptable . . . Deep concern is expressed at the lack of effort by the authorities to collect information regarding the situation of indigenous ethnic and other minorities which could serve as an indication of the practical implementation of the Convention, particularly when there appears to be clear evidence that the indigenous minorities live in conditions of extreme economic marginalization. (A/50/18)

## CONCLUDING OBSERVATIONS

The adoption of concluding observations expressing the collective view of the Committee has moved the dialogue with Latin American states onto a new plane that increases expectations of them. Thus in 1992 the Committee observed of the report from Costa Rica that:

There were too few practical examples or relevant statistics, particularly on cases of complaints and convictions for acts of racial discrimination. There were also omissions in the presentation of the actual situation of ethnic minorities, especially indigenous peoples and Blacks, the 'social indicators' of the non-integration of those population groups, the difficulties and discrimination to which they were exposed (right to land, right to health, freedom of movement, education, etc.), the damage caused to the environment of the Indians and the obstacles they might encounter in claiming compensation for such damage. (A/47/18, para. 112)

In Chapter 8 reference was made to the revolt in the Chiapas region of Mexico which was headline news in 1993. It is therefore appropriate to recall that in 1991 the Committee reported that members had asked about:

the continuing conflicts, acts of violence, illegal arrests, expulsions and other human rights violations of which peasants and indigenous persons had been victims, in particular in the states of Oaxaca and Chiapas. In that regard, members wished to know what measures the Mexican Government had taken to solve conflicts between landowners and indigenous peoples; whether the recommendations of the National Human Rights Commission were legally binding; and whether they were followed by the legal and administrative authorities concerned in cases in which the statutory time-limit for sentencing had been exceeded.

In its concluding observations the Committee reported

that there were in Mexico economic and social disparities between the different categories of the population that led to serious discrimination that

ought to be remedied, even if it was not of a directly racist character . . .
It regretted that Mexico had not modified its position with regard to the
interpretation of article 4 of the Convention. (A/46/18, paras. 350, 363)

Concerning article 4, the government maintained that the Convention could be invoked before national courts, particularly in
criminal cases, and any offender could be punished for violation of
a constitutional guarantee, but some members of the Committee
were not satisfied. They maintained that this was insufficient to implement an obligation under the Convention.

   In 1995 CERD reported that, 'As regards the Chiapas conflict,
it is noted with satisfaction that in January 1994, the government
decided to take steps to seek a political rather than a military
solution.' It went on

The Committee reaffirms that the provisions of article 4, paragraphs (*a*)
and (*b*), of the Convention are of a mandatory character . . . The Committee wishes the government of Mexico to provide, in its next report,
detailed information on the implementation of article 5 of the Convention . . . The Committee draws the attention of the State party to the
necessity of adopting indicators to evaluate the policies and programmes
aimed at the protection and promotion of the indigenous peoples' rights.
(A/50/18)

   In the same year the combined eighth to eleventh periodic reports
of Peru were presented by a delegation led by that country's Minister of Justice. The delegation brought the text of a draft law
currently before the parliament which had been drawn up so as to
meet the requirement of article 4. The Minister said that for six
years his government's priority had been to combat terrorism and
drug trafficking and rebuild a shattered economy. Now attention
could be given to other problems and the incidence of allegations
of human-rights violations had been greatly reduced. The Committee recommended that

effective monitoring mechanisms be introduced to assess progress achieved
in the protection of the rights of indigenous communities . . . special efforts
be made within the armed forces to terminate any unlawful violence
towards civilians, including persons belonging to indigenous communities,
and to secure that perpetrators of human rights violations are brought to
justice . . . [and that the government] provide, in its next report due on
30 October 1994, detailed information on the actual implementation of
articles 4, 5 and 6 of the Convention. (A/50/18)

Guatemala is another state which, after falling behind, submitted in 1995 a single document in place of five periodic reports. It ran to 127 pages, reproducing a variety of laws for the protection of human rights, but saying little about the manner of their implementation. Nor was the state representative able to answer questions on this point. Indeed, when asked if he could identify any article of the Convention which his government actually implemented, he chose not to respond. The Committee's concluding observations included:

Profound concern is expressed regarding widespread discrimination affecting the indigenous communities and excluding them from the enjoyment of their civil, political, economic, social and cultural rights . . .

Concern is expressed at the numerous excesses by elements of the military and the Civilian Defence Patrols (PACs) against indigenous peoples, including summary executions, and other cruel, inhuman or degrading treatment, threats and forcible recruitment into the armed forces.

The failure to investigate these crimes and to prosecute the perpetrators is particularly deplored.

The lack of awareness of members of indigenous communities about recourse procedures, the shortage of practical facilities for them to use their own language in court procedures and the weaknesses of the judicial system are also regretted as well as the resulting relative impunity for the perpetrators of such violations. (A/50/18)

Other concerns mentioned included the effects of poverty and illiteracy in the indigenous communities. There followed a set of 'suggestions and recommendations' based upon the concerns mentioned. The Committee took note with satisfaction of the government's invitation to send one of its members to Guatemala to advise them on implementation of the Convention, and of its intention to submit a further report very soon.


## IMPROVED PROTECTIONS

This review offers some support for the conclusion that over the past quarter-century international norms of human rights have had an increasing and positive influence upon the policies of Latin American states affecting indigenous peoples. Those states now to a greater extent accept that they have a duty to protect indigenous cultures and are subjected to greater pressure to demonstrate that they take this duty seriously.

Protections are best embodied in a country's constitution. In 1995 CERD reported of El Salvador that it regretted 'that no references to the rights of indigenous persons are made in the Constitution, including their right to participate in decisions affecting their lands, culture, traditions and the allocation of natural resources'. The Committee welcomed the 1987 constitution of Nicaragua in that it recognized 'for the first time the multi-ethnic character of the Nicaraguan population and grants to all persons the enjoyment of the rights proclaimed in various international and regional instruments'. Regarding Mexico it noted with particular satisfaction that the January 1992 amendment to article 4 of the constitution represented

a fundamental shift in the State party's policy towards indigenous peoples, since it states that the Mexican nation has a multicultural composition originally based on its indigenous peoples and recognizes, for the first time since Mexico's independence, special constitutional rights for the indigenous people living in its territory. (A/50/18)

In the South-West Africa cases before the International Court of Justice, Judge Tanaka stated that protection 'cannot be imposed upon members of minority groups, and consequently they have the choice whether to accept it or not'. Therefore the manner in which the state fulfils its duty to protect has to be negotiated. In practice, this is a relation between parties of very unequal power, and consultation is often one-sided. An example of an enlightened policy of this kind is furnished by the Colombian policy of self-administration, but such a policy may be more impressive on paper than in reality. Protections are particularly weak in the Amazon Basin. There, as in other parts of Latin America, the land of the indigenous peoples has been invaded by colonists and the state has been unable to provide the promised protection. The police and the military tend to side with the colonists and are not effectively disciplined by the government. Indigenous leaders have been assassinated. Such problems are magnified many times in the areas affected by the narcotics trade. In many regions (including the Pacific Coast region of Colombia) the rain forest is being destroyed by logging and mining companies. The government has made concessions to transnational corporations in order to attract investment from outside. The sacrifice of the rights of the indigenous peoples in this and other Latin American countries has been attributed to an underlying attitude that a Japanese sociologist (Mushakoji 1993) calls development racism.

CERD has not been silent on these issues. In 1992 it took favourable note of Colombia's plans for the conservation of the Amazon region and its programmes for improving the conditions of the indigenous population but remarked that similar programmes had been launched before and that the Committee had not been told whether they had achieved their objectives. Its observations continued:

the report lacked information on the actual economic, social and educational situation of the indigenous population . . . only on the basis of such data would the Committee be in a position to assess accurately the situation of the indigenous population . . . [and] the black community . . . article 4 of the Convention was not properly reflected in the national penal law . . . about ongoing violence . . . the measures that had been taken by the Colombian Government did not seem to be sufficient so far to effectively protect the life, health and property of the citizens, and especially of members of its indigenous population. (A/47/18, paras. 156–9)

Circumstances in the highland regions of Bolivia and Ecuador, and in countries like Argentina, are obviously different from the Amazon, but some of the same issues arise, even if they are less marked. It may also be advisable to add that CERD receives information from non-governmental sources about abuses that are rarely mentioned in state reports, and that it asks states for additional information about what they have done to investigate such allegations and try to prevent their recurrence.

Indigenous peoples in Costa Rica, Ecuador, and Peru could use article 14 of the Convention to maintain that the state has not protected their individual or shared rights. In so doing they would be drawing upon the international cultural capital built up by the human-rights movement. Such action requires both legal and emotional support for the complainant, but is the more likely now that organizations of indigenous peoples have come together in the World Council for Indigenous Peoples. Their Sixth General Assembly was held in Norway (Henriksen 1991: 191–200).

If indigenous persons make use of their rights of petition, there will be cases from Latin America which resemble that which Ivan

Kitok brought to the Human Rights Committee against Sweden mentioned in Chapter 3 (Thornberry 1991: 211–13). There will be similar conflicts wherever the state vests collective rights to land and other resources in bodies representing indigenous peoples, but this may still be the better policy.

It is probable that the future responses of persons of indigenous descent will depend upon whether they see themselves as members of indigenous peoples or of classes or of nations. All over Latin America there is a substantial migration from the countryside to the towns. The migrant may see the move as temporary, but the economic base is unlikely to sustain any return migration. In Latin American societies, even more than in those of Western Europe and North America, birth into a relatively wealthy and educated family confers a great advantage. There is a massive transmission of social inequality from one generation to the next.

Many of the migrants to Latin American cities have swelled the population in the *barriadas*, the squatter settlements on the urban periphery. In Peru this movement has led to a growth in the proportion of persons who would elsewhere be called *mestizos* but in Peru are called *Cholos*, i.e. persons of partially Indian origin who are now likely to work as truck drivers, market workers, waiters, clerks, traders, or as university students. They are locked into the urban system of socio-economic status, having entered it at the bottom. They seek to advance as individuals, speaking Spanish and wearing European-style costume. But they are also resentful of the attitudes towards them of so many whites and *mestizos* and therefore the more ready to respond to changes which reflect mountain culture as against creole culture (Mangin 1973). If they become dissatisfied with the rate at which they can advance, socially, economically, and politically, as individuals, they may well adopt other strategies of a collective character based upon their shared class interests. Some university students now take pride in wearing indigenous costume (Valencia Rodriguez 1993: 54).

So far those people of indigenous origin who have come to the towns have chosen the path of individual mobility. This is in accordance with a prevalent intellectual view on Ecuador:

Ecuador is not a country inhabited by white folk, for as an ethnic minority they only add up to scarcely one-tenth of the total population. Neither is it a country of Indians, for in that case its history would be one of regression, or else, of stratification . . . the nation is *Mestizo* . . . Once the Indians enter civilized life . . . the *Mestizo* part of the population will be more homogeneous. (quoted in Whitten 1975: 58)

This process may not continue. In areas where there is no upper-class *blanco* culture, some *mestizos* are becoming *blancos*, and this tends to increase the disjunction between *indios* and *mestizos* (Whitten 1975: 59–60). Another study reports that in some other parts of Ecuador the townspeople are all accounted *blancos* in distinction from the *indigenas*. The two categories are distinguished by self-identification through dress and language use, and in the 1960s and 1970s the boundary was frequently crossed in both directions, often by people from the bottom stratum of their category. By the 1980s literacy programmes in the indigenous language were flourishing. Educated persons of indigenous origin were returning from the universities maintaining their ethnic alignment. The *blancos* encouraged any *indigena* to transculturate and become a *blanco*, but a new ethnic pride pulled in the opposite direction. Those who changed were no longer seen as trying to better themselves but as betraying their people. A process of ethno-genesis was in train (Belote and Belote 1984).

According to one line of analysis, nationalism has been used in Western Europe as an ideology which enables the ruling class to buy the support of the working class by highlighting a shared national interest opposed to the competition from foreigners. It has also been a basis on which the working class has increased the price for its loyalty. Such a form of nationalism seems unlikely in Latin America. National sentiment has not grown very fast because of the magnitude of the internal differences relative to external conflicts. This reduces the speed of operation of governmental policies for nation-building, while at the same time such policies remain central to any attempt to integrate the members of the indigenous groups into a larger whole.

Latin American governments have not formulated any policies of multiculturalism with respect to immigrants from European countries. Why should they be so different from Australia and Canada? Is multiculturalism in those countries to be regarded as primarily a rhetorical idiom used by political parties to attract new voters? Or is it something more substantial?

Perhaps because of its use in the First World, some Latin American governments are now employing the idiom of multiculturalism to show a willingness to protect the cultures of indigenous peoples. It looks as if the publicity for international norms has been influential in this. Like states in many other regions, they declare national integration to be their overriding policy. Bolivia, Colombia, Ecuador, Mexico, Nicaragua, and Peru have done most to give official recognition to indigenous languages, while some have introduced measures of self-administration in the territories of indigenous peoples, but scarcely any explicit attention has been given to persons of indigenous origin who move to the cities, either to live in the poorer neighbourhoods or for higher education. Governments may develop nationalist ideologies to demand the loyalty of indigenous leaders, but they will no longer be able to confine these issues to the domestic political arena, for these leaders will increasingly appeal to international norms. The notion of multiculturalism can be turned to so many purposes that it may well become a more common coin of Latin American political rhetoric.

## CARIBBEAN STATES

The relations between persons of different racial and ethnic origin are more harmonious in the Caribbean than in most regions. Among the states of this region, it is Cuba which has been the most diligent in its actions to implement the Convention and to report on them. Others have not seen this matter as a priority. For example, when the seventh report of Barbados was considered in 1991, the Committee regretted that the government had sent no representative to present it. Members noted that the mandatory requirements of article 4

were not met either by Constitutional provisions or the Public Order Act. Members of the Committee also wished to know whether any cases of violations of fundamental rights and freedoms had been brought before the High Court since the submission of the sixth report and what type of High Court decisions were appealable to the Privy Council. (A/46/18, para. 44)

Since they were seriously overdue in the submission of periodic reports, the situations in both Jamaica and the Bahamas were considered under the review procedure. Jamaica sent a representative who declared that his government had intended to adopt legislation implementing article 4, after which it could withdraw its reservation. Since then it had decided instead to consider taking the Convention into account by amending section 24 of the Constitution. The Committee hoped that Jamaica would soon be in a position to withdraw the reservation and to submit a report in accordance with the reporting guidelines (A/48/18, paras. 152–61). Since the Bahamas had not responded, the Committee reported that it had

recalled that the previous reports had not conformed to the reporting guidelines and were somewhat imbalanced in that they were largely devoted to a discussion of the application of article 5 of the Convention. The Committee also noted that no specific legislation had been enacted to make the provisions of the Convention directly enforceable before the courts, on the grounds that the measures set out in the Constitution were adequate; that the definition of the expression 'discriminatory' in article 26 of the Constitution should be brought into line with that contained in article 1 of the Convention; and that no information had been provided on measures for securing the advancement of certain backward racial or ethnic groups. (A/46/18, para. 345)

## NORTH AMERICA

The federal structure of government in Canada results in variation from one province to another in some of the measures taken to implement the Convention. In its eleventh periodic report the federal government stated that responsibility for implementing the Convention 'is shared by the Government of Canada, the provincial governments and, following a delegation of authority by the Parliament of Canada, the territorial governments'. This led the Committee to raise the difficult issue of relations between the federal government and other governments in the discharge of legal obligations. According to international law, a party may not invoke the provisions of its internal law as justification for the failure to perform a treaty. CERD questioned the statement in the report and 'expressed concern . . . that the Federal Government cannot compel the provincial and territorial governments to align their laws with the requirements of the Convention'.

After considering together the eleventh and twelfth reports of Canada, CERD also expressed concern about

the slowness at which negotiations have been undertaken to further define aboriginal rights to land and resources in many parts of the country; the limited scope of the Employment Equity Act of 1986 which covers only 10% of the workers in Canada and does not fully guarantee the equal opportunity for aboriginal peoples and their representation at high level employments; the treatment of immigrants from Asian and African regions, which, according to various non-governmental sources, appears to be not adequately protected against discrimination; and the existence of racist organizations.

In addition, it is noted with concern that in spite of various positive measures taken by the Canadian authorities on both the provincial and federal levels to ensure an adequate development and protection of the aboriginal people, certain social indicators concerning especially alcoholism, drug abuse, suicide and the incarceration rate show that aboriginal peoples may be more affected by social problems than other social groups in the country.

The Committee recommends that legal provisions at both the federal and provincial level concerning human rights be harmonized to avoid any possible difference in treatment; that equality in access to and treatment by courts be fully guaranteed; that the Employment Equity Act be extended to larger categories of workers, including the federal civil servants . . . the authorities should strengthen their efforts . . . with a view to fully implementing articles 2, 4, 5 and 6 of the Convention. In particular, measures should be undertaken to ban racist organizations, to improve the employment and health situation of aboriginal people, to speed up negotiations on aboriginal land claims, to actually enforce remedies existing under the law, and to protect immigrants, especially those of African and Asian origin, against discrimination. (A/49/18, paras. 325–6, 328–9)

The initial report of the USA was expected during 1995. When it is considered, particular attention will centre upon the reservations made upon ratification. The question of reservations has been concerning all the treaty bodies, but particularly the Committee on the Elimination of Discrimination Against Women. That Committee believes that some reservations to its convention are incompatible with the spirit and purpose of the Convention and should not have been permitted. The same concern has been raised with regard to the Convention on the Rights of the Child. Treaty bodies have no power either to object to questionable reservations or to refer them to the International Court of Justice. The Fifth Meeting of Persons Chairing Human Rights Treaty Bodies recommended

that treaty bodies state clearly that certain reservations to international human rights instruments are contrary to the object and purpose of those instruments and consequently incompatible with treaty law. Treaty bodies should also bring this to the attention of the States parties . . . (A/49/18, para. 30)

The Human Rights Committee has issued a General Comment on the question of reservations (CCPR/C/21/Rev.1/Add.6) which is currently the most authoritative statement on the question of reservations to human-rights instruments. It states, *inter alia*:

3. . . . If a statement . . . purports to exclude or modify the legal effect of a treaty in its application to the State, it constitutes a reservation . . .

6. . . . A State may make a reservation provided it is not incompatible with the object and purpose of the treaty . . .

8. . . . provisions . . . that represent customary international law (and *a fortiori* when they have the character of peremptory norms) may not be the subject of reservations. Accordingly, a State may not reserve the right . . . to permit the advocacy of national, racial or religious hatred . . .

12. . . . Of particular concern are widely formulated reservations which essentially render ineffective all Covenant rights which would require any change in national law to ensure compliance with Covenant obligations. No real international rights or obligations have thus been accepted.

17. . . . the Vienna Convention on the Law of Treaties . . . the Committee believes that its provisions on the role of State objections in relation to reservations are inappropriate to address the problem of reservations to human rights treaties. Such . . . are not a web of inter-State exchanges of mutual obligations. They concern the endowment of individuals with rights. The principle of inter-State reciprocity has no place . . . The absence of protest by States cannot imply that a reservation is either compatible or incompatible with the object and purpose of the Covenant . . .

18. . . . It necessarily falls to the Committee to determine whether a specific reservation is compatible with the object and purpose of the Covenant . . .

19. Reservations must be specific and transparent, so that the Committee, those under the jurisdiction of the reserving State and other States parties may be clear as to what obligations of human rights

compliance have or have not been undertaken. Reservations may thus not be general, but must refer to a particular provision of the Covenant and indicate in precise terms its scope in relation thereto . . . reservations should not systematically reduce the obligations undertaken only to those presently existing in less demanding standards of domestic law. Nor should interpretive declarations or reservations seek to remove an autonomous meaning to Covenant obligations, by pronouncing them to be identical, or to be accepted only in so far as they are identical, with existing provisions of domestic law . . .

20. . . . It is desirable for a State entering a reservation to indicate in precise terms the domestic legislation or practices which it believes to be incompatible with the Covenant obligation reserved; and to explain the time period it requires to render its own laws and practices compatible with the Covenant, or why it is unable to render its own laws and practices compatible with the Covenant . . .

Ratification of the ICERD by the USA was subject to the following reservations:

(1) That the Constitution and laws of the United States contain extensive protections of individual freedom of speech, expression and association. Accordingly, the United States does not accept any obligation under this Convention, in particular under Articles 4 and 7, to restrict those rights, through the adoption of any legislation or any other measures, to the extent that they are protected by the Constitution and laws of the United States.

(2) That the Constitution and laws of the United States establish extensive protections against discrimination, reaching significant areas of non-governmental activity. Individual privacy and freedom from governmental interference in private conduct, however, are also recognized as among the fundamental values which shape our free and democratic society. The United States understands that the identification of the rights protected under the Convention by reference in Article 1 to fields of 'public life' reflects a similar distinction between spheres of public conduct that are customarily the subject of governmental regulation, and spheres of private conduct that are not. To the extent, however, that the Convention calls for a broader regulation of private conduct, the United States does not accept any obligation under this Convention to enact legislation or take other measures under paragraph (1) of Article 2, subparagraphs (1)(c) and (d) of Article 2, Article 3 and Article 5 with respect to private conduct except as mandated by the Constitution and laws of the United States.

(3) That with reference to Article 22 of the Convention, before any dispute to which the United States is a party may be submitted to the jurisdiction of the International Court of Justice under this article, the specific consent of the United States is required in each case.

These reservations show no understanding of the Convention and what it is attempting to achieve, nor do they meet the standards quoted from paragraphs 8, 12, 19, and 20 above. The obligations of the ICERD, like those of the ICCPR, have autonomous meanings. A ratifying state has to act in good faith, indicating an acceptance of the object and purpose of the Convention, and, if it enters a reservation, it should meet the standards of paragraphs 19 and 20 above. It may well be that those responsible for implementing the Racial Convention in the United States will act in this spirit, but it is indeed regrettable that a major power should display such a grudging attitude towards an international movement against a major evil, especially when that power has long been reproached for its own history of racial discrimination.

## CONCLUSIONS

Many of the conclusions drawn from the dialogue between the Committee and the states in the WEOG apply also to the American group. However, since the conception of race as dividing one section of the population from others is foreign to the states of Latin America, their governments have experienced less internal pressure for action against racial discrimination. As has been seen, some of them prepared their first reports in the belief that racial discrimination characterized only other regions. Most were persuaded to take their reporting obligations more seriously, but some have maintained their original position. There have accordingly been variations in the productiveness of their dialogue with the Committee. The most distinctive feature for many states parties in this group has been the development of their policies regarding indigenous peoples. CERD has apparently made a significant contribution here with respect to the form of the legislation, but much of the progress is probably attributable to internal pressure.

Many states of the Caribbean have been less conscientious in their reporting, but the incidence of racial discrimination in this region is relatively low. Article 4 has not generated as much discussion with American states, partly because (with the partial exception of anti-Jewish activity in Argentina) there are relatively few racist organizations. Canadian jurisprudence has considered the issues of free speech in detail. With the accession of the USA to the Convention, the dialogue on this topic will doubtless be interesting.

# 11

# Dialogue with African States

REPRESENTATIVES of black African states took the lead in pressing
for action in the General Assembly against racial discrimination
and apartheid. It was a member of the Ghanaian delegation, Mr
George Lamptey, who coordinated the drafts of the Convention
put before the Assembly. African states were equally prominent in
discussion of the programme for the first Decade of Action to
Combat Racism and Racial Discrimination, so that when Daniel
Patrick Moynihan (1979: 181) wrote about it he referred to it as
'their Decade'. Underlying African claims to leadership in this field
was the view expressed in the General Assembly debate by the
representative of Togo that 'if there was today any race which
suffered discrimination more than any other, it was the Negro
race'.

For the African states, implementation of the Convention was
more a matter of their foreign than of their domestic policies. None
of their delegates in the 1965 debate said anything about how it
might be used in regulating relations between ethnic groups within their own boundaries. The Convention was part of a campaign
against the remnants of colonialism, and against racist regimes
in southern Africa. The newly independent states were in confident
mood. Their governments enjoyed popular support, they were
mostly in effective control of their national territories, and their
administrations were reasonably efficient. Twenty years later, their
political and economic circumstances had changed for many
of them. Table 4 (which can be found at the end of Chapter 8)
shows, among other things, that many had fallen seriously behind
in the submission of their reports to CERD. Implementation of
the Convention depends upon the capacity as well as the will of
governments to introduce effective prohibitions of, and remedies
for, racial discrimination. For a variety of reasons, the capacity of
many African governments to do this declined in the post-colonial
period.

## DATA ON ETHNIC ORIGINS

The successful implementation of a policy of eliminating racial discrimination requires the collection of data on the ethnic origins of people to see if disadvantage is being reduced. Some states collect such data as part of decennial censuses but others find this objectionable. A representative of Algeria stated in the General Assembly that the collection of information on the ethnic origins of people was contrary to Islamic ethics (A/40/18, para. 19). As already mentioned in Chapter 9, France has made it a criminal offence to store data on the racial origins of people. Many African states believe that the recording of ethnic origins in a census is undesirable because it stimulates interethnic competition; politicians seize on such information to demand a greater share of resources for the ethnic groups they claim to represent and this hinders the development of sentiments of common citizenship.

On the other hand, states are under an obligation to pursue effective policies. CERD, in its general recommendation IV of 1973, invited states to include in their reports information on the demographic composition of the population relevant to the provisions of article 1 of the Convention, and it has persistently reiterated that it needs information of this kind if it is to monitor state policies. The current version of its reporting guidelines states:

The ethnic characteristics of the country are of particular importance . . . Many States consider that, when conducting a census, they should not draw attention to factors like race lest this reinforce divisions they wish to overcome. If progress in eliminating discrimination based on race, colour, descent, national or ethnic origin is to be monitored, some indication is needed of the numbers of persons who could be treated less favourably on the basis of these characteristics. States which do not collect information on these characteristics in their censuses are therefore requested to provide information on mother tongues as indicative of ethnic differences, together with any information about race, colour, descent, national and ethnic origins derived from social surveys. In the absence of quantitative information, a qualitative description of the ethnic characteristics of the population should be supplied. (CERD/C/70/Rev.3, para. 8)

The association between race (or ethnic origin) and unequal development was particularly important in many African states. Frequently the first Western-style schools were established in particular regions, usually by Christian missions. Young men of the local ethnic group benefited, and then acquired posts first as clerks, and then as administrators, or obtained further education and entered the professions. In this way their groups obtained a more than proportionate share of privileged positions and evoked the jealousies of members of other groups, especially since privilege in one generation was easily transmitted to the next generation.

One of the first occasions when the question of 'tribalism' was considered by CERD was in 1978, in connection with the initial report of Zaïre. The state reported that political parties had been suppressed because most of them were of a tribal character. The government 'accepted the existence of tribes, but was opposed to tribalism' (A/33/18, para. 157). Members of the Committee thought that this action could not be justified as a measure to implement article 4(*b*). Some members asked whether tribalism could be assimilated to racism? Some suggested that a tribal form of society had many positive features which could enrich cultural life, and that it was only when tribalism became a form of exclusivism and discrimination that it constituted an evil. Mr Lamptey said that he did not share the view, reflected in the report of Zaïre, that tribalism could be equated with racial discrimination. Zaïrians were of the same racial stock, and the problem of welding peoples into a single nation faced by many African countries was not within the purview of the Convention. Information on the methods being used to forge a national identity, which was what the Mouvement Populaire de la Révolution was trying to do, should not have been included in the report (SR 370).

Mr Lamptey's assertions are easily disputed. If a Mukongo (i.e. someone belonging to the ethnic group called Kongo) treats less favourably a Luba, Lunda, Mongo, Nandi, or Zande because of that person's ethnic origin, then that is discrimination as defined in the Convention, and the government of Zaïre is obliged to see that everyone in the country is protected from such treatment. A state is required to have a policy for eliminating racial discrimination. In many states that policy is part of a larger policy of promoting national unity, and the narrower policy cannot be understood unless it is seen as part of the broader one, so there was nothing inappropriate in Zaïre's description of its policy to forge a national identity.

Even so, problems remain. Chapter 9 discussed the difficulty of deciding whether an action has been 'based on race . . . or ethnic origin' when it seems to have sprung from multiple motives. For the action to have been in breach of the Convention, must ethnic origin have been the sole ground, a dominant ground, or just one of the grounds? It can be difficult to distinguish ethnic origin as one ground of action in a society composed of ethnic groups in the manner of many black African societies. If a group distinguished by ethnic origin seeks to secede from the state, and its movement is repressed by the state, is the repression based on the group's ethnic distinctiveness or is the action political? It could be argued that any secessionist movement would be suppressed, and therefore the state's action is not unlawful. But if, say, the state seizes land that has traditionally belonged to a particular ethnic group in order to turn it into a national park and cater to the tourist trade, it is possible that members of a group regarded as 'unprogressive' may be treated less favourably than other groups which participate actively in market relations and are better able to defend their interests. Some governments seem to believe that the right to development is a right of the majority population which may at times override the rights of a minority, especially one which appears unprogressive. If, in such circumstances, it appeared that the action of state officials was influenced by a contempt for the way of life of a particular group, their action might be contrary to the Convention. Anyone inquiring into an allegation of a breach would have to study the manner in which the government used its powers, to see if any prejudicial motive was subject to proper control.

Within CERD, different members have attributed different priorities to economic development. Some members have tended to stress the right of peoples to maintain a distinctive identity, whereas others have emphasized the obligation of governments to help all groups benefit from progress. Such differences were illustrated in 1986 in connection with the seventh report of the Central African Republic. Mr Öberg expressed doubts about the wisdom of the government's efforts to introduce the Pygmies to civilization. He feared that they might be subject to coercion since they had resisted persuasion. Mr Song wondered whether the Pygmies had equal access to education and recalled that governments had an obligation to rectify any inequalities in this respect. Mr Karasimeonov commended in particular the government's efforts to hasten the development of the Pygmies. Mr Öberg replied that his view were based on three considerations: the Pygmies lived in harmony with nature; they were happy; and they did no harm to other groups. Why could they not be left as they were (SR 751)?

The capacity of a treaty body to form an independent estimate of the potential for ethnic conflict in a state party and to draw attention to the nature of the problem is limited. Its capacity is even less when the government employs autocratic methods to suppress the conflict and its ministers or officials use their office to advance their personal interests. Some idea of the difficulties can be obtained by taking, as a case study, CERD's dealings with Rwanda and Burundi, countries that acceded to the Convention in 1975 and 1977 respectively.

## REPORTS FROM RWANDA AND BURUNDI

Rwanda and Burundi are similar in respect of size, total population (six and five million), and ethnic composition (the two main ethnic groups being Hutu and Tutsi, splitting 89–10 per cent in Rwanda and 83–16 per cent in Burundi). Regional divisions are rather more important among the Burundi Tutsi than they are in Rwanda, and these often overlie ethnic tensions. What sorts of group are the Hutu and Tutsi? It would appear that an agricultural people, called Hutu, were established in the region before the sixteenth century when the immigration commenced of several pastoralist ethnic groups collectively known as Tutsi. By the end of the eighteenth century sacred monarchies with Tutsi kings had been established in what were earlier known as Ruanda and Urundi. Each king was at the top of a social pyramid built by a web of interdependent relationships involving both Hutu and Tutsi but giving precedence to the latter. Tutsi and Hutu speak a common language and it can be misleading to refer to them as tribal groups in the sense which this expression has acquired in other parts of Africa. It may be more helpful to compare the social structure as it existed in the nineteenth century with that of European feudalism.

The two countries first became part of German East Africa but fell into Belgian hands during the First World War. The League of Nations gave Belgium a mandate to administer Ruanda–Urundi, and the inhabitants, after a few years of administration in German, had to adapt themselves to French and Flemish. It is said that the Belgian style of indirect rule strengthened the power of the Tutsi.

From 1926 every citizen in Rwanda was required to have an identity card which specified the bearer's ethnic group. Allegedly those with ten or more cows were classified as Tutsi and those with fewer as Hutu, or possibly Twa (de Waal 1994). In Burundi the recording of ethnic group membership was later abolished. In neighbouring Uganda separate kingdoms were merged within a larger framework, but this did not happen in Ruanda–Urundi. Under the UN both countries became trusteeships.

Between 1955 and 1958 Tutsi extremists in Rwanda feared Belgian plans for political reform as a threat to their position. They repressed the Hutu movement and murdered several of its leaders. After the death of the Tutsi king in 1959, and an attack on one of their leading figures, the Hutu struck back. According to reports quoted in the Minority Rights Group booklet (Lemarchand and Martin 1974) but disputed by the government of Rwanda, as many as 20,000 Tutsi were killed and 100,000 fled into Burundi and Uganda. The Belgian authorities began to replace Tutsi officials by Hutu. In 1960 leaders of the Hutu Emancipation Movement (Parmehutu) established a provisional government, recognized a year later by Belgium. The UN, hoping to preserve the ethnic–economic union of Rwanda and Burundi, ruled it unlawful and ordered free elections. These confirmed the Parmehutu government. Rwanda and Burundi became independent as separate states in 1962.

During the period 1961–6 Tutsi exiles invaded Rwanda a dozen times. Each time there were reprisals against those Tutsi who had remained in the country. After the attacks of 21 December 1963, for example, some 10,000 Tutsi were killed. After each such incident, more Tutsi left Rwanda to join the exiles, to the number of some 500,000. In 1973 an army officer and minister of defence, Juvénal Habyarimana, led a *coup d'état* to restore national unity, and the second republic was inaugurated.

Rwanda's initial report under the ICERD was considered in 1976 (A/31/18, paras. 129–31). It explained that an international convention took full effect internally without the need for additional legislation. When the second report was considered in 1979 (A/34/18, paras. 460–4) information was requested 'on the current situation with regard to refugees', a topic that has come up repeatedly, as with the third report in 1981 (A/36/18, paras. 305–10) and the fourth report in 1984 (A/39/18, paras. 157–67).

When the fifth report was considered in 1986, the government representative stated that actions in respect of refugees were governed by the relevant international conventions. He maintained that 'the basic cause of inequality among the three ethnic groups had been eliminated when the monarchy had been abolished in 1961' (A/42/18, para. 78). Ten committee members took part in the discussion, asking about the government's policies towards the Twa (the smallest ethnic group of forest-dwellers) and the policy of balance to ensure the equitable allocation of jobs in the public and private sector as well as in teaching in order to avoid the preponderance of certain ethnic or social groups. They asked how the country's main ethnic groups were represented in its single political party and whether any single ethnic group was dominant in that party. The representative of the government did not answer those questions.

The sixth and seventh reports were considered in 1989 (A/44/18, para. 196–212) when seven committee members posed questions, some of them about the refugee situation. The government representative then said that the policy of equitable distribution of posts involved both target figures and quotas but provided no figures; ethnic classification was by self-identification. There was still no answer about ethnic power-sharing (A/44/18, esp. para. 200; SR 839, paras. 22, 39–40).

On 1 October 1990 the army of the Front Patriotique Rwandais (FPR) invaded from Uganda with a force of 7,000 soldiers, some of whom were Tutsi exiles who had deserted from the Ugandan army. On the night of 4–5 October shots were fired in the capital, Kigali. The following day President Habyarimana announced that this was the work of FPR terrorists who had infiltrated the city. As a result some 8,000–10,000 persons were arrested. Some were tortured. After interventions from diplomats accredited to Kigali, most were released. There were attacks on Tutsi elsewhere in Rwanda. In 1993 the government lost control of the situation.

In Burundi the main source of change was the ballot box. Voting by individuals challenged the highly complex traditional structure, and those who enjoyed privilege within that structure sought to retain it. After an election resulting in an overwhelming victory for the Hutu parties, there was a sequence of assassinations, mutinies, and massacres in which 2,500–5,000 Hutu died. This led to the abolition of the monarchy in 1966 and the establishment of the first republic under President Michel Micombero. His government introduced a measure of power-sharing between Tutsi and Hutu but did not succeed in preventing ethnic conflict. This erupted again in 1972 and occasioned the slaughter of some 100,000 persons, possibly 4 per cent of the population. Tutsi killed those who were or might have become Hutu leaders, so that the events have been called a selective genocide. Power-sharing ceased, Tutsi domination was reinforced, and many Hutu fled to Rwanda. The second republic, from 1976, attempted a policy of reconciliation, but the Hutu remained very much disadvantaged.

When Burundi submitted its initial report to CERD in 1980, its representative referred to the more detailed report which his government intended to submit as soon as possible (A/35/18, paras. 155–64). CERD's report to the General Assembly made no mention of any tension between Hutu and Tutsi. The second report was considered in 1981 (A/36/18, paras. 234–48). Committee members posed many questions but added that they were 'aware of the difficulties of national unity in the African countries caused by ethnic or tribal problems inherited from the colonial era'. The year 1987 saw a military *coup* and the establishment of the third republic under President Pierre Buyoya, who sought to improve ethnic relations. In the north there were Hutu who feared trouble when army manœuvres started. They thought they needed to defend themselves, but only stimulated suspicion and attacks; 2,000–3,000 were slain. The following year, in 1989, CERD considered the combined third, fourth, and fifth reports (A/44/18, paras. 370–84). The government gave a different account of the events, as springing from external aggression and being in no way a result of ethnic domination. Extremists, mostly from outside, had incited the people to commit atrocities. Had the army not restored order, the country might have been destroyed. CERD reported that 'it was observed by several members that the most serious problem in Burundi would be to combat discrimination, particularly in the army, public administration and in education' (A/44/18, para. 378). Mr Banton, the country rapporteur, spoke in stronger terms than the four other members who took part in the discussion (SR 847–8). Mr Ahmadu (Nigeria) stated that Burundi was doing its utmost to resolve its problems. It had allowed its internal affairs to be discussed in the Organization of African Unity and many other forums. It had submitted one of the most candid reports he had ever seen. Burundi needed encouragement. Mr Banton thought it was not encouragement but a warning that was needed:

from my knowledge about ethnic conflicts in other regions, I conclude that a solution to Burundi's problems will require more radical measures than those so far contemplated. Some features of Burundi's situation are unique but others are common to all situations of acute bi-ethnic conflict. The biggest problem concerns the army. This has been recruited overwhelmingly from the Hima, a section of the Tutsi who inhabit the locality in which the army's training school is to be found. This means that all 31 members of the *Comité militaire pour le salut nationale*, a very powerful body, are Tutsi. Hutu are unwilling to join the army. Their fears will not be allayed so long as this situation continues. If Hutu confidence is to be cultivated the government will need to publish for the army, and for other State institutions, including the *Sureté nationale*, specific goals and monitoring procedures. They will need to adopt a target of, say, 10 per cent Hutu representation in the army by 1995 and 20 per cent by the year 2000. They will need to explain how the figures are collected and to publish them. I understand the arguments for saying that people should be appointed and promoted on the basis of individual merit, but I do testify, on the basis of experience elsewhere, that this principle is insufficient to solve problems such as Burundi's.

The problem of the army is interwoven with another, that of the political psychology of reconciliation. In Burundi now there are many people, both Hutu and Tutsi, who remember the slaughter of their kinsfolk. There are children and young people whose bodies bear the signs of mutilation. Their memories will not die. I come from the United Kingdom. People in my country are repeatedly reminded of the grievances of both Catholics and Protestants in Ireland. Events that happened three hundred years ago are important in the lives of Irish people *today*. Also at this very time the British government is considering a proposal to change the law in order to permit the trial of persons for war crimes committed between 1939 and 1945 for which evidence has only recently become available. Other European countries have been going through the same travail in the hope of purging their history of evil-doing. On the fortieth anniversary of the ending of the war the President of the Federal Republic of Germany told his parliament 'We must understand that there can be no reconciliation without remembrance.' It is our duty to future generations to investigate, to publish the facts, and to bring suspects before public courts. Otherwise memories fester. Similar examples could be quoted from other regions. Let me mention only one. The belief that in 1916 a Middle Eastern ethnic group was massacred is still today a cause of bombings, assassination and bitter controversy. So I conclude that if Burundi is to achieve reconciliation it must at the very least ascertain whether in 1988 any soldiers were given unlawful orders, and which soldiers were responsible for atrocities. Those apparently responsible must be brought before the appropriate tribunals.

Burundi's sixth report described the actions taken to implement the recommendations of a commission on national unity. When it was considered by CERD in 1991, one of the state representatives said that his country had endured a period characterized by personal greed and the dominance of a single social group. Instead of partnership there had been bloody confrontations, tension between Church and State, and discrimination at all levels in justice, employment, and credit. Because of the many new initiatives the country now looked forward to the restoration of justice in education and employment. Mrs Sadiq Ali, as country rapporteur, commended the new measures, observing that half the cabinet were now Hutu. The biggest challenge would be to tackle institutional discrimination in the army and educational system where Tutsi held all the senior positions. Mr Rhenan Segura, Mr Wolfrum, Mr de Gouttes, and Mr Banton also posed questions, but spoke more briefly (SR 894). The Committee reported that 'there was as yet no concrete evidence to suggest that the conditions that had caused the events of 1988 had changed significantly'. With regard specifically to those events, members wished to know what judicial proceedings had been taken; they asked whether penalties had been imposed on military personnel guilty of violence and noted that 'requests for details of action taken by Burundi on the Committee's recommendations had gone unheeded . . .' (A/46/18, para. 82).

In its concluding observations on the sixth report CERD expressed the hope that it would be given more details about the implementation of the Convention through judicial and administrative measures: 'specific information could also be given on the representation of the Hutus in the army, the public service, the UPRONA [Union for National Progress] party, the Parliament and the Government to measure progress in realizing national unity. The repatriation of refugees and the gradual elimination of institutionalized discrimination in education augured well for the future' (A/46/18, para. 92).

## FURTHER INFORMATION REQUESTED

In May 1992 Amnesty International published two reports: *Burundi: Appeals for an Inquiry into Army and Gendarmerie Killings and Other Recent Human Rights Violations* and *Rwanda: Persecution of Tutsi Minority and Repression of Government Critics, 1990–1992*. The first document presented the reports of killings as a continuation of the similar killings which had taken place in 1965, 1969, 1972, and 1988. The second document stated that in Rwanda since 1990 more than 1,000 Tutsi had been extra-judicially executed, while dozens of others had 'disappeared' or been tortured while detained without trial. Those responsible for extra-legal action had been able to act with impunity. CERD used its powers under article 9(1) to call for further information from these two states by 1 March 1993. Mrs Sadiq Ali reported at this time that the foreign ministers of the two countries were holding meetings to restore calm along the border between them. The information requested was not submitted by the due date, so CERD decided to reconsider the situation at its forty-third session.

Five Rwandan human-rights associations appealed for an international investigation of human-rights abuses in the period following 1 October 1990. This was answered by four associations in Paris, New York, Ouagadougou, and Montreal. With the support of nine associations (including the Commission of European Communities) they were able to establish an international commission of inquiry composed of ten experts from eight countries; at least six were judges or lawyers, one was a medical specialist; six of them had never previously visited Rwanda. President Habyarimana welcomed their appointment, but the commission remained independent. It visited Rwanda from 7 to 21 January 1993 to conduct interviews and other investigations. On 8 March 1993 it published *Rapport de la Commission Internationale d'Enquête sur les violations des droits de l'homme au Rwanda depuis le 1er Octobre 1990*.

The report is a document of 123 pages, full of factual information. It starts with an investigation of events in Kibilira, less than three hours by road to the west of the capital. In the course of forty-eight hours there in October 1990 at least 348 persons were massacred; more than 550 houses were burnt down and all the goods belonging with them pillaged. The report passes next to a region in the north-west, one associated with the President and his family, also the home of a group of Tutsi called Bagogwe; they had for a long time kept themselves separate from the dominant Tutsi groups. It would appear that the massacres carried out in this region in January 1993 were planned by a group involving members of the government. Details are also provided of the killing of 277 persons in a third region about an hour's drive south of the capital, in March 1992. In Rwanda as a whole the number of victims since 1 October 1990 was estimated at 2,000. They were mostly Tutsi but included Hutu. Many Tutsi were hidden or otherwise saved by Hutus, some of whom paid with their lives for these acts of courage. Tutsi were killed just because they were Tutsi, in actions which were genocidal even if the total number of deaths is considered insufficient for the whole sequence to be accounted a genocide.

The report next described violations of human rights committed by the armed forces on both sides. Because the Rwandan soldiers could look forward to only one meal every two days, the army terrorized the local population. Rape was commonplace. The size of the Rwandan army was not given, but it cannot have been large. (According to the *UN Development Report for 1992*, expenditure on the armed forces relative to expenditure on education—the soldier/teacher ratio—for Rwanda was 28, much lower than the average of 64 for developing countries.) The Commission's report noted that, if the soldiers behaved in an arbitrary and ill-disciplined way towards the civilian population, their internal discipline was strong and they displayed effective organization when this was required of them.

At the time of the Commission's visit there were some 350,000 displaced persons in camps, but the total of displaced persons must have been much higher. Some of these camps were bombarded in December 1991 and March 1992.

The Commission concluded that the massacres were not spontaneous movements arising from the relations between two groups. Too much evidence pointed to prior planning: the identification of targets, the dissemination of incitements in the forms of tracts and in radio messages which justified attacks, and the apparent staging of provocations. Certain agitators were named. The territorial administration was clearly implicated. Armed militias maintained contrary to a law of 18 June 1991 (particularly that of the Mouve-

ment Républicain Nationale pour la Démocratie et le Développe-
ment (MRND), the party of which President Habyarimana was
also president) exercised an evil influence; they established road
blocks and the traveller who could not show a card of membership
in the MRND or its ally ran the risk of being murdered. Members
of the Commission themselves had experience of these road blocks.
(When exercising police powers the military and militias are bound
by the UN Code of Conduct for Law Enforcement Officials.
Rwanda has reported to ECOSOC on its implementation of this
Code (E/.57/1988/8, para. 5) and was due to report again in 1993.)
According to the Commission's report on 15 November 1992,
President Habyarimana described the Arusha agreements as being
only pieces of paper and invited the MRND militia to serve as a
strike force in his electoral campaign. The prime minister protested
about this.

The judicial system had been paralysed. Relatively few magistrates were legally qualified; they were protected by no security
of tenure; there was no independent bar. Murderers had enjoyed
impunity. The prisons were old, dilapidated, and overpopulated.
Prisoners were subjected to degrading treatment. Many of those
detained in 1990–1 lost their employment. According to the Commission the policy of equitable distribution of posts mentioned on
page 255 above was a sham. CERD should surely have pressed the
government harder for figures about the implementation of its
policy.

The Commission found that human-rights violations had been
committed on a massive scale; they were deliberately directed
against Tutsi and against political opponents. The Rwandan state
had operated so as to exacerbate ethnic tensions. Despite the
power-sharing, the head of state had almost total control through
the army, the territorial administration, the judiciary, and an illegal
militia. The actions of ministers who did not belong to the MRND
were constantly frustrated.

Meantime there had been developments in the diplomatic sphere
affecting Rwanda, starting with the reaching of an agreement on a
ceasefire at Arusha (in Tanzania) on 12 July 1992. This was signed
by the Foreign Minister of Rwanda, a representative of the Front
Patriotique Rwandais (FRP, sometimes identified as the Rwandan
Patriotic Front (RPF)), the Facilitator (the Foreign Minister of
Tanzania), and the representative of the Secretary-General of the

OAU. It built upon meetings of the Heads of State of the Region held earlier in Tanzania and Zaïre which had involved a delegate of the UNHCR. The agreement provided for the establishment of a neutral corridor separating the areas occupied by the two forces. The Groupe d'Observateurs Militaires Neutres (GOMN) was to include officers from Nigeria, Senegal, Zimbabwe, and one other country. Further meetings were held in Arusha from 24 November to 9 January attended by the same officials as previously but with the addition of representatives of Burundi, Uganda, Belgium, France, Germany, and the USA. An agreement was signed on 9 January on arrangements for power-sharing within the framework of a transitional government of an enlarged character. They included provisions for a transitional assembly, the distribution of portfolios in the new government, and the formation of a new national army. It seems that the resettlement of the refugees was discussed without any text having been adopted on this problem. Apparently a coalition government along the agreed lines was formed shortly afterwards. A new prime minister, belonging to a party opposed to that of the president, declared that his government's main task was to negotiate peace with the exiles and facilitate the repatriation of the refugees.

On 13 February the president and the prime minister gave a new undertaking about the implementation of the Arusha agreements. The FPR was ready to maintain its former positions provided that the Rwandan army did not try to advance and the territory between them was kept under the control of the GOMN.

These developments were brought to the attention of the Security Council, which on 12 March 1993 adopted resolution SCR 812 welcoming a communiqué issued in Dar es Salaam on 7 March concerning a new ceasefire and the situation of displaced persons. It invited the Secretary-General to consult with the OAU about a UN contribution to the strengthening of the peace process and decided to remain actively seized of the matter.

CERD was due to reconsider the situation in August 1993. The representatives of the two states in Switzerland had not received instructions from their governments and the position in Burundi following upon the election was still uncertain. The Committee was pressed for time because (as already mentioned in Chapter 8) it wished to prepare its response to the Secretary-General's *An Agenda for Peace* (UN 1992*a*). So the Committee postponed this item until March 1994. This may have been unfortunate. CERD might have drawn attention to the report of the international commission and endorsed its conclusions (though this might have been difficult since the report was available only in French and eight committee members therefore could not read it). Had CERD done this, would it have made any difference to events in Rwanda? The Committee's report would have been studied at the time of the General Assembly debate in October. Conceivably it could have led to more pressure to implement the Arusha accords, but it could scarcely have prevented the massacres in Burundi.

At its forty-fourth session in March 1994, CERD heard of new developments in both Burundi and Rwanda. While it was meeting, the press was reporting further slayings in Burundi. There an election had resulted in the installation of a president of Hutu origin, Melchior Ndadaye, who included many Tutsi in his government. The prime minister, Mrs Sylvie Kiniji, was a Hutu who was a member of the previous president's party. Yet the new president had been assassinated on 21 October 1993 in the course of a failed *coup* by soldiers from Bururi, the district from which the three previous presidents had originated. In reaction, many Hutu groups had started killing Tutsi and those Hutu who supported political parties which favoured Hutu–Tutsi collaboration. In some areas the army killed Hutus, but in general terms the massacres (in which by the end of the year 50,000 people lost their lives) differed from previous ones in that more of the victims were Tutsi. According to a document prepared by a collective of opposition parties, and entitled *Le Genocide d'octobre 1993*, Hutu political sentiment had been mobilized by an extremist ideology. 'Throughout the country, the militants seek to recruit support by saying that the Tutsi ought to go back to Egypt from which they originate.'

A new president, Cyprien Ntaryamira, took office in February, but his two months in power were tumultuous. According to a press report, hardline members of his own party stopped listening to him. Ex-President Buyoya was quoted in the *Guardian* as saying:

There's never been any ethnic conflict between the groups on the level of the village. There was no ethnic war before independence. It's the politicians who transfer their political conflicts onto the hillsides. If the leaders say nothing the killings don't happen . . . The events in October were created by ethnic extremists on both sides who want exclusive power. But the thing which really led to the conflict was the violence in Rwanda—the massacre of the Tutsis. The Hutus chased them and exterminated them. The Hutu saw power there as their natural right, and this led to all the subsequent violence. Ever since, power has been ethnicised. It's exactly the same in Rwanda as in Burundi.

Rwandan leaders were quoted on the same occasion as saying something very similar about their own country:

Rivalry between the groups always comes from the élite. It never comes from the population. The political class wants to completely polarize political life. In this country the ethnic problems are not as strong as people say . . . The bigger problem is economic—rich against poor, and the rich encouraging the poor to fight.

The ambassador of Burundi to the UN in Geneva attended the meeting of CERD. She appealed to the international community, not for humanitarian aid, but for help to restore democratic government. Mrs Sadiq Ali, as country rapporteur, provided a detailed chronology of recent events and concluded by stressing the need to reform the army and the judicial system. Mr de Gouttes asked his colleagues, 'had we predicted such events, what could we have done?' Mr Aboul-Nasr asked who was currently in charge, and the ambassador replied that the army had a veto over government proposals. Twelve committee members took part in the discussion, which concluded that CERD should propose to the UN that a tribunal should be established capable of trying crimes against humanity such as those which had been committed in Burundi. This seemed to be in line with the ambassador's appeal. There was, however, one notable dissentient, Mr Chigovera (Zimbabwe). He insisted that the UN should not start by 'witch-hunting'.

Zimbabwe's experience, which was matched in Mozambique, Angola and South Africa, had been that concentration on the investigation, prosecution and punishment of past violations could be counterproductive and could, with an additional heavy cost in human lives and suffering, prolong rather than interrupt the spiral of violence. Some principles sometimes had to be sacrificed for the common good. With or without international assistance, a measure of accommodation and compromise must be accepted. (SR 1027)

The ambassador relied that 'we understand the need to compromise'. A dialogue had been in progress but it had not included the army, and the army would never accept proposals that its composition be regionally based. The Committee then set up a working group to elaborate a proposal for a tribunal (see Chapter 8).

Following its consideration of Burundi, CERD turned to the situation in Rwanda. The country rapporteur, Mr Banton, summarized the events leading to the Arusha accords, adding that one ugly feature of the situation in Rwanda was the ready availability of weapons. Large quantities had been purchased. A Western diplomat in Kigali had been quoted as saying, 'The country is flooded with weapons. Two beers will get you one grenade.' (Later soldiers were accused of selling weapons or giving them to their political allies.) He asked the Committee to note the recommendations of the Commission of Inquiry as well as the action of the Security Council. He said that the FPR had a Hutu president and that two-fifths of their ministers-designate were Hutu, so the problems were more political than ethnic. Doubts had been cast upon the good faith of the president and his willingness to implement the Arusha accords. So far attention had necessarily been concentrated upon short-term action, but:

Racial discrimination will continue in Rwanda so long as no solution has been found to the problem presented by the exiles. Because they, and the FPR, are such a threat to the state as matters now stand, anyone who criticizes the government runs the risk of being accused of siding with the rebels. The Commission's report describes many situations in which Tutsi were accused of supporting the FPR. Many were killed for this reason. If, because of threats, they fled, this was taken as proof that they were FPR supporters. MRND office-holders constantly highlight the dangers presented by the presence of an internal enemy. The situation . . . has an international dimension such that the problem cannot be solved by the government of Rwanda acting alone. The last two decades have demonstrated that.

As of June, talks have been continuing in Arusha which appear to be narrowing the differences between the Rwandan government and the RPF. CERD should nevertheless express its concern to the Secretary-General, inviting him (1) to study the report of the international commission; (2) to consider convening an international conference to build upon the Arusha agreements, possibly by drafting an international treaty involving Rwanda and neighbouring states which would (*a*) provide for the resettlement in Rwanda of the exiles and displaced persons; (*b*) provide effective protections for ethnic minorities; and (*c*) satisfy the government's legitimate concerns for the long-term viability of the state and its institutions.

Mr de Gouttes supported these views and asked for further information about implementation of the accords. Mr Wolfrum stressed the breakdown in the rule of law throughout the subregion. The state representative responded, saying that there had been no progress since January but that he did not know where the blockage was. The president was not the only one responsible. The parties seemed to be at fault. 'We ask the same questions as you . . . if the international community can exert pressure this might enable me to report from a more tenable position. I have come here with a guilty plea. You may be better informed than I am of where the truth lies.' He saw nothing against the proposal to convene a conference involving all the countries of the subregion. In its quite lengthy concluding observations the Committee expressed concern 'over the failure to identify and punish those responsible for the ethnically motivated murders which have taken place in Rwanda' and 'deep concern that an atmosphere of impunity continues to prevail in Burundi'. It referred to the parallels between Rwanda and Burundi, adding that 'it doubts whether one State can resolve the conflict within its borders unless there is a resolution covering the sub-region'.

## THE GENOCIDE STARTS

Shortly after CERD's session, on 6 April 1994, the presidents of Rwanda and of Burundi were returning to Kigali from negotiations in Tanzania when their aeroplane was apparently destroyed by a rocket. Hutu in Rwanda believed that this was the work of the RPF and commenced a wave of carnage in which over half a million people were killed in three months. The Rwandan prime minister, Mrs Agathe Uwiligiyimana, was suspected of collaboration in the attack and assassinated. It is notable that, in both Rwanda and Burundi, Hutu who sought power-sharing with the Tutsi were singled out for killing. This tends to support Tutsi claims about the spread of an extremist ideology amongst Hutu in both countries. Subsequent developments are discussed in Chapter 13.

No one who seeks an explanation of the violence should fall into the trap of assuming that ethnic differences of themselves are causes of such conflicts. People often live together with others quite unconscious of any differences in ethnic origin. Consciousness of common ethnic origin of itself does nothing, but when there are insecurities it can be whipped up and made important by those who wish to assume positions of leadership or to obtain the rewards that can go with them. Hence the greater responsibility of those who hold official positions or belong to the élite. The most dangerous exploitation of ethnic consciousness is that which insists 'this is our territory; others have no place here'. That doctrine is preached in other regions of the world too, but it has a special potency in many parts of Africa.

## SOME WEST AFRICAN STATES

The cases of Rwanda and Burundi suggest limits to the effectiveness of treaties between states as a way of protecting human rights. Weak states with internal conflicts are unlikely to be greatly influenced by the comments of a treaty body. Perhaps more important, other states do not act when other parties to a convention neglect their obligations. For example, in 1974 CERD reported concern over a provision in the constitution of Sierra Leone, namely:

subsection 4(g) of section 13 of the Constitution, which provided that the anti-discrimination provisions of subsection 1 should not apply to any law so far as that law makes provision 'for the limitation of citizenship to persons of negro African descent'—which appeared to be incompatible with article 1, paragraph 3, of the Convention . . . The Committee decided to reconsider the question when the report requested from Sierra Leone came up . . . (A/9618, para. 193)

Yet that report has never been submitted and Sierra Leone's fourth periodic report, due in January 1976, had not been received nineteen years later. The states parties to the Convention have taken no action to discipline one of their number and, presumably, a representative of the defaulting state has continued to vote in elections to the Committee.

Some of the states in this group which have continued to report have had little new to say, despite major changes in their legal order. Ghana's legislation, as reported in the *Global Compilation* (UN 1991a), consists of an Avoidance of Discrimination Act of 1957, which prohibits any body or group of persons having a common racial origin and whose membership is substantially restricted to any body or group of persons to have as one of its objectives the exposure of any other association of persons or any part of the community to hatred, contempt, or ridicule on account of their race. Conviction under the act can result in a fine or imprisonment.

The last report from Ghana was considered in 1992, when it was observed that, because of current political changes, the information in it was out of date. The Committee asked for copies of the new constitution and the new laws recently introduced so that it could make a proper assessment of the situation (A/47/18, para. 141).

In Nigeria protections against discrimination are embodied in the Constitution. According to article 3,

The State shall direct its policy towards ensuring that

> (*a*) all citizens without discrimination on any ground whatsoever have the opportunity for securing adequate means of livelihood as well as adequate opportunity to secure suitable employment.

According to article 39:

A citizen of Nigeria of a particular community, ethnic group, place of origin, sex, religion or political opinion shall not, by reason only that he is such a person

> (*a*) be subjected . . . to disabilities or restrictions to which citizens of Nigeria of other communities, ethnic groups, places of origin, sex, religions or political opinions are not made subject . . .

However, it is doubtful whether these provisions are in practice implemented in such a manner that individuals are protected from discrimination on the basis of ethnic origin. Many Nigerians believe that the distribution of resources, whether by the state or by private bodies, is heavily influenced by considerations of ethnicity.

The tenth, eleventh, and twelfth periodic reports of Nigeria were considered in 1993. In its concluding observations the Committee

expressed its concern over the ongoing interethnic conflicts . . . particularly over reports that the Nigerian Police Force had, in some circumstances of violence, been ineffective in protecting the rights of civilians. The Committee found that national legislation . . . did not fully meet the requirements of article 4 of the Convention and that the provisions of article 5 were not adequately implemented.

In the light of all information available to it, the Committee found that the actual situation in Nigeria warranted a closer monitoring of the implementation of the Convention and decided to request the Government of Nigeria to provide the Committee with additional information to be considered at its spring session in 1994. (A/48/18, paras. 325–9)

Somewhat later, in August 1995, a delegation from Nigeria attended to present two documents, one responding to the request for further information and the other a thirteenth periodic report. Some of the Committee's questions concerned allegations that the security forces had perpetrated human-rights violations against members of the Movement for the Survival of the Ogoni People who had been protesting about conditions deriving from the extraction of oil in their area. The state representative insisted that these allegations were groundless. Those arrested and charged with criminal offences were part of a group which had transformed an originally peaceful movement into one of violence. CERD nevertheless reiterated some of its anxieties about the inadequacy of Nigerian legislation and its implementation in practice. Four of the concerns it expressed in its report may be singled out. The first was that 'in circumstances such as those of Nigeria, in which political and religious differences may easily be associated with ethnic differences, any breakdown in law and order can exacerbate ethnic tension'. The second was over allegations that 'agents of the Government have contributed to ethnic tensions in the course of attempts to maintain law and order, particularly in the Rivers State'. The third and fourth expressed 'particular concern' that a decree of the Federal Military Government ousted courts of jurisdiction over acts of that government, which could affect proceedings invoking protection against racial discrimination, and that trial by special tribunals could counter the right to equality before the law in accordance with article 5 of the Convention.

Among other suggestions and recommendations, CERD recommended a review of the effectiveness of protections under article 5, and of recourse measures in accordance with article 6. Moreover:

The Committee recommends that the State party investigate situations of ethnic disorder and the causes thereof, including any possible unlawful orders, with a view to taking the necessary remedial measures in accordance with the Convention and to ensure that no one can act with impunity in these circumstances.

The Committee recommends that the Government, when promoting projects of economic development, undertake the necessary measures to effectively protect the identity of ethnic groups in the areas concerned.

Further dialogue on some of these matters may depend upon whether there is a return to civilian rule.

Senegal provides an example of fairly comprehensive legislation on the French model. In August 1989 representatives of this state took their places at CERD's committee table to present their state's eighth periodic report, dated May 1987. Only in response to a question from Mr Lamptey did they refer to the clashes in April 1989 between Senegalese and Mauretanians, that is to say, between darker- and lighter-skinned Africans. Mauretania had become a party to ICERD in January 1989, but its initial report is overdue. The Committee was told:

Cattle had strayed onto land belonging to Senegalese and Mauretanian cattle-rearers had come to collect them, accompanied by Mauretanian soldiers. Shots had been fired: two Senegalese had been killed and others taken away as hostages. The aggressors had, moreover, committed the humiliating act of having the corpses dragged behind horses. Senegal, anxious not to exacerbate the situation, had refrained from retaliating . . . Incidents had then followed in eastern Senegal, where the population had attacked Mauretanians on learning that Senegalese had been attacked in Mauretania . . . There were at present between 100,000 and 110,000 persons in Senegal who had been displaced as a result of these occurrences, including some 45,000 to 50,000 Mauretanians who had been expelled from Mauretania because of their colour [perhaps persons of Senegalese origin and appearance but Mauretanian nationality?] . . . An African Mediation Commission had been appointed on the initiative of the OAU. (SR 844)

Nothing further was said about this in the next periodic report. The experience does not suggest that Senegal, at least, would see value in the use of ICERD article 11 in such circumstances. After consideration of that report, CERD noted with satisfaction that the Convention had been incorporated into Senegalese law but expressed concern about the lack of information as to its actual implementation. It recommended that the government intensify efforts at finding a solution to the problems in its Casamance region, where there had been a continuing conflict that had an ethnic dimension.

Among the states brought into the review procedure on which CERD has recently agreed concluding observations have been Botswana, Burkina Faso, Cape Verde, Central African Republic, Côte d'Ivoire, Lesotho, Mali, Mauritius, Togo, and Uganda. In the case of Zambia, the government responded by submitting its five overdue reports in a single document. When, in the course of the dialogue, the state representative was asked about the abuse of their powers by the police, he replied that the police continued with bad habits learnt under the colonial regime. Since he himself had been maltreated and unlawfully detained by them for several days, he could not deny that there were abuses, though attempts were being made to rectify them (SR 988). In its concluding observations the Committee recommended that appropriate consideration should be given to:

the effective incorporation of the provisions of the Convention in municipal law, particularly those of article 4(*b*) and (*c*) . . . that law enforcement officials should receive intensive training . . . For that purpose, as well as for the preparation of the next report, the Government should request the assistance of the Centre for Human Rights. (A/48/18, paras. 255–6)

The breakdown of the legal order in Mozambique has prevented CERD from doing much more than express its concern about trends in that country. There has been more detailed consideration of implementation of the Convention in Chad and Sudan.

When, in 1993, the Committee considered the implementation of the Convention in Chad, the state representative was the Minister of Humanitarian Affairs. He described the ways in which human rights were protected in the Republic's new Charter. He maintained that there was no pattern of racial discrimination; there were 110 tribes and currently thirty-three political parties, each of which was required by law to have members in at least ten of the country's fourteen regions. It seemed as if the situation was on the mend, and in its concluding observations: 'The Committee took note with satisfaction of the commitment made by the representative of Chad to submit the written report in the prescribed manner at the next session . . .' (A/48/18, para. 170). Yet in the following week new reports were received of mass human-rights abuses. No report having been received, CERD in 1994 reconsidered the situation. No state representative attended. It was reported that:

It is noted with concern that according to information available two years after the end of the change of government in Chad, tensions between ethnic groups persisted, and violent acts and multiple violations are still being committed, *inter alia*, by the military forces and security units.

The members of the Committee also express concern regarding information on the impunity enjoyed by perpetrators of human rights violations who, despite the Government's promises, have still not been prosecuted by the authorities.

The members of the Committee note with concern information received about the paralysis in the administration, which affects all sectors of the public service, including the judicial sector. They express their concern over the attacks on the independence of the judicial authorities . . .

The Committee recommends that the State party include in its next periodic report information on developments in the situation within the country, the strengthening of the rule of law in Chad, the composition of the population, the introduction of legislation to combat racial discrimination (article 4 of the Convention), the means available to individual victims of human rights violations to obtain justice and reparation (article 6 of the Convention) and the measures taken to promote education with a view to combating racial discrimination (article 7 of the Convention). (A/49/18, paras. 559–61, 563)

In 1995 a document representing the fifth to ninth periodic reports of Chad was presented by a delegation able to supplement it in many ways. CERD welcomed the resumption of dialogue but expressed concern about the ethnic dimension to the continuing human-rights violations within the state. It requested the government to do all in its power to enable the judicial system to function properly and to improve the training about the observance of human rights of the armed forces, police, gendarmerie, and other agents of the state (A/50/18).

These examples suggest that CERD has been doing what it can to encourage the states of the region to keep up the reporting process and in this way to ensure that state obligations under the Convention are not neglected.

## SOME NORTH AFRICAN STATES

After considering the tenth report of Morocco, CERD expressed concern that the provisions of ICERD article 4 were not fully implemented. It asked for information on the number of complaints of racial discrimination, the situation of the rural population, and information on the protection of the right, without discrimination, to freedom of thought, conscience, and religion (A/49/18).

When the tenth report of Algeria was considered in 1993, it was thought that the report contained too little on actual practice (SR 927). CERD observed:

Taking into account the fact that the report was oriented especially towards legislative texts, the Committee considered that the next report should contain more demographic and statistical information on social indicators reflecting, in particular, the situation of ethnic and racial groups, in particular Berbers and blacks, as well as on judicial or administrative decisions taken to give effect to the Convention. It was also considered necessary to clarify the effect of emergency measures taken by the Government with regard to the application of the Convention.

The Committee considered, in particular, that the next report should clarify the place of the Berber population in Algerian society with respect to identity, language, participation in public life and the social benefits provided for in article 5 of the Convention. (A/48/18, paras. 184–5)

The ninth report of Tunisia provided CERD with much information about the laws which could be used against racial discrimination, but too little information about their application in practice. The Committee recommended that specific legislation be introduced to meet the requirements of article 4. A similar set of requests was directed to Egypt in 1994.

In 1987 the Committee considered the fourth report of the Sudan. Somewhat unusually, a committee member from the reporting state took the floor. Mr Mohammed Omar Beshir observed that an autocratic, inhuman, violent, and corrupt military regime had been replaced by a democratic one. But in spite of its promises, the new government had taken no steps to modify the laws of September 1983. They were responsible for the punishment by amputation of between 150 and 300 persons between 1983 and 1985, while another 400 were still awaiting trial. Those so punished seemed to have been mostly young men from the south. These laws were the main source of the prevailing conflict and the main obstacle to peace negotiations. Mr Beshir, as the author confirmed in a private conversation, was not concerned about whether such matters were within the purview of the Convention; for him, issues of human rights had a priority of their own. The state representative did not answer Mr Beshir's questions; nor did he express irritation over the stance he had taken up, but Mr Beshir had difficulty leaving his country in order to attend CERD's next session, and he was not renominated at the end of his elected term of membership.

The Committee continued to be concerned about conditions in the Sudan. After considering that country's eighth report in 1993, it

expressed its deep concern at the serious human rights violations . . . noted the statement of the representative that violations of human rights had been occurring and, in view of the Committee's anxieties, attached particular significance to the statement that the Government was taking every step to prevent further occurrences . . . The Committee regretted the lack of information on the ethnic dimension to the current conflict and the insufficiency of demographic data . . . took note of the information supplied concerning Sudanese legislation, but observed that there often appeared to be a disjunction between those provisions and the manner of their implementation. It expressed its concern about the situation in the Nuba mountains and that of the Fur and wished to learn about the finding of the Commission of Inquiry appointed on 25 November 1992. In accordance with article 9, paragraph 1, of the Convention, the Committee requested further information . . . not later than 31 January 1994 . . . (A/48/18, paras. 124–6)

The information was supplied as requested, and the following year CERD welcomed the government's characterization of Sudanese society as multiracial, multireligious, and multicultural. It is difficult to disentangle the ethnic from the political and religious dimensions of the conflict there, but the Committee recommended that the government more clearly define racial discrimination in the law and ensure that there were no legal barriers to closer association between communities. It emphasized the responsibility of the state for ensuring that law-enforcement officials observe the requirements of the Convention.

## CONCLUSION

The potential for discrimination on the basis of ethnic origin in many African states is high. It is possible, however, that in many places a man is disinclined to seek a job, a house, or some other service from someone belonging to an ethnic group he sees as in competition with his own; he assumes that the other man will show preference on the basis of ethnic origin (as he would himself) and therefore he does not perceive this as a matter for complaint. Tension is more likely to arise from conflicts between ethnically based political movements and from competition for resources. Has a minister ensured that more hospitals or schools have been opened, or better roads built, in the region from which he or she originates? When tensions rise, a person may feel safe only in the company of others of the same ethnic origin as himself or herself.

Many of these same states are administratively weak, and some are troubled by civil disorders. The central government may not be supported by compliant local-government bodies in all parts of state territory. It may have only limited resources to distribute. The relevant ministries in the capital may be short of personnel able to identify ways in which the Convention might be better applied, to implement plans to this end, or to write a report for the UN on the measures undertaken. Such circumstances are bound to affect dialogue with CERD, but if contact is maintained, better implementation may be achieved in the future.

Some other states are administratively stronger, and some of these, as in northern Africa, are less heterogeneous with respect to ethnic origin. To judge from the reports they submit, they do not need to introduce such elaborate measures as the European states in order to meet their obligations.

# 12

## Dialogue with Asian States

THE reasons which brought states in the UN's Asian group to ratify the Convention were varied. Many of them, like India and Pakistan, identified with the pressure for decolonization and were sympathetically disposed towards the new states of the 1960s. Many wished to be in the forefront of a progressive movement, but were also jealous of their own sovereignty. It is notable that China did not accede until 1981 and that Japan, Indonesia, Malaysia, Myanmar, Singapore, and Thailand had not acceded by 1995. The more authoritarian a government, the less likely it is to accept any international supervision. The Muslim states were affronted by the great wrong done to their co-religionists in Palestine, but still had grounds for hesitation. Islam is not a private religion (as Protestant Christianity can be). It expects the state to be devoted to the ends of the faith, and denies that non-believers can question those ends. Saudi Arabia, which tries to be an exemplar in these matters, has not acceded to any human-rights treaty.

The states of the Asian group include a larger population than that of any other group; their population is very diverse, including, as it does, followers of all the world's major religions. Within this group are some micro-states of the Pacific Ocean, including the tiny state of Tonga, which, though not a member state of the UN, has been a state party to the Convention since 1972. The Asian group includes Cyprus and most of the Arab states, as well as those of the Indian subcontinent, China, and Japan. The diversity is increased when, as for this chapter, Australia and New Zealand are added. The representative of New Zealand in the General Assembly in 1965 stated that 'few if any moral issues were of greater consequence to the international community than that of racial prejudice and discrimination'. Other Asian and Pacific states, including Malaysia, expressly testified that they had no problems of racial discrimination.

In Europe and America the relations between groups distinguished by race or ethnic origin have often had a legal basis. There were treaties between states and sometimes between immigrant and indigenous peoples. The enslavement of Africans and Indians in the New World was authorized by law. In the Asian states, by contrast, there were many forms of group inequality authorized by custom and religious belief, most notably the Hindu caste system, which were never rationalized in legal form. There were no treaties that could be the basis for minorities to claim rights, with the exception of New Zealand, where, 135 years after the signing of the 1840 Treaty of Waitangi, that document was given a new constitutional significance.

Representatives of some Asian states have criticized Western views of human rights as too individualistic. Often, as is usually the case with relations within the family or between friends, it is for the better if a person chooses not to exercise a right and keep quiet about some minor wrong in the belief that matters will balance out in the long run. Whether or not a right is exercised depends upon the desires of the individual who possesses that right. Many individual desires are not satiable, so, if individual rights are unrestrained and those who possess them keep on demanding that they be observed to the full extent, the collectivity may be less well off as a result. Somehow society must restrain and channel individual desires and this must affect the recognition accorded to individual rights. An implicit understanding of this argument may underlie such criticisms.

Among the UN member states in 1965 which were in or near the East Asian region, only the Philippines took an enthusiastic part in the preparation of the Convention. It was one of the first states to ratify (in 1967), and one of its nationals (Mr José D. Inglès) was elected to the Convention's monitoring committee that started work in 1970. China's contributions to the General Assembly debate consisted of a series of brief questions (like an enquiry as to what was meant by a reference to 'nationalities'). China acceded at the end of 1981. Cambodia took no part in the debate but acceded in 1983. Malaysia took a very small part and has not acceded (nor has Singapore, which had only just become independent at the time the debate started). Japan and Thailand attended the debate and voted on resolutions but did not take the floor and have not acceded. Indonesia withdrew from the UN between January 1965 and September 1966, and has also never acceded. Viet Nam became a UN member state in 1977 and acceded to the Convention in 1982. The Philippines apart, this group of states has displayed less interest in action against racial discrimination than any other regional group.

This chapter will review the Committee's dialogue with states, taking them in a sequence similar to that followed in Chapter 5 and adding substance to Table 5 (which can be found at the end of Chapter 8). While allowing that state action may have been influenced primarily by considerations of foreign policy and response to internal pressures, nevertheless the dialogue may have had some influence in improving state observance of obligations under the Convention.

## COLONIZATION IN THE PACIFIC

There are good reasons for starting the review with New Zealand, because of the imaginative use there of an 1840 treaty as a basis for the reconciliation, in the late twentieth century, of the conflicting interests of the two main sections of the population. In 1840 the increasing number of settlers from Britain had prompted the signing of a treaty at Waitangi in the north of the country by which the chiefs ceded the sovereignty of their country to Queen Victoria. The English text was translated into Maori by a missionary, but there is at least one significant difference between the two versions. A modern reconstruction in English of the principal Maori-language version of the treaty was used by the New Zealand Court of Appeal in 1987, and reads as follows:

Victoria, the Queen of England, in her concern to protect the chiefs and subtribes of New Zealand and in her desire to preserve their chieftainship and their lands to them and to maintain peace and good order considers it just to appoint an administrator one who will negotiate with the people of New Zealand to the end that their chiefs will agree to the Queen's government being established over all parts of this land and (adjoining) islands and also because there are many of her subjects living on this land and others yet to come.

So the Queen desires to establish a government so that no evil will come to Maori and European living in a state of lawlessness.

So the Queen has appointed me, William Hobson a captain in the Royal Navy to be Governor for all parts of New Zealand (both those) shortly to be received by the Queen and (those) to be received hereafter and presents to the chiefs of the Confederation, chiefs of the subtribes of New Zealand and other chiefs these laws set out here.

The first
The chiefs of the Confederation and all the chiefs who have not joined that Confederation give absolutely to the Queen of England for ever the complete government of their land.

The second
The Queen of England agrees to protect the chiefs, the subtribes and all the people of New Zealand in the unqualified exercise of their chieftainship over their lands, villages and all their treasures. But on the other hand the Chiefs of the Confederation and all the chiefs will sell land to the Queen at a price agreed by the person owning it and by the person buying it (the latter being) appointed by the Queen as her purchase agent.

The third
For this agreed arrangement therefore concerning the Government of the Queen, the Queen of England will protect all the ordinary people of New Zealand and will give them the same rights and duties of citizenship as the people of England.

Much of the settlement was regulated by the New Zealand Company, a private body, whose officials regarded the treaty with cynicism. As in so many colonies of settlement, there was tension between the settlers and the Colonial Office in Whitehall. Looking at affairs from a distance, those in London took a more enlightened view of the policies to be pursued than some of those on the spot.

New Zealand acceded to ICERD in 1972, having passed a Race Relations Act the previous year. This was also a time of growing Maori protest, which focused attention on the neglect of the treaty of Waitangi. As a result in 1975 the Waitangi Tribunal was established to consider claims deriving from the treaty. Ten years later its powers were extended to cover claims retrospective to 1840, while in subsequent years many statutes have recognized the treaty as a source of law. It is now widely accepted as the founding document of the nation and the most important instrument in the continuing evolution of relations between Maori and non-Maori.

In its ninth periodic report in 1990, the government summarized its published statement *Principles for Crown Action on the Treaty of Waitangi*. This includes:

'the Kawanatanga Principle' which recognizes that article 1 of the Treaty gives expression to the right of the Crown to make laws and to its obligation to govern in accordance with constitutional process. This sovereignty is qualified by the promise to accord the Maori interests specified in article II of the Treaty an appropriate priority. Article II ('the Ranga-tiratanga Principle') guarantees to *iwi* Maori (Maori tribes) the control and enjoyment of those resources and *taonga* (prized possessions) which it is their wish to retain. The preservation of a resource base, restoration of *iwi* self-management, and the active protection of *taonga*, both material and cultural, are necessary elements of the Crown's policy of recognizing *rangatiratanga*.

The Third Article of the Treaty (as noted in the third principle—the 'principle of equality' adopted by the Government) constitutes a guarantee of legal equality between Maori and other citizens of New Zealand. This means that all New Zealand citizens are equal before the law. Under the 'Principle of Co-operation', the fourth principle, the Treaty is regarded by the Crown as establishing a fair basis for two peoples in one country. Duality and unity are both significant. Duality implies distinctive cultural development and unity implies common purpose and community. The relationship between community and distinctive development is governed by the requirement of co-operation which is an obligation placed on both parties to the Treaty. Reasonable co-operation can take place only if there is consultation on major issues of common concern and if good faith, balance, and common sense are shown on all sides. The outcome of reasonable co-operation will be partnership.

Under the fifth principle articulated by Government, 'the Principle of Redress', the Crown accepts a responsibility to provide a process for the resolution of grievances arising from the Treaty. This process may involve courts, the Waitangi Tribunal, or direct negotiations. (New Zealand's ninth periodic report, paras. 9–11)

The Tribunal has made some important recommendations, including, for example, one that ownership of a disputed block of land near the centre of Auckland, New Zealand's major urban centre, be restored to the original owners and financial compensation be paid. This and other recommendations were accepted by the government. The chairman of the Waitangi Tribunal has said that claimants show a readiness to modify their claims so as to cause as little upset as possible, while non-Maori have been equally intent to reach decisions that are fair. 'There is much goodwill. The main intransigence had not come from the Maori and Pakeha involved in the proceedings, but from commentators passing judgement from outside.'

These developments have been important to the reduction of racial discrimination and disadvantage. They have been generated by pressures and enlightened policies within the country and not by any dialogue with CERD. Indeed in 1987, when the seventh report was under consideration, one committee member who had held an ambassadorial post in the region said in public that he had never heard of the treaty of Waitangi, which did not suggest that he had prepared his contribution to the discussion very carefully. In 1990 the Committee commended the ninth report with particular warmth, and the country rapporteur suggested that it be given wide circulation in libraries for its comprehensive account of developments.

The position in Australia has been very different. European settlement in that country was not based on a treaty with any of the five hundred or so indigenous peoples. The International Convention has played a decisive part in the recent development of relations with the descendants of those peoples. Legislation has also been needed to prohibit racial discrimination between sections of the white population, which is more varied than in New Zealand.

Until 1967 Aboriginal people in Australia were not counted as citizens; they could not vote and were not as of right included in the national census. Legislation concerning Aboriginals was a responsibility of the state governments until that date. In many parts of Australia all part-Aboriginal children were forcibly removed by native welfare patrols from their families and taken to missions or government settlements to be brought up. This was done under the cover of laws for their 'protection', but is now more commonly seen as having been part of a policy of destroying the traditional languages and culture of the Aboriginal people. One consequence of this is the presence in Australia of a so-called 'lost generation' of persons of part-Aboriginal descent who may in some periods of their lives or in some circumstances have identified themselves as Aboriginal but not in others, and who cannot be identified as definitely Aboriginal by other people. Rather more than 250,000 persons are accounted Aboriginal, about 1.5 per cent of the total population. About one-third live in rural areas, where they may preserve some of the distinctive features of the original peoples (of the approximately 250 Aboriginal languages spoken in 1788, only some twenty are still spoken and transmitted to the next generation). About two-thirds live in the cities, where a new culture common to all who identify as Aboriginal has been forming; this has been a political reaction based upon claims about racism, heritage, and identity. There is a tension between this conception of Aboriginality as based upon self-identification and Aboriginality as based upon ancestry; in law persons whose ancestors are predominantly non-Aboriginal may not qualify as Aboriginal with respect to land rights.

In 1982 Eddie Mabo and some other residents of Murray Island in the Torres Strait filed a claim to ownership of land in their island under 'native title', as a right independent of the system of land tenure introduced by the British. The government of Queensland attempted to invalidate this action by passing a Queensland Coast Island Declaratory Act. On appeal, the federal High Court held in 1988 that if, under state law, a right is denied to people of one racial group, or limited by comparison with other racial groups, then by virtue of the Commonwealth Racial Discrimination Act, 1975, those people shall enjoy that right to the full extent. Possibly there have been no legal proceedings in any country in which the International Convention has exercised a more important influence. Legislation enacted to fulfil obligations under the ICERD provided the only protection against a parliament that sought to extinguish native title.

The substance of Mabo's claim was upheld in 1992 by a decision which established that pre-existing land rights ('native title') survived the extension of British sovereignty over Australia and may still survive today, provided that (*a*) the relevant native group maintains sufficient ties with the land in question, and (*b*) the title has not been extinguished as a consequence of valid governmental action. Following the view of Professor Garth Nettheim of the Aboriginal Law Centre, University of New South Wales, it can be concluded that, wherever British sovereignty has been extended to new places, the Common Law has generally recognized and protected pre-existing rights of the inhabitants while acknowledging the ultimate power of government to extinguish or displace such rights. Until 1992 Australia had been an exception to this principle, although there had been very little judicial authority for what was assumed to be the position. Now Australia is no longer an exception.

The Mabo decision cast doubt upon the legal validity of governmental land grants made between 1975 and 1992. To regularize them it appeared that it might be necessary to suspend the Racial Discrimination Act. Though another solution was eventually adopted, this meant that the Act, and Australia's obligations under the Convention, attracted much more attention than has happened in many states parties. At much the same time, in July 1992, a former prime minister, Mr Gough Whitlam, delivered a public lecture attacking the inaction of successive governments in discharging these obligations. He concluded that the Commonwealth government's declaration under article 14 would be the most effective means of persuading police and magistrates to heed the recommendations of the Royal Commission into Aboriginal Deaths in Custody. He answered his own question '*Quis custodiet ipsos custodes?* The answer may well be the Committee on the Elimination of Racial Discrimination.'

It should also be noted that the Australian government made some unsuccessful moves to try to conclude a legal arrangement with Aboriginal Australians that might substitute for an original treaty. It also maintains a distinctive process whereby allegations of racial discrimination are first subject to conciliation; if this does not succeed, there is then a public hearing. For example, when two Aboriginal women were refused service in a hotel and the case went to a hearing, the complaints were upheld and the hotel ordered to pay compensation and publish an apology.

In 1994 (as on the previous occasion) the state report was presented by the Minister for Aboriginal Affairs but this time he was accompanied by the Social Justice Commissioner, who was from the indigenous population and was permitted to express views diverging from the minister's; this was commended by the Committee as an example to other states. CERD expressed concerns about the ability of the Commonwealth government to ensure that other governments within the federation cooperated in implementing the Convention. It went on to note that:

Aboriginals continue to die in custody at a rate comparable to that which led to the appointment of the Royal Commission . . . that persons who identify as Aboriginal but whose ancestors are predominantly non-Aboriginal may not qualify as Aboriginal with respect to land rights . . . [that] Aboriginals continue to suffer disadvantage in such areas as education, employment, housing and health services. Their participation in the conduct of public affairs is disappointing. It is, once again, noted that, according to various social indicators, Aboriginals are more deeply affected by social problems such as alcoholism, drug abuse, delinquency and incarceration than any other social groups in the country. (A/49/18, paras. 543, 545)

The Committee's 'suggestions and recommendations' offered encouragement for the policies recognizing Aboriginal rights and furnishing compensation for past discrimination. They included recommendations that measures to remedy any discrimination suffered by members of non-English-speaking minorities be strengthened and that law-enforcement officials 'receive more effective training to ensure that in the performance of their duties they respect as well as protect human dignity and maintain and uphold the human rights of all'. The quality of the dialogue between the Committee and Australia appears to have been unusually high. The state has supplied a wealth of information and appears to take very seriously the opinions expressed in the Committee. Concluding his replies in 1994, the minister encouraged the Committee to 'tell us which of the current policies you approve', as if this would be important to discussions between the Commonwealth and state governments and the various agencies.

In other Pacific countries the Convention has not attracted so much attention as in Australia. For example, in Fiji there has been a significant conflict between the traditional rights of the indigenous Polynesian people and the democratic rights of people of immigrant Indian ethnic origin. When in 1987 the governing party lost an election, the army intervened. It was as if the traditional holders of power were unwilling to share that power on a democratic basis. Constituency boundaries had already been drawn in such a way that it took fewer Polynesian than Indian votes to elect a member of the legislature and Indians were unable to buy land; so, from the outset, there had been obvious racial discrimination. The obligations of the government under the Convention seemed to have had very little influence and the international dimension to the domestic conflict had not been accorded importance.

Since the periodic report was seriously overdue, CERD reconsidered implementation of the Convention in Fiji at its fortieth session in 1991. The country rapporteur, Mr Wolfrum, reviewed developments since the *coup d'état* in 1987. Racial inequalities in the electoral system had been institutionalized. In the General Assembly India had charged Fiji with racial discrimination against its citizens of Indian origin. Mr de Gouttes observed that the Committee had rarely encountered racial discrimination of such a character. Mr Banton struck a different note, maintaining that, if the Committee wanted the Fijian government to resume dialogue, it would have to indicate an awareness of its viewpoint. The ethnic minority introduced during colonial rule had been left exposed on its termination when the majority reasserted what it saw as its rights, as in Malaysia, Indonesia, and Myanmar. It was noteworthy that a number of countries in this position had not ratified the Convention. It might be that other states parties had failed to object to Fiji's reservations or to take action under article 11 of the Convention on this account. Fiji's adoption of a British-style electoral system had threatened the indigenous population with permanent minority status, but the discrimination in the present electoral arrangements could not be excused by reference to article 1(2) of the Convention. Mr Ferrero Costa proposed that the Committee request the government to withdraw its reservations. Mr Yutzis argued that CERD should do everything possible to induce the government to resume dialogue. Mr Rechetov cautioned that political representation strictly proportional to country's demographic composition existed nowhere, and that members had hardly mentioned the current racial tensions in Fiji. Mrs Sadiq Ali observed that the party ejected by the *coup d'état* had been the country's first multiracial political alliance. The landowners' movement was in effect a racist organization (SR 925–6). The Committee then agreed:

Having discussed the new constitutional developments which have taken place in Fiji, the reservations it had made on ratification, and taking note of the express concern of members of the Committee about possible discrimination against Indians in respect of political and economic rights, the Committee calls upon the Government of Fiji to resume its dialogue with the Committee by filing the reports which are due . . . (A/46/18, para. 343)

A special problem for the Committee has been posed by reports of violence in Papua New Guinea. Since no report had been received from the government since 1983, the Committee in 1992 reviewed the position there and formally requested further information on the situation in Bougainville (A/47/18, para. 266). When this was not forthcoming, the Committee 'requested that information concerning the human rights situation in the whole territory of Papua New Guinea that was available to the Secretary-General should be shared with the Committee' (A/48/18, para. 572). Having received no response, in 1994 it reported:

The Committee is gravely concerned at reports of serious human rights violations, including summary executions and population transfers in Bougainville where the population is ethnically distinct.

The Committee continues to be concerned about the possible resumption of large-scale mining operations in Bougainville without due regard to the rights of the population and the effects of environmental degradation.

The Committee strongly urges that the Government resume its dialogue . . . (A/49/18 para. 102)

## EAST ASIA

Passing now to the Asian mainland, it may be noted that China has reported to the UN:

Among China's many nationalities, the Han are the largest group, numbering 1,040 million or 91.96 per cent of the total population; besides the Han there are a further 55 separate minority nationalities together numbering 91,200,000 people or 8.04 per cent of the population, including Mongols, Hiu, Zang (Tibetans), Uighurs, Miao, Yi, Zhuang, Puyi, Koreans, Mon, Dong, Yao, Bai, Tuchia, Hani, Kazakhs, Dai and Li, all of which number over 1 million. There are 24 different nationalities living in Yunnan Province, and 12 in the Xinjiang Uighur Autonomous Region. (HRI/CORE/1/Add.21)

The largest nationality after the Han would appear to be the Zhuangs, with a population of 13,378,162 in 1982. According to the second periodic report in 1985, 'Over 17 million minority people, or 25 per cent of the total minorities, live in mingled or scattered communities in large, medium-sized and small cities or townships'. The government's policy for minorities concentrates upon the areas regarded as minority territory and it is doubtful whether the protections against racial or ethnic discrimination of those who live in mingled or scattered communities are very effective. According to the third periodic report:

The principal legal instruments regulating ethnic relations in China are the Self-Government Laws of Nationality Regions. National autonomous areas and provinces with large minority populations comply with the provisions of these laws. In addition, each minority area, according to its own conditions and characteristics, also formulates its own self-government regulations as well as concrete measures for their implementation. This is the way minority peoples exercise their equal and self-government rights.

When this report was considered by CERD there was an animated discussion of allegations of racial or ethnic discrimination in Tibet. The country rapporteur, Mr Ferrero Costa, stated that

information received from non-governmental sources indicated that the Chinese Government was guilty of racial discrimination in Tibet. For instance, a paper submitted to the Commission on Human Rights at its forty-sixth session by the Minority Rights Group had stated that the large-scale movement of Chinese settlers to Tibet was a deliberate policy of the Government . . . The large influx of Han Chinese settlers had affected the life and culture of the Tibetans and was rapidly reducing them to an insignificant and second-class minority in their own country . . . [following references to income from the extraction of timber and minerals, and the sale of works of art and religious artefacts abroad] the central Government seemed to have earned at least 10 times as much from Tibet as it had granted in state aid.

Ordinary Tibetans who were not residents of Lhasa could not visit the capital without obtaining passes from three different local authorities and a permit from the city authorities, for which they were required to pay an exorbitant fee. Tibetan pilgrims visiting Lhasa were given a temporary registration permit valid for 15 days, whereas all Chinese received a permit valid for up to three years . . . Tibetan Buddhist monks had been subjected to new rules and regulations which were often totally at variance with their ancient traditions . . .

Tibetans complained of massive unemployment . . . Acute discrimination prevailed in the field of housing and public health . . . there was a marked difference in the quality of education provided to Chinese and to Tibetan children . . . (SR 896)

Mrs Sadiq Ali endorsed some of these points and maintained that the Muslim population was subjected to various forms of segregation. Mr Rhenan Segura, Mr Wolfrum, and Mr de Gouttes also expressed concern regarding Tibet, while Mr Banton drew attention to the reference to 'the peaceful liberation of Tibet in the early 1950s' and stated that, if this was not a mistranslation from the original Chinese text but was intended as a statement of historical fact, then it was grotesque. The state report maintained that the root cause of the riots in Lhasa was neither nationalism, nor religious faith, nor any question of human rights. 'The riots were perpetrated by a small group of separatists with the aim of splitting China . . . Most Tibetans as well as Chinese of other nationalities are strongly opposed to this kind of chaos instigated by a small handful of people.' In response Mr Banton observed that there were small groups of separatists in many countries, but the question was why such people received the support of substantial sectors of the population. A different note was struck by Mr Lechuga Hevia, who asked why Tibet was given preferential treatment with regard to the retention of foreign-exchange income earned from foreign trade. Mr Vidas and Mr Rechetov wanted China to understand that the remarks of Committee members were intended to be constructive and did not constitute criticism of China.

In that they were unsuccessful. When discussion resumed, Mr Song objected that the comments of some members had not displayed goodwill. The state representative said that his delegation would not reply to comments or questions which sought to teach China a lesson. He reiterated the positions stated in the report and quoted a series of statistics at variance with those used earlier by Committee members. Mr Wolfrum, Mr de Gouttes, and Mr Ferrero Costa noted that some questions remained outstanding, while Mr Yutzis observed that, with respect to freedom of religion, the documents of the Commission of Human Rights gave a different picture (SR 871).

When, in 1993, CERD came to report on its examination of the seventh report of the Republic of Korea, it explained that the national legislation still did not meet all the requirements of the Convention, and requested further information

on the situation of children of mixed parentage and foreign workers and the general social attitude towards them; on the actions taken to assure equal provision of education, medical and other care and employment opportunities for those persons living in the south-western region . . . on the effectiveness of legal remedies for those who suffered from discriminatory practices and on specific cases where compensation had been provided to victims of such discrimination. (A/48/18, paras. 234–5)

Viet Nam, for reasons that will be well known, has been experiencing economic difficulties. Its initial report under the Convention, considered in 1984, was chiefly concerned with the government's policy for the fifty ethnic minorities which accounted for 12.3 per cent of the population (A/39/18, paras. 353–66) and did not cast much light on Vietnamese conceptions of race. When it was brought within the review procedure, a state representative appeared to explain the difficulties and to discuss the Convention's requirements. A full report was then considered in 1993. CERD noted with satisfaction the moves towards a fuller establishment of the rule of law but expressed concern that the state legislation did not cover the whole of article 4.

The remaining states on the East Asian mainland to have reported under the Convention are the Lao People's Democratic Republic (reviewed in 1992) and Cambodia. Democratic Kampuchea, as it was then called, reported in 1987 that, because of Vietnamese occupation of much of its territory, it could not prepare a proper report. The Committee drew attention to the possibility, under article 11 of the Convention, for a state party to invoke a procedure for interstate disputes concerning racial discrimination, but the state representative did not wish to pursue this (A/42/18, paras. 435–48). Here, again, there is little indication of what is understood by 'race'.

The Philippine government in its 1989 periodic report under ICERD asserted that there was no racial discrimination among ancient Filipinos. Western imperialism led to unequal development, so that 'our Muslim brothers in the South and other national cultural minority groups, were largely left behind in the general movement for development and social advance' and these disparities 'resulted in apparent racial distinctions or perceived instances of racial discrimination'.

## SOUTH ASIA

At the time of writing, in July 1995, both India and Pakistan were seriously overdue in the submission of periodic reports and had been sent letters to say that implementation of the Convention in their territories would be considered under the review procedure. Sri Lanka had just responded to a similar letter by submitting a single document which combined its third to sixth reports. The Committee had welcomed this resumption of dialogue; it noted the variety of human-rights organs functioning in the country but wanted more systematic information about how their mandates interrelated, how their activities were coordinated, and how they in practice implemented the various articles of the Convention. The Committee wanted more information concerning the implementation of articles 4(b) and 5(e), more attention paid to sensitizing members of the law-enforcement agencies and armed forces about human rights, and a further report covering the points listed.

No reports from India and Pakistan have therefore been considered since CERD adopted the practice of formulating concluding observations expressing the collective view of the whole Committee. But some impression of the contrast between CERD's old and new reporting styles can be obtained from the 1987 report (A/42/18), which includes thirty-nine paragraphs on India and twenty-two on Pakistan. Many of them raise questions of dubious relevance to the Convention and few generate pressure for its better implementation. By way of example, and with reference to India:

749. . . . members were gratified to note the measures taken in support of the scheduled castes and tribes, in particular, the establishment of two states inhabited by scheduled tribes. The fact that those two states had been established in India was a sign of progress, which proved that the principle of federalism could be applied to developing countries. Within that context, it was asked whether those two states were in the region of the Sino-Indian conflict. One member pointed out that there was a boundary dispute.

750. . . . It was noted that the Constitution provided that the State could set aside jobs in the public services for the backward classes. The fact that that provision applied to the scheduled castes and tribes was highly appreciated, but it was felt that it should also apply to other groups. In that context, information was requested about the representation of the various communities in the public services.

757. Members also wished to know, in general, what India was doing to preserve and encourage the cultural identity of the various Indian states, and, in particular, of the State of Sikkim, the population of which was mostly of Mongolian descent . . .

759. Concerning the implementation of article 4 of the Convention, it was noted that the Government had enacted appropriate legislation. It was asked whether the Indian Penal Code, which predated the Convention, had been amended following the entry into force of the latter so as to reflect more precisely the provisions of that article.

764. In reply to the questions asked . . . the representative of India stated . . .

775. With reference to Sikkim, he explained that that region had become a full state of the Indian Union in 1975. There were four principal languages but all, except Nepali, were dialects with no written literature and could never therefore be used as official languages. The social and economic development of all the frontier states had rightly received attention out of all proportion to the population of the area . . .

778. Regarding article 4, the representative said that, since the submission

of the seventh periodic report, there had been no new developments in India, as existing laws were deemed adequate with any problem of implementation that might arise.

Concerning the ninth report of Pakistan, it was reported:

794. With regard to the implementation of articles 4 and 6 of the Convention, members of the Committee pointed out that no response had been forthcoming regarding the criticisms expressed by the Committee during consideration of the previous report concerning shortcomings in the application of article 4 of the Convention. In particular, section 153A of the Pakistan Penal Code, which was mentioned in the annex to the report, showed that certain aspects of article 4(*b*) of the Convention had still not been incorporated into the domestic law of Pakistan. They wished to know whether the provisions of the Pakistan Penal Code concerning discrimination were frequently applied and asked to be provided with a few significant court decisions . . . Members wished to know whether an individual citizen could appeal directly to the courts, whether penal, civil or administrative, to seek redress.

796. In reply . . . the representative of Pakistan stated . . .

803. Regarding Pakistan's obligations under article 4 of the Convention, amendments had been made to the Penal Code and the Code of Criminal Procedure in 1973 to bring them into conformity with the provisions of the Convention. The amendments included provisions penalizing incitement to disharmony or feelings of enmity, hatred or ill will between different communities and which disturbed public tranquillity. The word 'disharmony' was considered broad enough to cover every conceivable act of racial incitement and no further legislation had been thought necessary.

When, in 1986, the representative of Sri Lanka presented his country's second periodic report, he said that a very small minority urged separation of the country into two racially homogeneous states. No meaningful steps towards a political dialogue could be undertaken until most members of the minority Tamil community could exercise their free will unhindered by terrorist action. Yet, according to the Committee:

The central problem seemed to be not just the violence of certain groups of the Tamil community, but the fact that the Government was not addressing the underlying causes. Explanations were requested regarding the three rather different elements which were amalgamated in the report, namely terrorist violence, communal disturbance and the minority Tamil community. Those three categories should be clearly distinguished and terrorism should be considered quite separately . . . Combating [ethnic] polarization required political responsibility . . .

Compliance [with articles 2 and 5] was not a matter of terrorism requiring a military solution, but a matter arising from an increasing sense of frustration among the Tamil population and from legitimate social, economic and political grievances, particularly in such areas as denial of equal status for their language, the problem of land settlement, education, employment and a growing sense of insecurity . . .

Members wished to know what were the prospects of lifting the sixth amendment to the Constitution, so as to enable moderate members of the Tamil United Liberation Front to participate in Parliament and work towards a political solution to the ethnic crisis . . . nothing was to be found in the report concerning measures called for in article 4 . . . clarifications were sought on the manner in which effective protection and remedies were implemented . . . implementation of article 7 was of special significance in Sri Lanka . . .

In reply, the state representative denied that the Tamil community had been blamed; only a small number of Tamils were involved. The only issue on which the Government was not prepared to negotiate was that of the territorial integrity of Sri Lanka (A/42/18, paras. 268–98).

Occasionally there is a disagreement between a state party and members of the Committee concerning the requirements of the Convention and their respective roles in its implementation. As an illustration it may be illuminating to rehearse a dispute in 1992 over the sixth report of Bangladesh. The state representative, introducing the report, declared that there was no racial discrimination in Bangladesh

since there was but one mixed race . . . Some details had been given in the report about the integrative process in Bangladesh simply to emphasize the country's success in dealing with the problems of a 'post-racial' society . . . some tiny tribal groups had difficulties, at the instigation of their foreign mentors, in identifying themselves with the polity of Bangladesh. That was a problem of national integration and nothing else. Marginal problems of tribal terrorism had complicated and hindered democratic dialogue with a view to a political solution.

The country rapporteur, Mr Yutzis, objected that racial definition was defined by the Convention; using that definition, he could not accept that there was no racial discrimination in Bangladesh. The government had stated that no measures to implement article 4 had 'been considered necessary', but that article created mandatory obligations. According to the information available to him, from a variety of sources, including reports of the International Labour Organization and annual and specific reports of Amnesty International for 1991 and 1992, there were at least 27 ethnic groups in Bangladesh, 13 of them living in the Chittagong Hill Tracts . . . the recent history of these peoples had been one of gradual encirclement and dispossession . . . The period 1979 to 1983 had seen a policy of large-scale settlement by Bengali colonists from the plains. The result had been the further impoverishment and marginaliz-ation of the indigenous peoples, a situation which had led to armed uprising. Guerrilla groups were now active in the Hill Tracts, and the authorities had responded by virtually militarizing the area, so that the ethnic groups found themselves the victims, not only of economic deprivation, but also of institutionalized violence in reprisal for attacks on settlers and military personnel by guerrilla groups. There were an estimated 35,000 or more security troops and police operating in the Hill Tracts, and the Amnesty International reports gave details of widespread torture and other human rights violations. In one recent incident, several hundred defenceless villagers had been murdered in reprisal for the killing by guerrillas of a Bengali soldier. A policy of forced resettlement had been pursued in the context of the authorities' counter-insurgency strategy. In the areas of resettlement, curfews and restrictions on movement were such that conditions resembled those in military-run camps. The undeclared low-intensity warfare amounted virtually to State terrorism. (SR 942)

He requested the delegation of Bangladesh to confirm or deny the reports he had just mentioned in regard to the Chittagong Hill Tracts, to state whether a distinction could be made between the problems posed by armed struggle and respect for civilian popu-lations, and to indicate how far the process of militarizing the region was to go, to what point a colonization policy directly harmful to the inhabitants was to be pursued, how long the forced resettlements imposed on the latter were to continue, what measures the government intended to take to protect the ethnic groups of the region and to ensure that their holy places, their heritage and culture were respected, and lastly, what were to be the powers of the district councils. The government had stated that the special protective regulation of 1900 was operative, but more information was needed about its application (SR 943).

Mrs Sadiq Ali, speaking next, observed that the return to democ-racy in Bangladesh was encouraging, 'although the military was always in the background and intervention on its part could not be completely ruled out'. She referred to a fact-finding mission to the Chittagong Hill Tracts headed by a senior member of the European

Parliament which spoke of 'countless cases of gross human rights violations . . . The report had been suppressed, and the police had also seized a large number of copies of reports of the international human rights commission.' She continued:

The Prime Minister, during her visit in May 1992, had been handed a memorandum calling for a political solution to the problems of the region, respect for the land rights of its inhabitants, dissolution of the district councils, rehabilitation of the 60,000 refugees who had fled the country, creation of a safe environment for the hill people and the setting up of a judicial commission to investigate the Longang massacre.

Was any solution in sight?

Referring specifically to article 3 of the Convention, about segregation, Mrs Sadiq Ali went on to say that local authorities had

indicated that the collective farms had a twofold objective: to cut communications between the indigenous Jumma people and the Shanti Bahini forces, and to ensure the future rehabilitation of repatriated refugees. They had indicated that in some areas all returning refugees had been interned in cluster camps for 'civilizing' and protection purposes. According to the Chittagong Hill Tracts Students' Council, those living in such camps were subject to very severe restrictions and could not travel without permission. The movements of Jumma villagers were controlled by the military, who had the power to cut them off from essentials such as medicine, clothing and food . . . government policy aimed to convert the Jummas to the Islamic faith . . .

Among the succeeding speakers, Mr Diaconu found the government's report too vague as to legal measures. Mr Song asked about population numbers and access to education. Mr de Gouttes joined in the criticism of the reports legal deficiencies. Mr Banton asked about the observation of certain laws governing property in the tribal areas and why the legal assistance project of Caritas Bangladesh had been stopped prematurely by the government. Mr Fererro Costa observed:

First, while Bangladesh was undeniably encountering special difficulties, those difficulties in no way justified the perpetration of acts of racial discrimination, and did not preclude the Committee from making observations and recommendations with regard to that country. Secondly, while it was important to have information on minorities, general information was also needed on the various regions and races in the country mentioned in the report. Thirdly, the fact that ethnic minorities in Bangladesh represented only a small proportion of the total population did not mean that the country could evade its responsibility for taking measures to guarantee their protection. Fourthly, the statement in regard to article 4 of the Convention that the authorities in Bangladesh had not considered it necessary to take any specific measures was unacceptable. Lastly, the Committee was also unable to accept claims as general and vague as those to the effect that racial discrimination was unknown in the country.

Mr van Boven said that any idea that the inhabitants of poor countries might have fewer rights than those of rich countries was unacceptable where human rights were concerned. He asked about official policy regarding population transfers, concerning consultation and compensation. Mr Lechuga Hevia enquired why the inhabitants of the Chittagong Hill Tracts were not subject to the same administrative regulations as the rest of the population.

Since no other member of the Committee wished to speak at this stage, the Chairman turned to the state representative, who said that he was not for the moment in a position to respond to all the questions raised. There then followed a general discussion as to whether the Committee should ask for replies later during the session, within one year, or wait for the next periodic report. But Mr Aboul-Nasr struck a different note. He said that the Committee might have gone too far in its questions. It was not entitled to pass judgements or make accusations, like that of state terrorism. Mr Ahmadu then argued for abandoning the system of country rapporteurs because it did not reduce the number of questions and the Committee was showing a tendency to turn itself into a court of law. Delegations of states parties, particularly those from Third World countries, were intimidated.

Mr Yutzis defended himself by saying that he had cited his sources, which had referred to a massacre of over 200 women, children, and old men. The least that could be done was to check the truth of that allegation. In such a situation, which concerned the right of minorities, it was essential that the Committee should be in a position to reach a decision on the basis of the procedures it had adopted. If that was to be done, the reply of the state concerned should be provided as speedily as possible.

The state representative said that he would reply to the questions at a later stage, but that with reference to observations on such matters as terrorism and the take-over of indigenous lands, he pointed out that, under article 9 of the Convention, the Committee was required to examine the reports of states parties, not extraneous information.

The reader who consults the Committee's summary record will find that later in the session (SR 956) it considered draft concluding observations presented by the committee rapporteur. He proposed, *inter alia*, that a footnote be added to the report to the General Assembly, stating: 'Subsequently the Committee received from the Permanent Mission of Bangladesh a communication denying a variety of allegations made during consideration of the report.' Mr Aboul-Nasr noted that the Committee was duty-bound to refer to the letter. Originally the Mission had demanded official apologies from Mr Yutzis and Mrs Sadiq Ali as well as the publication of its letter, and had threatened to pursue the matter in the General Assembly. These demands had been dropped and there would now be no follow-up. It was most important that any confrontation should be avoided. Mr de Gouttes, however, maintained that either the Mission had withdrawn its letter, in which case there was no need to make any reference to it, or it had not. He expressed concern

that the Committee was now discussing at a public meeting a matter which had been dealt with the previous day at a closed meeting. As he understood it, the representative of Bangladesh had agreed not to take the matter further, but had not offered formally to withdraw its letter. That being so, he proposed that the Rapporteur should read out the preliminary draft of the reply considered the previous day, so that the Committee could hold that reply in reserve for use at the next session in the event of the original letter being made public.

Mr Fererro Costa took a similar view. The letter from the Mission had referred very specifically to duties and responsibilities of individual members; it had offered an interpretation of article 1, paragraph 1, of the Convention that was open to question, and the Committee ought not to remain silent. The Committee did not agree, preferring the proposal of the rapporteur. Mr Shahi remarked that the summary record should refer to its decision of the previous year that the Committee, as a body of independent experts, should have access to a variety of sources. In its concluding observations:

The Committee expressed grave concern at reports on the human rights of the ethnic minorities in the Chittagong Hill Tracts, including the forced transfer of population. Since the state representative was not in a position to respond to questions, the Committee looked forward to receiving further information. (A/47/18, para. 127)

This episode illustrates a series of points bearing upon the work of the Committee. In sequence, they include: a state that reports on the basis of its own understanding of the nature of racial discrimination instead of the definition in the Convention; the failure of a state to appreciate the mandatory character of article 4; the difficulties that can be created when Committee members do not use 'diplomatic' language and express unusually sharp criticism; a state response which distracts attention from what should be the main issues in implementation of the Convention; the variation between Committee members in the way they balance their understanding of the difficulties of some reporting states with their obligations towards those intended to be protected by the Convention; the desire of members both to maintain their independence and to avoid unnecessary disputes with states. It may also be concluded that, while the Committee's report has to be adopted in a public session, some matters are better settled in private, and the episode casts some light on how a committee's work can move between private and public meetings. It may be recalled that the state representative spoke of the 'foreign mentors' of the tribal groups. This may have been a reference to an alleged influence from India, and therefore have added an extra element to the objection to the remarks of Mrs Sadiq Ali.

## SOUTH-WESTERN ASIA

A dispute between a reporting state and the state of which a committee member is a national was reflected in the consideration of the initial report of Afghanistan in 1985. In 1978 there had been a change of government in Afghanistan. At the end of the following year the Red Army took over the capital. At this time Mr Aga Shahi, a member of CERD since 1978, was Adviser for Foreign Affairs (and from 1980 to 1982, Minister for Foreign Affairs) in the government of Pakistan. In the course of the dialogue with Afghanistan in 1985, Mr Shahi asked whether conditions were being created to enable refugees to return home in honour and safety. He noted that the special rapporteur of the Commission on Human Rights had expressed profound concern over grave and massive violations of human rights, including torture, bombings, and crop destruction, in the context of the continuing armed conflict in Afghanistan. Two other members endorsed his comments. The state representative replied that Mr Shahi had raised points unrelated to the work of the Committee. He had quoted an estimate of the numbers of refugees which had been inflated. Inasmuch as Mr Shahi had occupied a high position in his government when Pakistan and Afghanistan had been discussing the return of refugees, he should have had no doubts as to the truth of the matter. Mr Shahi responded by saying that he had no desire to enter into polemics and by explaining how he had estimated the number of refugees. Mr Partsch objected that it was not for the representative of a state party to censure a member of the Committee. Afghanistan's representative then contested some further observations, and, in particular, the report of the Commission's special rapporteur, Mr Ermacora.

It was well known that Mr Ermacora was an individual of dubious integrity. He had served the Nazis in the Second World War, still attended Fascist meetings and was the supporter of a neo-Nazi organization. The facts surrounding his appointment were common knowledge. The real question was how could the Committee, which was charged with promoting the elimination of violations of some of the most basic human rights, give credence to a report prepared by a well-known Fascist. (SR 719).

A later record (SR 742) contains a note of Mr Ermacora's reply to these reflections upon him.

Since no further periodic report had been received, CERD in 1994 reviewed implementation of the Convention in the country. It expressed 'deep concern about the tragic circumstances prevailing in Afghanistan, which include conflicts based upon descent', but could do little else.

Islamic states have on occasion looked to the Qur'an for a lead concerning racial discrimination and have quoted from it (as Yemen did in its tenth report) the passage 'We created you male and female and divided you into peoples and tribes so that you may know each other.' This passage must have an esoteric meaning because otherwise it might be thought that it would be easier for humans to know one another were there none of the physical differences that sometimes cause people to deny their common humanity with others.

After consideration of the combined ninth to twelfth reports of Iran, the Committee concluded with the recommendation that 'its comments . . . should be studied by the authorities of the State party with a view to their adopting the necessary legal, judicial and administrative measures to give effect in practice to all the provisions of the Convention' (A/48/18, para. 275). Somewhat similar views were expressed in 1991 regarding implementation of the Convention in Iraq. These have already been quoted in Chapter 8 as an illustration of the new-style concluding observations.

On the report from Kuwait considered in 1993 the Committee observed that it was

particularly concerned about expulsions and other discriminatory measures against especially vulnerable groups of foreigners, including Palestinians, stateless Arabs, Bedoons, Iraqis and nationals of countries which did not participate in the coalition, and the treatment of foreign domestic servants. The Committee was concerned that no specific measures had been envisaged to eliminate discrimination with respect to descent, national or ethnic origin. In that connection the Committee referred to official discrimination made between two categories of Kuwaiti citizens: those who possessed longstanding Kuwaiti nationality and those who have acquired Kuwaiti nationality in more recent times. Furthermore, the Committee expressed its concern about the lack of penal legislation to implement the provisions of article 4 of the Convention. (A/48/18, para. 376)

Equally, the United Arab Emirates were asked in 1994 to supply more precise information on

the measures taken to give effect to the provisions of article 4 of the Convention; the situation of foreign workers, including domestics; the protection of the freedoms of religious expression and of assembly; the effect of the Gulf war on the exercise of fundamental rights and freedoms; the reform of the Penal Code; and the respective competencies of non-religious and religious courts regarding cases of racial discrimination. (A/49/18, para. 293).

## THE MIDDLE EAST

Some Muslim states have maintained that, as no forms of racial discrimination existed in their countries, legislation to implement article 4 was unnecessary. They have been told, as Yemen was told, that 'that was not a legally defensible interpretation of the obligations that a State assumes on acceding to the Convention' (A/47/18, para. 178).

Lebanon had to cope with the influx of Palestinian refugees, some of whom used Lebanese territory to attack Israel. The Israeli army invaded Lebanon in 1978 and 1982. Different groups within Lebanon, aided by outside interests, engaged in hostilities that amounted to civil war. Late in 1989 Lebanese deputies met in Saudi Arabia and there adopted a document of national understanding which established a special relationship with Syria. CERD reviewed the situation in 1991. The country rapporteur, Mr Wolfrum, rehearsed the recent history and proposed steps to reinstitute dialogue. All other speakers supported his proposals (SR 923).

Chapters 6 and 7 have discussed the manner in which political tensions in the Middle East affected the Committee's reception of reports from Israel and its neighbours. CERD is still far from satisfied that Israel has done enough to implement the Convention. The situation may be illustrated by a summary of the consideration on 15 August 1991 of a document constituting that country's fifth and sixth periodic reports.

Presenting those reports, the first Israeli representative referred to the Iraqi missile attacks during the Gulf War. He maintained that the absence of any supporting response from Israel's Arab citizens, who made up 16 per cent of the population and who enjoyed equality before the law, had demonstrated Israeli pluralism. The intake of Ethiopian and Soviet Jews showed that there was no racism or xenophobia in Israel. A recent Supreme Court decision had described the International Bill of Human Rights as a heritage common to all enlightened people. A second representative then provided many social statistics on the participation of Arab citizens in various spheres of society.

The country rapporteur was Mr Yutzis. He asked a series of questions about the meaning of certain passages in the report and a further series about reported incidents in Israel and the occupied territories. Twelve other members followed, posing questions which were too detailed to be summarized here, many of them relating to the legal basis of policy in the occupied territories. It may also be noted that Mr Aboul-Nasr repeated an observation made in connection with earlier reports. He saw no reason other than racism to explain the fact that an Arab, whether Muslim or Christian, should be denied the right to return home, whereas considerable efforts were made to settle Ethiopian and Russian Jews who had never set foot in Israel. Could it not be said that to grant Israeli citizenship automatically to any Jew settling in Israel, while denying Arabs the right to return there, amounted to a legalization of discrimination? Mr Banton observed that there was a political conflict in which the parties could be identified by both religion and ethnic origin. It might happen, therefore, that Israeli courts would have to determine whether the grounds for discriminatory treatment were those of race, religion, political opinion, or, as Mr Wolfrum had mentioned, military necessity. Any decision on such points would be of interest in view of parallel situations elsewhere (the conflict in Kashmir could have been mentioned).

In its concluding observations CERD

reiterated that the Government of Israel had implemented in the occupied territories neither the Geneva Convention Relative to the Protection of Civilian Persons in Time of War nor the International Convention on the Elimination of All Forms of Racial Discrimination. The Committee expressed great concern about the situation in the occupied territories. The Committee urged the Government of Israel to answer, in its seventh periodic report, all the questions asked and concerns raised during the consideration of its sixth and earlier reports. (A/47/18, paras. 387–8)

As already mentioned (Chapter 8), on 7 March 1994 CERD adopted decision 1(44) to request an urgent report. This read:

1. The Committee expresses its shock at the appalling massacre committed by Israeli settlers against Palestinian worshippers in the Abraham mosque at Hebron on 25 February 1994.

2. In accordance with article 9, paragraph 1(*b*), of the International Convention on the Elimination of All Forms of Racial Discrimination and with reference, in particular, to article 5(*b*) of the Convention, the Committee requests the Government of Israel to send it an urgent report, no later than 30 June 1994, on measures taken to guarantee the safety and protection of the Palestinian civilians in the occupied Palestinian territory and to bring to an end the illegal action of Israeli settlers and to disarm them.

Israel responded to CERD's request by forwarding extracts from the report of the official inquiry into the shooting, but without accepting the Committee's right under the Convention to request such information, or supplying information on measures taken to guarantee the safety of Palestinians. It sent no representative to meet the Committee. CERD was not prepared to accept the description of the shooting as an 'isolated incident', given the context in which it had occurred. In its concluding observations the Committee reaffirmed its competence to examine the manner in which Israel discharged its obligations and regretted that the report requested had not been submitted:

The Committee regards the Israeli settlements in the occupied territories as not only illegal under international law but also as obstacles to peace and to the enjoyment of human rights by the whole population in the region without distinction as to national or ethnic origin in accordance with the Convention.

It requested the government to expedite its seventh and eighth periodic reports, 'due on 2 February 1992 and 1994 respectively, and to include in them a response to these observations' (A/49/18, paras. 87, 91).

The government of Israel replied that it would supply a copy of the report of its committee of inquiry into the Hebron massacre without prejudice to the competence of the Committee in the matter. When the Committee acknowledged receipt of these materials, it observed that they did not constitute the report requested. Israel then expressed surprise at the Committee's response and requested that the materials it had submitted be published as Israel's report. The Committee replied in the terms of its decision 8(46) that

Third, on the basis of this qualification by Israel itself of the materials supplied, the Committee had good reason to assume that these materials did not constitute the urgent report the Committee had requested. The assumption was confirmed by the fact that Israel preferred to be absent when the question was discussed by the Committee. Fourth, now that Israel has indicated that it wishes to see that the materials supplied to the Committee be treated as the urgent report requested by the Committee, the Committee is ready to treat these materials on the same footing as urgent materials requested from other States parties. Fifth, recalling the final paragraph of the concluding observations adopted by the Committee on 18 August (A/49/18, para. 91) the Government of Israel is again requested to expedite its 7th and 8th periodic reports, due on 2 February 1992 and

1994 respectively, and to include in them a further response to the observations in question. They should be submitted in time for consideration at the Committee's 47th session.

Those who drafted the Convention had in mind the problems of their time and did not consider how racial grounds were to be distinguished from other grounds of action in the circumstances of the Asian states. It may not be so easy at present to see the application of the Convention to some of the conflicts in this region, but the situation will change with time. Much will depend upon the courts in those countries and the extent to which the victims of discrimination on grounds of descent, or national or ethnic origin, have access to them.

## CONCLUSION

As previous chapters have exemplified, there is always a political dimension to the dialogue between a state party and CERD, and that dimension comes more to the forefront when there is any doubt about the application of the Convention to the circumstances of a particular state. Fewer such doubts have arisen with respect to the Pacific states with a history of European colonization than with respect to the states of the Asian mainland and the Middle East. In no case have the differences of opinion been sharper than in the recent exchange with Bangladesh, where the government has claimed to represent a 'post-racial society', neglecting the manner in which the Convention covers discrimination based upon descent or ethnic origin. A further factor tending to elevate the political dimension is that general human-rights questions have at times been confounded with the more specific questions of racial discrimination. Given the heterogeneity of the states parties in the Asia–Pacific regional grouping, it is doubtful if any other general conclusions can be drawn that would differentiate the dialogue with these states from that with states in other regions.

As in the case of some of the states considered in the previous chapter, there are states in Asia which do not have the ability effectively to prohibit racial discrimination in all circumstances, particularly discrimination in effect and discrimination on the grounds of ethnic origin in the private sector, and to provide victims with satisfactory remedies and opportunities to secure compensation. Indeed, any suggestion that they should do so might appear to some of these states yet another example of the attempt to apply Western norms of human rights to societies which have quite different needs and values. These states may enact legislation to comply with article 4, but they may well doubt whether it is really suited to their circumstances where differences of ethnic origin are often confounded with other social and cultural differences.

# 13

## States Parties

THE adoption and implementation of ICERD has been an attempt to expand the realm of law at the expense of the realm of politics. Nothing quite like it had ever been tried before, but providence seems to have smiled upon the venture. Seen in retrospect, it is remarkable that those who promoted the Convention should have been able to take a legal definition of racial discrimination from an ILO instrument adapted to the circumstances of the workplace, and marry it to the political thrust against racial discrimination as that was conceived on the international plane. It is for this reason that Chapter 4 presented the Convention as founded upon a 'noble lie'. The lie was that racial discrimination *as defined in article 1.1* could be eliminated. It was noble because it made possible the mobilization of international opinion to combat a nearly universal evil.

Most of the states which acceded to the Convention in the early years apparently regarded racial discrimination as a social pathology which afflicted other states than their own, one which had been caused by either colonialism or the dissemination of racist ideology. This led them to see the struggle against racial discrimination as belonging primarily within their foreign policy. The form of the Convention was that of a contract between states parties. Accession was seen as an exercise that would bring states credit on the international stage without making many domestic demands upon them. The text of the contract contained no clauses specifying sanctions that could be applied to parties that failed to keep their promises. This assisted the process of accession, but there was a price to be paid in the longer term.

The Convention was promptly used by some states parties in pursuit of foreign-policy objectives. Panama led the way in 1971 by employing it to publicize a grievance against the USA. This was followed by similar disguised interstate grievances voiced by the Syrian Arab Republic, Jordan, and Egypt complaining about Israel, and by Cyprus complaining about Turkey. The Convention was also used with some success as part of an international campaign against colonial rule and racist regimes in southern Africa, but suggestions that similar principles might apply to Chinese rule in Tibet, or to the 'internal colonialism' that affects indigenous peoples, have been vigorously resisted.

States parties have assembled every two years to elect the Committee. After the UN's budgetary crisis at the end of 1985 they had an additional reason to use the occasion in order to consider ways of disciplining those of their own number who were threatening the Convention by their failure to fulfil their financial and reporting obligations. They never used this opportunity. When their representatives met in 1994 they could have acted to get more states parties to deposit notes indicating acceptance of the amendments to the Convention, but that again was not their priority. Muslim states sympathetic to the plight of Bosnia and Herzegovina used the occasion to express disapproval of the policies of the Belgrade government. The states barred the representative of Yugoslavia (Serbia and Montenegro) from the meeting, but not the representatives of states which had long neglected their financial and reporting obligations. This is not to say that the states parties' action was not justified. It is simply to point out the underlying priorities of those who operate the human-rights treaty system. Most states parties look upon the Convention with goodwill, but they are often unable to align their domestic policies with their foreign policies. They created a treaty body and then left it to get on with its task unaided, raising their voices only when they thought the treaty body had acted beyond its mandate.

## CERD'S CONTRIBUTION

CERD has done more than was originally expected of it. At its first session in 1970 it was told by Mr N. K. Tarassov, in words that have already been quoted in Chapter 6, that 'All the Committee could do was to detect an incompatibility between the domestic laws of a country and a specific provision of the Convention.' Mr Tarassov was subsequently appointed a judge of the International Court of Justice so his views demand particular respect, but events have proven him wrong.

CERD has done much more than compare the texts of a country's laws with the obligations set out in the Convention. In accordance with articles 2 and 9 of the Convention, it has tried to determine whether the state has taken *effective* measures as part of a policy for the elimination of racial discrimination. To *examine* the information and reports received from states parties, it has studied the problems and social conditions in the states in order to ascertain whether the measures are put into practice in a manner that actually promotes the elimination of discrimination. CERD now speaks *with a collective voice* on the effectiveness of state policies as well as the texts of laws, and it has been contributing to general UN human rights activities, most notably with the Decades to Combat Racism and Racial Discrimination.

From its first meeting, CERD has been making a significant contribution to the extension of the rule of law. The Convention incorporated what was then the novel obligation of periodic reporting. Since many, perhaps most, states did not appreciate the extent and significance of that requirement, this book began by describing the Committee's struggle with Venezuela over the nature and extent of those obligations. Later passages have offered further examples (such as the further information requested from Israel). CERD has used every opportunity to explain the autonomous meaning of the obligations set forth in the Convention (which will lead to a further struggle over the reservations entered by the USA), and it has drawn particular attention to those provisions which have a mandatory character. Chapters 6–8 have described how progress has often arisen from struggles within the Committee itself, none of them more important than that over permissible sources. Very useful information is assembled by non-governmental bodies. Other information is often featured in the press, sometimes in a sensationalized manner and often selectively. Some governments are powerful and secure enough to accept criticism of this kind (though, as has been seen in the case of Britain's trading relations with Malaysia, a government's vital interests can be threatened by the kind of press reporting that offends ministers in foreign governments). Members of CERD receive information from sources other than state reports and they use it responsibly. They do not have the research or clerical support available to diplomats and legislators in many countries, so, if they are to discharge their duties faithfully and conscientiously, it is important that NGOs should be able to feed information to them.

Article 5 is the most far-reaching in the Convention, especially when coupled with the obligation in article 6 to provide effective remedies for any breach of its provisions. States parties are allowed some discretion in determining what means of implementation are required by their circumstances in order to eliminate racial discrimination in respect of the many rights listed, but they are contracted in the long run to eliminate racial discrimination from every field of public life. Many proposals to this end will collide with the wishes of the majority of their electorates. All over the world majority ethnic groups see minority ethnic groups as making unreasonable demands. They are inclined to see their own privileges as the product of their ancestors' struggles, and are reluctant to vote for anyone who proposes to restrict those privileges. So it is unsurprising if those who are responsible for a country's domestic policies are unaware or neglectful of the undertakings their government has assumed as part of its foreign policy. It is CERD's duty to see that they are reminded of them, and that they are helped to learn from the lessons of experience elsewhere, because those who accede to the Convention are 'resolved . . . to build an international community free from all forms of racial segregation and racial discrimination'.

CERD has found in the Convention much law that the parties, or many of them, appear not to have perceived when they acceded to it, and which they would not have found for themselves. Interpretation of the Convention may in law be for the states parties, and, if they so choose, for the International Court of Justice, but the situation is changing. In the first place, as the Human Rights Committee has stated in its General Comment 24 on reservations, human-rights treaties 'are not a web of inter-State exchanges of mutual obligations. They concern the endowment of individuals with rights.' So a special responsibility falls upon the monitoring committee. In the second place, the practice of the states parties hitherto has been to leave any problems of interpretation to the Committee and to show interest in them only when their own interests are affected.

CERD is not a court, but it serves a similar function in its dialogue with states, in its reports to the General Assembly, and in the opinions it issues in response to article 14 communications. In face-to-face dialogue with state representatives, as well as through its reports, CERD has explained the implications of accession to the Convention in relation to the circumstances of each particular state party. Its reporting guidelines, its general recommendations, and its specific suggestions to reporting states all go well beyond the comparison of one legal text with another. It has done all this publicly, calling attention to deficiencies in the way states implement their obligations. The public to which CERD's reports have been directed has been the General Assembly. The messages contained in those reports have been so phrased that the mass media have found in them little that is worth publicizing to a wider audience. That might be about to change. Concluding observations which express a collective view on particular points are better suited to dissemination by the mass media and should engage public opinion in the country concerned. They can be used by private citizens and groups which lobby for change.

Within the UN, CERD is accounted a committee of experts, to distinguish it from the many political bodies. Some of its members are indeed experts in their own fields, notably the international lawyers, but members generally can be considered as experts in racial discrimination only in respect of the knowledge they have built up in the course of examining state reports. In 1995 the membership included five serving and four retired diplomats, two government lawyers, and seven other persons. When deciding whom to nominate in the future, states parties might consider that, while CERD benefited during the years 1970–8 from having a high proportion of diplomats among its members, circumstances have since changed. The Committee might benefit in the future from having more members experienced in the implementation of domestic policies against racial discrimination, particularly in their legal aspects. On general grounds it would be better were there more female members, and perhaps some with experience of life as a member of a racial minority or an indigenous people. States parties might also note that the Committee now has a greater need for members able and willing to devote time to preparing for committee meetings.

As a committee, CERD is not very well equipped to play a specialist part in the 'early-warning' process. Its members are not necessarily well informed about current problems in particular countries. The Committee is unlikely ever to be given investigatory powers because of the opportunity available in the Commission on Human Rights for the appointment of a special rapporteur. Yet sometimes other states block such proposals in the Commission. CERD is more independent and has the right mandate to issue an early warning of ethnic conflicts. Its membership reflects all the major regions of the world and its proceedings are not partizan after the fashion of the Commission on Human Rights, or its Sub-Commission on Prevention of Discrimination and Protection of Minorities. CERD's starting-point is that of legal obligation, which can be the more important in view of the high emotional charge of any accusation of racial discrimination. So, if CERD calls attention to the dangers in a particular situation, it ought to be listened to.

CERD is also better placed than any other UN body to form judgements about the kinds of measures that are likely to be effective in reducing racial discrimination, and it could in future play a more active part in ensuring that experience in one country is passed on to other countries that seek to tackle similar problems. Anyone who seeks to do this will have to step beyond the strictly legal field and assess the contribution that laws can make in conjunction with other measures as parts of wider policies. Future developments will depend upon the course of international politics. As the Committee's history already shows, at certain moments there is a readiness to move forward which can be utilized if the parties make good use of the opportunity

The treaty-body system is only one wing of UN action in the field of human rights. The other wing, as was explained in Chapter 3, is that of the Charter-based bodies, particularly the Commission on Human Rights. Treaty bodies try to engage states parties in a dialogue that will promote state compliance with obligations. If this is unsuccessful, the treaty body can report the state's non-compliance to the states parties. The conflicts in the former Yugoslavia and in Rwanda could have been taken up by invoking article 11 of ICERD, but the states parties would have seen such a course as risky and slow; they are unlikely to utilize it when they have the alternative of raising an issue in the Commission. This can involve states which are not parties to a treaty. It is a body with a well-understood place in a political structure and it is better equipped to deal with interstate problems. CERD may be the body best placed to press for preventive action, but once conflicts intensify the time for prevention may pass and only remedial action may be effective. Remedial action may require intervention authorized and controlled by the Security Council, though before this is contemplated there may be a role for the Commission on Human Rights.

## REMEDIAL ACTION

In the former Yugoslavia remedial action might have been undertaken before Croatia's declaration of independence, and at the time of writing it might still be appropriate in Kosovo. In Rwanda (and possibly Burundi) the time for such action would have been in 1993. In both Croatia and Rwanda the conflicts escalated quickly, but the UN's political organs are rarely able to respond equally fast. In both cases, too, UN action would doubtless have been better had it been in support of action taken by regional bodies, the Organization for Security and Cooperation in Europe and the OAU. An indication of what can be expected from the states that would have to bear the burden of any collective action was given by the outcome of the Human Rights Commission's third special session held in 1994.

The session, convened on a Canadian proposal, adopted a resolution which stated that the Commission believed that genocidal acts had occurred in Rwanda, called for a cessation of hostilities, welcomed the decision of the Security Council to increase the UN force in the country, and stated that 'the international community will exert every effort to bring those responsible [for human-rights violations] to justice, while affirming that the primary responsibility for bringing perpetrators to justice rests with national judicial systems'. It requested the appointment of a special rapporteur to be assisted by human-rights field officers. The resolution was adopted without a vote, but several delegations expressed their opposition to the way that the proposed action was linked with the Security Council.

On the one side in the debate were states like Mauritius which spoke of their feelings of guilt, shame, and moral responsibility:

Among the questions which the Commission must address were how the tragedy in Rwanda could have occurred so shortly after the conclusion of its fiftieth session and without the human rights machinery and institutions being able to do anything to prevent so blatant a violation of the right to life itself, despite the warning issued by the Special Rapporteur on extrajudicial, summary or arbitrary executions, Mr Ndiaye, and why the Commission had decided to maintain the confidential procedure when the situation had already been so precarious.

The representative of Venezuela insisted 'that the Rwandese conflict was not a war between rival tribes, as was too often alleged, but the result of a mutual extermination policy . . . the cruellest genocide . . .'. Speakers on this side stressed the international responsibility for the punishment of murderers who had enjoyed impunity for too long. The representatives of NGOs, several of them Rwandese, when given the floor, added compelling testimony. One asserted: 'As long as emphasis was placed on ceasefires and negotiations rather than punishing criminals, impunity would continue to reign and the massacres would only recur.' The director of one NGO, the International Service for Human Rights, said that:

for at least two years, everyone in the Commission had known what was happening in Rwanda but nobody had done anything about it. That inertia was due to the fact that the Member States of the Commission were more inclined to protect their own interests than to be moved by the fate of peoples. Although the NGOs that dared to denounce the many serious and mass violations of human rights came in for much abuse, restraint was the order of the day when it was a question of taking action . . . Several Western countries had a heavy responsibility in Rwanda, while the African countries were trying to avoid further opprobrium.

On the other side of the argument were states like China, Iran, Cuba, and Malaysia which were opposed to intervention by the Security Council in the internal affairs of states. The Sudan was critical of proposals for any international tribunal, since no such tribunal had begun its task with regard to the Bosnian conflict. These delegations did not press their views to a vote. Then the Chairman announced the appointment as special rapporteur of Mr René Degni-Ségui, dean of the law faculty at the University of Abidjan, Côte d'Ivoire (E/CN.4/S-3/SR.4). By the end of June he had visited Rwanda and presented an impressive report describing the nature of the genocide, analysing its causes, and advancing proposals for UN action of immediate, short-term, and medium-term character (E/CN.4/1994/7). The newly appointed High Commissioner for Human Rights also visited the country more than once.

At the same time ethnic relations in neighbouring Burundi have continued to deteriorate. Tutsi and Hutu used to live side by side, but insecurity has been causing a degree of physical separation. Part of the trouble is that, if a system of majoritarian democracy is to operate, the parties that lose an electoral contest must be assured that their opponents will not use their victory to exclude all others from any prospect of sharing in the government. International oversight could give them such assurance.

The recent instances of conflict in and between the states of the former Yugoslavia, and in Rwanda, have demonstrated once again that prevention is much better than cure. This is no novel proposition. How is it that a clear recognition of a general interest may evoke no sufficient response from states? In the Commission debate the director of the International Service for Human Rights attributed the Commission's previous inaction to a state of inertia. This is to borrow an analogy from mechanics, when the condition may be better understood by drawing upon economic reasoning as expressed in the theory of collective action, notably in the analogy of the 'free rider'. This is often illustrated by wage-bargaining in circumstances in which, if a trade union secures a wage increase, it will be paid to all persons in a particular job irrespective of whether or not they are union members. A man who had not so far joined the union might set out to calculate whether it was worth while joining. He would ascertain what it would cost to pay the subscriptions or dues required. Then he would work out the extent to which the union's power to win a wage rise was increased by his joining. Next he would compare the likely benefit of his joining with the cost of doing so. Usually he would conclude that his economic interest was not to join but instead to take a 'free ride' at the expense of his fellow employees who bore the costs of maintaining the union. Mancur Olson (1965) generalized this to show that in a whole range of situations rational self-interested individuals would not act to advance their common interests. In international affairs every state might be better off (or no less well off) if a particular course of action were adopted, yet it might not be worth the while of any state to try to get the others to agree to it.

Industrial workers recognize the logic of free-riding when they act to create a 'closed shop' and to restrict employment in it to union members. They vote to restrict their own freedom. Their action can be compared with that of the Spanish invaders of Mexico, when, before starting on the expedition into the interior, Cortez ordered the burning of their boats. He cut off an avenue of escape and obliged all his party to commit themselves to the success of the expedition if they were ever to return home. The essence of commitment is the elimination of an alternative, so that a doubtful participant is obliged to go through with a course of action. This is where the law enters, because the enactment of a law gives certain persons the power to oblige others to observe the norm or pay the penalty—provided the law is enforced. A state's accession to a treaty gives others powers to make that state keep its promises, though, as has been shown, states may be loath to use their powers if they fear that they themselves are open to criticism for not keeping all their own promises. Their actions in international bodies may respond less to the problems confronting those bodies than to electoral considerations at home. So political considerations frequently govern the use that is made of law.

## DECISION-TAKING

One of the problems of meetings between representatives of states is the procedure for reaching decisions in the absence of any power to oblige a state to abide by the undertaking of its representative. States insist upon their sovereignty and independence. So there has been a general preference at the UN for reaching decisions by consensus. The alternative is majority voting, which leads on to the problems of proportionality and the size of the majority desirable for decisions of great importance. If a micro-state like Andorra, Liechtenstein, Maldives, Monaco, or San Marino casts one vote, how many votes should China be able to cast? Is it just that a meeting should be able to take a majority decision when the outcome will have negative implications for the minority voting against it, although it will not affect the interests of the others? Yet if the decision has to be by consensus, that gives every voter present the opportunity to exercise a veto power, and that power can be exercised in pursuit of objectives distinct from the matter at issue. Veto power may also be exercised in the form of a filibuster, a way of using up time to prevent others reaching a decision. So, while the arguments for some kind of majority voting are strong, they will be persuasive only when the parties trust one another not to exercise majority power without careful attention to minority concerns.

Members of CERD do not meet as the representatives of states, so they should be less troubled by any attempts to exercise a veto power. But many members are, or have been, diplomats serving at UN headquarters and they bring to the Committee the habits of that place. Though trust appears to have increased since 1988, there are nevertheless occasions when business is held up or diverted for reasons that are difficult to understand. For example, the World Conference on Human Rights in 1993 discussed interim proposals presented by Mr Alston for improving the effectiveness of human-rights instruments (see Chapter 3). It resolved that the views of the treaty bodies should be taken into account. In March 1994 CERD was supplied with copies of the text and invited to express its views. One member objected, claiming to know nothing of the Alston report, and asking why he should be expected to read it. He asserted that it would be a waste of time to discuss a document that had not been finalized. He was not answered effectively; time was wasted on incidental issues, and the Committee abandoned the attempt to discuss the matter (SR 1011). The Committee's search for consensus can sometimes give an individual member a kind of veto power.

The Convention has to be implemented by the states parties, and it cannot be effective when those states are unable or unwilling to legislate or to enforce the laws that are on the statute book. Many governments have too feeble a hold upon power, and are too anxious to retain it, for them to be much concerned with the Convention. Some governments have their eyes on the next election and are reluctant to do anything that might cost them votes. Hence the importance in the long term of article 7 of the Convention and of educational measures generally, because it is much easier for a government to act against discrimination when it has the support of the mass of the population. Hence, too, the value of noting that, when people line up alongside others of the same ethnic origin as themselves, this can result in two different kinds of group. The distinction earlier drawn between majority and minority ethnicity (Banton 1983: 165) might be reformulated as one between primary and secondary ethnicity.

The ethnicity of the French or the Germans is a primary ethnicity in which ethnic alignment coincides with national alignment. The ethnicity of the Polish-Americans or the Welsh is a secondary ethnicity in which ethnic groups compete with one another within a framework of shared citizenship. In disputed cases (for example, Tibet, or Kosovo Albanians) there may be variable proportions of a group which claim a primary ethnicity while others, either inside the group or within the state claiming sovereignty, oppose the claim). As their circumstances change, individuals alter the significance they accord to national and ethnic identities. In the former republic of Yugoslavia there was a significant number of people for whom being a Yugoslav was their national identity, but this identity was destroyed and they had to define themselves as Serbs, Croats, or the like, as this became for them a new national identity and an example of primary ethnicity.

The significance of the distinction should now be apparent. It is much easier for states to prohibit discrimination based upon secondary than primary ethnicity. It is also easier to distinguish a racial motivation or conflict from a political one at the level of secondary ethnicity than at the level of primary ethnicity. The conflicts in the former Yugoslavia and Rwanda–Burundi have been political conflicts in which differences of ethnic origin have been exploited for political ends. There is nothing special about differences of ethnic origin that they should occasion conflict. The key often lies in the relation between the boundaries of the ethnic group and the state.

Formally, all states parties are equal. Each state has the same number of votes when Committee members are elected. Committee members are conscious of what article 1.2 of the UN Charter calls 'the principle of the sovereign equality of all its Members'. The reader who studies Tables 2–5 might well conclude that CERD does not treat all states equally. It spends far more time on the reports of some states than others. Yet the principle of equal treatment is not one that requires identical treatment. The most basic meaning of the word equality is that of a mathematical relation. Before deciding what the treatment has to be equal to, it is necessary to recognize that some states face much greater challenges than others with respect to racial discrimination. Some are more conscientious than others. CERD's practice is to treat states equally in the light of the challenges that face them and the adequacy of their responses in relation to the resources available to them. This requires the exercise of political, not legal, judgement.

In the drafting of the Convention racial discrimination was separated from discrimination on the grounds of religion and treated on its own. The prohibition of discrimination against women came later. Now they have all three to be seen as examples of the more general principle of non-discrimination. This provides that certain criteria cannot legitimately be used when applying the right to equality before the law. The unequal treatment of persons differentiated by race, sex, age, religion, and disability has often been taken for granted as 'natural', but the introduction of legal remedies has brought historical assumptions into the open and required that they be justified. This has improved the public understanding of the nature of racial discrimination and it may continue to do so since the right to equality before the law is a dynamic right and could serve as the basis for the recognition of new rights. As the number of communications addressed to CERD under article 14 of the Convention increases, this will enable the Committee to contribute to the developing jurisprudence on discrimination.

## PROSPECTS

Further action to develop the potential of the Convention will require a greater commitment from states parties acting within the General Assembly. As has been explained, CERD is now involved in the dynamics of a larger system of treaty bodies. It is affected by the attitudes of states towards that system as well as towards the problems presented by racial discrimination. All the six main treaty bodies are responsible for the examination of state reports. The Human Rights Committee and the Committee Against Torture can issue opinions on complaints from either states or individuals wherever they have been empowered to do by states parties. CERD can issue opinions on complaints from individuals in like circumstances. The other human-rights treaties which have not yet opened up possibilities of this kind may be amended and they may all come to work in a more uniform manner.

Chapter 3 made reference to the study of the work of the treaty bodies by Mr Alston, to its calculations of the growth in overdue reports, and its conclusion that the reporting system had reached a critical crossroads. Yet the whole treaty system has been in continuous crisis from its inception, being subject to threats from so many quarters. It would be unfortunate were reporting requirements to be weakened before all states have adhered to the six core treaties and procedures for consideration of state and individual complaints are operating under all of them. Once that goal has been reached, it may be time to simplify the system.

Effective implementation of a human-rights convention like ICERD depends upon a triangular relationship between the states parties, the treaty body, and members of the public within the states parties. In a democratic society the state needs the support of its citizenry to carry through its policies, and the public needs to keep the pressure upon the politicians to see that the state fulfils its obligations. The relationship between the state and the citizenry has to be mediated through the press. Effective implementation requires that the state party report conscientiously on whatever progress has been made and that the treaty body carefully examine its reports, drawing attention to shortcomings. This process will be more effective when the public in the state party is aware of the obligations that have been assumed by its government and is able to supply, perhaps through some NGO, information additional to that in the state's report. It will be the more inclined to do this when the results of the treaty body's examination are publicized in the country concerned. Human-rights law is an inheritance of past struggles which does not work by itself. It offers means for building commitment and implementing it, but it is fully effective only when a broad range of the public inform themselves about its potentialities and utilize them.

This book has presented CERD as one of several UN organs engaged in a struggle to extend the rule of law. The outcome of the struggle will be decided by the states. Even those which are most committed to the human-rights movement are far from sure that the institutions they have created will always be impartial, for the UN does not always act in an even-handed manner and the expert committees are not free from political influence. Yet gross violations of human rights occur with such distressing frequency and no means other than those of international law can offer even a long-term means for countering them. Will states be willing to give up enough of their sovereignty to make the system effective? Are they ready now to discipline those of their own number who fail to discharge their obligations? As the twentieth century comes to a close, it is the states which must decide on the next steps.

# APPENDIX I

## International Convention on the Elimination of All Forms of Racial Discrimination

*Adopted* by the General Assembly of the United Nations in resolution 2106 A (XX) of 21 December 1965.

*Opened for Signature* at New York on 7 March 1966.

*Entered into Force* on 4 January 1969, on the thirtieth day after the date of the deposit with the Secretary-General of the United Nations of the twenty-seventh instrument of ratification or instrument of accession, in accordance with article 19 of the Convention.

---

*The States Parties to this Convention,*

*Considering* that the Charter of the United Nations is based on the principles of the dignity and equality inherent in all human beings, and that all Member States have pledged themselves to take joint and separate action, in co-operation with the Organization, for the achievement of one of the purposes of the United Nations which is to promote and encourage universal respect for and observance of human rights and fundamental freedoms for all, without distinction as to race, sex, language or religion,

*Considering* that the Universal Declaration of Human Rights proclaims that all human beings are born free and equal in dignity and rights and that everyone is entitled to all the rights and freedoms set out therein, without distinction of any kind, in particular as to race, colour, or national origin,

*Considering* that all human beings are equal before the law and are entitled to equal protection of the law against any discrimination and against any incitement to discrimination,

*Considering* that the United Nations has condemned colonialism and all practices of segregation and discrimination associated therewith, in whatever form and wherever they exist, and that the Declaration on the Granting of Independence to Colonial Countries and Peoples of 14

December 1960 (General Assembly resolution 1514 (XV)) has affirmed and solemnly proclaimed the necessity of bringing them to a speedy and unconditional end,

*Considering* that the United Nations declaration on the Elimination of All Forms of Racial Discrimination of 20 November 1963 (General Assembly Resolution 1904 (XVIII)) solemnly affirms the necessity of speedily eliminating racial discrimination throughout the world in all its forms and manifestations and of securing understanding of and respect for the dignity of the human person,

*Convinced* that any doctrine of superiority based on racial differentiation is scientifically false, morally condemnable, socially unjust and dangerous, and that there is no justification for racial discrimination, in theory or in practice, anywhere,

*Reaffirming* that discrimination between human beings on the grounds of race, colour or ethnic origin is an obstacle to friendly and peaceful relations among nations and is capable of disturbing peace and security among peoples and the harmony of persons living side by side even within one and the same State,

*Convinced* that the existence of racial barriers is repugnant to the ideals of any human society,

*Alarmed* by manifestations of racial discrimination still in evidence in some areas of the world and by government policies based on racial superiority or hatred, such as policies of *apartheid*, segregation or separation,

*Resolved* to adopt all necessary measures for speedily eliminating racial discrimination in all its forms and manifestations, and to prevent and combat racist doctrines and practices in order to promote understanding between races and to build an international community free from all forms of racial segregation and racial discrimination,

*Bearing in mind* the Convention concerning Discrimination in respect of Employment and Occupation adopted by the International Labour Organisation in 1958, and the Convention against Discrimination in Education adopted by the United Nations Educational, Scientific and Cultural Organization in 1960,

*Desiring* to implement the principles embodied in the United Nations Declaration on the Elimination of All Forms of Racial Discrimination and to secure the earliest adoption of practical measures to that end,

*Have agreed* as follows:

# PART I

*Article 1*

1. In this Convention, the term 'racial discrimination' shall mean any distinction, exclusion, restriction or preference based on race, colour, descent, or national or ethnic origin which has the purpose or effect of nullifying or impairing the recognition, enjoyment or exercise, on an equal footing, of human rights and fundamental freedoms in the political, economic, social, cultural or any other field of public life.

2. This Convention shall not apply to distinctions, exclusions, restrictions or preferences made by a State Party to this Convention between citizens and non-citizens.

3. Nothing in this Convention may be interpreted as affecting in any way the legal provisions of State Parties concerning nationality, citizenship or naturalization, provided that such provisions do not discriminate against any particular nationality.

4. Special measures taken for the sole purpose of securing adequate advancement of certain racial or ethnic groups or individuals requiring such protection as may be necessary in order to ensure such groups or individuals equal enjoyment or exercise of human rights and fundamental freedoms shall not be deemed racial discrimination, provided, however, that such measures do not, as a consequence, lead to the maintenance of separate rights for different racial groups and that they shall not be continued after the objectives for which they were taken have been achieved.

*Article 2*

1. States Parties condemn racial discrimination and undertake to pursue by all appropriate means and without a delay a policy of eliminating racial discrimination in all its forms and promoting understanding among all races, and, to this end:

(*a*) Each State Party undertakes to engage in no act or practice of racial discrimination against persons, groups of persons or institutions and to ensure that all public authorities and public institutions, national and local, shall act in conformity with this obligation;

(*b*) Each State Party undertakes not to sponsor, defend or support racial discrimination by any persons or organizations;

(*c*) Each State Party shall take effective measures to review government, national and local policies, and to amend, rescind or nullify any laws and regulations which have the effect of creating or perpetuating racial discrimination wherever it exists;

(*d*) Each State Party shall prohibit and bring to an end, by all appropriate means, including legislation as required by circumstances, racial discrimination by any persons, group or organization;

(*e*) Each State Party undertakes to encourage, where appropriate, integrationist multi-racial organizations and movements and other means of eliminating barriers between races, and to discourage anything which tends to strengthen racial division.

2. States Parties shall, when the circumstances so warrant, take in the social, economic, cultural and other fields, special and concrete measures to ensure the adequate development and protection of certain racial groups or individuals belonging to them, for the purpose of guaranteeing them the full and equal enjoyment of human rights and fundamental freedoms. These measures shall in no case entail as a consequence the maintenance of unequal or separate rights for different racial groups after the objectives for which they were taken have been achieved.

*Article 3*

States Parties particularly condemn racial segregation and *apartheid* and undertake to prevent, prohibit and eradicate all practices of this nature in territories under their jurisdiction.

*Article 4*

States Parties condemn all propaganda and all organizations which are based on ideas or theories of superiority of one race or group of persons of one colour or ethnic origin, or which attempt to justify or promote racial hatred and discrimination in any form, and undertake to adopt immediate and positive measures designed to eradicate all incitement to, or acts of, such discrimination and, to this end, with due regard to the principles embodied in the Universal Declaration of Human Rights and the rights expressly set forth in article 5 of this Convention, *inter alia*:

(*a*) Shall declare an offence punishable by law all dissemination of ideas based on racial superiority or hatred, incitement to racial discrimination, as well as all acts of violence or incitement to such acts against any race or group of persons of another colour or ethnic origin, and also the provision of any assistance to racist activities, including the financing thereof;

(*b*) Shall declare illegal and prohibit organizations, and also organized and all other propaganda activities, which promote and incite racial discrimination, and shall recognize participation in such organization or activities as an offence punishable by law;

(*c*) Shall not permit public authorities or public institutions, national or local, to promote or incite racial discrimination.

*Article 5*

In compliance with the fundamental obligations laid down in article 2 of this Convention, States Parties undertake to prohibit and to eliminate racial discrimination in all its forms and to guarantee the right of everyone, without distinction, as to race, colour, or national or ethnic origin, to equality before the law, notably in the enjoyment of the following rights:

(*a*) The right to equal treatment before the tribunals and all other organs administering justice;

(*b*) The right to security of person and protection by the State against violence or bodily harm, whether inflicted by government officials or by any individual, group or institution;

(*c*) Political rights, in particular the rights to participate in elections—to vote and to stand for election—on the basis of universal and equal suffrage, to take part in the Government as well as in the conduct of public affairs at any level and to have equal access to public service;

(*d*) Other civil rights, in particular:

  (i) The right to freedom of movement and residence within the border of the State;

  (ii) The right to leave any country, including one's own, and to return to one's country;

  (iii) The right to nationality;

  (iv) The right to marriage and choice of spouse;

  (v) The right to own property alone as well as in association with others;

  (vi) The right to inherit;

  (vii) The right to freedom of thought, conscience and religion;

  (viii) The right to freedom of opinion and expression;

  (x) The right to freedom of peaceful assembly and association;

(*e*) Economic, social and cultural rights, in particular:

  (i) The rights to work, to free choice of employment, to just and favourable conditions of work, to protection against unemployment, to equal pay for equal work, to just and favourable remuneration;

  (ii) The right to form and join trade unions;

  (iii) The right to housing;

  (iv) The right to public health, medical care, social security and social services;

  (v) The right to education and training;

  (vi) The right to equal participation in cultural activities;

(*f*) The right of access to any place or service intended for use by the general public, such as transport, hotels, restaurants, cafes, theatres and parks.

## Article 6

States Parties shall assure to everyone within their jurisdiction effective protection and remedies, through the competent national tribunals and other State institutions, against any acts of racial discrimination which violate his human rights and fundamental freedoms contrary to this Convention, as well as the right to seek from such tribunals just and adequate reparation or satisfaction for any damage suffered as a result of such discrimination.

## Article 7

States Parties undertake to adopt immediate and effective measures, particularly in the fields of teaching, education, culture and information, with a view to combating prejudices which lead to racial discrimination and to promoting understanding, tolerance and friendship among nations and racial or ethnical groups, as well as to propagating the purposes and principles of the Charter of the United Nations, the Universal Declaration of Human Rights, the United Nations Declaration of the Elimination of All Forms of Racial Discrimination, and this Convention.

## PART II

### Article 8

1. There shall be established a Committee on the Elimination of Racial Discrimination (hereinafter referred to as the Committee) consisting of eighteen experts of high moral standing and acknowledged impartiality elected by States Parties from among their nationals, who shall serve in their personal capacity, consideration being given to equitable geographical distribution and to the representation of different forms of civilization as well as of the principal legal systems.

2. The members of the Committee shall be elected by secret ballot from a list of persons nominated by the States Parties. Each State Party may nominate one person from among its own nationals.

3. The initial election shall be held six months after the date of the entry into force of this Convention. At least three months before the date of each election the Secretary-General of the United Nations shall address a letter to the States Parties inviting them to submit their nominations within two months. The Secretary-General shall prepare a list in alphabetical order

of all persons thus nominated, indicating the States Parties which have nominated them, and shall submit it to the States Parties.

4. Elections of the members of the Committee shall be held at a meeting of States Parties convened by the Secretary-General at United Nations Headquarters. At that meeting, for which two thirds of the States Parties shall constitute a quorum, the persons elected to the Committee shall be those nominees who obtain the largest number of votes and an absolute majority of the votes of the representatives of States Parties present and voting.

5. (*a*) The members of the Committee shall be elected for a term of four years. However, the terms of nine of the members elected at the first election shall expire at the end of two years; immediately after the first election the names of these nine members shall be chosen by lot by the Chairman of the Committee.

(*b*) For the filling of casual vacancies, the State Party whose expert has ceased to function as a member of the Committee shall appoint another expert from among its nationals, subject to the approval of the Committee.

6. States Parties shall be responsible for the expenses of the members of the Committee while they are in performance of Committee duties.

## Article 9

1. States Parties undertake to submit to the Secretary-General of the United Nations, for consideration by the Committee, a report on the legislative, administrative or other measures which they have adopted and which give effect to the provisions of this Convention: (*a*) within one year after the entry into force of the Convention for the State concerned; and (*b*) thereafter every two years and whenever the Committee so requests. The Committee may request further information from the States Parties.

2. The Committee shall report annually, through the Secretary-General, to the General Assembly of the United Nations on its activities and may make suggestions and general recommendations based on the examination of the reports and information received from the States Parties. Such suggestions and general recommendations shall be reported to the General Assembly together with comments, if any, from States Parties.

## Article 10

1. The Committee shall adopt its own rules of procedure.

2. The Committee shall elect its officers for a term of two years.

3. The secretariat of the Committee shall be provided by the Secretary-General of the United Nations.

4. The meetings of the Committee shall normally be held at United Nations Headquarters.

## Article 11

1. If a State Party considers that another State Party is not giving effect to the provisions of this Convention, it may bring the matter to the attention of the Committee. The Committee shall then transmit the communication to the State Party concerned. Within three months, the receiving State shall submit to the Committee written explanations or statements clarifying the matter and the remedy, if any, that may have been taken by that State.

2. If the matter is not adjusted to the satisfaction of both parties, either by bilateral negotiations or by any other procedure open to them, within six months after the receipt by the receiving State of the initial communication, either State shall have the right to refer the matter again to the Committee by notifying the Committee and also the other State.

3. The Committee shall deal with a matter referred to it in accordance with paragraph 2 of this article after it has ascertained that all available domestic remedies have been invoked and exhausted in the case, in conformity with the generally recognized principles of international law. This shall not be the rule where the application of the remedies is unreasonably prolonged.

4. In any matter referred to it, the Committee may call upon the States Parties concerned to supply any other relevant information.

5. When any matter arising out of this article is being considered by the Committee, the States Parties concerned shall be entitled to send a representative to take part in the proceedings of the Committee, without voting rights, while the matter is under consideration.

## Article 12

1.(a) After the Committee has obtained and collated all the information it deems necessary, the Chairman shall appoint an *ad hoc* Conciliation Commission (hereinafter referred to as the Commission) comprising five persons who may or may not be members of the Committee. The members of the Commission shall be appointed with the unanimous consent of the parties to the dispute, and its good offices shall be made available to the States concerned with a view to an amicable solution of the matter on the basis of respect for this Convention.

(b) If the States parties to the dispute fail to reach agreement within three months on all or part of the composition of the Commission, the members of the Commission not agreed upon by the States parties to the dispute shall be elected by secret ballot by a two-thirds majority vote of the Committee from among its own members.

2. The members of the Commission shall serve in their personal capacity. They shall not be nationals of the States parties to the dispute or of a State not Party to this Convention.

3. The Commission shall elect its own Chairman and adopt its own rules of procedure.

4. The meetings of the Commission shall normally be held at United Nations Headquarters or at any other convenient place as determined by the Commission.

5. The secretariat provided in accordance with article 10, paragraph 3, of this Convention shall also serve the Commission whenever a dispute among States Parties brings the Commission into being.

6. The States parties to the dispute shall share equally all the expenses of the members of the Commission in accordance with estimates to be provided by the Secretary-General of the United Nations.

7. The Secretary-General shall be empowered to pay the expenses of the members of the Commission, if necessary, before reimbursement by the States parties to the dispute in accordance with paragraph 6 of this article.

8. The information obtained and collated by the Committee shall be made available to the Commission, and the Commission may call upon the States concerned to supply any other relevant information.

## Article 13

1. When the Commission has fully considered the matter, it shall prepare and submit to the Chairman of the Committee a report embodying its findings on all questions of fact relevant to the issue between the parties and containing such recommendations as it may think proper for the amicable solution of the dispute.

2. The Chairman of the Committee shall communicate the report of the Commission to each of the States parties to the dispute. These States shall, within three months, inform the Chairman of the Committee whether or not they accept the recommendations contained in the report of the Commission.

3. After the period provided for in paragraph 2 of this article, the Chairman of the Committee shall communicate the report of the Commission and the declarations of the States Parties concerned to the other States Parties to this Convention.

*Article 14*

1. A State Party may at any time declare that it recognizes the competence of the Committee to receive and consider communications from individuals or groups of individuals within its jurisdiction claiming to be victims of a violation by that State Party of any of the rights set forth in this Convention. No communication shall be received by the Committee if it concerns a State Party which has not made such a declaration.

2. Any State Party which makes a declaration as provided for in paragraph 1 of this article may establish or indicate a body within its national legal order which shall be competent to receive and consider petitions from individuals and groups of individuals within its jurisdiction who claim to be victims of a violation of any of the rights set forth in this Convention and who have exhausted other available local remedies.

3. A declaration made in accordance with paragraph 1 of this article and the name of any body established or indicated in accordance with paragraph 2 of this article shall be deposited by the State Party concerned with the Secretary-General of the United Nations, who shall transmit copies thereof to other States Parties. A declaration may be withdrawn at any time by notification to the Secretary-General, but such a withdrawal shall not affect communications pending before the Committee.

4. A register of petitions shall be kept by the body established or indicated in accordance with paragraph 2 of this article, and certified copies of the register shall be filed annually through appropriate channels with the Secretary-General on the understanding that the contents shall not be publicly disclosed.

5. In the event of failure to obtain satisfaction from the body established or indicated in accordance with paragraph 2 of this article, the petitioner shall have the right to communicate the matter to the Committee within six months.

6.(a) The Committee shall confidentially bring any communication referred to it to the attention of the State Party alleged to be violating any provision of this Convention, but the identity of the individual or groups of individuals concerned shall not be revealed without his or their express consent. The Committee shall not receive anonymous communications.

(b) Within three months, the receiving State shall submit to the Committee written explanations or statements clarifying the matter and the remedy, if any, that may have been taken by the State.

7.(a) The Committee shall consider communications in the light of all information made available to it by the State Party concerned and by the petitioner. The Committee shall not consider any communication from a petitioner unless it has ascertained that the petitioner has exhausted all available domestic remedies. However, this shall not be the rule where the application of the remedies is unreasonably prolonged.

(*b*) The Committee shall forward its suggestions and recommendations, if any, to the State Party concerned and to the petitioner.

8. The Committee shall include in its annual report a summary of such communications and, where appropriate, a summary of the explanations and statements of the State Party concerned and of its own suggestions and recommendations.

9. The Committee shall be competent to exercise the functions provided for in this article only when at least ten States Parties to this Convention are bound by declarations in accordance with paragraph 1 of this article.

*Article 15*

1. Pending the achievement of the objectives of the Declaration of the Granting of Independence to Colonial Countries and Peoples, contained in General Assembly resolution 1514 (XV) of 14 December 1960, the provisions of this Convention shall in no way limit the right of petition granted to these peoples by other international instruments or by the United Nations and its specialized agencies.

2.(*a*) The Committee established under article 8, paragraph 1, of this Convention shall receive copies of the petitions from, and submit expressions of opinion and recommendations on these petitions to, the bodies of the United Nations which deal with matters directly related to the principles and objectives of this Convention in their consideration of petitions from the inhabitants of Trust and Non-Self-Governing Territories and all other territories to which General Assembly resolution 1514 (XV) applies, relating to matters covered by this Convention which are before these bodies.

(*b*) The Committee shall receive from the competent bodies of the United Nations copies of the reports concerning the legislative, judicial, administrative or other measures directly related to the principles and objectives of this Convention applied by the administering Powers within the Territories mentioned in sub-paragraph (*a*) of this paragraph, and shall express opinions and make recommendations to these bodies.

3. The Committee shall include in its report to the General Assembly a summary of the petitions and reports it has received from United Nations bodies, and the expressions of opinion and recommendations of the Committee relating to the said petitions and reports.

4. The Committee shall request from the Secretary-General of the United Nations all information relevant to the objectives of this Convention and

available to him regarding the Territories mentioned in paragraph 2(*a*) of this article.

## Article 16

The provisions of this Convention concerning the settlement of disputes or complaints shall be applied without prejudice to other procedures for settling disputes or complaints in the field of discrimination laid down in the constituent instruments of, or in conventions adopted by, the United Nations and its specialized agencies, and shall not prevent the States Parties from having recourse to other procedures for settling a dispute in accordance with general or special international agreements in force between them.

## PART III

### Article 17

1. This Convention is open for signature by any State Member of the United Nations or member of any of its specialized agencies, by any State Party to the Statute of the International Court of Justice, and by any other State which has been invited by the General Assembly of the United Nations to become a Party to this Convention.

2. This Convention is subject to ratification. Instruments of ratification shall be deposited with the Secretary-General of the United Nations.

### Article 18

1. This Convention shall be open to accession by any State referred to in article 17, paragraph 1, of the Convention.

2. Accession shall be effected by the deposit of an instrument of accession with the Secretary-General of the United Nations.

### Article 19

1. This Convention shall enter into force on the thirtieth day after the date of the deposit with the Secretary-General of the United Nations of the twenty-seventh instrument of ratification or instrument of accession.

2. For each State ratifying this Convention or acceding to it after the deposit of the twenty-seventh instrument of ratification or instrument of accession, the Convention shall enter into force on the thirtieth day after the date of deposit of its own instrument of ratification or instrument of accession.

*Article 20*

1. The Secretary-General of the United Nations shall receive and circulate to all States which are or may become Parties to this Convention reservation made by States at the time of ratification or accession. Any State which objects to the reservation shall, within a period of ninety days from the date of the said communication, notify the Secretary-General that it does not accept it.

2. A reservation incompatible with the object and purpose of this Convention shall not be permitted, nor shall a reservation the effect of which would inhibit the operation of any of the bodies established by this Convention be allowed. A reservation shall be considered incompatible or inhibitive if at least two thirds of the States Parties to this convention object to it.

3. Reservations may be withdrawn at any time by notification to this effect addressed to the Secretary-General of the United Nations. Such notification shall take effect on the date on which it is received.

*Article 21*

A State Party may denounce this Convention by written notification to the Secretary-General of the United Nations. Denunciation shall take effect one year after the date of receipt of the notification by the Secretary-General.

*Article 22*

Any dispute between two or more States Parties with respect to the interpretation or application of this Convention, which is not settled by negotiation or by the procedures expressly provided for in this Convention, shall, at the request of any of the parties to the dispute, be referred to the International Court of Justice for decision, unless the disputants agree to another mode of settlement.

*Article 23*

1. A request for the revision of this Convention may be made at any time by any State Party by means of a notification in writing addressed to the Secretary-General of the United Nations.

2. The General Assembly of the United Nations shall decide upon the steps, if any, to be taken in respect of such a request.

*Article 24*

The Secretary-General of the United Nations shall inform all States referred to in article 17, paragraph 1, of this Convention of the following particulars:

(*a*) Signatures, ratifications and accession under articles 17 and 18;

(*b*) The date of entry into force of this Convention under article 19;

(*c*) Communications and declarations received under articles 14, 20 and 23;

(*d*) Denunciations under article 21.

*Article 25*

1. This Convention, of which the Chinese, English, French, Russian and Spanish texts are equally authentic, shall be deposited in the archives of the United Nations.

2. The Secretary-General of the United Nations shall transmit certified copies of this Convention to all States belonging to any of the categories mentioned in article 17, paragraph 1, of the Convention.

# APPENDIX II

## Selected General Recommendations

By September 1995 CERD had adopted eighteen general recommendations. This appendix reprints those which bear upon the interpretation of articles 1-6 of the Convention, arranged in the sequence of those articles. It summarizes the bearing of general recommendation VIII upon article 1.1, of general recommendation III and decision 2(XI) upon article 3, and that of general recommendation V upon article 7.

### ARTICLE 1.1

1. Non-discrimination, together with equality before the law and equal protection of the law without any discrimination, constitutes a basic principle in the protection of human rights. The Committee wishes to draw the attention of States parties to certain features of the definition of racial discrimination in ICERD 1.1. It is of the opinion that the words 'based on' do not bear any meaning different from 'on the grounds of' in preambular paragraph seven. A distinction is contrary to the Convention if it has *either* the purpose *or* the effect of impairing particular rights and freedoms. This is confirmed by the obligation placed upon States parties by article 2.1(*c*), to nullify any law or practice which has the effect of creating or perpetuating racial discrimination.

2. The Committee observes that a differentiation of treatment will not constitute discrimination if the criteria for such differentiation, judged against the objectives and purposes of the Convention, are legitimate or fall within the scope of article 1.4 of the Convention. In considering the criteria that have been employed, the Committee will acknowledge that particular actions may have varied purposes. In seeking to determine whether an action has an effect contrary to the Convention, it will look to see whether that action has an unjustifiable disparate impact upon a group distinguished by race, colour, descent, or national or ethnic origin.

3. Article 1, paragraph 1, of the Convention also refers to the political, economic and social and cultural fields; the related rights and freedoms are set out in article 5. (general recommendation XIV adopted in 1993)

In its general recommendation VIII of 1990 the Committee stated that, after having considered reports from states parties about the ways in which individuals were identified as being members of racial or ethnic groups, it 'is of the opinion that such identification shall, if no justification exists to the contrary, be based upon self-identification by the individual concerned'.

## ARTICLES 1.2 AND 1.3

1. Article 1.1 defines racial discrimination. Article 1.2 excepts from this definition actions by a State party which differentiate between citizens and non-citizens. Article 1.3 qualifies article 1.2 by declaring that, among non-citizens, States parties may not discriminate against any particular nationality.

2. The Committee has noted that article 1.2 has on occasion been interpreted as absolving States parties from any obligation to report on matters relating to legislation on foreigners. The Committee therefore affirms that States parties are under an obligation to report fully upon the legislation on foreigners and its implementation.

3. The Committee further affirms that article 1.2 must not be interpreted to detract in any way from the rights and freedoms recognized and enunciated under other international instruments, especially the International Bill of Human Rights. (general recommendation XI adopted in 1993)

## ARTICLE 3

In its general recommendation III of 1972 the Committee 'expresses the view that measures adopted on the national level to give effect to the provisions of the Convention are interrelated with measures taken on the international level to encourage respect everywhere for the principles of the Convention'. By that recommendation and by its decision 2(XI) of 1975 the Committee 'invites all States parties to include in their periodic reports information on the status of their diplomatic, economic and other relations with the racist regimes of southern Africa'.

1. The Committee on the Elimination of Racial Discrimination calls the attention of States parties to the wording of article 3, by which States parties undertake to prevent, prohibit and eradicate all practices of racial segregation and *apartheid* in territories under their jurisdiction. The reference to *apartheid* may have been directed exclusively to South

Africa, but the article as adopted prohibits all forms of segregation in all States parties.

2. The Committee believes that the obligation to eradicate all practices of this nature includes the obligation to eradicate the consequences of such practices undertaken or tolerated by previous governments in the State or imposed by forces outside the State.

3. The Committee observes that while conditions of complete or partial racial segregation may in some countries have been created by governmental policies, a condition of partial segregation may also arise as an unintended by-product of the actions of private persons. In many cities residential patterns are influenced by group differences in income, which are sometimes combined with differences of race, colour, descent, national or ethnic origin, so that inhabitants can be stigmatized and individuals suffer a form of discrimination in which racial grounds are mixed with other grounds.

4. The Committee therefore affirms that a condition of racial segregation can arise without any initiative or direct involvement by the public authorities. It invites States parties to monitor all trends which can give rise to racial segregation, to work for the eradication of any negative consequences that ensue, and to describe any such action in their periodic reports. (general recommendation XIX (47) adopted in 1995)

## ARTICLE 4

1. When the International Convention on the Elimination of All Forms of Racial Discrimination was being adopted, article 4 was regarded as central to the struggle against racial discrimination. At that time there was a widespread fear of the revival of authoritarian ideologies. The proscription of the dissemination of ideas of racial superiority, and of organized activity likely to incite persons to racial violence, was properly regarded as crucial. Since that time the Committee has received evidence of organized violence based on ethnic origin and the political exploitation of ethnic difference. So implementation of article 4 is now of increased importance.

2. The Committee recalls its general recommendation VII in which it explained that the provisions of article 4 are of a mandatory character. To satisfy these obligations, States parties have not only to enact appropriate legislation but also to ensure that it is effectively enforced. Because threats to and acts of racial violence easily lead to further such acts and generate an atmosphere of hostility, only immediate intervention can meet the obligations of effective response.

3. Article 4(*a*) requires States parties to penalize four categories of misconduct: (i) the dissemination of ideas based upon racial superiority or hatred; (ii) incitement to racial hatred; (iii) acts of violence against any race or group of persons of another colour or ethnic origin; (iv) incitement to such acts.

4. In the opinion of the Committee, the prohibition of the dissemination of all ideas based upon racial superiority or hatred is compatible with the right to freedom of opinion and expression. This right is embodied in the Universal Declaration of Human Rights (article 19) and is recalled in ICERD article 5(*d*)(viii). Its relevance to article 4 is noted in the article itself. The citizen's exercise of this right carries special duties and responsibilities, specified in article 29.2 of the Universal Declaration, among which the obligation not to disseminate racist ideas is of particular importance. The Committee wishes furthermore to draw to the attention of States parties article 20 of the International Covenant on Civil and Political Rights, according to which any advocacy of national, racial or religious hatred that constitutes incitement to discrimination, hostility or violence, shall be prohibited by law.

5. Article 4(*a*) penalizes the financing of racist activities, which the Committee takes to include all the activities mentioned in paragraph 3 above, that is to say, activities deriving from ethnic as well as racial differences. The Committee calls upon States parties to investigate whether their national law and its implementation meets this requirement.

6. Some States have maintained that in their legal order it is inappropriate to declare illegal an organization before its members have promoted or incited racial discrimination. The Committee is of the opinion that article 4(*b*) places a greater burden upon such States to be vigilant in proceeding against such organizations at the earliest possible moment. Organizations, as well as organized and other propaganda activities, have to be declared illegal and prohibited. Participation in these organizations is of itself to be punished.

7. Article 4(*c*) outlines the obligations of public authorities. Public authorities at all administrative levels, including municipalities, are bound by this paragraph. The Committee holds that States parties must ensure that they observe these obligations and report on this. (General Recommendation XV of 1993)

## ARTICLE 7

In its general recommendation V of 1977 the Committee requested States parties to report on their measures to give effect to the provisions of article 7.

The Committee invited States parties to include in their periodic reports information on the 'immediate and effective measures' which they have adopted 'in the fields of teaching, education, culture and information' with a view to (*a*) 'combating prejudices which lead to racial discrimination'; (*b*) 'promoting understanding, tolerance and friendship among nations and racial or ethnical groups', and (*c*) propagating the purposes and principles of the Charter of the United Nations, the Universal Declaration of Human Rights, and the United Nations Declaration on the Elimination of All Forms of Racial Discrimination as well as the International Convention on the Elimination of All Forms of Racial Discrimination'.

# APPENDIX III

## Elections to the Committee

Members of CERD are elected by secret ballot at meetings of states parties in New York. The first such meeting was held on 10 July 1969. By that date seventeen nominations had been received. Those candidates were declared elected and further nominations were solicited for the last seat. Two nominations were then received, and at a second meeting on 20 November 1969, the states parties elected Mr F. A. Sayegh, who was in the Kuwaiti diplomatic service. He went on to become the Rapporteur of the Committee from 1970 to 1979 and an important influence within it.

According to article 8.1, states parties are obliged, when electing to the Committee, to consider equitable geographical distribution. The Committee they elected in 1969 included 4 nationals of African states, 5 of Asian states, 5 of East European states, 2 from states which were members of the Latin American group, and 2 from the West European and Other Group (WEOG). At the Committee's first meeting in 1970 the Chairman drew lots to decide which members would serve for two years only. The first name he drew was his own. The nine members selected for a two-year term included all the 5 from the East European group, 3 from Asia, and 1 from Latin America. This made it possible to achieve a more equitable distribution at the 1972 election, and caused the Nigerian member to remark in an audible whisper: 'The Holy Ghost has had a hand in this!' (Partsch 1994: 106). So from 1972 the Committee consisted of 4 members from Africa, 4 from Asia, 3 East European, 3 Latin American, and 4 WEOG; this distribution was maintained until 1986. It meant that in 1976, 1980, 1984, and so on, elections were held to fill nine vacancies to seats previously held as follows: Africa 0, Asia 2, Eastern Europe 3, Latin America 2, WEOG 2. In 1974, 1978, 1982, and so on there were nine vacancies in seats previously held as follows: Africa 4, Asia 2, Eastern Europe 2, Latin America 1, WEOG 2. That the distribution achieved in 1972 was maintained shows that groups do not collectively attempt to increase their representation in years when they have no retiring members. However, sometimes a group is not able to agree on a slate of candidates. One state (or its diplomats) may believe that they have a better candidate than another state in the same group and insist upon nominating him or her. At every election between 1972 and 1994 there were between two and six more candidates than places (an average 'excess' of 4.6). The East

European group has been the most successful in producing an agreed slate, as can be seen from the distribution of 'excess' nominations: Africa 12, Asia 12, Eastern Europe 1, Latin America 12, WEOG 9. On at least one occasion, after a group meeting, a letter has been sent nominating 'group' candidates and the secretariat has had to point out that it is only states parties than can nominate.

A state may be concerned to press the cause of one of its own nationals because it believes it has a special interest in having a national on the Committee. Cyprus may be a case in point. At times a state may press its claim within its regional group because it does not have a national on any other treaty body: it argues for a fair distribution as between the various elective bodies. At election times diplomats either in the capitals or in the missions to the UN headquarters press their views upon diplomats of other countries, and seek their support. In 1986 one seat had been vacated by a Latin American and there were two candidates from the group, from Cuba and Uruguay. Neither was elected, presumably because the Latin American diplomats had been unable to agree a group priority and communicate it to others. The 'extra' place went to the candidate from the UK, Mr Banton. Representatives of Latin American states protested that the reduction in their representation on the Committee showed that not all states parties had voted in an equitable manner. They attracted support from the East European group. To conclude the discussion it was suggested that groups should increase their efforts to present agreed slates.

In 1988 only one WEOG candidate was nominated although two seats had been vacated. This made it easier for another Latin American to be elected and for the balance to be restored. In 1990 there were four African retirements, three of the members being renominated. Two nominations for the fourth seat were submitted too late for either candidate's *curriculum vitae* to be circulated. This makes it the less surprising that neither was elected and that more votes went to a Cuban candidate who had earlier been his country's ambassador to the UN. From 1990 to 1993 the Latin American group had one more seat than earlier, and the African group one fewer. The Latin American group did not act as the WEOG had done in 1988 and put up one fewer candidate in 1992, presumably because all their three candidates wished to continue as members. In the 1994 election the retiring Cuban member was renominated and re-elected, so that there continued to be four Latin American members and three African members. Perhaps the African governments failed to campaign sufficiently vigorously about the case for returning to the previous distribution of seats.

The names of those elected have been printed as an appendix to the Committee's little history entitled *The First Twenty Years* (UN 1991c). From this list it can be seen that seven states had one of their nationals serving as a committee member from 1970 through to 1994: Egypt, the FRG, India, Nigeria, and the USSR. Ghana had a seat from 1970 to 1994,

Yugoslavia from 1970 to 1992, while Pakistan has had a serving national for all but two years. Other states to have provided members have been, from Africa: Burkina Faso, Morocco, Senegal, Sudan, Swaziland, and Zimbabwe (with the following having nominated unsuccessful candidates: Burkina Faso, Libya, Madagascar, Sierra Leone, Uganda, and Zambia); from Asia: China, Iran, Kuwait, Philippines (with Iraq, Syria, and Yemen having nominated unsuccessful candidates); from Eastern Europe: Bulgaria, Czechoslovakia, Poland, and Ukraine (with Croatia having nominated an unsuccessful candidate); from Latin America: Argentina, Costa Rica, Cuba, Ecuador, Panama, and Peru (with Barbados, Bolivia, and Mexico having nominated unsuccessful candidates); and WEOG: Austria, Canada, Denmark, France, Greece, Malta, Netherlands, Sweden, and UK (with Belgium, Iceland, Malta and New Zealand having nominated unsuccessful candidates). Israel nominated a candidate in 1994 who fell a few votes short of election. Thus so far, fifty-two states have participated in the nomination of candidates.

In order to discover what sorts of candidate are nominated, a distinction may be drawn between nominees who are directly in the employment of governments (mainly diplomats) and those who are judges, lawyers in private practice, university teachers, or private citizens. Each of these two categories may be divided into those who are qualified lawyers and others. Some candidates have been renominated many times. It seems best to count nominees who have recently retired after a long period of government service as if they were still in government employment. A calculation then shows that, from 1969 to 1990, African and East European states have nominated government employees more than twice as often as private citizens, contrasting with the WEOG states, which have nominated thirty-one private citizens by comparison with four persons in government employment. In all groups no less than half the nominations of government employees have been of legally qualified persons. Among the private citizens nominated more than four in every five have been lawyers. Consideration of the particular candidates, and of the number of votes they have received, suggests that candidates who are known to UN diplomats in New York may enjoy an advantage in competition with others. Candidates who have served on the Committee are often but not always renominated if they wish this; on nine occasions former members have failed to be re-elected.

# APPENDIX IV

## Legal and Educational Measures Against Racial Discrimination

Public understanding of the nature and causes of racial discrimination has grown dramatically in the last seventy years as a result of discoveries in the social sciences, though these are not usually seen as discoveries since so much new social science is assumed, after the event, to be only common sense. In the 1920s it was widely, and reasonably, believed that racial prejudices were inherited. One of the achievements of the 1920s and 1930s was the marshalling of evidence showing that racial prejudices were learnt, and that, if they were passed from one generation to the next, they were culturally transmitted. Research influenced by the insights of psychoanalysis showed in the post-war years how prejudice could be rooted in individual psychopathology and there was at this time a tendency to see prejudicial attitudes as the causes of discriminatory behaviour. Such arguments could not satisfactorily account for the persistence of institutionalized discrimination and they neglected the causal power of economic interest.

By the time the UN was founded, interest was growing in the potential of law as a means of combating racial discrimination, partly, perhaps, because in the USA the law had become the prime means of enforcing such discrimination. This interest was reflected in the Secretary-General's memorandum of 1949 mentioned in Chapter 4. However, at that time many sceptics maintained that racial prejudice could be eliminated only by education. Influenced in part by the civil-rights movement in the USA, a better understanding spread of the ways in which unequal relationships generated attitudes supportive of such inequalities. Events since then have shown that effective legislation is essential to policies for the reduction of discrimination and that law can have an educational value in establishing norms of conduct. When they decide cases, courts educate the public in the nature of these norms and their application in particular circumstances. In the industrialized countries public understanding of the nature of racial discrimination has also grown as a result of the increased demand for, and use of, legal measures to combat other forms of what are now seen as discriminatory practice, including less favourable treatment on grounds of sex, age, religion, and disability. The unequal treatment of persons in such categories used often to be taken for granted as 'natural', but the introduction of legal remedies has brought historical assumptions into the open and required that they be justified.

The revocation of discriminatory laws has not led to any very rapid changes of attitude; laws against discrimination are proving no more effective than the laws against crime, and are sometimes implemented so feebly that they are less effective. They appear even weaker because consciousness of the incidence of discrimination is rising. A contemporary account would stress the extent to which most forms of inequality are transmitted within families from one generation to the next, racial inequalities being bound up with others. In such circumstances it is hardly surprising that within the UN more voices are speaking of the need for legislation to be complemented by education. Those who argue this cannot say what kinds of educational programme are likely to be effective because the study of just how legal and educational measures can interact with one another has been neglected.

Many public-opinion surveys in Europe and North America have found statistically significant associations between education and racial tolerance. The longer a person has spent in the educational system, the less likely it is that he or she will express racial prejudice. Yet this does not mean that the level of expressed prejudice has been lowered by the content of the lessons in the classroom. It could also have been lowered because those who study longer have an expectation of better jobs and are less disposed to vent frustrations upon a scapegoat group. The chains of cause and effect are complicated.

The content of lessons learnt in school, from the mass media and from other members of the society, can all be important. Children learn that they belong to a nation or to some section of it, and that they should identify with other people who in past generations were members of the same group. Many lessons which appear apolitical carry concealed messages of this kind (some of Shakespeare's historical dramas, for example, implicitly justified the claims of the Tudor dynasty to the English throne). As a result of socialization, individuals grow up sharing the preferences and prejudices of their peer group and are inclined to conform to the norms of that group. In identifying with 'their' group, children learn to disparage others. Education can both generate ethnic prejudices and reduce them, for it can help pupils to an insight into the processes by which people acquire images of those who belong to stranger groups.

Everyone has preferences as to the kinds of people with whom they wish to associate. While members of any group will share such preferences, there will also be variation from one person to another. Some enjoy mixing with people of a different culture more than others do. Some like to meet members of other groups only in those relationships in which they can maintain a certain distance. In most societies preferences for a given degree of ethnic mixture will have to be weighed against other preferences. To take a very practical example, a mother might like her daughter to attend a school in which she would meet a small number of classmates who come from other ethnic groups, but dislike the prospect of a school in which most of her daughter's classmates would be from other groups. The same mother might want her daughter to attend a school with a good academic record, or one not too far away from the family home. In practice the mother may have to make a choice between particular schools so as to meet her several preferences to the extent that is possible. The example serves to illustrate how ethnic preferences may have to be weighed against other preferences.

The logic of preferences plays an important part in economic analysis where an indifference curve describes an abstract relationship. Everyday decisions respond to a more complicated set of circumstances in which a person's preferences as between two alternatives would be better represented by a band of variable width than a line. Faced with two or three equally attractive or equally unattractive possibilities, the mother might in practice be indifferent as between the alternatives. An overheard conversation between two other mothers who did not want their daughters associating with children of a different colour or who praised the teachers in a particular school could be sufficient to settle the issue.

Consideration of such an example teaches several lessons. One is that in everyday life the margin of indifference for people faced with choices of this kind is often quite large; the outcome can then be influenced by the leaders of public opinion, whether they be politicians, clergy, community figures, or those who devise the messages in the mass media. This is the point of entry at which the exercise of political responsibility is so important. Whatever decision the ordinary citizen reaches can set a pattern for that person's future behaviour and the behaviour of others. If the decision is one that promotes interethnic contact, preferences may alter as a result of that contact. (Just as people who move from one country to another may take over the preferences of people in the new country, so their preferences may change over time along with those of their peer group.)

People are influenced by what they believe to be the opinions of their peers, but they may err in their estimates of what these opinions are. Studies in North America and several European countries have shown the importance of what psychologists call 'pluralistic ignorance'. Research has shown that people regularly believe their peers to be less well disposed towards interethnic social contacts than they really are. Thus, in Detroit in 1969 and 1971, whites were asked if a mother should allow her daughter to play with Negro children, and whether they thought that other whites would agree with their views on this subject. Seventy-six per cent of white respondents thought it acceptable for the daughter to invite her Negro playmate to her house, yet only 33 per cent believed that most people in the Detroit area would agree with them about this. Similar findings were obtained in both years. It transpired that relatively liberal whites under-estimated the support of their peers by around 60 per cent, while relatively illiberal ones estimated the support of their peer group as being twenty times greater than it actually was. Not only is there much inaccuracy in the perception of group norms, but the errors follow a socially determined pattern (Banton 1986).

An invitation to a child to come and play in the house does not come within any definition of 'public life' and will not be governed by laws against racial discrimination, but comparable situations within the public realm can arise over the purchase of housing in particular communities, over admission to social clubs, and over jobs. When ethnic preferences are very strong, it may be impossible to introduce or enforce laws which seek to neutralize them, but in many situations ethnic preferences will be only one kind of preference among many others and fall within a margin in which many outcomes are possible. In such circumstances legal norms have a decisive influence either to facilitate or to discourage interethnic contact because they influence ideas about peer-group expectations and the sanctions they can generate.

Those who designed the systems of apartheid in southern Africa, and of racial segregation in the Deep South of the USA, well understood that there were many circumstances in which even whites with high preferences for avoiding equal-status contacts with blacks might act in accordance with preferences of higher priority (e.g. of financial advantage) and ignore or circumvent norms of segregation. Therefore they legislated to deprive members of the public of the non-discriminatory alternative by making some kinds of transaction illegal or dangerous (e.g. to sell a house in a 'white' neighbourhood to a black purchaser). One of the merits of the 'consumer society' is that it allows individuals freedom to put their own prices upon their ethnic preferences. With increasing contact, these prices are likely to fall.

Ethnic preferences may appear to be constant, but that is only when they are maintained by the constructions individuals put upon their everyday experience and the information that comes their way. Recent events have shown how the flow of information can be manipulated so as to change preferences. A sad example was furnished in the former Yugoslavia. With the weakening of federal authority, politicians in the republics seized con-trol of the mass media and used them to increase ethnic antagonisms (documented in Hampson 1993, Thompson 1994, and the report of the UN special rapporteur, A/CN.4/1995/54). Reports about the insidious influence of Radio Mille Collines in the Rwandan genocide of 1994 were confirmed by the UN special rapporteur, who wrote that 'the generally illiterate Rwandese rural population listens very attentively to broadcasts in Kinyarwanda; they hold their radio sets in one hand and their machetes in the other, ready to go into action' (E/CN.4/1994/7, para. 59). Experience also indicates that the power of the mass media to promote ethnic tolerance scarcely compares with their power to promote hostility.

A French writer, Maurice Harriou, once declared that 'a little sociology leads away from the law, but much sociology leads back to it'. This stimulated one of his successors (Gurvitch 1947: 2) to observe that, while a little law leads away from sociology, much law leads back to it. The current state of empirical research on the interrelation between legal and educational measures against racial discrimination does not yet demonstrate the truth of these fine words, but such research offers a good place in which to start.

# REFERENCES

Amnesty International (1992*a*), *Burundi: Appeals for an Inquiry into Army and Gendarmerie Killings and Other Recent Human Rights Violations*. London: International Secretariat.

——(1992*b*), *Rwanda: Persecution of Tutsi Minority and Repression of Government Critics, 1990–1992*. London: International Secretariat.

Banton, Michael (1983), *Racial and Ethnic Competition*. Cambridge: Cambridge University Press.

——(1986), 'Pluralistic Ignorance as a Factor in Racial Attitudes', *New Community*, 13: 18–26. Also note 'Correction', *New Community*, 14: 313.

——(1994), *Discrimination*. Buckingham: Open University Press.

Beetham, David (1991), *The Legitimation of Power*. London: Macmillan.

Belote, Linda Smith, and Belote, Jim (1984), 'Drain from the Bottom: Individual Ethnic Identity Change in Southern Ecuador', *Social Forces*, 63: 24–50.

Benthall, Jonathan (1992), 'A Study in Survivalry', *Anthropology Today*, 8(6): 1–2.

Bloed, Arie, and Van Hoof, Fried (1985), 'Some Aspects of the Socialist View of Human Rights', pp. 29–55 in Arie Bloed and Pietar Van Dijk (eds.), *Essays on Human Rights in the Helsinki Process*. Dordrecht: Martinus Nijhoff.

Brackman, Arnold C. (1987), *The Other Nuremberg: The Untold Story of the Tokyo War Crimes Trials*. London: Collins.

Brogan, Patrick (1989), *World Conflicts: Why and Where they are Happening*. London: Bloomsbury Books.

Buergenthal, Thomas (1977), 'Implementing the UN Racial Convention', *Texas International Law Journal*, 12: 187–221.

Commission Internationale d'Enquête sur les Violations des Droits de l'Homme au Burundi depuis le 21 octobre 1993, *Rapport final* (1994). Publisher not stated, but probably Fédération Internationale des Droits de l'Homme, Paris.

DeConde, Alexander (1992), *Ethnicity, Race, and American Foreign Policy: A History*. Boston: Northeastern University Press.

Fédération Internationale des Ligues des Droits de l'Homme (1993), *Rwanda. Violations massives et systématiques des droits de l'homme depuis le 1er octobre 1990. Rapport*. Paris.

Furnival, J. S. (1948), *Colonial Policy and Practice: A Comparative Study of Burma and Netherlands India*. Cambridge: Cambridge University Press.

Gomez del Prado, José L. (1985) 'United Nations Conventions on Human Rights: The Practice of the Human Rights Committee and the Committee on the Elimination of Racial Discrimination in Dealing with Reporting Obligations of States Parties', *Human Rights Quarterly*, 7: 492–513.

Gray, Andrew (1990), 'Report on International Labour Organisation Revision of Contention 107', pp. 173–91 in *IWGIA Yearbook 1989*. Copenhagen: International Workgroup for Indigenous Affairs.

Gurvitch, Georges (1947), *Sociology of Law*. London: Kegan Paul.

Hampson, Françoise (1993), *Incitement and the Media: Responsibility of and for the Media in the Conflicts in the Former Yugoslavia*. Colchester: University of Essex, Papers in the Theory and Practice of Human Rights 3.

Hannum, Hurst (1990), *Autonomy, Sovereignty, and Self-Determination: The Accommodation of Conflicting Rights*. Philadelphia: University of Pennsylvania Press.

HCI (Haut Conseil à l'Intégration) (1993), *Intégration à la française*. Paris: Documentation Française.

Henriksen, Georg (1991), 'Sixth General Assembly of the World Council for Indigenous Peoples', pp. 191–200 in *IWGIA Yearbook 1990*. Copenhagen: International Workgroup for Indigenous Affairs.

ILO (International Labour Office) (1988), *Equality in Employment and Occupation*. Geneva: ILO.

IWGIA (1989), 'IWGIA—20 Years', pp. 13-28 in *IWGIA Yearbook 1988*. Copenhagen: International Workgroup for Indigenous Affairs.

Lauren, Paul G. (1988), *Power and Prejudice: The Politics and Diplomacy of Racial Discrimination*. Boulder, Colo.: Westview Press.

Lemarchand, René, and Martin, David (1974), *Selective Genocide in Burundi*. London: Minority Rights Group.

Lerner, Natan (1980), *The UN Convention on the Elimination of All Forms of Racial Discrimination*. 2nd edn. Alphen an den Rijn: Sijthoff & Nordhoff.

McKean, Warwick (1983), *Equality and Discrimination under International Law*. Oxford: Clarendon Press.

Mahalic, Drew, and Mahalic, Joan Gambee (1987), 'The Limitation Provisions of the International Convention on the Elimination of All Forms of Racial Discrimination', *Human Rights Quarterly*, 9: 74–101.

Mair, Lucy Philip (1928), *The Protection of Minorities: The Working and Scope of the Minorities Treaties under the League of Nations*. London: Christophers.

Mangin, William (1973), 'Sociological, Cultural, and Political Characteristics of Some Urban Migrants in Peru', pp. 315–50 in Aidan Southall (ed.), *Urban Anthropology: Cross-Cultural Studies of Urbanization*. New York: Oxford University Press.

Meron, Theodore (1985), 'The Meaning and Reach of the International

Convention on the Elimination of All Forms of Racial Discrimination', *American Journal of International Law*, 79: 283–318.

Moynihan, Daniel Patrick (1979), *A Dangerous Place*. London: Secker & Warburg.

Mushakoji, Kinhide (1993), 'Development and Racism in Asia and the Pacific', pp. 15–30 in *Six Continents: Race and Unequal Development*, ed. Michael Banton, IMADR Yearbook: Peoples for Human Rights 1992. Tokyo.

Nettheim, Garth (1981), *Victims of the Law: Black Queenslanders Today*. Sydney: Allen & Unwin.

Öberg, Kjell (1990), *FN-konventionen om avskaffande av alla former av rasdiskriminering*. Lund: Raoul Wallenberg Institute, Report No. 8.

Olson, Mancur (1965), *The Logic of Collective Action: Public Goods and the Theory of Groups*. Cambridge, Mass.: Harvard University Press.

Oreskov, Claus (1989), 'Interview with Ed Burnstick, Treaty Six, Alberta', *IWGIA Yearbook 1988*. Copenhagen: International Workgroup for Indigenous Affairs.

Partsch, Karl Joseph (1979), 'Elimination of Racial Discrimination in the Enjoyment of Civil and Political Rights', *Texas International Law Journal*, 14: 191–250.

——(1992*a*), 'The Committee on the Elimination of Racial Discrimination', pp. 339–68 in Philip Alston (ed.), *The United Nations and Human Rights: A Critical Appraisal*. Oxford: Clarendon Press.

——(1992*b*), 'Racial Speech and Human Rights: Article 4 of the Convention on the Elimination of All Forms of Racial Discrimination', pp. 21–8 in Sandra Coliver (ed.), *Striking a Balance: Hate Speech, Freedom of Expression and Non-Discrimination*. London: Article 19.

——(1994), *Hoffen auf Menschenrechte: Rückbesinnung auf eine internationale Entwicklung*. Zurich: Interform.

——(1995), 'Racial Discrimination', pp. 1003–11 in Rüdiger Wolfrum (ed.), *United Nations: Law, Policies and Practice*. Dordrecht: Martinus Nijhoff.

Rechetov, Yuri (1992), 'Incitement of National Enmity in the Context of International Law: Foreign and Soviet Practice', *Israel Yearbook on Human Rights*, 22: 83–96.

République du Burundi, Collectif des Partis d'Opposition (1993), *Le Génocide d'octobre 1993*. Bujumbura.

Schwelb, Egon (1966), 'The International Convention of the Elimination of All Forms of Racial Discrimination', *International Comparative Law Quarterly*, 15: 996–1068.

Taylor, Telford (1993), *The Anatomy of the Nuremberg Trials*. London: Bloomsbury Books.

Thompson, Mark (1994), *The Media in Serbia, Croatia and Bosnia-Hercegovina*. London: Article 19.

Thompson, Peter (1994), 'Human Rights Reporting from a State Party's Perspective', pp. 329–64 in Philip Alston (ed.), *Towards an Australian Bill of Rights*. Canberra: Centre for International and Public Law.

Thornberry, Patrick (1991), *International Law and the Rights of Minorities*. Oxford: Clarendon Press.

Tusa, Ann, and Tusa, John (1983), *The Nuremberg Trial*. London: Macmillan.

UN (United Nations) (1949), *The Main Types and Causes of Discrimination (Memorandum submitted by the Secretary-General)*. New York. Sales No. 1949 XIV 3.

——(1950), *Definition and Classification of Minorities (Memorandum submitted by the Secretary-General)*. New York. Sales No. 1950 XIV 3.

——(1971), *Racial Discrimination*. Revised and updated version of the special study prepared by Mr Hernán Santa Cruz. New York. Sales No. E.76.XIV.2.

——(1979), *Committee on the Elimination of Racial Discrimination and the Progress Made towards the Achievement of the Objectives of the International Convention on the Elimination of All Forms of Racial Discrimination*. CERD/1. New York. Sales No. E.79.XIV.4.

——(1985), *Teaching, Education, Culture and Information as Means of Eliminating Racial Discrimination*. CERD/3. New York. Sales No. E.85.XIV.3.

——(1986), *Positive Measures Designed to Eradicate all Incitement to, or Acts of, Racial Discrimination*. CERD/2. New York. Sales No. E.85.XIV.2.

——(1991*a*), *Global Compilation of National Legislation Against Racial Discrimination*. New York. HR/PUB/90/8.

——(1991*b*), *Manual on Human Rights Reporting*. New York. HR/PUB/ 91/1. Sales No. E.91.XIV.1.

——(1991*c*), *The First Twenty Years: Progress Report of the Committee on the Elimination of Racial Discrimination*. New York. HR/PUB/91/4.

——(1992*a*), *An Agenda for Peace: Preventive Diplomacy, Peacemaking and Peacekeeping*. Report of the Secretary-General, Boutros Boutros-Ghali. New York.

——(1992*b*), *Human Development Report*. (Annual publication). New York.

——(1994), *United Nations Action in the Field of Human Rights*. New York. ST/HR/2/Rev 4. Sales No. E.94.XIV.11.

Valencia Rodriguez, Luis (1993), 'The Protection of the Rights of Indigenous People in Ecuador', pp. 42–55 in *Six Continents: Race and Unequal Development*, ed. Michael Banton, IMADR Yearbook: Peoples for Human Rights 1992. Tokyo.

Vincent, R. J. (1986), *Human Rights and International Relations*. Cambridge: Cambridge University Press.

de Waal, Alex (1994), 'Genocide in Rwanda', *Anthropology Today*, 10(3): 1–2.

Whitten, Norman E. (1975), 'Jungle Quechua Ethnicity: An Ecuadorian Case Study', pp. 41–69 in Leo A. Despres (ed.), *Ethnicity and Resource Competition in Plural Societies*. The Hague: Mouton.

Wolfrum, Rüdiger (1990), 'Das Verbot der Rassendiskriminierung im Spannungsfeld zwischen den Schutz individuelle Freiheitsrechte und der Verpflichtung des einzelnen im Allgemeininteresse', pp. 515–27 in Erhard Denninger *et al.* (eds.), *Kritik und Vertrauen: Festschrift für Peter Schneider*. Frankfurt am Main: Hain.

Zoller, Adrien-Claude (1993), 'The Political Context of the World Conference', *Human Rights Monitor*, 21: 2–4.

# INDEX OF STATES

The first date after the name of a state indicates the year in which it became a member of the United Nations; the second indicates the year in which its adherence to ICERD came into force. It is possible for a state which is not a UN member state to be a party to the Convention. Some states were admitted to the UN under other names than those they used at the time of acceding to ICERD; the names in current use have been preferred.

Afghanistan (1946–1983) 96, 297–8
Albania (1955–1994) 183
Algeria (1962–1972) 90, 125, 126, 163–4, 250, 272–3
Angola (1976– ) 88, 264
Antigua and Barbuda (1981–1988)
Argentina (1945–1969) 102, 104, 163, 229, 230, 231–2, 239, 248, 340
Armenia (1992–1993) 84
Australia (1945–1975) 8, 30, 33, 44, 75, 80, 90, 140, 170, 191–2, 281–4
Austria (1955–1972) 16, 33, 191–3, 194, 197, 203, 217, 221, 340
Azerbaijan (1992– ) 84

Bahamas (1973–1975) 33, 242–3
Bahrain (1971–1990) 97
Bangladesh (1974–1979) 44, 96, 97, 169, 292–7, 303
Barbados (1966–1972), 169, 242, 340
Belarus (1945–1969) 33, 124, 169
Belgium (1945–1975) 14, 30, 62, 85, 126–7, 193, 253, 262, 340
Belize (1981– )
Benin (1960– ) 41, 54
Bhutan (1971– )
Bolivia (1945–1970) 105, 107, 225, 228, 230, 232, 239, 242, 340
Bosnia and Herzegovina (1992–1993) 147, 152, 165, 189, 306
Botswana (1966–1974) 270
Brazil (1945–1969) 33, 60, 61, 139, 225, 226, 229, 232
Brunei Darussalam (1984– )
Bulgaria (1955–1969) 16, 33, 84, 125, 134–7, 143, 153, 186–7, 222, 340
Burkina Faso (1960–1974) 54, 270, 340

Burundi (1962–1977) 89, 152, 162, 253–67, 311, 312–13

Cambodia (1955–1983) 8, 93–4, 277, 289
Cameroon (1960–1971) 58
Canada (1945–1970) 7, 30, 33, 37, 39, 75, 85, 87, 208, 224, 243–4, 248, 311, 340
Cape Verde (1975–1979) 88, 270
Central African Republic (1960–1971) 54, 252, 270
Chad (1960–1977) 54, 89, 271–2
Chile (1945–1971) 7, 58, 111, 119, 129, 130, 131, 137, 230, 231, 233, 234
China (1945–1982) 9, 15, 22, 33, 92–3, 94, 95, 276, 277, 286–8, 312, 340
Colombia (1945–1981) 7, 33, 228, 229, 233, 238, 239, 242, 306
Comoros (1975– ) 88
Congo (1960–1988)
Costa Rica (1945–1969) 5, 230, 232, 235, 340
Cote d'Ivoire (1960–1973) 54, 270
Croatia (1992–1991) 152, 162, 189, 311, 340
Cuba (1945–1972) 33, 242, 312, 339, 340
Cyprus (1960–1969) 33, 75, 110, 111, 276, 306, 339
Czech Republic (1993–1993) [including references to Czechoslovakia (1945–1969)] 15, 16, 33, 60, 160, 203, 340

Dahomy, see Benin
Democratic Kampuchea, see Cambodia

Democratic People's Republic of Korea (1991– )
Denmark (1945–1972) 30, 33, 35, 36, 207–8, 222, 340
Djibouti (1977– ) 88
Dominica (1978– ) 33
Dominican Republic (1945–1983)

Ecuador (1945–1969) 33, 112, 138, 230, 232, 233, 239, 240–1, 242, 340
Egypt (1945–1969) 3, 5, 34, 71, 112, 163, 305, 339
El Salvador (1945–1979) 33, 230, 233, 234, 238
Equatorial Guinea (1968– )
Estonia (1991–1991)
Ethiopia (1945–1976) 90

Federated States of Micronesia (1991– )
Fiji (1970–1973) 87, 91, 117, 139, 284–5
Finland (1955–1970) 17, 33, 37, 81, 222
France (1945–1971) 18, 30, 33, 36, 81, 85, 184, 193, 196, 201, 293, 210–12, 214, 215–16, 217, 219, 220, 250, 262, 340

Gabon (1960–1980) 139
Gambia (1965–1979)
Georgia (1992– ) 84
Germany (1973–1969) 1, 7, 14, 16, 19, 30, 33, 36, 37, 41, 81, 85, 153, 169, 193–4, 196, 200, 212, 214, 216, 218, 220, 257, 262, 339
Ghana (1957–1969) 1, 33, 66, 267–8, 339
Greece (1945–1970) 16, 61, 115, 195, 198–9, 340
Grenada (1974– )
Guatemala (1945–1983) 162, 230, 233, 237
Guinea (1958–1977) 54
Guinea-Bissau (1974– ) 86
Guyana (1966–1977) 86, 151, 229

Haiti (1945–1973)
Holy See ( –1969) 8, 169
Honduras (1945– )
Hungary (1955–1969) 16, 33, 61, 222

Iceland (1946–1969) 1, 6, 99, 222, 340
India (1945–1969) 16, 25, 33, 61, 91, 95, 96, 97, 170, 276, 289, 290–1, 339
Indonesia (1950– ) 94, 276, 277, 285
Iran (1945–1969) 33, 96, 112, 115, 149, 299, 312, 340
Iraq (1945–1970) 9, 61, 147–8, 169, 299, 340
Ireland (1955– ) 30, 183
Israel (1949–1979) 7, 29, 30, 31, 61, 97, 110, 111, 114, 125, 129, 130, 137, 163, 170, 215, 300–3, 305, 307, 340
Italy (1945–1976) 16, 30, 203, 219, 222

Jamaica (1962–1971) 86, 242–3
Japan (1956– ) 15, 18, 25, 37, 91–2, 93, 95, 105, 168, 276, 277
Jordan (1955–1974) 61, 305

Kazakhstan (1992– )
Kenya (1963– ) 88
Kuwait (1963–1969) 29, 97, 111, 299, 340
Kyrgyzstan (1992– )

Lao People's Democratic Republic (1955–1974) 93–4, 289
Latvia (1991–1992)
Lebanon (1945–1971) 97, 300
Lesotho (1966–1971) 127, 270
Liberia (1945–1976) 151
Libyan Arab Jamahiriya (1955–1969) 6–7, 106
Liechtenstein (1990– )
Lithuania (1991– )
Luxembourg (1945–1978) 6, 14, 30, 100

Macedonia (the Former Yugoslav Republic of) (1993–1994) 151, 164, 189, 199
Madagascar (1960–1969) 107–8, 340
Malawi (1964– ) 33, 61
Malaysia (1957– ) 87, 94, 95, 276, 277, 285, 307, 312
Maldives (1965–1984)
Mali (1960–1974) 54, 270
Malta (1964–1971) 340
Marshall Islands (1991– )
Mauretania (1961–1989) 54, 58, 270

Mauritius (1968–1972) 33, 87, 270, 311
Mexico (1945–1975) 33, 66 n., 85, 163–4, 224, 229, 230–1, 233, 234, 235–6, 238, 242, 313, 340
Moldova (1992–1993)
Mongolia (1961–1969) 61
Morocco (1956–1971) 9, 48, 61, 89, 125, 272, 340
Mozambique (1975–1983) 88, 264, 271
Myanmar (1948– ) 94, 276, 285

Namibia (1990–1982) 88
Nauru (1993– ) 91
Nepal (1955–1971)
Netherlands (1945–1972) 30, 33, 42, 43, 85, 191–2, 197, 200, 202, 220, 222, 340
New Zealand (1945–1972) 30, 33, 75, 80, 90–1, 170, 276, 277, 278–81, 340
Nicaragua (1945–1978) 230, 233, 238, 242
Niger (1960–1969)
Nigeria (1960–1969) 25, 33, 61, 62, 153, 262, 268–9, 339
Norway (1945–1970) 33, 81, 197, 204, 206, 212–13, 218, 219, 221, 222

Oman (1971–1970) 97

Pakistan (1947–1969) 4, 16, 33, 95, 96, 97, 170, 276, 289, 291, 298, 340
Panama (1945–1969) 22, 33, 106, 110, 230, 232, 236, 242, 340
Papua New Guinea (1975–1982) 18, 91, 152, 285–6
Paraguay (1945– ) 229
Peru (1945–1971) 4, 116–17, 230, 231, 232, 236, 242, 340
Philippines (1945–1969) 7, 17, 18, 61, 94, 97, 131, 170, 277, 289, 340
Poland (1945–1969) 16, 33, 60, 81, 94, 125, 132, 170, 340
Portugal (1955–1982) 33

Qatar (1971–1976) 33, 97

Republic of Korea (1991–1979) 37, 91, 97, 170, 288

Romania (1955–1970) 16, 84, 120
Russian Federation (1945–1969) 161, 163–4
Rwanda (1962–1975) 19, 23, 47, 89, 152, 162, 219, 253–67, 310, 311–13

Saint Kitts and Nevis (1983– )
Saint Lucia (1979–1990)
Saint Vincent and the Grenadines (1980–1981)
Samoa (1976– ) 91
San Marino (1992– )
São Tomé and Principe (1975– ) 88
Saudi Arabia (1945– ) 61, 97, 276, 300
Senegal (1960–1972) 169, 262, 270, 340
Seychelles (1976–1978) 88
Sierra Leone (1961–1969) 81, 267, 377
Singapore (1965– ) 94, 95
Slovak Republic (1993–1992)
Slovenia (1992–1992)
Solomon Islands (1978–1982)
Somalia (1960–1975) 90, 150–1
South Africa (1945– ) x, 26, 28, 30, 33, 34, 61, 70, 88, 119, 120, 125, 127, 137, 165, 264
Spain (1945–1969) 33, 99, 213
Sri Lanka (1955–1982) 96, 99, 289, 291–2
Switzerland ( –1994) 99
Sudan (1956–1977) 44, 58, 61, 89, 271, 273–4, 312, 340
Suriname (1975–1984) 85, 87, 151, 229
Swaziland (1968–1969) 106, 340
Sweden (1946–1972) 7, 37, 39–40, 81, 85, 124, 138, 184, 197, 200, 201, 204–6, 217, 221, 223, 340
Syria (1945–1969) 71, 96, 97, 106, 110, 128, 130, 305, 340

Tajikistan (1992– )
Thailand (1946– ) 94, 97, 276, 277
Togo (1960–1972) 249, 270
Tonga ( –1972) 91, 117, 276
Trinidad and Tobago (1962–1973) 33, 86
Tunisia (1956–1969) 29, 63–4, 273
Turkey (1945– ) 16, 33, 41, 75, 85, 96, 97, 110, 128–9, 134, 306

Turkmenistan (1992–1994)
Tuvalu, 33

Uganda (1962–1980) 72, 89, 132–3,
255, 262, 270, 340
Ukraine (1945–1969) 33, 59, 105,
222, 340
Union of Soviet Socialist Republics 29,
33, 35, 56, 58, 60, 63, 68, 75, 81,
94, 96, 100, 101, 104, 130, 133,
185–6, 215, 339; *see also* Russian
Federation
United Arab Emirates (1971–1974)
33, 97
United Arab Republic [union of Egypt
and Syria from 1958–61] 59, 70
United Kingdom (1945–1969) 18, 25,
30, 31, 33, 81, 84, 106, 107, 130,
148–9, 163, 169, 183–4, 196–7,
203, 206–7, 213, 214–15, 216, 218,
222, 307, 340
United Republic of Tanzania
(1961–1972) 58
United States of America (1945–1994)
x, 15, 17, 18, 25, 31, 59, 60, 61, 71,

85, 86, 87–8, 93, 94, 110, 113, 133,
168, 203, 224, 244, 246–7, 262,
305, 307, 341, 344
Upper Volta, *see* Burkina Faso
Uruguay (1945–1969) 139, 229, 339
Uzbekistan (1992– ) 96

Vanuatu (1981– )
Venezuela (1945–1969) 1–6, 7, 33,
100, 112, 117, 228, 230, 232, 233,
307, 312
Viet Nam (1977–1982) 18, 93–4,
277–8, 288–9

Yemen (1947–1972) 298, 300, 340
Yugoslavia (1945–1969) 15, 16, 19,
23, 35, 36, 46, 60, 68, 81, 84, 125,
131, 152, 160, 162, 165, 169,
187–9, 219, 306, 310, 311, 316,
340, 344

Zaïre (1960–1976) 125, 251
Zambia (1964–1972) 270–1, 340
Zimbabwe (1980–1991) 88, 262, 264,
340

# INDEX OF PERSONS

In the case of members of CERD, brackets after the name give the dates during which the person was a member and the country of nationality. For a complete list up to 1990, see UN 1991c: 76–9.

Aboul-Nasr, Mahmoud (1970–8, 1986– , Egypt) 3–4, 5, 103, 135, 142, 150, 159, 160, 163, 194, 264, 295, 296, 301
Ahmadu, Hamzat (1984– , Nigeria) 162, 256, 295
Alston, Philip 40, 44, 315, 317
Amin, Idi 72

Bahnev, Yuli (1976–82, Bulgaria) 120, 133
Banton, Michael (1986– , United Kingdom) vii, 4, 52, 86, 130, 136, 137, 150, 158, 191, 193–4, 200, 218–19, 256–8, 265, 284–5, 287–8, 294, 301, 315, 339, 344
Beetham, David 131
Belote, Linda Smith & Jim 241
Bentham, Jeremy 13
Benthall, Jonathan 226
Bloed, Ari 14
Beshir, Mohamed Omer (1986–90, Sudan) 273
Boven, Theodoor van (1992– , The Netherlands) 66, 160, 189, 193, 202, 208, 295
Braunschweig, André (1986–90, France) 5, 135, 139
Brackman, Arnold C. 19
Brin-Martinez, Pedro (1976–80, Panama) 105
Brogan, Patrick 89, 90
Buergenthal, Thomas 108, 110, 121
Burke, Edmund 13

Capotorti, Francesco 35
Carter, Jimmy 224
Chigovera, Andrew (1994– , Zimbabwe) 264
Cicanovic, Nicola (1984–8, Yugoslavia) 132, 135, 137
Cremona, John J. (1984–8, Malta) 135, 136, 205

Deschenes, Jules 36
Dechezelles, André (1976–80, France) 123, 124, 125, 127, 131, 132
DeConde, Alexander 15
de Pierola y Balta (1984–8, Peru) 135, 136, 187, 205
Devetak, Silvo (1976–80, Yugoslavia) 127, 132
Diaconu, Ion (1992– , Romania) 159, 161, 294
Dulles, John Foster 224

Eide, Asbjørn 32, 228
Ermacora, Felix 298

Ferrero Costa, Eduardo (1988– , Peru) 4, 5, 285, 287, 288, 294–5, 296
Foighel, Isi (1988–92, Denmark) 6
Furnival, J. S. 94

Garvalov, Ivan (1988– , Bulgaria) 194
Gaitskill, Baroness 59, 68
Ghoneim, Abdel Moneim M. (1978–86, Egypt) 140
Glélé-Ahananzo, Maurice 41, 164
de Gobineau, Arthur 83
Gomez del Prado, José 120, 167, 176
de Gouttes, Régis (1990– , France) 161, 187, 219, 258, 264, 265, 287, 288, 294, 296
Gray, Andrew 227, 229
Gurvitch, Georges 345

Hampson, Françoise 344
Hannum, Hurst 139, 226
Hegel, G. W. F. 13
Henriksen, Georg 239
Hitler, Adolf 9, 11
van Hoof, Fried 14

Inglès, José D. (1970–8, 1980–4, Philippines) 102, 277

Karasimeonov, Matey (1982–8, Bulgaria) 127, 132–3, 136, 252
Knox, Robert 83

Lamptey, George O. (1984–94, Ghana) x, 1, 4, 5, 42, 63, 66, 67, 119, 124, 127, 128, 146, 249, 251, 270
Lauren, Paul 15, 224
Lemarchand, Réne 254
Lechuga Hevia, Carlos (1990– , Cuba) 288, 295
Lerner, Natan ix
Lester, Lord 222
Locke, John 12

Mahalic, Drew & Mahalic, Joan Gambee 167
Mair, Lucy Philip 16
Mangin, William 240
Martin, David 254
Marx, Karl 13
Mazowiecki, Tadeusz 164–5
McKean, Warwick ix
Meron, Theodore 104, 152
Moynihan, Daniel Patrick 29, 249
Murray, Gilbert 16
Mushakoji, Kinhide 239

Nettel, Erik (1976–80, Austria) 124, 133, 139
Nettheim, Garth 140, 282

Öberg, Kjell (1984–8, Sweden) 135, 137, 138–9, 187, 252–3
Olson, Mancur 313
Omar, Mr 9
Oreskov, Claus 87
Ortiz-Martin, Gonzalo (1970–6, Costa Rica) 105

Partsch, Karl Josef (1970–90, Fed. Rep. Germany) 4, 21, 102, 106, 110, 111, 120, 125, 130, 132–3, 135–6, 202–3, 204, 205, 209, 338
Plato 50, 53
Popper, Sir Karl 53

Rechetov, Yuri (1988– , USSR, then

Russian Federation) 5, 159, 162, 194, 205, 207, 285, 288
Rhenan Segura, Jorge (1988–92, Costa Rica) 5, 258, 287

Sadiq Ali, Shanti (1982– , India) 6, 135, 159, 258, 259, 264, 285, 287, 293–4, 296, 297
Safronchuk, Vasily S. (1972–6, USSR) 100, 103, 105
Santa Cruz, Hernán 74, 76, 103
Sayegh, Fayez A. (1970–82, Kuwait) 29, 102, 103, 106, 111, 120, 125, 130, 132–3, 135–6, 144, 338
Schwelb, Egon 66–7, 99, 183, 204
Shahi, Aga (1978– , Pakistan) 4, 128, 135, 136, 137, 146, 147, 159, 161, 296–8
Sherifis, Michael E. (1982– , Cyprus) 136
Song, Shuhua (1984– , China) 5, 135, 161, 187, 252, 288, 294
Staruschenko, Gleb Borisovich (1982–8, USSR) 132–3, 136, 138, 187, 188
Sviridov, Eduard Petrovitch (1979–80, USSR) 124

Tanaka, Judge 238
Tarassov, Nikolai K. (1970–4, USSR) 100, 103, 111, 306
Taylhardat, Rudolfo 1, 2, 4–5
Taylor, Telford 15
Thompson, Mark 344
Thompson, Peter 166
Thornberry, Patrick 34, 225, 226, 229, 240
Tomko, Jan (1970–6, Czechoslovakia) 104, 108
Tusa, Ann & John 17, 18

Valencia Rodriguez, Luis (1970–86, 1992– , Ecuador) 104, 105, 138, 240
Vidas, Kasimir (1988–92, Yugoslavia) 288
Videla-Escala, Frederico (1976–80, Argentina) 145
Vincent, R. J. 11, 12

Waal, Alex de 254
Whitten, Norman E. 241
Wilson, Woodrow 15

Wolfrum, Rüdiger (1990– , Germany)
153, 159, 162, 198, 205, 209, 258,
266, 284, 287, 288, 300, 301

Yutzis, Mario Jorge (1984– ,
Argentina) 3, 4, 135, 137, 141, 162,
285, 292–3, 295, 296, 300

Zoller, Adrien-Claude 48, 312

# INDEX OF SUBJECTS

accession to treaties 63, 99
African Charter on Human and Peoples' Rights 23, 30
Albanian minority in Greece 199
Albanians in Kosovo 162, 167, 188, 197, 316
American Convention on Human Rights 23, 222, 226
Amnesty International 23, 134, 259, 293
An Agenda for Peace 47, 152, 161, 164, 262
antisemitism 53, 60, 61, 68, 72, 221
apartheid 26, 28, 30, 31, 32, 33, 34, 58, 61, 75, 88, 109, 110, 112, 126–7, 165, 201, 214, 227, 344
Anti-Racism Information Service (ARIS) 166
assimilation 5, 134, 135, 226, 231
asylum-seekers 193, 213, 216

Bretons 36, 212

caste 77–8, 83, 92, 95, 277
Chechnya 163–4
Chiapas 163–4, 235–6
Cold War vii, 123, 134, 142, 182
colonialism 30, 58, 59, 60, 61, 68, 70, 71, 75, 98, 104, 105, 106, 112, 249
Committee Against Torture (CAT) and Convention Against Torture 40, 165, 317
Committee for the Elimination of Racial Discrimination (CERD):
   achievements of 8, 121, 306–11
   annual report of 8, 43, 125, 133, 140, 143, 145, 161, 231, 256
   autonomy of 8, 101, 120, 121, 126
   cancellation of sessions 9, 100, 141, 143
   chairmanship 137, 155
   closed meetings 149, 188, 296–7
   communications to: Demba Talib Diop v. France 157; L.K. v. the Netherlands 157, 208, 213;

Narrainen v. Norway 157–8, 212; C. P. v. Denmark 158; Yilmaz-Dogon v. the Netherlands 156–7
   concluding observations 145, 147–9, 167, 189, 199, 206, 211, 212–13, 235, 239, 258, 299
   considered effective 121
   considered ineffective 42
   costs of meeting 144, 154
   country rapporteurs 3, 6, 145, 146–7, 153, 154–5, 281, 295
   decisions 110, 127, 128, 137, 147, 153, 302, 333–7
   dialogue with states 3, 7, 107, 168–71, 223, 232
   diplomat members of vii, 7, 67, 120, 138–9, 147, 160, 309, 315, 340
   division of labour in 144, 146
   early warning and urgent procedures 161, 309–10
   elections to 100, 142, 152, 338–40
   funding of 9, 43, 167–8
   further information requested 107–8, 133, 152–3, 163, 189, 274, 285, 301
   general recommendations 5, 64, 107, 152, 158–60, 162, 194, 199, 201–2, 204, 206, 212, 214, 250, 333–7
   general recommendations, narrative form 160, 202
   independence of members 4, 100, 120, 140, 160, 273, 297
   languages 2, 9, 140, 147
   length of speeches 3, 144, 155
   meeting place 143–4, 167
   members who are nationals of reporting states 137, 149–50
   membership vii, 100, 121, 123, 138, 142, 153, 309
   missions of 162, 237
   non-self-governing territories 144, 158
   officers of 102, 137, 143
   permissible sources 102–3, 106, 109, 131–3, 153, 307

political constraints upon 142, 144, 167, 185, 187
preventive action a priority 161
quorum for meetings 101, 141
questions asked 115, 153, 154
records 5, 8–9
relations with General Assembly 120–1
relations with non-governmental organizations 41, 103
relations with states parties 109–10, 118, 121, 245
reporting guidelines 7, 44, 102, 107, 243, 250
reports, time taken 6–7, 8, 160–71
review procedure 150–1
rules of procedure 102, 132, 155
sessions of 101
state representatives attending 7, 8, 109–10, 111, 115, 116, 128, 145, 152, 154
suggestions and recommendations 5, 103, 149, 198, 212, 237, 284
working methods 9, 107, 144, 154
Committee on Economic, Social and Cultural Rights 40, 159
Committee on the Elimination of Discrimination Against Women (CEDAW) and Convention on the Elimination of Discrimination Against Women 40, 47, 244
Committee on the Rights of the Child (CRC) and Convention on the Rights of the Child 40, 47, 99, 244
Conference on Security and Cooperation in Europe (CSCE) (from 1994, Organization for Security and Cooperation in Europe, OSCE) 38, 184
constitutional protections from racial discrimination 2, 16, 196, 238, 243
Convention against Discrimination in Education 24, 53
core document 44
Council of Europe 38, 182, 184

data protection laws 210–11, 250
Decades for Action to Combat Racism and Racial Discrimination 28–34, 105, 119, 127, 165, 249, 307

Declaration on the Elimination of Racial Discrimination 55
Declaration on the Rights of Persons Belonging to National, Ethnic, Religious and Linguistic Minorities 23, 38, 47, 228
decolonization 9, 43, 55, 56, 70, 89, 276
development racism 239, 252
Discrimination (Employment and Occupation) Convention 25

educational measures 218, 221, 315, 337, 341–5
empires 15, 18, 96
*Encyclopedia Britannica* 14
equality of states 15, 118, 149, 153, 155, 188, 232, 316
ethnic cleansing, defined 188
ethnic dimension to conflicts 164, 270, 316
ethnic groups 15, 80, 84, 89, 159
ethnic monitoring 200, 210–11, 219, 235, 236, 250, 257
ethnic origin 36, 111, 194–5, 198, 250–2
ethnicity, primary and secondary 315–16
eugenics 84
European Community 30
European Parliament 38, 293–4
European Commission against Racism and Intolerance 41 n.
European Convention for the Protection of Human Rights and Fundamental Freedoms 23, 182, 207, 222
European Union 38, 184
explanation of vote 29, 31

federal states, problems of 90, 187–8, 243–4, 281, 283
Fédération Internationale des ligues des droits de l'homme 377

Geneva Convention Relative to the Protection of Civilian Persons in Time of War 18, 162, 301
genocide 66, 84, 93, 256, 260, 263, 266–7, 311–12
*Global Compilation of National Legislation* 33, 166, 267
Gypsies, (or Roma) 37, 84, 106

Hague Convention 18
*Haut Conseil a l'intégration* 196, 219
Hebron, massacre in mosque 163,
    301–2
Human Rights Committee 22, 23, 39,
    40, 159, 202, 317
    comment on minorities 37
    comment on reservations 245–6,
    308

immigration laws 183, 193, 211, 216
inalienable rights 12, 82
incitement to racial hatred 205
incorporation of ICERD 63, 231
indigenous peoples 2, 31, 32, 34, 37,
    46, 47, 70, 80, 82, 86, 92, 225–6,
    229, 233–9, 283
    treaties with 87, 91, 228, 277,
    278–81
    Working Group on 37, 229
integration, perfect 105
integration, policies of 196–7, 230,
    232
International Bill of Human Rights 22,
    300, 334
International Commission of Jurists
    93, 167
International Convention for the
    Elimination of All Forms of Racial
    Discrimination (ICERD):
    adoption of vii, 28, 50, 57–62, 66,
    227
    amendments to 44, 160, 167–8
    individual complaints under 63,
    109, 156–8, 185, 208–9, 222,
    239, 283, 317
    interpretation of 104, 116, 125,
    126, 308
    key article of 202, 209
    non-compliance with 118, 136, 159
    overdue reports under 150–2
    reasons for acceding to vii, viii, 1, 3,
    5, 50, 99–100, 112–13, 183, 276,
    305
    reporting interval 44, 150, 166
    reporting under 2, 6, 44, 108, 113,
    116–21, 131, 134
    reservations to 66, 118, 128, 203–4,
    206, 246–7, 307
    states parties to vii, 99, 101, 106,
    107, 119, 141
    training in preparation of reports
    152

International Convention on the
    Suppression and Punishment of
    Apartheid 26, 40, 70
International Court of Justice 26, 48,
    63, 104, 116, 117, 238, 245, 308
International Covenant on Economic,
    Social and Cultural Rights 22,
    226, 245–7
International Covenant on Civil and
    Political Rights 22, 35–8, 39–40,
    207, 208, 225, 226
International Day for the Elimination
    of Racial Discrimination x, 28, 34
International Labour Organization
    (ILO) 22, 25, 32, 52, 57, 98,
    225–6, 293, 305
International Law Commission 19
International League for Human Rights
    42, 131
International Service for Human Rights
    312–13
International Tribunal 19, 162, 189,
    264–5, 312
International Work Group for
    Indigenous Affairs 226–7
International Year to Combat Racism
    and Racial Discrimination 28, 71
inter-state disputes 103, 108–12,
    128–9, 270, 289, 305–6, 310
Islam 33, 96, 106, 118, 135, 158,
    212

*Jersild* v. *Denmark* 207–8
Jews 37, 61, 84, 129, 130, 170, 195,
    215
juries, selection for 158, 212

Kellogg–Briand Pact 16–17
*Kitok* v. *Sweden*, before Human Rights
    Committee 39–40, 197, 240
Kurds 41, 96–7, 148, 149

law, conceptions of 11–14
law enforcement officials, training of
    160, 212
    UN Code of Conduct for 261
law, rule of 9–10, 14, 122, 140, 305,
    318
League of Nations 15, 16, 21, 37, 81,
    253
legitimacy of governments 111, 130,
    131
linguistic rights 32, 37, 225, 231, 237

*Lovelace* v. *Canada*, before Human
   Rights Committee 39

mass media 219–20, 318, 342–5
Meetings of Persons chairing Human
   Rights treaty bodies 40, 146, 152,
   245
migrant workers 31, 32, 34, 40, 47,
   97
minorities:
   definition of 32, 35, 36, 37, 38, 225
   protection of 31, 32, 34, 40, 47, 96,
   97
   treaties 16
model legislation 32, 166
multiculturalism 87, 229, 241–2
multiethnic society 72, 97, 148, 165,
   233, 238, 274

nation-building 229, 241, 251
nationality and national origins
   distinguished 194
nationality, right to 215–6
nation state 80–2, 96, 242
native title to land 91, 244, 252,
   282–3
Nazis, Nazism 17–18, 29, 31, 53, 59,
   60, 68, 70, 76, 105, 112, 182, 298
noble lie 50, 305
non-citizens 160, 193–4, 334
non-governmental organizations 23,
   24, 31, 41, 42, 45, 47, 103, 154,
   166, 185, 226, 307–8
Nuremberg Tribunal 17–19, 76

Organization for Security and
   Cooperation in Europe (OSCE)
   38, 184, 311
Organization of African Unity (OAU)
   256, 262, 270, 311

Palestine, Palestinians 30, 31, 34, 97,
   129, 163, 170, 276, 301–2
pariah states 60, 119, 137
paradigm cases 225, 230, 234
Paris, Pact of 16–17
philosophical nominalism 69
philosophical realism 67
plural society 84, 94
police 157, 215, 238, 261, 271, 289
political myth 73
protected classes 64
protected fields 64

public life 195, 246, 344

Qur'an 97, 298

race, meaning given to 52, 69, 76–7,
   80, 83, 87–8, 92–3, 97–8, 251,
   289, 292, 297
racial classification 80, 83
racial consciousness 77–9, 83, 84,
   266–7
racial discrimination:
   and disadvantage 70, 202, 219, 280
   as a characteristic of states vii, 171,
   305
   as sickness or crime 53–4, 57, 68–9,
   71, 73, 75
   claims as to absence of 2, 102,
   106–17, 116–17, 230, 232, 234,
   276, 292, 295
   conceptions of 50, 52, 58–62,
   67–71, 104, 114, 156, 230, 234–5
   definition of viii, 50, 51–2, 52–3, 57,
   64, 77
   direct and indirect 66, 191, 192,
   193
   forms of 29, 53–4, 60–2, 67, 71, 72
   grounds of 52, 65–6, 191–2, 252,
   301, 333
   in private life 64
   normal or pathological 53, 59, 61,
   67–71, 114–15
   purpose and effect 53, 64–5, 71,
   112, 160, 191, 192, 193, 222, 333
   test for 191, 195
racial prejudice 24–5, 34, 54, 55,
   341–2
racism 29, 68, 71–2, 73, 85, 92, 105,
   119, 124, 125, 214, 251, 301
racist acts of terrorism 163
racist ideologies 75, 76, 105, 263, 305
religious discrimination 34–5, 54, 192,
   195
recognition of states 130–1
remedies, criminal and civil 197,
   220–1
reservations to treaties 47, 245–6, 308
resolutions, manoevring on 31
rhetoric 28, 30, 45, 73, 242
right to development 33, 46
right of rebellion 13

Saami (or Sami) 37, 39–40, 197
schools, privatization of 195

segregation 200–2, 219, 334–5
self-determination, principle of 15, 30,
    130, 164, 186, 188, 226
Sharpeville x, 26, 28, 88
Sikhs 195
slavery 24, 86–7, 112
socialism 106, 124, 138
soldier/teacher ratio 260
sovereignty viii, 1, 2, 4, 13
special rapporteurs:
    appointment 23, 24, 41
    on Former Republic of Yugoslavia
        164–5
    on indigenous populations 228
    on racism and xenophobia 41, 48,
        165
    on Rwanda 312, 344
states parties, meetings of 151, 161,
    163, 306
successor states 63, 89, 160–1

*The First Twenty Years* 158, 165, 198,
    339
transmitted inequality 71, 200, 209,
    240, 251, 342
treaty bodies vii, 16, 39–43, 44, 138,
    142, 145, 151, 166, 167, 245, 310
treaty-making 63, 99, 195–6, 231,
    254; *see also* Incorporation of
    ICERD
tribalism 88, 251
Turkish minority in Greece 198

unequal development 70, 71, 230,
    234, 250–1, 289
United Nations (UN):
    budgetary crisis of 1985 9, 141, 306
    Charter 15, 21, 26, 39, 51, 52, 109,
        117
    Commission on Human Rights 22,
        23, 26, 36, 39, 41, 47, 48, 57, 74,
        152, 165, 171, 202, 228, 288,
        298, 309, 311

Economic and Social Council
    (ECOSOC) 22, 24, 25, 35
High Commissioner for Refugees
    132–3
High Commissioner for Human
    Rights 47, 312
General Assembly vii, 8, 9, 19, 22,
    25, 26, 29, 30, 31, 32, 34, 35,
    40, 43, 45, 50, 54, 55, 57, 66,
    70, 71, 101, 109, 114, 120, 124,
    125, 126, 127, 140, 142, 148,
    151, 152, 160, 161, 202, 249,
    263, 309
regional groups 27, 71, 102, 338–9
Security Council 20, 22, 26, 34, 47,
    48, 127, 161, 171
Sub-Commission on Prevention of
    Discrimination and Protection of
    Minorities 24, 35, 51, 53, 54,
    55–7, 72, 74, 228, 310
Universal Declaration of Human
    Rights (UDHR) 22, 35, 51, 203,
    225
United Nations Educational, Scientific
    and Cultural Organization
    (UNESCO) 22, 24–5, 31, 32, 51,
    57, 76

Vienna Convention on the Law of
    Treaties 3, 245
Vienna Declaration, 1993 x, 46

war crimes 11, 14, 17–19
World Conferences to Combat Racism
    and Racial Discrimination 29,
    30–1, 119, 123
World Conference on Human Rights
    45–7, 48, 315
World Council for Indigenous Peoples
    239

Zionism 29, 30, 45, 53, 59, 60, 61,
    68, 70, 72